CompTIA®
Server+®
Certification (2009 Objectives)

Bhaumik Patel

CompTIA® Server+® Certification (2009 Objectives)

Part Number: 085055
Course Edition: 1.0

NOTICES

HELP US IMPROVE OUR COURSEWARE

Your comments are important to us. Please contact us at Element K Press LLC, 1-800-478-7788, 500 Canal View Boulevard, Rochester, NY 14623, Attention: Product Planning, or through our Web site at **http://support.elementkcourseware.com.**

CompTIA® Server+® Certification (2009 Objectives)

**Appendix A: Mapping Server+ Course Content to the CompTIA®
Server+® Exam Objectives**

Appendix B: CompTIA® Server+® Acronyms

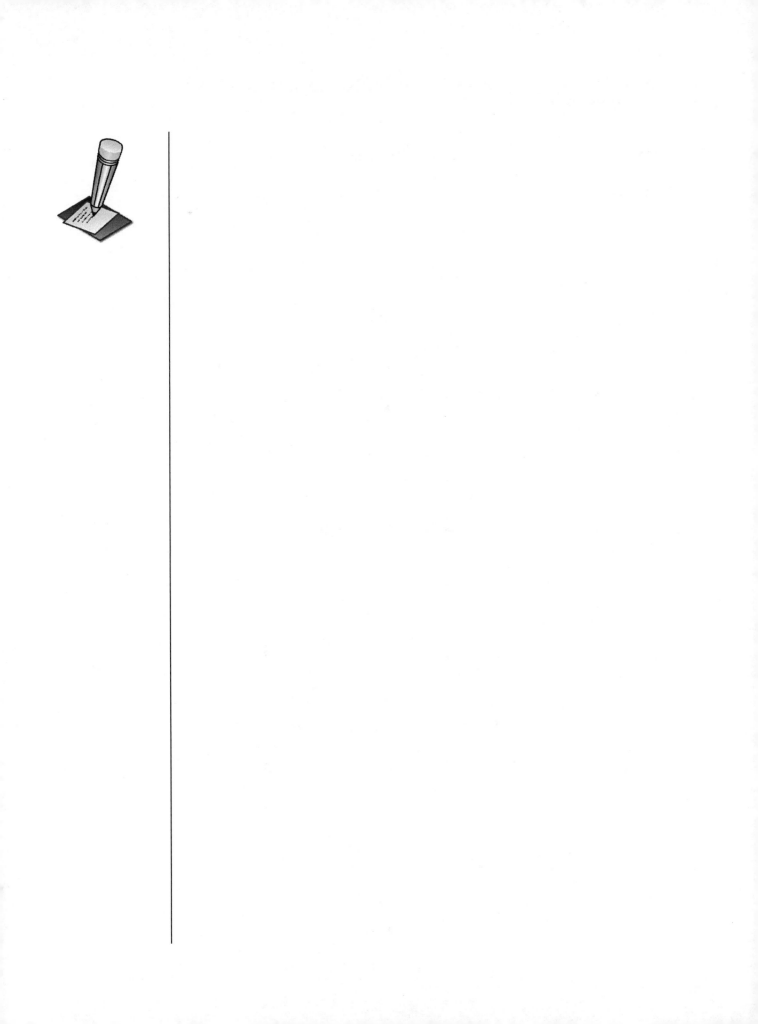

About This Course

The CompTIA® Server+® Certification course is aimed at building upon your experience with personal computer operating systems and networks and validating advanced skills and concepts that you will use on the job in dealing with server technologies. In this course, you will examine the various CompTIA objectives related to server hardware, software, data storage, IT environment, troubleshooting, and disaster recovery.

The Server+ Certification course can benefit you in two ways. If your job duties include installation, configuration, upgrading, maintenance, troubleshooting, or disaster recovery of servers, it validates the advanced-level technical competencies required to be successful. Or, it can assist you if you are preparing to take the CompTIA® Server+® certification examination based on 2009 objectives (exam number SK0-003).

Course Description

Target Student

The CompTIA® Server+® certification exam is targeted at IT professionals, network support technicians, and server hardware specialists having 18-24 months of experience in the information technology industry and hands-on experience with the installation, configuration, diagnosis, and troubleshooting of PC hardware.

Course Prerequisites

Students taking this class or preparing for the Server+ 2009 examination should have 18 to 24 months of hands-on experience with the installation, configuration, diagnosis, and troubleshooting of PC hardware and network operating system issues. It is recommended that they also hold the CompTIA® A+® certification.

In addition to these exam requirements, to ensure your success with this course, we recommend you first take the following Element K courses or have equivalent knowledge: *CompTIA® A+® Certification: A Comprehensive Approach for 2009 Objectives* and *CompTIA® Network+® Certification (2009 Objectives)*.

How to Use This Book

As a Learning Guide

Each lesson covers one broad topic or set of related topics. Lessons are arranged in order of increasing proficiency with *Server+*; skills you acquire in one lesson are used and developed in subsequent lessons. For this reason, you should work through the lessons in sequence.

We organized each lesson into results-oriented topics. Topics include all the relevant and supporting information you need to master *Server+*, and activities allow you to apply this information to practical hands-on examples.

You get to try out each new skill on a specially prepared sample file. This saves you typing time and allows you to concentrate on the skill at hand. Through the use of sample files, hands-on activities, illustrations that give you feedback at crucial steps, and supporting background information, this book provides you with the foundation and structure to learn *Server+* quickly and easily.

As a Review Tool

Any method of instruction is only as effective as the time and effort you are willing to invest in it. In addition, some of the information that you learn in class may not be important to you immediately, but it may become important later on. For this reason, we encourage you to spend some time reviewing the topics and activities after the course. For additional challenge when reviewing activities, try the "What You Do" column before looking at the "How You Do It" column.

As a Reference

The organization and layout of the book make it easy to use as a learning tool and as an after-class reference. You can use this book as a first source for definitions of terms, background information on given topics, and summaries of procedures.

Course Icons

Icon	Description
	A **Caution Note** makes students aware of potential negative consequences of an action, setting, or decision that are not easily known.
	Display Slide provides a prompt to the instructor to display a specific slide. Display Slides are included in the Instructor Guide only.
	An **Instructor Note** is a comment to the instructor regarding delivery, classroom strategy, classroom tools, exceptions, and other special considerations. Instructor Notes are included in the Instructor Guide only.
	Notes Page indicates a page that has been left intentionally blank for students to write on.
	A **Student Note** provides additional information, guidance, or hints about a topic or task.
	A **Version Note** indicates information necessary for a specific version of software.

Certification

This course is designed to help you prepare for the following certification.

Certification Path: CompTIA® Server+® (2009 Objectives)

● Exam: SK0-003

Course Objectives

In this course, you will install, configure, upgrade, maintain, and troubleshoot servers. You will also examine the server hardware and software, server IT environment, disaster recovery concepts, and learn information and skills that will be helpful on the job.

You will:

● examine server fundamentals.

● identify the hardware components of a server.

● describe the features of server software.

● examine the various types of storage systems used in servers.

- install hardware components on a server.
- configure servers.
- examine the issues in upgrading server components.
- identify some of the industry's best practices for deploying a server and the various strategies of securing, accessing, and remotely managing the server hardware.
- troubleshoot servers.
- describe disaster recovery concepts and techniques.

Course Requirements

Hardware

- At least one server-class computer, toolkit, and ESD kit (with extra straps, if possible) for every three or four students attending the class. These computers should have at least one processor installed, but be dual-processor capable. In addition to the requirements for the network operating system (at least 1 GHz (x86 processor) to 1.4 GHz (x64 processor) of clock speed, at least 512 MB of RAM, a DVD drive, and at least 20 GB of free hard disk space), the server should have the capability to add at least one additional SATA/SCSI hard drive. For each server, you will also need a keyboard, mouse, and monitor; a network adapter card; a spare power supply; a RAID controller card; and at least one additional hard drive (two is preferable).
- A desktop computer for every student attending the class.
- At least one external hard disk per server to be used for the backup and restore activities. In addition, these can be used if students will need to install any device drivers during the class.
- Enough cabling and network-connection devices to connect the computers.
- An Ethernet port with enough number of ports so as to connect the server and client computers in a group.
- Optionally, a desktop-class system that can be taken apart so that students can compare server hardware components with their desktop counterparts, a server rack system, a blade server system, a UPS, memory modules, additional processors, tape drives, a Wake-on-LAN system, dial-up connection configuration information and modems, external peripherals such as Zip or Jaz drives, KVM switches and cables, and SNMP management software.

Software

- Windows Server 2008 Standard Edition.
- Microsoft® Windows® XP SP2.
- Device drivers for the hardware components that students install or upgrade during the class.
- Optionally, other network operating systems such as Windows 2003 Server, Novell Open Enterprise Server 2, and various flavors of UNIX or Linux, if required.

Class Setup

The classroom setup needs to be performed depending on the feasibility of providing the required number of servers and other related hardware and software to the students. The lab administrator or the instructor should decide on which type of setup needs to be followed based on the two scenarios listed below:

Scenario 1: Set Up the Server Computer

If there is a single server computer, the instructor can choose to operate the server computer and demonstrate the tasks to the students. The students will be provided a client computer.

The setup instructions for the instructor computer are as follows:

1. Power on the server and insert the bootable DVD provided by the manufacturer into server while running for the first time.

2. Format the hard disks of the server computer to delete any data present on them.

3. Connect the server computer to an Ethernet hub using an Ethernet cable. The Ethernet hub should have enough number of ports so as to connect the server and all the client computers in the classroom.

Scenario 1: Set Up the Client Computers

The setup instructions for the client computer are as follows:

1. Install Windows® XP Professional SP2 in all client computers with the following settings.

    - **Computer Name:** *clientsys 01* through *clientsys 12* (or more if required).
    - **Administrator Password:** *password*
    - **IP Address:**
        - Students: *192.168.1.101* through *192.168.1.112* (or more if required)
    - **Subnet Mask:** *255.255.0.0*
    - **Default Gateway:** *192.168.1.100*
    - **Preferred DNS server:** *192.168.1.100*

2. Connect each client computer to the common hub using Ethernet cables.

3. Ensure that the Ethernet hub is powered on.

Scenario 2: Set Up the Server Computer

If it is possible to provide one server-class computer, Ethernet bridge, and ESD kit (with extra straps, if possible) for every single student or for a group, with each group consisting of three or four students, then follow the following setup instructions for the server computer of each group:

1. Power on the server and insert the bootable DVD provided by the manufacturer into server while running for the first time.

2. Format the hard disks of the server computer to delete any data present on them.

3. Connect the server computer to an Ethernet hub using an Ethernet cable. The Ethernet hub should have enough number of ports so as to connect all the server and client computers for a group of students.

Scenario 2: Set Up the Client Computers

The setup instructions for the client computer are as follows:

1. Install Windows® XP Professional SP2 in all client computers with the following settings.
   - **Computer Name:** *clientsys 01* through *clientsys 04* (or more if required).
   - **Administrator Password:** *password*
   - **IP Address:**
     - Students: *192.168.1.101* through *192.168.1.104* (or more if required)
   - **Subnet Mask:** *255.255.0.0*
   - **Default Gateway:** *192.168.1.100*
   - **Preferred DNS server:** *192.168.1.100*
2. Connect each client computer in a group to a common hub using Ethernet cables.
3. Ensure that each group of students use their own Ethernet hub. Do not interconnect with the Ethernet hubs or computers of other groups.
4. Ensure that the Ethernet hub is powered on.

Course CD-ROM

This course comes with an interactive CD-ROM that contains several simulations and simulated guided activities that can be used in lieu of the hands-on activities in the course. It also includes data files, PowerPoint slides, and the course assessment.

To install the data files, insert the interactive CD-ROM into the CD drive and click the Data Files button. This will install a folder named ServerPlus on your C drive. This folder contains all the data files that you will need to complete this course as well as a copy of the simulations.

List of Additional Files

Printed with each activity is a list of files students open to complete that activity. Many activities also require additional files that students do not open, but are needed to support the file(s) students are working with. These supporting files are included with the student data files on the course CD-ROM or data disk. Do not delete these files.

1 | Introduction to Servers

Lesson Time: 1 hour(s), 30 minutes

Lesson Objectives:

In this lesson, you will examine server fundamentals.

You will:

● Describe the various types of computers and common network architecture types.

● Identify the functions of some common types of servers.

Introduction

CompTIA Server+™ certification requires that you have wide knowledge and skills pertaining to all types of server-related job roles. You can begin your study by learning some basic server concepts. In this lesson, you will describe the various types of computers, network architectures and the classification of servers into different types.

Any CompTIA Server+ professional will usually have many career options open. Whether you choose to become a network support technician or a server hardware specialist, you will still have to draw upon the basics of CompTIA Server+ concepts and information. In any case, a good grasp of the types of computers, network architectures, servers, and their functions will help you to succeed in any server-related job role.

This lesson covers all or part of the following CompTIA Server+ (2009) certification objectives:

● Topic A:

■ Objective 2.4: Explain different server roles, their purpose and how they interact.

● Topic B:

■ Objective 2.4: Explain different server roles, their purpose and how they interact.

TOPIC A
Examine the Network Architecture

As a Server+ technician, you must be familiar with the basic elements of a network and the network architecture. Before getting into full fledged server concepts, revisiting some basic concepts relating to computers and networks would help you move towards learning core server related concepts with ease. In this topic, you will identify the types of computers and the networks where servers would have a role.

As a Server+ technician, you may be involved in setting up or maintaining the network infrastructure of an organization. Knowing the basic concepts related to servers, workstations, and desktops will help you to choose the right combination of computers for your network. Also, knowing the various network architectures will help you to choose the architecture that best suits the client's requirements.

Desktop Computers

From the perspective of a Server+ technician, a *desktop computer* is a general term used to designate any system deployed as a general purpose computer to be operated directly by a single user. Desktop systems can utilize traditional desktop-style hardware, or may be laptops or even tablet-style PCs. Desktop computers can support simple applications such as word processing, spreadsheets, databases, web browsers, email clients, and games, but may not be capable of running complex scientific or commercial applications. In networks, desktop systems generally function as client computers that request services from a server, and run general purpose operating systems such as Windows Vista or Macintosh OS.

| Laptop | Desktop | Tablet PC |

Figure 1-1: *Different types of computers.*

Multiuser PCs

Though most desktops or PCs are operated by one user, most modern PCs come with the capability to support multiple users through a multi-user operating system such as UNIX or Linux. Most multi-user PCs can support a maximum of six to eight users.

Workstations

A *workstation* is a general term sometimes applied to a class of higher-end computers designed for technical, scientific, and commercial applications. While there is no strict dividing line between a desktop-class computer and a workstation, a computer marketed as a workstation would generally have higher processing power, memory, and multitasking capability than a desktop system. Workstations are optimized for visualizing and manipulating complex data, such as 3D mechanical designs, engineering simulations, animation and image rendering, and mathematical plots. As with desktop systems, workstations typically function as clients on the network and are primarily meant for use by one person at a time. However, given their higher performance capabilities, it is also common for workstations to be shared among users through a multiuser operating system or to be otherwise deployed as lower-end servers running a server operating system.

Desktop   Workstation

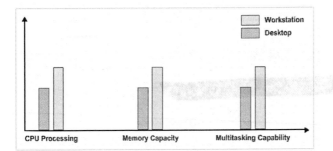

Figure 1-2: *Comparison of a workstation with a PC.*

A workstation console consists of a high resolution display, keyboard, and mouse. The configuration can also be extended to support multiple displays, graphics tablets, and special devices for manipulating 3D objects and navigating scenes. Due to their sophistication, workstations are more expensive than PCs.

Desktops vs. Workstations

Though the terms workstation and desktop PC are different, most modern PCs systems are powerful enough to qualify as workstations and therefore, the difference between the two classes of systems is not always obvious. Most manufactures do not distinguish between the two terms and use the term workstation solely for marketing purposes.

Servers

A *server* is a computer that provides services to client computers as well as to other servers on a network. Services provided by servers often include: facilitating the sharing of resources such as printers, data processing for clients, and filtering unwanted data from the network. While any class of computer can be configured to provide network services, server-class computer hardware is optimized for good network performance and includes fast CPUs, high-performance RAM, and often multiple large hard drives. Other features include redundancy in power supplies, network connections, and even the servers themselves to ensure uninterrupted services in the event of a breakdown. Other server features may be supplied by server operating systems such as Windows Server 2008 or UNIX, or by server-specific applications.

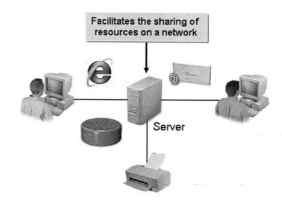

Figure 1-3: A computer network with a server.

Desktop PCs and Workstations as Servers

Most modern day PCs and workstations can be used as servers by configuring them with a network operating system such as Windows Server 2008. However, the performance of such servers will be lower when compared to a server running on server class hardware and therefore, the use of such servers is restricted to networks containing very few computers. Using PCs and workstations as servers on large networks will lead to frequent breakdowns or delay in services.

Computer Networks

Definition:

A *computer network* is a group of computers connected to communicate with each other and share resources, such as files and printers. Networks include a network medium, such as a cable, to carry network data; network adapter hardware to translate data between a computer and the network medium; a network operating system to enable computers to recognize the network; and some network protocols to control network communication.

Example:

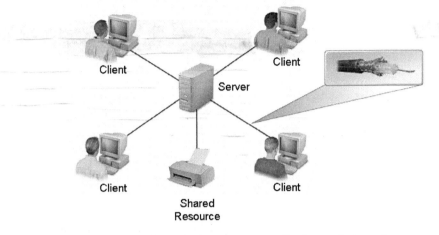

Figure 1-4: A computer network comprises servers, clients, and shared resources.

The Open System Interconnection Model

The Open Systems Interconnection (OSI) model is a seven-layer framework that defines and describes how software or hardware operating at each layer will act on a data packet before it is sent. The model consists of two functional blocks: application support and network support. The seven layers of the OSI model are Physical layer, Data-link layer, Network layer, Transport layer, Session layer, Presentation layer, and Application layer.

The TCP/IP Network Model

The TCP/IP model is a four-layer network model that loosely follows the seven-layer OSI model. The Application layer maps to the Application, Presentation, and Session layers in the OSI model. The Transport layer maps to the Transport layer in the OSI model. The Internet layer maps to the Network layer in the OSI model, and the Network layer maps to the Data-link and Physical layers in the OSI model.

Types of Network Architectures

The network architecture may vary from one organization to another.

Network Architecture	Description
Client/Server Networks	A *client/server network* is a network in which a server provides services to its clients. In most networks, workstations or PCs are used as clients due to lower performance requirement of the clients as compared to servers, though a server class computer too can be configured to act as a client of other servers.
	Typically, there is at least one server providing central authentication services to the clients. Servers also provide access to shared files, printers, hardware, and applications such as databases. In a client/server network, processing power, management services, and administrative functions can be concentrated in the server wherever needed, while clients can still perform many basic end-user tasks on their own.
	As a Server+ certified professional, most of the servers you support will be found in client-server environments.
Centralized Computer Networks	A *centralized computer network* is a network in which a single computer or server controls all network communication and performs data processing and storage on behalf of its clients. Unlike a client/server network, clients in a pure centralized computer network do not have any processing capabilities of their own. Users connect to the server through dedicated terminals. Centralized networks provide high performance and centralized management, but they are expensive to implement, and pure centralized networks have become rare as the power and flexibility of the client-server architecture has increased.
Peer-to-Peer Networks	A *peer-to-peer network* is a network in which resource sharing, processing, and communications control are completely decentralized. All clients on the network are equal in terms of providing and using resources, and users are authenticated by each individual workstation. Peer-to-peer networks are easy and inexpensive to implement. However, they are only practical in very small organizations due to the lack of centralized data storage and administration. Because these networks do not employ dedicated servers, you will not deal with them often in the context of your role as a Server+ certified professional.

The Disadvantage of Centralized Computer Networks

Pure centralized computer networks have a major disadvantage. Because these networks rely totally on the central server computer, a fault in the central server may shut down the entire network by making the services unavailable. Due to the increasing computing capabilities of computers, the centralized computer network model is more of a legacy architecture and has been replaced by other models or integrated into client-server architectures to a large extent.

ACTIVITY 1-1
Discussing the Types of Computers and Network Architectures

Scenario:

In this activity, you will discuss the types of computers and common network architectures.

1. **Match the type of computer to its description.**

    _a_ Server

    _c_ Workstation

    _b_ Desktop Computer

    a. High-end computers designed for technical or scientific applications.

    b. A system deployed as a general purpose computer to be operated directly by a single user.

    c. Computers that are designed to facilitate the sharing of resources between other computers on the network.

2. **Which statements are valid for a peer-to-peer network?**

    a) Access to shared files is controlled by centralized servers.

    b) No centralized server is required.

    c) Clients in a peer-to-peer network do not have any processing power of their own.

    d) No centralized data storage is used.

3. **True or False? A server computer can support a multiuser operating system.**

    ✓ True

    ___ False

4. **Which networks are based on a type of interaction between the server and client computer?**

    a) Client-server networks

    b) TCP/IP networks

    c) Centralized computer networks

    d) Peer-to-Peer computer networks

TOPIC B

Identify Common Server Types and Functions

You are familiar with the role of servers in a given network architecture. Servers can be classified based on their features and capabilities. In this topic, you will identify the functions of several types of servers.

As a server specialist, you will work in environments that use different types of hardware for numerous functions and services. Although some of these server types may be more prevalent than others, it is important to have sufficient knowledge to identify and understand the systems that are in place in any environment.

Server Form Factors

The form factor of a server specifies the physical dimensions and shape of the server hardware or its major components. Servers come in multiple form factors to meet varying needs, such as physical space, access, availability, organization, and cooling and power requirements.

Tower

Rackmount

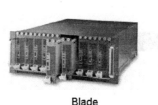
Blade

Figure 1-5: The various form factors of servers.

Form Factor	Description
Tower	A *tower server* looks like a traditional desktop tower PC but includes more opportunities for the expansion of processing capabilities. Tower servers take up more physical space than newer form factors, but they often provide the best value for smaller companies and departmental networks.

Form Factor	Description
Rackmount	A *rackmount server* provides sliding rails and hinged cases for easy access, and many components such as hard drives, power supplies, expansion cards, and fans are usually hot-swappable, enabling you to replace faulty parts without shutting down the server. Rackmount servers hold more devices than tower servers, use less physical space, and provide better organization, but they cost more than their tower counterparts.
Blade	A *blade server* consists of a chassis that contains one or more server blades. A *server blade* consists of a single circuit board holding components such as processors, memory, and network connections that are usually found on multiple boards. Server blades are stacked side-by-side and interconnected in a blade server chassis. The chassis supplies power and cooling to the connected blades.

U size or Rack Unit

A rack unit or U size is a unit of measurement used to describe the height of an individual rack mounted equipment. One rack unit is 1.75 inches (44.45 mm) high and is commonly denoted as 1U: similarly 2 rack units are 2U and so on. The standard width of most rack mounted servers is either 19 inches or 23 inches. A standard rack server can support a maximum of 42 rack units.

Transition to Blade Servers

While the transition from tower servers to rackmount was strictly a difference in form factor, blade servers offer unique advantages in server management and availability. In addition, blade servers provide even more physical space savings than rackmount servers, are easier to install and remove, and consume less power than traditional box-based servers. Although there has been significant growth in the sales of blade server systems, a factor that has held the market in check is a lack of standards for blade formats. Every vendor has their own proprietary format, so customers need to be very careful when committing to a blade server solution.

Power Requirements

Servers have power supplies and modules of varying sizes and technologies. Although components used in smaller devices draw less power than their larger counterparts, their design requires them to manage power more efficiently.

Cooling Requirements

Primarily the responsibility of the manufacturer, the design of a server's components impacts its cooling requirements. The components that are of the greatest concern are the processor and the power supply. Smaller components, typically found in rackmount or blade servers, run hotter than the components in the standard tower server. This issue compounds itself when you consider that the fans and heat sinks that keep the components cool also receive size reductions. In addition, there is generally not much room in a smaller server for air circulation.

General Use Servers

Servers play an important role in many general computing tasks and services, such as file storage, printing, email and network security, and client data processing.

Server Type	Description
File server	*File servers* are computers that store the programs and data files intended to be shared by multiple users. Many file servers use high-speed LAN or WAN links to keep data moving at optimal rates. Simply put, a file server acts like a remote disk drive.
Print server	A *print server* enables many network users to share the common printers.
Mail server	A *mail server,* also called the message server, provides "post office" facilities by storing incoming mails or messages for distribution to users and forwards outgoing mails or messages through appropriate channels. Many of today's mail servers also provide other services such as document collaboration, chat, web access, and file storage. The term may refer to just the software that performs this service while residing on a machine with other service functions.
Fax server	A *fax server* provides a bank of fax modems, allowing users to fax out messages and remote users to fax in messages over the next available modem. It may be a dedicated machine or implemented on a file server that is providing other services.
Application server	An *application server* performs the data processing in a client/server environment. Generally, client/server environments are either two- or three-tiered. The difference between a file server and an application server is that the file server stores programs and data, while the application server runs programs and processes data.
	The application server can act as an interface between the web server and a database, or between legacy applications. Application servers are also used for monitoring resources and maintaining a log of their usage.

Server Type	Description
Database server	A *database server* holds the database management system (DBMS) and databases. It is dedicated to database storage, updating, and retrieval, and is a key component in a client/server environment. Upon requests from the client machines, it searches the database for selected records and passes them back over the network. A database server and file server may be one and the same because a file server often provides database services. However, the term implies that the system is dedicated to database use only and not a central storage facility for applications and files.
Terminal server	A *terminal server* is designed to be capable of emulating multiple hosts at the same time and allotting separate virtual sessions for each host. It is widely used in centralized computing networks where multiple clients may need to access the server at the same time. If the demands of the client are low, then the companies can use terminal services as a way of extending the lives of their outdated computers.
	Because a terminal server can support hundreds of sessions, companies can spend money on upgrading the server and use older clients, thereby, saving money.

Server Application Models

Software applications on a network can be implemented in three different server application models.

Server Application Model	Description
Dedicated	A *dedicated application* is a program designed to run primarily on one computer. In an application server environment, the server itself performs what is known as the business logic (or data processing), often pulling information from a database server and then manipulating it to complete the client's request.
Distributed	A *distributed application* is a program designed to run on more than one computer, typically with functionality separated into tiers such as client, service, and data storage.

Server Application Model	Description
Peer-to-peer	A *peer-to-peer application* is one that does not need a server to act as a go-between among participating clients. Examples include real-time programs such as Netscape, AOL Instant Messenger, and Microsoft NetMeeting.

Authentication Servers

There are different types of authentication servers that provide network security by verifying the identity of users.

Authentication Server	Description
Remote Access Service (RAS) server	The *Remote Access Service (RAS)* server provides a subset of wide area networking services, including packet forwarding and remote connections for Windows-based clients, and enables users to implement VPNs over the Internet or other public networks. Types of connections that are supported include ISDN, modem, and X.25 links. In Windows Server 2003 and Windows Server 2008, RAS server functionality is also known as Routing And Remote Access Service server (RRAS).
Remote Authentication Dial-In User Service (RADIUS)	The *Remote Authentication Dial-In User Service (RADIUS)* stores permissions and configuration information for RADIUS-compatible hardware to authenticate remote network users. When a network contains several remote access servers, you can configure one of the servers to be a RADIUS server and all of the other servers as RADIUS clients. The RADIUS clients will pass all authentication requests to the RADIUS server for verification, alleviating the need for configuring remote access policies on multiple remote access servers. In Windows, RADIUS implementation is accomplished through the Internet Authentication Service.
802.1X server	The *802.1X server* uses one of several certificate-based mechanisms to authenticate wireless users on a network. An 802.1X provides an authenticated user with an encryption key that can be either static or dynamic. Dynamic encryption keys are less vulnerable because they are changed automatically during a session with no user involvement.
LDAP server	The *LDAP server* uses *Directory System Agents (DSAs)* or Directory Services Server (DSS) to process queries and updates to an LDAP directory. DSAs supply the services that provide access to data stores. LDAP servers are simple to install, easy to maintain, and can be optimized to provide an efficient and scalable means for storing, managing, searching, and retrieving data that is rarely modified. In Windows operating systems, the LDAP feature is known as Active Directory Domain Services (ADDS).

Lightweight Directory Access Protocol.

Internet Services

Servers are used for providing several Internet services, such as web, DNS, DHCP, and FTP services.

Function	Description
Web	Provides World Wide Web services on the Internet. The web server provides functions such as database searching and e-commerce transactions. If the web server is used internally and not by the public, it may be known as an intranet server. The term may refer to just the software and not the entire computer system. In such cases, it refers to the HyperText Transfer Protocol (HTTP) server that manages web page requests from the browser and delivers HTML documents (web pages) in response.
DNS	Provides name resolution for IP networks, including the Internet. The DNS server maintains a database of domain and host names, and their corresponding IP addresses. For example, if www.mycompany.com were presented to a DNS server, the IP address 204.0.8.51 might be returned. DNS has replaced the manual task of updating HOSTS files in an in-house UNIX network, and of course, it would be impossible to do this manually on the global Internet given its size.
Dynamic Host Configuration Protocol (DHCP) server	Dynamic Host Configuration Protocol (DHCP) server runs software that automatically assigns IP addresses to client stations logging on to a TCP/IP network. It eliminates the need to manually assign permanent IP addresses. DHCP software typically runs on servers and is also found in network devices such as firewalls, ISDN routers, and modem routers that allow multiple users access to the Internet. You can also configure DHCP servers to provide additional client settings such as default gateways and DNS server addresses. Newer DHCP servers dynamically update the DNS servers after making assignments.
Windows Internet Name Service (WINS)	The *Windows Internet Name Service (WINS)* is Microsoft®'s NetBIOS name resolution service, which was developed to reduce the number of NetBIOS name resolution broadcasts on networks that use NetBIOS naming. The WINS server uses a name resolution table to map NetBIOS names to protocol addresses. WINS clients are configured with the IP address of the WINS server so that they automatically register their names in the WINS database when they come online. They can also resolve names by targeted requests to the WINS server. There has been talk of phasing out WINS for years, and Microsoft began to move in that direction with the release of Windows Server 2008. The WINS service is replaced in Windows Server® 2008 with a new type of DNS zone that will still support older WINS clients.
File transfer Protocol (FTP)	*File Transfer Protocol (FTP)* stores files for download from, or upload to, the Internet or an intranet running the TCP/IP protocol stack. FTP designates that the server is using the File Transfer Protocol to copy files from one host to another.
Network Time Protocol (NTP)	*Network Time Protocol (NTP)* synchronizes the clocks of computer systems over packet-switched data networks. The latest version of NTP can usually maintain time to within 10 milliseconds (1/100 s) over the public Internet, and can achieve accuracies of 200 microseconds (1/5000 s) or better in local area networks under ideal conditions.

[handwritten margin note: What's the differn Internet vs Intranet]

Function	Description
Proxy	A proxy server enables a sender and a receiver to communicate without actually setting up a direct connection between the computers. Proxies are applications that act as go-betweens to provide security. All input is forwarded out from a different port, closing a straight path between two networks and preventing a hacker from obtaining internal addresses and details of a private network. Because the proxy servers can be used for the selective filtering of content accessed by the users, they are also known as *filtering servers.*. Proxies are only one tool that can be used to build a firewall.

Internetworking Devices

Servers can also be used as internetworking devices, such as gateways, routers, and firewalls.

Gateway

Router

Firewall

Figure 1-6: *The various types of internetwork devices.*

Internetworking Device	Description
Gateway	A *gateway* performs conversion between different types of networks or applications. Three main types of gateways are protocol, address, and format. For example, a protocol gateway can convert a TCP/IP packet to a legacy protocol such as NetWare IPX packet and vice versa. An address gateway connects networks with different directory spaces, and a format gateway connects networks with different data encoding and representation schemes, such as ASCII and EBCDIC. Gateways function at every layer in the OSI model, but are sometimes referred to as functioning at the Application layer (Layer 7). In most instances, gateway functionality is achieved by using a combination of hardware and software.

Internetworking Device	Description
Router	A *router* manages the exchange of information from network to network, or between network cabling segments. Based on routing tables and routing protocols, routers read the network address in each transmitted frame and make a decision on how to send it based on the most expedient route (traffic load, line costs, speed, bad lines, and so forth). Routers work at the Network layer (Layer 3) of the OSI model and are used to segment LANs in order to balance traffic within workgroups and to filter traffic for security purposes and policy management. Routers are also used at the edge of the network to connect remote offices. Multiprotocol routers support several legacy protocols such as IPX, AppleTalk, DECnet and modern day IP. Most routers are specialized computers optimized for communications, but router functions can also be implemented by adding routing software to other servers like file servers or authentication servers.
Firewall	A firewall filters out unwanted data packets from a network or subnetwork. Companies employ firewall technology to provide Internet access to internal users and company website access to external users, while keeping outsiders from accessing proprietary internal data. A firewall can restrict access to a certain portion of a network, such as the Accounting or Research areas, from unauthorized access from internal users. A firewall can be implemented as both hardware or software running on a server designated for filtering purposes.

Nonroutable Protocols

Routers can only route a message that is transmitted by a routable protocol such as IP or IPX. Messages in nonroutable protocols, such as NetBIOS and LAT (Logical Address Translation), cannot be routed, but they can be transferred LAN to LAN via a bridge. Because routers have to inspect the network address in the packets, they do more processing and add more overhead than a bridge or a switch, which both work at the Data Link (MAC) layer.

Firewall Implementations

Firewalls can be implemented to include packet filtering (using a router to block traffic based on IP address or port number), proxy servers (using a server as a go-between to gather external data and forward it to the internal user without allowing an unlimited connection between the two networks), Network Address Translation (NAT) (using one IP address to gather external information, thus keeping internal IP addresses secret), and tracking transactions in order to verify that the destination of an inbound packet matches the source of a previous outbound request.

ACTIVITY 1-2
Discussing Common Server Types and Functions

Scenario:
In this activity, you will discuss common server types and functions.

---

1. **Which server type can be used as part of a firewall solution?**

   a) File

   b) Proxy

   c) Print

   d) DHCP

---

2. **Which of these are server form factors?**

   a) Rackmount

   b) Blade

   c) Database

   d) Tower

---

3. **Match each application server model to its description.**

   C Peer-to-peer   a. They are designed to run primarily on a single computer.

   B Distributed   b. They are designed to run on more than one computer.

   a Dedicated   c. They do not need a server to act as a go-between among participating clients.

---

4. **Which Internet functionality allows a server to assign IP addresses to clients that log on to the network?**

   a) FTP

   b) Proxy

   c) DHCP → Dynamic host Configuration Protocol

   d) DNS

---

5. **Match each internetworking device with its description.**

_c_	Gateway	a.	Prevents unwanted data from entering into the network.
_b_	Router	b.	Manages the exchange of information from network to network, or between network segments.
_a_	Firewall	c.	Translates the protocols between dissimilar networks.

Lesson 1 Follow-up

In this lesson, you described the fundamental concepts related to servers. A good understanding of the fundamental concepts related to different types of computer, network architectures, server form factors, and server roles will help you to succeed in any server-related job role.

1. **What are the various factors that you would take into consideration while choosing a server form factor?**

2. **What are the various general server types that you have come across?**

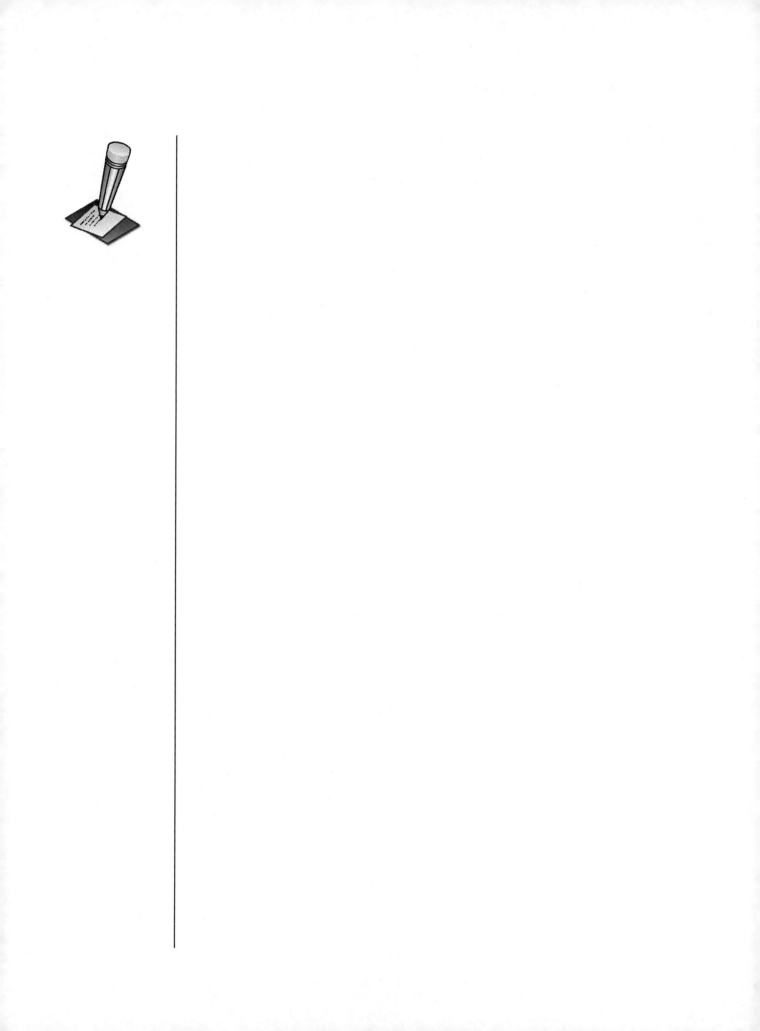

2 Exploring the Server Hardware

Lesson Time: 3 hour(s)

Lesson Objectives:

In this lesson, you will identify the hardware components of a server.

You will:

- Identify the system board components of a server.
- Explore the system processing core.
- Explore the memory hardware used in servers.
- Describe the server cooling systems and power supply.

Introduction

You examined the common network architecture, server types, and server applications. Before learning how to install a server, you must know more about the internal hardware components that constitute a server. In this lesson, you will explore different hardware components of a server.

Server hardware has various components that form the core of its processing subsystem. Being familiar with the different types of processors, memory, and other support tools will help you to identify the server that best suits your need.

This lesson covers all or part of the following CompTIA Server+ (2009) certification objectives:

- Topic A:
  - Objective 1.1: Differentiate between system board types, features, components and their purposes.
  - Objective 1.4: Explain the importance of a Hardware Compatibility List (HCL).
  - Objective 1.6: Given a scenario, install appropriate expansion cards into a server while taking fault tolerance into consideration.
- Topic B:
  - Objective 1.5: Differentiate between processor features / types and given a scenario select the appropriate processor.
- Topic C:

- ■ Objective 1.3: Differentiate between memory features / types and given a scenario select appropriate memory.
- ■ Objective 1.4: Explain the importance of a Hardware Compatibility List (HCL).
- ● Topic D:
  - ■ Objective 1.2: Deploy different chassis types and the appropriate components.

TOPIC A
Identify Server System Board Components

You examined servers as a complete system. However, each server is made up of a set of hardware subsystems. In this topic, you will identify the components of a system board and examine the operation of a server's core processing subsystem.

It is good practice to begin examining individual components of a complex device such as a server system board. The system board of the server houses vital components that communicate with the server. You will need to understand the roles played by these components to have a clearer view of the working of a system board.

System Board

The *system board,* also referred to as the *motherboard,* is a printed circuit board that houses processor or memory chips, controller circuits, buses, slots, and sockets. It provides a platform for components and peripherals to communicate with each other.

Figure 2-1: Components of a system board.

In addition to basic components such as the processor and memory, server system boards contain other specialized components.

System Board Component	Description
Human Interface Device (HID)	A Human Interface Device (HID) is a type of server device that interacts directly with the user—it takes input and delivers output. Most operating systems recognize standard HID devices, such as the keyboard and mouse, without needing a special driver.

System Board Component	Description
Dual Inline Package (DIP) switches or jumpers	To configure older system boards, you used either dual inline switches more commonly called Dual Inline Package switches (DIP) or jumpers. DIP switches are switches on a card used to configure hardware settings. These are usually rocker switches (like light switches) that turn on or off. Jumpers are pins and connectors used for configuring hardware settings. You physically connect or disconnect a circuit by adding or removing a jumper block, which is a small rectangular connector, from a pair of pins attached to the system board or add-on card. You might have used these switches to specify the multiplier and the CPU bus frequency. The most recent system boards enable you to use software to configure these values through the BIOS setup program.
Backplane	An interconnecting device consisting of a series of sockets for printed circuit boards. Backplanes are used in servers to provide the required connection between logic, memory, input/output modules, and other printed circuit boards. They are categorized into two types: ● **Passive backplane:** This backplane adds no processing functionality to the circuit. You may also encounter servers that use the passive backplane technology—where the chipset, processor, and cache reside on a separate card, leaving the system board as a physical connection point for the other components to be plugged. ● **Active backplane:** This backplane contains a microprocessor or controller-driven circuitry with processing functionality.

System Board Component	Description
Chipset	A set of embedded chips that supports the processor. Server system boards are more often characterized by their chipsets. Chipset architecture, including the number, function, name, and placement of the various chips in a chipset, will vary depending on the type and manufacturer of the system board. For example, on many Intel Pentium computers, the two main chips in the chipset are known as the Northbridge and the Southbridge. • The Northbridge controls the system memory and the AGP video ports, and it may also control cache memory. The Northbridge is closer to the processor and communicates directly with it using the system bus. • The Southbridge controls input/output functions, the system clock, drives and buses, APM power management, and various other devices. The Southbridge is further from the CPU and uses the PCI bus to communicate with the Northbridge. Newer Intel systems employ the Intel Hub Architecture (IHA) chipset. This also has two main chips, now named the Graphics and AGP Memory Controller Hub (GMCH) and the I/O Controller Hub (ICH), which perform functions roughly analogous to the Northbridge and Southbridge, but the communication between the two new chips is designed to be faster.
System clock	A circuit that discharges a continuous stream of precise high and low pulses of equal length. One clock cycle is the time that passes from the start of one high pulse until the start of the next. If several events are supposed to happen in one clock cycle, the cycle is subdivided by inserting a circuit with a known delay in it, thus providing more high and low pulses. The system clock synchronizes tasks in a server; for example, loading data before manipulating it.

Types of System Boards

The form factor of the system board describes its general shape, the cases and power supplies it can use, and its physical organization. Based on a form factor, system boards are classified into different types.

Type	Form Factor
Full-size AT (Advanced Technology)	This form factor was used in older tower systems. It was designed from the original XT motherboard, which itself was designed for use in the second version of the IBM PC released in 1983. These original full-size systems took up a large amount of server space, unless placed vertically on the floor. The full size AT board was 12 inches by 13.8 inches. A transfer bus of 16-bit or better was required.
Baby AT	As with the full-size AT, this form factor was used in older server systems. It was the scaled down version of the full size AT designed so that manufacturers could build a smaller PC. It also helped to free up desk space. The board was usually 13 inches by 8.5 to 9 inches. This was an extremely popular design even though it was never developed as a standard but as a variety of sizes.
ATX	ATX boards introduced by Intel in 1995 provided better I/O support, lower cost, easier use, and better processor support than earlier form factors. The dimensions of a standard ATX board are 12 inches wide by 9.6 inches long. Some of the features of the ATX board are: <ul><li>Power supply with a single, keyed 20-pin connector. Rather than requiring Voltage Regulator Modules (VRMs) to reduce voltage down from 5 volts to 3, 3 VDC is available directly from the power supply.</li><li>The CPU is closer to the cooling fan on the power supply. Also, the cooling circulation blows air into the case instead of blowing air out of the case.</li><li>I/O ports are integrated into the board along with PS/2 connectors (instead of 5-pin DIN connectors).</li><li>You can access the entire motherboard without reaching around drives. This was accomplished by rotating the board 90 degrees.</li><li>This board cannot be used in Baby AT or LPX cases.</li><li>The board is 12 inches by 9.6 inches.</li></ul>
BTX	Intended to be the replacement for the ATX system board form factor in 2005, the BTX form factor was designed to fix some of the issues that arose from using newer technologies (which often demand more power and generate more heat) on system boards compliant with the circa-1996 ATX specification. BTX features include: <ul><li>**Low profile:** The backplane is inches lower than the ATX.</li><li>**Thermal design:** The BTX layout establishes a straighter path of airflow with fewer obstacles, resulting in better overall cooling capabilities.</li><li>**Structural design:** The emerging need for heat sinks, capacitors, and other components dealing with electrical and thermal regulation has resulted in devices that can physically strain some motherboards. The BTX standard addressed this issue by specifying better locations for hardware mounting points.</li></ul>

Type	Form Factor
Micro BTX (µBTX)	The Micro BTX is similar to the standard BTX system board, measuring 10.4 by 10.5 inches. The main difference between the standard board and the micro board is the smaller size and that the micro board has fewer expansion slots.
Pico BTX	The Pico BTX system board form factor is a smaller version of the standard BTX board measuring 10.5 inches by 8 inches. The pico board is designed with the same rear panels as the standard board and is used for half height applications. Pico boards usually include only one or two expansion slots.
NLX	The NLX system board is a small form factor designed around the Pentium II processor. It supports advances in memory and graphics technology such as DIMMs and AGP. This board was designed to fit slimline design systems. The board is 8 to 9 inches by 10 to 13.6 inches.

Form Factor Example

A company can make two motherboards having basically the same functionality but with a different form factor. The only real difference will be the physical layout of the board and the position of components.

System Board Cards

There are various interface cards soldered onto the motherboard to support basic server functions such as display, sound, and network connections.

Interface Card	Description
Video Interface Card or Video Card	This card is an interface between the computer monitor and the motherboard and its subcomponents, such as the microprocessor and memory. This card may be included as part of the motherboard or it may plug into a card slot on the motherboard.
Sound Card	This card is an interface between the computer speaker set and the motherboard and its subcomponents such as the processor and memory. This card may be included as part of the motherboard or it may plug into a card slot on the motherboard.
Network Interface Card (NIC)	This card transfers information across the network. For servers to be able to communicate with other computers on the network, you need at least one NIC. Some servers include two or more on-board network adapters (a network interface built into the system board); for others, you'll have to install one to enable basic network communications. Multiple NICs help reduce network congestion, by splitting the load over several cables, or provide some basic routing functions between separate networks.

The Processor

Definition:

The *processor*, also called the Central Processing Unit (CPU), is the main chip on the system board that executes program instructions that control the server. On most computers, the CPU is housed in a single microprocessor module and is inserted directly into a CPU socket on the motherboard. The processor consists of a control unit and an Arithmetic and Logic Unit (ALU). The control unit retrieves program instructions from memory and then decodes them for execution; the ALU performs mathematical operations.

Example:

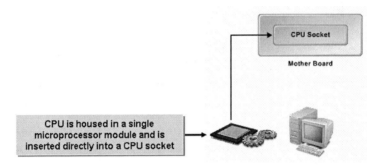

Figure 2-2: *The processor controls the server.*

Memory

Definition:

Memory is a repository that allows the temporary storage of information required by the processor to perform calculations, run programs, or open documents. Each memory chip contains millions of transistors, which are etched on one sliver of a semiconductor. Transistors are switches that can be opened or closed. When a transistor is closed, it conducts electricity; this is represented by the binary number 1. An open transistor does not conduct electricity; this is represented by the binary number 0. Although the term "Computer Memory" is commonly used to refer to the RAM, there are various other forms of memory inside a server; for example, the hard disk drive.

Example:

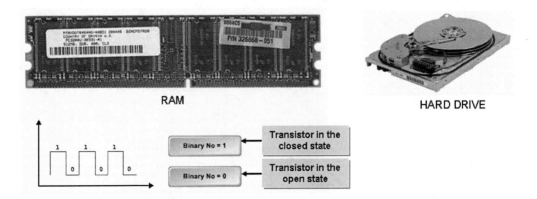

Figure 2-3: *Memory allows the temporary storage of information required by the processor.*

Volatile and Nonvolatile Memory

Memory can be considered either volatile or nonvolatile:

- Volatile memory requires a constant source of electricity to keep track of the data stored in it. When the power is no longer available, the data stored in volatile memory is lost. The computer's main *RAM* (Random Access Memory) is an example of volatile memory. The computer can both read the data stored in RAM and write different data into the same RAM. Any byte of data can be accessed without disturbing other data, so the computer has random access to the data in RAM.

- Nonvolatile memory retains the information stored on it whether or not electrical current is available. ROM (Read-Only Memory) is an example of nonvolatile memory.

Single-Sided and Double-Sided Memory

Single-sided RAM does not refer to the literal number of sides that a RAM module has, rather it means that an expansion bank of RAM has all of its available memory accessible by the computer. Double-sided RAM might have two banks of memory, but only one can be accessed at a time by the computer.

Single-Sided and Double-Sided Media

Depending upon the media type, single-sided and double-sided have two meanings when discussing server memory. Single-sided removable media refers to a disc (floppy, CD, or DVD) that can be read and written to one side only. Double-sided discs or DVDs can read from and write to both sides, thus doubling the storage capacity of the media.

BIOS Chip

The *Basic Input Output System (BIOS) chip* is either a ROM or an Electrically Erasable Programmable ROM (EEPROM) chip with the BIOS program code. This code allows system devices to communicate with each other. The BIOS chip also contains the code that executes the Power On Self Test (POST), in which the computer conforms to a number of tests. After the POST is successfully executed, the control of a system's boot process is taken over by the BIOS.

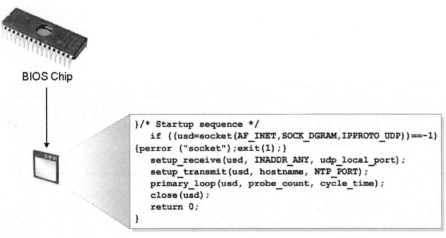

BIOS Chip

```
}/* Startup sequence */
   if ((usd=socket(AF_INET,SOCK_DGRAM,IPPROTO_UDP))==-1)
{perror ("socket");exit(1);}
   setup_receive(usd, INADDR_ANY, udp_local_port);
   setup_transmit(usd, hostname, NTP_PORT);
   primary_loop(usd, probe_count, cycle_time);
   close(usd);
   return 0;
}
```

BIOS Program Code

Figure 2-4: The system BIOS code allows system devices to communicate with each other.

Physical Ports

A *physical port* is a hardware interface that helps external devices to communicate with servers. The port is either an electrically wired socket or a wireless transmission device. Ports can vary based on their shape, the number and layout of pins or connectors, signals carried, and location. There are ports for both internal and external devices.

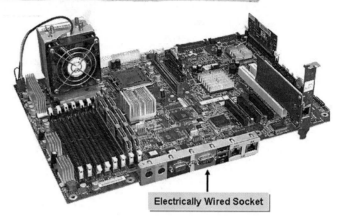

Electrically Wired Socket

Figure 2-5: Ports help external devices to communicate with servers via a hardware interface:

There are various types of physical ports available for a server.

Physical Port	Description
Serial	Enables data transfer over a single wire at the rate of one bit per unit time. Serial connections support two-way communications and are typically used for devices such as fax cards or external modems.
	Legacy serial ports have either 9-pin (DB-9) or 25-pin (DB-25) male connectors. A legacy serial cable ends with a female connector to plug in to the male connector on the system board.
	Serial ports are typically called COM1, COM2, COM3, and COM4, where COM is short for communications port. On system boards that have color-coded ports, the serial port is teal-colored.

Physical Port	Description
Parallel	Enables data transfer over eight or more wires at the rate of eight or more bits per unit time. Any component connected by multiple data pathways may be considered to have a parallel connection, but the term is generally used to refer to a standard legacy parallel port that uses eight data wires, and is typically used to connect a printer to a system board.
	Standard parallel ports have 25-pin female connectors. A parallel cable has a 25-pin male connector to plug into the system unit and a 36-pin male Centronics connector at the other end to attach to the external device. On system boards that have color-coded ports, the parallel port is burgundy or dark pink.
Universal Serial Bus (USB)	Enables connecting multiple peripherals to a single port with high performance and minimal device configuration. USB connections support two-way communications. All modern systems have multiple USB ports and can support up to 127 devices per port.
	USB 2.0 card is the most commonly implemented standard. It can communicate up to 480 Mb/s. The original USB 1.1 card is still commonly found in devices and systems. It can communicate up to 12 Mb/s. A USB 2.0 card connected to a USB 1.1 hub or port will communicate at only USB 1.1 speeds, even though it might be capable of faster speeds. Generally, the operating system will inform you of this when you connect the device.
	USB 3.0 card, also called SuperSpeed USB, is the latest USB standard released and features a maximum transfer rate of 5.0 Gb/s. It is 10 times faster than the USB 2.0, has enhanced power efficiency, and is compatible with USB-enabled devices currently in use. USB cards also incorporate plug-and-play technology that allows devices to self-configure as soon as a connection is made.
FireWire/IEEE 1394	A fast peripheral interconnect standard that enables data transfer at a rate of up to 400 Mb/s. It is used to connect multimedia peripherals such as DV (Digital Video) cameras and other high-speed devices like the latest hard disk drives, CD/DVD burners, and printers. FireWire can support up to 63 devices on one FireWire port. FireWire 400 card transmits data at 400 Mb/s and uses either a 6-pin bullet-shaped powered connector or a 4-pin square-shaped unpowered connector. FireWire 800 card transmits at 800 Mb/s and uses a 9-pin connector.

Riser Cards

Definition:

A *riser card* is a board plugged into the system board and provides additional slots for adapter cards. Because it rises above the system board, the riser card enables you to connect additional adapters to the system in an orientation that is parallel to the system board, thereby saving on space within the system case.

Example:

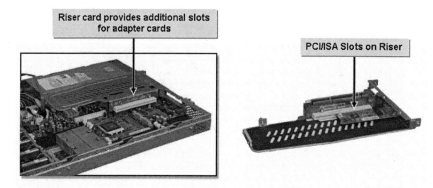

Figure 2-6: *System board with a riser card.*

Daughter Boards

A *daughter board* is an expansion board connected directly to the motherboard to facilitate the computer with an added feature such as modem capability. In personal computing, a daughter board can be used as a more general term for adapter cards. Sometimes, in casual usage, the term daughter board is used interchangeably with the term riser card, but technically they are not the same.

Riser Card vs. Onboard Card

Riser card allows you to connect additional cards to the system in an orientation that is parallel to the system. Onboard cards are directly inserted perpendicular to the system board slots.

Bus

A *bus* is an electrical pathway to which various server components are connected in parallel so that signals can be transferred. Buses are broadly classified into three types.

Bus Type	Description
Processor bus	Handles traffic between the CPU and the chipset. It transfers data between the CPU and the I/O bus, as well as between the CPU and any external cache memory that is on board. Its purpose is to get information to and from the CPU as fast as possible, so it functions at a much faster rate than any other bus in the server. You will seldom find bottlenecks at the processor bus.

Bus Type	Description
Memory bus	Also known as system bus, front side bus, local bus, or host bus. It handles traffic between the CPU, the chipset, and RAM. It can be a dedicated chipset that transfers data between the processor bus and the memory, but sometimes it's incorporated right into the processor bus. The memory bus can be a source of bottlenecks, because the CPU runs faster than the RAM.
I/O bus	Also known as main bus or expansion slot bus. It handles traffic between hardware components and the processor (via the memory bus). Most servers have at least two I/O buses: local and standard. The local I/O bus services performance-critical peripherals such as disk systems, video cards, and high-speed NICs, while the standard I/O bus services other peripherals such as pointing devices, modems, and standard NICs. I/O buses can experience bottlenecks in many circumstances, such as when disks and disk arrays cannot handle I/O requests quickly enough, or network interface cards are overloaded.

Single Channel and Dual Channel Architecture

Single channel versus dual channel architecture refers to the capability of a system bus to access multiple memory modules either in series or in parallel. In single channel architecture, memory modules can be installed in a wide variety of configurations on the system board, and are accessed in series. Dual-channel compatible system boards require pairs of memory modules to be installed in color-coded memory slots and are accessed by the system bus in parallel, in order to double the data transfer rate.

Types of Expansion Buses

System boards include several buses, or data paths, to transfer data to and from different computer components, including all adapter cards.

Expansion Bus Type	Description
PCI	Created by Intel in 1993 as a general-purpose local bus, a PCI local bus uses 32-bit technology and runs at 33 MHz. Newer PCI systems use 64-bit technology and runs at 66 MHz. PCI is the highest performance general I/O bus that is currently used on modern computers.
	• Physical characteristics of cards: 33 or 66 MHz. 133 Mb/s throughput at 33, 66, or 133 MHz. Up to eight functions can be integrated on one board. Card size varies, but must have a PCI edge connector. Slot on the system board is white.
	• Configuration: Supports up to five cards per bus and a system can have two PCI buses for a total of ten devices per system. It can share IRQs, and it uses Plug and Play.
	• Used for all current adapters in client and server systems.
	• Number of data lines: 64-bit bus often implemented as a 32-bit bus.
	• Communication method: Local bus standard; 32-bit bus mastering. Each bus uses 10 loads. A load refers to the amount of power consumed by a device. A PCI chipset uses three loads. Integrated PCI controllers use one load. Controllers installed in a slot use 1.5 loads.

Expansion Bus Type	Description
PCI eXtended or PCIx	As PCI, PCIx uses a parallel interconnect along a bus that is shared with other PCIx devices. In fact, it is an extension of the legacy PCI 32-bit format, with which it is backward-compatible. It differs mainly in the fact that the bus is now 64 bits wide, and runs at higher frequencies (now up to 533MHz, compared to 66MHz the fastest PCI frequency). PCIx is used in the server as a bus for high-bandwidth server peripherals such as RAID controllers and Gigabit Ethernet.
PCIe	An implementation of the PCI bus that uses a faster serial physical-layer communications protocol. It uses a point-to-point bus topology to ensure that devices have constant access to the system bus. ● Used for high-speed graphics cards and high-speed network cards. ● Number of data lines: Each device has a serial connection consisting of one or more lanes. Each lane offers up to 250 Mb/s of throughput. An x16 slot (16 lanes) can handle 4 GB/s of bandwidth in one direction. ● Communication method: Local serial interconnection.

Interrupts

Interrupts are requests that warrant immediate response and are usually created by external devices. Interrupts are generally classified as:

● **Maskable interrupt**: A type of hardware interrupt that enables the processor to handle requests from devices or applications. Generally known as IRQs (interrupt requests), these interrupts can be enabled and disabled by software.

● **Non-maskable interrupt** (**NMI**): A type of hardware interrupt that cannot be disabled by another interrupt. NMIs are often used to report hardware malfunctions such as parity errors. If an NMI is returned, it's highly likely that a hardware component has failed.

Determine the Data Transfer Rate in PCI BUS

When the bus width is known, simply multiply it by the bus speed. For example, if the bus width is 32 bits and the bus speed is 33MHz, then:

● PCI data transfer rate = bus width × bus speed, which is $32 \times 33,000,000$ = 1,056,000,000 b/s or 1,056,000,000 bps/8 or 132MB/s

Suppose the width of the PCI data bus is 64 bits and the speed of the bus is 66MHz. The data transfer rate is then:

● PCI data transfer rate = bus width × bus speed, which is $64 \times 66,000,000$ = 4,224,000,000 b/s or 4,224,000,000 bps/8 or 528MB/s

Expansion Slots

An *expansion slot* is a socket on the system board that is designed to hold expansion cards. Expansion slots come in two sizes: Half-size expansion slots, which can transfer 8 bits of data at a time, and Full-size expansion slots, which can transfer 16 bits of data at a time. Expansion slots provide a means of adding enhanced features and additional memory to a system. They allow you to expand the capabilities of a server by adding a wide variety of peripheral devices.

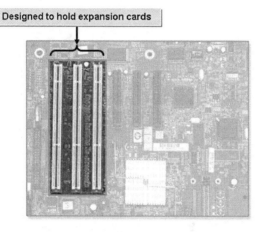

Figure 2-7: An expansion slot is a socket on the system board.

Different types of expansion slots are used for a variety of applications.

Type of Expansion Slot	Description
Industry Standard Architecture or ISA	Introduced by IBM, it is the earliest type of expansion slot that supports both 8-bit and 16-bit expansion cards. ISA slots, which are usually black, are twice as big as PCI slots. Although 16-bit cards use the entire slot, 8-bit cards use only the first half of the slot.
	An 8-bit ISA slot transfers data at the rate of 0.625MB/s, whereas a 16-bit ISA slot transfers data at the rate of 2MB/s. This is still slow compared to today's standards; however, for cards such as modems, the speed is adequate.
Peripheral Component Interconnect (PCI)	Introduced by Intel, the PCI slots extend the computer's functionality with its capability to add general purpose expansion cards. Examples of PCI expansion cards are network, graphics, and sound cards. The slot is either white or ivory colored.
	The standard PCI slot is a 32 bit, 5V slot that operates at 33 MHz. Later, a 64 bit, 3.3V PCI slot that operates at 66 MHz was designed to handle data transfer at the rate of gigabits.

Type of Expansion Slot	Description
PCI eXtended	Jointly developed by IBM, HP, and Compaq, PCIx slot doubles the speed and amount of data exchanged between computer processor and peripherals. PCIx was designed mainly for servers that handle large amount of data.
	The PCIx is a 64-bit 3.3V slot and can handle data at the speed of 66 or 133 MHz. It is fully backward compatible with the existing PCI architecture. PCI expansion cards can be used in PCIx slots and PCIx adapters can be used in PCI slots.
PCI Express or PCIe	Designed by Intel, PCIe slots are used strictly for video cards. PCIe slots will not accept PCI cards and vice versa. The PCIe architecture provides for extremely high bandwidth at low cost.
	PCIe slots come in different sizes: PCIe x1, PCIe x2, PCIe x4, PCIe x8 and PCIe x16. PCIe slots look similar to the standard PCI slot but are usually smaller. Generally, the PCIe slot will have more pins than a PCI slot and is separated from the group of PCI slots.
Accelerated Graphics Port or AGP	Introduced by Intel, AGP speeds up data transfers to video cards. The advent of 3D graphics led to limit the utilization of PCI slot because of its restricted performance for graphic applications such as 3D animation. Therefore, AGP was designed to exclusively meet this requirement.
	An AGP slot is smaller than a PCI slot, is usually brown in color, and is located in line and beside the bank of PCI slots. AGP slots and cards come in four different modes. Some cards and slots are capable of running in more than one mode. AGP 1x transfers data at 266MB/s. AGP 2x mode transfers data at 533MB/s. AGP 4x mode transfers data at 1.07GB/s. The latest AGP mode is AGP 8x. It transfers data at 2.14GB/s.

Expansion Bays

Expansion bays provide space to connect additional drives such as CD, DVD, or additional hard drive storage devices. Additionally, expansion bays provide users with the ability to add other specialized equipment such as cards to improve video, sound, or to add scanners or other devices. Typically, slots are in the back of the server and bays are in the front.

Expansion Cards

An *expansion card* is a circuit board inserted into an expansion slot on the main motherboard, to add a new feature to the server. The expansion card contains I/O circuits for devices, such as printers, scanners, and sound cards.

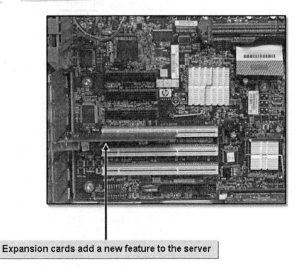

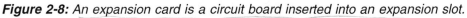

Expansion cards add a new feature to the server

Figure 2-8: An expansion card is a circuit board inserted into an expansion slot.

There are various types of expansion cards.

Type of Expansion Card	Description
Network Interface Card	Adds networking capabilities to servers that require additional NICs apart from the built-in NICs.
Host Bus Adapter (HBA)	Connects a server to the Storage Area Network (SAN). HBAs improve the performance time of the server because the HBA relieves the host microprocessor of both data storage and retrieval tasks. An HBA and its associated disk subsystems are also called disk channel.
Video card	Speeds up both 2D and 3D graphics rendering. Few programs such as CAD design programs and video games rely so heavily on the video card that they will not run if a supported video card is not installed. Video cards are typically installed in either the PCI or AGP slots in the back of a computer. Video cards are also called graphics accelerators.

Type of Expansion Card	Description
Sound card	Delivers audio input and output capabilities. Any type that produces an analog output must include a digital-to-analog converter (DAC) to convert the outgoing signal from digital to analog, which can be played through most speaker systems. Moreover, sound cards that support analog input also warrant an analog-to-digital converter (ADC). This digitizes the incoming analog signal, so the computer can process it. In some computers, the sound card is soldered onto the motherboard, whereas some machines have an expansion sound card that resides in a PCI slot.
Fax card	Enables a computer to be connected to a phone line and thereby transmit or receive fax messages. Using fax card and its associated software allows screen content to be converted into a fax image and transmitted, just like a fax machine.
PBX card	Enables a PBX server to receive and send calls to a standard analog line.
Camera card	Transfers images or graphics from a camera to the server.
VOIP card	Enables you to transmit voice over the Internet using VOIP technology.

Port Expansion Cards

Port expansion cards are additional interfaces added to the PCI slot of the system board to extend the port functionality of the server. When a server requires extra port to connect additional peripheral devices to the system board, port expansion cards are added to the PCI slots. The architecture and the functionality of a port expansion card are similar to that of the actual physical ports themselves. The various port expansion cards include serial, parallel, USB, and FireWire/IEEE 1394.

Expansion Card Compatibility

Expansion cards can cause bottlenecks on a server, so selecting the proper expansion card for your server can actually help performance. When you're installing an expansion card, you need to match the physical hardware characteristics of the system bus, drivers, and network topology. In a Windows-only environment, this is fairly easy; when other operating systems such as UNIX or NetWare are present, the job becomes a little more complicated.

One of the first things you need to consider when selecting an expansion card is the system bus architecture of the server, and the types of expansion slots that are available. If you have both ISA and PCI slots in the server, it's recommended that you use a PCI adapter, because doing so will enable you to take advantage of bus mastering, a technology that takes the control of the bus away from the CPU to transfer data directly to the RAM or other devices.

ACTIVITY 2-1
Identifying System Board Components

Scenario:

In this activity, you will identify system board components.

1. A 32-bit PCI bus is operating at a clock speed of 66 MHz. What is the total bandwidth of the bus?

   a) 264 Mb/s

   b) 512 Mb/s

   c) 528 Mb/s

   d) 544 Mb/s

2. Which PCI technology uses a point-to-point bus topology to ensure that devices have constant access to the system bus?

   a) Bus mastering

   b) PCIe

   c) PCIx

   d) AGP

3. True or False? Server system boards are most often identified by their form factors.

   ___ True

   ___ False

4. Match a bus type to its description.

   ___ Processor bus   a. Handles traffic between the CPU, chipset, and RAM.

   ___ Memory bus   b. Handles traffic between the CPU and the chipset.

   ___ I/O buses   c. Handles traffic between hardware components and the processor.

5. What is the advantage of using a riser card?

TOPIC B
Explore System Processing Core

In the previous topic, you described the various system board components of a server. Among these components, the processor is considered to be the computer's brain. In this topic, you will examine the features of the system processing core.

One of the important components of a server is its processor, which plays an important role in defining the performance of a system. Based upon the performance requirements of a server, an appropriate processor needs to be chosen and installed. A server technician must be equipped with knowledge of the processor types and their features in order to choose the right one to install or upgrade.

Features of a Processor

Every server processor will have various features that can be implemented based on your specific requirements. The features include:

- Multiprocessing
- Cache levels
- Execute Disable (XD) and No Execute (NX) Bits
- Hyperthreading
- Virtualization Technology (VT) or AMD Virtualization (AMD-V)

 The processor can also be referred to as system processing core or CPU.

Types of Processors

Both Intel and AMD offer a variety of processors to suit varied requirements.

Intel offers Pentium Pro, Pentium II, Celeron, Pentium II Xeon, Pentium III, Pentium II and III Xeon, Pentium IV, Pentium M, Intel Core, Dual Core Xeon LV, Intel Pentium Dual Core, Intel Core 2, Pentium Duo, Pentium Dual Core, Core 2 Quad, and Intel Pentium 2 Dual Core Processor.

AMD processors include AMD Athlon, AMD Athlon 64, AMD Athlon X2, AMD Athlon XP, AMD Duron, AMD Sempron, AMD Turion, MD Opteron, and AMD Phenom 1.

Slots and Socket Types

CPUs use either sockets or slots to connect to the system board. Many varieties of sockets and slots have been developed over the years.

The following table describes some of the slots you might encounter.

Slot Type	Description
Slot 1	Contains a 242-pin edge connector. Used for Celeron SEPP (Single Edge Processor Package), Pentium II SECC (Single Edge Contact Cartridge) and SECC2, and Pentium III processors.
Slot 2	Contains a 330-pin edge connector. Used for Pentium II Xeon and Pentium III Xeon processors. Designed for multiprocessor systems.
Slot A	Contains a 242-pin edge connector. Used for AMD Athlon processors. Pinouts are incompatible with Slot 1.
Slot M	Used for Itanium processors.

The difference between an Intel and AMD processor lies in the socket used. AMD processors use Socket A (462 pins) while Intel processors use Socket 478 (478 pins). The following table describes some of the common sockets types.

Socket Type	Description
Super Socket 7	• Pin layout: 321 pin Staggered PGA (SPGA) arranged in 37 x 37 grid • Processor used for: AMD K6-2 and K6-III
Socket 423	• Pin layout: SPGA • Processor used for: Pentium IV
Socket 478	• Pin layout: SPGA • Processor used for: Pentium IV, Celeron, Pentium IV EE, Pentium M
Socket 462/Socket A	• Pin layout: Supports Plastic PGA (PPGA) • Processor used for: AMD Athlon, Duron, Athlon XP, and Sempron
Socket 603	• Pin layout: 603 pins arrayed around the center of the socket • Processor used for: Xeon
Socket 754	• Pin layout: 754-pin PGA • Processor used for: Athlon 64, Sempron, Turon 64
Socket 771	• Pin Layout: 771-pin contact Land Grid Array (LGA) • Processor used for: Intel Xeon
Socket 775 (or LGA 775, or Socket T)	• Layout: 775 pin-contact LGA • Processor used for: Pentium 4, Celeron D, Pentium Extreme Edition, Core 2 Duo, Core 2 Extreme
Socket 939	• Pin layout: 939 pin PGA • Processor used for: Athlon 64, Athlon 64FX, Athlon 64X2, and Opteron 100 series
Socket 940	• Pin layout: 940 pin PGA • Processor used for: Opteron, Athlon 64FX

Socket Type	Description
Socket F (or Socket 1207)	• Layout: 1207 pin contact LGA • Processor used for: Opteron
Socket AM2	• Pin layout: 940 pin PGA • Processor used for: Athlon 64, Sempron, Turon 64, Athlon 64FX, Athlon 64X2, Opteron 100-series
PAC418	• Pin layout: 418 pin Very Low Insertion Force (VLIF) • Processor used for: Itanium
PAC611	• Pin layout: 611 pin VLIF • Processor used for: Itanium, Itanium 2
FCPGA6	• Pin layout: 479 pin PGA • Processor used for: Core Solo, Core Duo, Dual-Core Xeon, Core 2 Duo
Socket AM3	• Pin layout: 941 pin PGA • Processor used for: Phenom II, Athlon II
Socket 1155	• Pin layout: 1155 pin LGA • Processor used for: Core i5
Socket 1156	• Pin layout: 1156 pin LGA • Processor used for: Core i5
Socket 1167	• Pin layout: 1167 pin LGA • Processor used for: Xeon

Processor Chip Packaging

The Pin Grid Array, or the PGA, is the arrangement of pins on the integrated circuit packaging. In a PGA, the pins are arranged in a square array that may or may not cover the bottom of the package. The pins are commonly spaced 2.54 mm (0.1″) apart. PGAs are typically ceramic (CPGA), but plastic cases are also used (PPGA). The underside of a PGA package looks like a "bed of nails." In a staggered PGA (SPGA), the pins are not lined up in perfect rows and columns.

The Land Grid Array (LGA) is a type of surface-mount packaging used for integrated circuits. It is a chip package with a very high density of contacts. An LGA chip has flat pads on the bottom of its package that contacts the motherboard socket. Intel favors the LGA arrangement because the pinless processor package can better withstand rough handling.

Multiprocessing

Many mid-range and upper-range servers have the ability to use more than one processor for routine processing tasks. This ability is referred to as parallel processing or *multiprocessing*. Although computers are built with various overlapping features, such as executing instructions while inputting and outputting data, the term "multiprocessing" refers specifically to the concurrent execution of instructions by more than one processor.

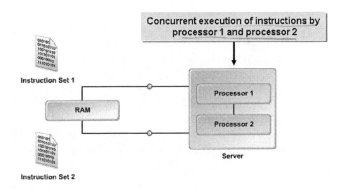

Figure 2-9: Multiprocessing provides an ability to use more than one processor for routine processing tasks.

Symmetric multiprocessing (SMP) is a technology used for large databases, data warehousing, and decision support systems. SMP treats all processors as equals. Any processor can do the work of any other processor, and applications are divided into threads that can run concurrently. SMP improves the performance of the application itself, as well as the total throughput of the system. SMP requires some form of shared memory and local instruction caches. But most importantly, SMP systems require applications that can take advantage of the multi-threaded technology.

Multi-threaded Technology

Multi-threaded technology is a technique that enables an operating system to execute different parts of a program or application, called threads, simultaneously. These threads are concurrently processed by the various CPU's in the server.

SMP Limitations

The main limitation to SMP is that all individual processors share the same memory bus. Some higher-end systems attempt to overcome that limitation by including a separate high-speed memory cache for each processor, but you're generally limited to using two, four, or eight processors; however, Windows NT/2000 Server/Server 2003/ Server 2008 and Linux provide SMP support for up to 32 processors. To use more than eight processors, you'll probably need to move to Massive Parallel Processing (MPP) or server clustering.

Multicore Processing

Multicore processor is a single chip that contains two or more distinct CPUs that process simultaneously. Current common options include dual-core (two CPUs), triple-core (three CPUs), and quad-core (four CPUs), though octo-core chips are becoming more common. Once you start adding tens or hundreds of CPUs, the terminology changes from "multi-core" and become "many-core."

To employ multicore processing effectively requires:

- **Motherboard Support**: A motherboard capable of handling multiple processors. It requires sockets or slots for the extra chips, and a chipset capable of handling the multi-processing arrangement.
- **Processor Support**: Processors those are capable of being used in a multiprocessing system.
- **Operating System Support**: An operating system that supports multiprocessing, such as Windows 2003/2008 or one of the various flavors of UNIX and LINUX.

Processor Speed

Processor speed is the number of processing cycles that a microprocessor can perform in a given second. Some CPUs require several cycles to assemble and perform a single instruction, whereas others require fewer cycles. The clock speed, indicated by MHz, is a technical and theoretical rating, whereas the actual performance speed can vary from the published clock speed rating.

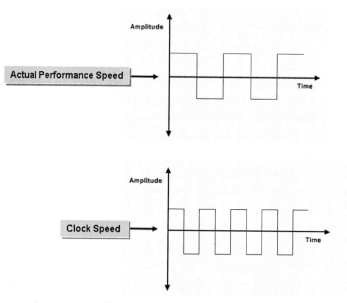

Figure 2-10: Processing speed refers to the processing cycles that a microprocessor can perform in a given second.

32-Bit vs. 64-Bit

32-bit operating systems support applications that use data units up to 32 bits wide, but no larger. 64-bit operating systems can support applications that use data units up to 64 bits wide, making 64-bit operating systems backwards-compatible (able to support 32-bit programs). 64-bit operating systems require a 64-bit processor and use memory more efficiently. Because they can use more memory, they can increase the use of RAM and decrease the amount of time spent using the hard disk. Windows Vista® comes in both 32-bit and 64-bit versions.

x86 and x64

x86 is the most common and successful instruction set architecture which supports 32-bit processors. If something is referred to as x86, it means that it supports 32-bit software, and can also support 64-bit. The term x86-64 (also referred as x64) explicitly refers to the 64-bit x86 architecture.

Cache Levels

Cache memory—the temporary storage space—is described in levels of closeness and accessibility to the processor.

Cache Level	Description
Level 1/L1	A fast memory that the CPU uses first for quick storage and calculation. Level 1 is also referred to as internal or primary cache because it resides inside the processor. However, level 1 cache is not very large in storage capacity. Its storage capability ranges from 8 KB to 64 KB.
Level 2/L2	It feeds the L1 cache. L2 is either integrated into the CPU chip or is available as a separate bank of chips on the system board. It is slower than level 1 cache but can provide more than 512 KB of storage space. A popular L2 cache memory size is 1,024 kilobytes (one megabyte).
Level 3/L3	Some microprocessor manufacturers now provide CPUs with both level 1 and level 2 cache memory integrated in the processor chip. In that case, the cache memory that resides outside the processor and on the motherboard is called the level 3 or L3 cache.

Stepping

Stepping is the revision level of a processor. When multiprocessor system boards are manufactured, they're tested to ensure that they will work when the speed and L2 cache size are the same for each processor. As processors are updated, they're tested to see if the new stepping will work with the previous one.

You can get the stepping, speed, and cache information about processors from the manufacturer. For instance, Intel provides an S-spec number on the face of their Pentium III processors that you can use in conjunction with the Quick Reference Guide found on the Intel website to determine the stepping, voltage, timing, packaging, and other information specific to the processor.

With multiple processors, it is important to verify N+1 stepping, meaning that if the processor steppings do not match or fall within one stepping of each other, then it's recommended that you replace one of them so that stepping, speed, and cache all match.

The Execute Disable Bit

The *Execute Disable (XD)* bit, also called the No Execute (NX) bit, is a security feature that provides protection against buffer overflow attacks. When this feature is enabled, the CPU segregates areas of memory for storing processor instructions, code, or data, and ensures that the execution of code in the segregated memory space does not take place. However, when this feature is disabled, the processor will not restrict code execution in any memory area. This makes the processor more vulnerable to malicious attacks. The BIOS feature is actually a toggle for the processor's XD bit feature.

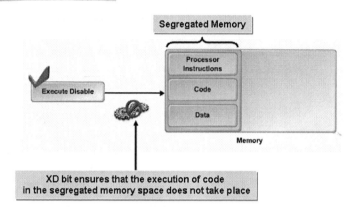

Figure 2-11: XD bits provide protection against buffer overflow attacks.

Buffer Overflow Attacks

Buffer overflow occurs when the program writes more information into the buffer than the space it has allocated in the memory. This allows an attacker to overwrite data that controls the program execution path and hijack the control of the program to execute the attacker's code instead of the process code.

Wait States

A *wait state* is a period during which the CPU or bus becomes idle, often due to differences in clock speeds among various components. Due to the introduction of faster microprocessors, there are major performance bottlenecks surrounding the usage of the system bus. Consider the fact that a PCI bus can run at around 66 MHz speeds, while a microprocessor can operate at 300 MHz and above. This disparity forced system designers to include up to five wait states between each memory access.

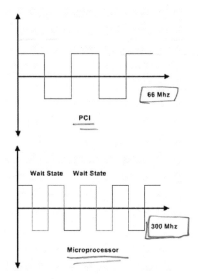

Figure 2-12: The CPU or bus becomes idle during the wait state.

Wait State Example

For example, if the CPU is much faster than memory chips, it may need to sit idle during some clock cycles so that memory chips can catch up. Likewise, buses sometimes require wait states if expansion boards run slower than the bus. In 1998, Intel introduced a new Pentium II chipset (the 440BX) that increased the system bus speed to 100 MHz. Today, some system buses can run at speeds over 1600 MHz.

Hyperthreading

Hyperthreading is a technique developed by Intel to enable a single CPU to act like multiple CPUs. In multiprocessing systems, the CPU is made up of many smaller components. At any given time, one of these components might be busy while the rest wait to be utilized. Therefore, the processor can handle only one instruction—called the thread—from a program at any instant.

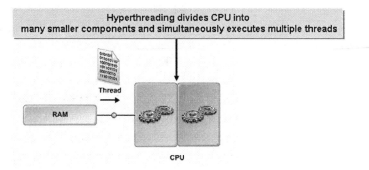
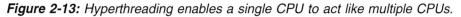

Figure 2-13: Hyperthreading enables a single CPU to act like multiple CPUs.

Moreover, processors are never 100% utilized even when their loads peak. By implementing the hyperthreading feature, various threads can be simultaneously processed by multiple CPUs, thereby increasing the system's efficiency to 90%. The benefits of hyperthreading can be realized only by using operating systems that support multiple CPUs. These operating systems consider each CPU as two units. Operating systems that support hyperthreading include Microsoft Windows NT 4.0, Microsoft Windows 2000/2003/2008, Microsoft XP Professional, Unix, and Linux.

 To determine if a CPU supports hyperthreading, look for the special "HT" marking on the CPU logo.

Instruction Sets

An *instruction* is a fundamental operation that a processor executes. A collection of instructions is called an instruction set. Instructions are stored in the main memory and are not processed.

Server processors are often categorized by the type of instruction set they use. Manufacturers have their own instruction sets, which can be categorized into three types.

Generally, the type of system board you have dictates the type of processor you'll need, and vice versa.

Instruction Set	Description
Complex Instruction Set Computer (CISC)	A design strategy for computer architecture that depends on hardware to perform complicated instructions. Does not require instructions to be of a fixed length. Allows for more complicated functions to be executed in one instruction. Most Intel and AMD processors fall into this category.
Reduced Instruction Set Computer (RISC)	A design strategy for computer architecture that depends on a combination of hardware and software to perform complicated instructions. Requires instructions to be of a fixed length. RISC instructions are simpler and less than CISC, but more instructions are required to carry out a single function. Macintosh, IBM RS/6000, and Sun Microsystems computers use RISC. IBM, Motorola, and Sun manufacture RISC chips.
Explicitly Parallel Instruction Computing (EPIC)	A design strategy for computer architecture that is meant to simplify and streamline CPU operation by taking advantage of advancements in compiler technology and by combining the best of the CISC and RISC design strategies. EPIC-based processors are 64-bit chips. Intel IA-64 architecture, including Intel Itanium processors, is based on EPIC.

Virtualization Technology

Virtualization Technology (VT) or AMD Virtualization (AMD-V) is a feature that enhances the processor design by implementing virtualization on it. Virtualization supports two or more virtual computing environments that run different operating systems and applications on the same hardware. For example, VT enables you to run both a Linux virtual machine and a Microsoft Windows virtual machine on one system. Launched in 2006, AMD-V was originally named "Pacifica."

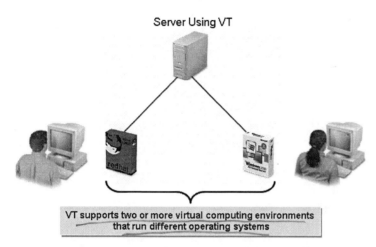

Figure 2-14: VT enables the user to run both a Linux virtual machine and a Microsoft Windows virtual machine on one system.

Intel refers to virtualization as VT AMD-V

Voltage Regulator Module

The *Voltage Regulator Module (VRM)* is a replaceable module installed on the system board to stabilize the voltage fed into the processor. In a server, if one power supply fails, there is a secondary power supply unit ready to feed the server components. The VRM card regulates these power supply sources.

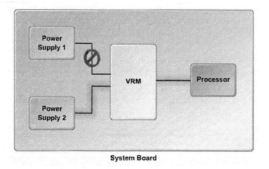

Figure 2-15: VRM stabilizes the voltage fed into the processor.

CPU Installation Considerations

There are several factors you should keep in mind when installing a CPU.

Factor	Description
Power	Make sure to review the CPU's power requirements to verify that it is compatible and that you aren't overloading the computer's power supply.
Removal	Review the computer's documentation to determine how to properly remove the existing processor from the system board. Most new processors use *Zero Insertion Force (ZIF)* sockets, which is a type of processor socket that uses a lever to tighten or loosen the pin connections between the processor chip and the socket. So there is no force required when you insert or remove the chip. The chip is easily dropped into the socket's holes, and a lever is pulled down to lock it in.
Cooling	Verify that you have the necessary equipment to cool the new processor. Some CPUs come equipped with a heat sink and fan; others don't. If necessary, follow the new CPU manufacturer's instructions to install any fan or heat sink on the new CPU. You will probably need to apply thermally conductive gel between the CPU and the heat sink.

CPU Selection Tips

There are two key factors you must consider when selecting a CPU for a server.

Factor	Considerations
Hardware compatibility	The design of the server's system board determines the type of CPU you can install. For example, you can't install an AMD processor into a system board designed to support an Intel processor. Most importantly, you should review the documentation for the computer's system board to determine its compatibility with other CPUs. Keep in mind that most original equipment manufacturers (OEMs) do not typically provide you with the system board's documentation. To obtain this documentation, try contacting the server's manufacturer or the manufacturer of the system board.
Performance	In addition, you should keep in mind that there is a trade-off between price and performance when selecting a CPU. The greater the performance requirements of the user, the more powerful CPU you should select. And more powerful CPUs are simply more expensive. When selecting a CPU for a user, you should ask the user the budget for the purchase. This budget can help you narrow down the choices for selecting a processor.

Vendor Standards for Hardware

Vendor standards specify the hardware requirements that are necessary for a server setup. These standards vary depending on the server application.

For a medium range server to support 10 to 15 workstations, the following hardware configuration is required:

- Processor: Minimum Quad Core Intel® Xeon® E5310, 2x4MB Cache, 1.60GHz, 1066MHz FSB
- Memory: Minimum 4 GB (Application Dependent)
- Type: Rack or Blade
- Hard drives: Minimum 180 GB (Application dependent)
- RAID Controllers: RAID 5
- Ports:
  - Rear: Two Universal Serial Bus (USB) 2.0, 9-pin serial, video (chassis compatible)
  - Front: Two Universal Serial Bus (USB) 2.0, (chassis compatible)
- Cooling: Hot-plug, redundant cooling fans
- Power: 1,470W, hot-plug redundant power (1+1), 200-240
- Input devices: USB mouse, USB keyboard, USB KVM dongle

ACTIVITY 2-2
Exploring the System Processing Core

Scenario:
In this activity, you will explore the system processing core.

---

1. **Which feature provides protection against buffer overflow attacks?**

   a) XD

   b) AMD-V

   c) Hyperthreading

   d) Mutliprocessing

2. **True or False? The processor first checks the L1 cache residing on the processor.**

   ___ True

   ___ False

3. **Match an instruction set to its description.**

   ___ CISC   a. A design strategy for computer architecture that is meant to simplify and streamline CPU operation by taking advantage of advancements in compiler technology and by combining the best of two design strategies.

   ___ RISC   b. A design strategy for computer architecture that depends on a combination of hardware and software to perform complicated instructions.

   ___ EPIC   c. A design strategy for computer architecture that depends on hardware to perform complicated instructions.

4. **Which feature enhances the processor design by implementing virtualization on it?**

   a) XD

   b) Mutliprocessing

   c) AMD-V/VT

   d) Hyperthreading

5. **What is the key factor that you must consider when selecting a CPU for a server?**

   a) Power supply

   b) Expansion slots

   c) RAM

   d) System board

6. **What are the factors that you should keep in mind when installing a CPU?**

   a) Power

   b) Removal

   c) Cooling

   d) RAM

TOPIC C
Explore Server Memory

In the previous topic, you examined the system processing system. The processing system requires an area called memory to retrieve and store the processed data. In this topic, you will explore the various types of memory associated with the server.

Adding memory is a simple and cost effective way to increase server performance. Upgrading memory is a frequent task for server hardware professionals. Before knowing how to upgrade memory, you need to have knowledge on the various types of memory installed on a server.

Memory Form Factors and Slot Types

Memory modules come in several form factors, and each module will connect to the system board through a compatible memory slot only.

Memory Form Factor	Description
Single In-line Memory Module (SIMM)	Generally found in older systems, SIMMs have a 32-bit data path. Because most processors now have a 64-bit bus width, they required that SIMMs be installed in matched pairs so that the processor could access the two SIMMs simultaneously. SIMMs generally have eight memory chips per module. Only SIMMs can be installed into SIMM slots on the system board.
Dual In-line Memory Module (DIMM)	DIMMs are found in many systems, and they have a 64-bit data path. The development of the DIMM solved the issue of having to install SIMMs in matched pairs. DIMMs also have separate electrical contacts on each side of the module, while the contacts on SIMMs on both sides are redundant. DIMMs generally have 16 or 32 chips per module.
Small Outline Dual In-line Memory Module (SODIMM)	SODIMMs are half the size of DIMMs and, therefore, cannot fit into a DIMM slot. SODIMMs are most often seen in laptops, small networking devices (such as routers), and PCs with smaller system boards. They have either 32 or 64-bit data paths.
Rambus Inline Memory Module (RIMM)	RIMMs have a metal cover that acts as a heat sink. Although they have the same number of pins, RIMMs have different pin settings and are not interchangeable with DIMMs and SDRAM. RIMMs can be installed only in RIMM slots on a system board.

Types of RAM

There are several types of RAM.

RAM Memory Type	Description
Dynamic RAM (DRAM)	A type of RAM that needs to be refreshed. The standard DRAM design is set up as a matrix of bits, where each bit is assigned a row and column address. When the memory controller wants specific data, it uses this address. A DRAM module that's rated at 60 nanoseconds provides requested data to the memory controller within 60 nanoseconds, but other factors such as setting up the addresses and receiving the data, can expand the memory cycle to 85 to 120 nanoseconds. With Fast Page Mode, the memory controller can access multiple data bits, as long as the bits have the same row address.
Extended Data-Out (EDO)	It provides improved performance over equivalent Fast Page Mode devices, but the performance increase isn't available unless the computer's chipset supports EDO. If you install EDO memory into a computer system that doesn't support it, it functions as a Fast Page Mode memory module. EDO memory goes one step further than DRAM by enabling the memory controller to start a new column address instruction while data is being read from the current address. Memory access cycles overlap, saving about 10 nanoseconds per bit of data accessed.
Synchronous DRAM (SDRAM)	It runs at high clock speeds and is synchronized with the CPU bus. SDRAM was originally packaged on a 168-pin DIMM.
Double Data Rate SDRAM (DDR)	It transfers data twice per clock cycle and is a replacement for SDRAM. DDR uses additional power and ground lines and is packaged on a 184-pin DIMM module. The difference between SDRAM and DDR RAM is that instead of doubling the clock rate it transfers data twice per clock cycle which effectively doubles the data rate. DDRRAM has become mainstream in the graphics card market and has become the memory standard.
Double Data Rate SDRAM 2 (DDR2)	The next-generation DDR memory technology that features faster speeds, higher data bandwidths, lower power consumption, and enhanced thermal performance. DDR2 memory modules are currently offered in two frequency ranges, 400MHz and 533MHz. The form factor most appropriate for servers is a registered ECC DIMMs (240 pin) module. DDR2 DIMM memory modules are not backward-compatible with DDR DIMM due to incompatible pin configurations, core voltage, and memory chip technology.
DDR3 SDRAM	It transfers data at twice the rate of DDR2 and uses 30% less power in the process. Like DDR2, DDR3 chips use 240-pin connections, but cannot be used interchangeably because of differences in notch location and electrical requirements.
RAMBUS DRAM (RDRAM)	It utilizes a narrow, high-speed bus. It has been adapted to high-bandwidth applications that can read from or write large blocks of data to memory. The RAMBUS data rate is higher than SDRAM and DDR and is similar to DDR. An 800 MHz RDRAM chip can handle two operations per clock cycle.

DDR2 Advantages

The advantages of DDR2 memory compared to DDR include the following:

- Higher speed and improved electrical and thermal performance
- Lower power consumption and heat dissipation
- Improved signal and integrity
- Higher module bandwidth
- Speed above 400 MHz
- Larger chip sizes

Types of ROM

ROM is memory that is nonvolatile. The original ROM chips could not be altered after the program code was placed on the ROM chip. As time went by, users needed the ability to update the information stored on ROM chips. Over the years, various chips have been created to perform the function of ROM, and can be updated one way or another. These are referred to as programmable ROM (PROM). Types of ROM include:

- **PROM:** A blank ROM chip that is burned with a special ROM burner. This chip can be changed only once. After the instructions are burned in it, the chip cannot be updated or changed.

- **EPROM (erasable PROM):** Like PROM, except that the data can be erased through a quartz crystal on top of the chip. After removing the chip from the system, a UV light is used to change the binary data back to its original state, all 1s.

- **EEPROM (electronically erasable PROM):** A chip that can be reprogrammed using software from the BIOS or chip manufacturer using a process called flashing. Also known as Flash ROM, the chip does not need to be removed in order to be reprogrammed.

Memory Standard Specifications

The following table summarizes the memory standard specifications.

Standard	Characteristics
PC100	- Clock speed: 100 MHz - Bus width: 8 bytes - Voltage: 3.3 V - Form factor: 168-pin DIMM and 144-pin SO-DIMM - Transfer rate: 763 MB/s - Backwards-compatible with PC66
PC133	- Clock speed: 133 MHz - Bus width: 8 bytes - Voltage: 3.3 V - Form factor: 168-pin DIMM and 144-pin SO-DIMM - Transfer rate: 1,015 MB/s - Backwards-compatible with PC100 and PC133

Standard	Characteristics
DDR-333 or PC2700	• Clock speed: 166 MHz • Bus width: 8 bytes • Voltage: 2.5 V • Form factor: 184-pin DIMM • Transfer rate: 2,533 MB/s • Backwards-compatible with slower DDR SDRAM DIMMs
DDR-400 or PC3200	• Clock speed: 200MHz • Bus width: 8 bytes • Voltage: 2.6 V • Form factor: 184-pin DIMM • Transfer rate: 3,052 MB/s • Backwards-compatible with slower DDR SDRAM DIMMs
DDR2–667, PC2-5300, or PC2-5400	• Clock speed: 166 MHz • Bus width: 8 bytes • Voltage: 1.8 V • Form factor: 240-pin DIMM • Transfer rate: 5,066 MB/s • Backwards-compatible with slower DDR2 SDRAM DIMMs
DDR3–1600 or PC3-12800	• Clock speed: 200 MHz • Bus width: 8 bytes • Voltage: 1.5 V • Form factor: 240-pin DIMM • Transfer rate: 12,207 MB/s

Cache Memory

Cache memory, or CPU cache, is static random access memory (SRAM) located near the processor. It allows the processor to execute instructions and to read and write data at a higher speed than the regular RAM. Cache memory has the fastest storage capability because it is built into a chip with zero wait-state interface to the processor's execution unit. Cache memory is limited in size, though. Instructions and data are transferred from the main memory to the cache in blocks to enhance performance.

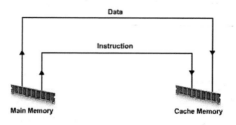

Figure 2-16: *Cache memory allows the processor to execute instructions and to read and write data at a higher speed than the regular RAM.*

There are several types of cache memory.

Type	Characteristics
Processor cache	A type of high-speed memory that is directly linked to the CPU. This link enables the CPU to access information faster from the processor cache than from the main memory. The cache is a buffer of sorts between the processor and the relatively slow memory that serves it. The presence of the cache enables the processor to do its work without having to wait for memory.
Write-back cache	A caching method where changes to data stored in L1 cache aren't copied to the main memory until absolutely necessary. Write-back caching is available on many microprocessors, including all Intel processors since 80486. A write-back cache is also called a copy-back cache.
Write-through cache	It performs all write operations in parallel; data is simultaneously written to main memory and the L1 cache. Write-back caching can provide increased performance over write-through caching because it reduces the number of write operations to main memory; however, this performance improvement introduces the risk that data can be lost if the system crashes.
RAID cache	A form of disk or peripheral cache. Although implementing RAID can increase fault-tolerance and availability of data, performance can suffer. RAID controllers often include cache memory that is used to store the most recently accessed files, thus decreasing access time if those files are needed again by the system. With RAID cache, I/O occurs at the speed of the PCI bus, not at the speed of the hard disk.

Write-Back Cache vs. Write-Through Cache

Write-back caching can provide increased performance over write-through caching because it reduces the number of write operations to main memory; however, this performance improvement introduces the risk that data can be lost if the system crashes.

Memory Compatibility Factors

There are various factors to be considered for ensuring memory compatibility.

Factor	Description
Speed	Memory must be compatible with bus speed. In servers, generally, memory that can run at the speed of 800 MHz or 1333 MHz is used.
Size	The size of RAM used must be compatible with the server. The most widely used RAM size is 8 GB or 16 GB.
Pins	The number of pins available in the system board slot must be compatible with the pins used in memory. For instance, 240-pin DIMMs are used in the newest and fastest DDR3 memory servers.
	DDR3 is the latest generation of memory with improved architecture that allows it to transmit data more quickly. To use DDR3 memory, the system motherboard must have 240-pin DIMM slots and a DDR3-enabled chipset.
Column Access Strobe (CAS) latency	The amount of time taken to retrieve data from a particular column of a specified row in a memory module. CAS latency is the clock cycles between the issuance of the read command and its subsequent data retrieval.
	CAS2 latency essentially means that there is a two cycle delay, and CAS3 has a three cycle delay. Therefore, to achieve better performance, CAS memory modules must be able to support low-latency settings.
Memory timing	The time taken by memory to produce the required data from the start of the access until the data is available for use. The current memory timing varies from 5 to 70 nanoseconds. The memory timing must be compatible with the processor speed.
Vendor specific memory	Installing and upgrading RAM from the same vendor helps you to reduce problems that crop up due to incompatibility.

Column Access Strobe (CAS) latency

CAS

DDR → Double Data rate

Memory Pairing

Memory pairing is a technique of coupling two physical memory banks and enhancing server performance. Although two different DIMMs with identical specification must technically work together, there are a few bottlenecks. To eradicate huge compatibility problems, the RAM speed or timing must be adjusted to a slower setting. You can operate any memory type at slower clock speeds and more conservative timings than its actual specification. This caution will help you to reduce the probability of any risks.

If you pair 1 GB DDR2-667 with 1 GB DDR2-800 DIMM, then both will run at DDR2-667 speed. All memory controllers—whether they are integrated into an AMD Athlon 64 X2 or a Phenom X3/X4 processor, or are part of a chipset northbridge—are capable of running in the dual-channel mode. In other words, they utilize two memory banks in order to double the bandwidth by widening the memory data path from 64 bits to 128 bits.

Memory Interleaving

Memory interleaving is the process of splitting main memory into several physically separate components called banks or modules. This process increases performance by enabling the CPU to make several concurrent memory requests, each to different but identical modules, and helps to alleviate the processor-memory bottleneck that is a major limiting factor in overall performance. Theoretically, system performance is enhanced because the read-and-write activity occurs nearly simultaneously across the modules, similar to hard drive striping. With this process, it's the memory addresses that are interleaved.

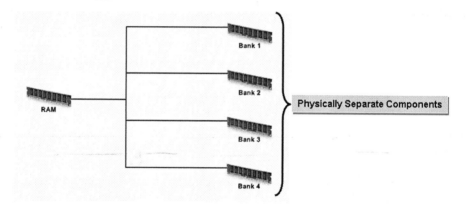

Figure 2-17: *Memory interleaving splits main memory into several physically separate components to increase the system performance.*

High-Order and Low-Order Interleaving

In high-order interleaving, consecutive memory addresses are stored on the same physical memory module, while in low-order interleaving, consecutive memory addresses are stored on consecutive memory modules.

Error Checking and Correction Memory

Error Checking and Correction (ECC) memory is a type of RAM that includes a fault detection/correction circuit to test the accuracy of data passing in and out of the memory. The detection technique used in ECC memory is different than that used in parity memory. The parity memory technique is used for detecting the bit that was flipped during the memory read process and for displaying a "Parity Error" message. ECC memory detects and corrects all single-bit errors, or it can detect errors in two bits. ECC RAM provides more reliable data transfer, resulting in greater system stability. Therefore, high-end servers and workstations may use ECC memory to minimize crashes and system downtime. Although, using ECC decreases a server's performance by about 2%, its use is important in applications in which data integrity is a major concern.

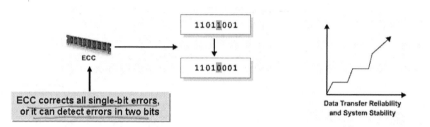

Figure 2-18: ECC memory is fault detection/correction circuit to test the accuracy of data passing in and out of the memory.

Non-ECC Memory

Non-ECC is a type of RAM that is usually located in client workstations, where data integrity is not such a major concern. Obviously, there is usually a lower efficiency associated with the requirement to fix memory errors because it does not include any mechanism to check or fix errors.

Parity Checking

Another type of memory error detection is called parity checking. It provides single-bit error detection but doesn't have any correction capabilities. ECC was developed to go beyond parity checking.

ECC Cost and Recovery

ECC uses a special algorithm to encode information in a block of bits that contains sufficient detail to permit the recovery of a single-bit error in the protected data. It uses 7 bits to protect 32 bits, or 8 bits to protect 64 bits. When ECC corrects a detected single-bit error in a 64-bit block of memory, the computer continues functioning as if no error occurred. However, if an error is corrected, it can be useful to know this; a pattern of errors can indicate a hardware problem that needs to be addressed. Chipsets that support ECC mode usually include a way to report corrected errors to the operating system, but it's up to the operating system to support this. ECC will detect (but not correct) errors of 2, 3, or 4 bits, in addition to detecting (and correcting) single-bit errors. ECC memory handles these multiple-bit errors similarly to how parity checking handles single-bit errors; a Non-Maskable Interrupt (NMI) instructs the system to shut down to avoid data corruption. Multiple-bit errors are extremely rare in memory. ECC can cause a system's performance to be degraded, because the ECC algorithm is more complicated than parity checking, and time must be allowed for ECC to correct any detected errors. The penalty is usually one extra wait state per memory read, which translates to a real-world performance hit of about 2 to 3 percent.

Although non-ECC systems may save on cost, implementing ECC memory is recommended to ensure data integrity.

Registered and Unregistered Memory

Based on the buffering status, RAM is classified into various types.

Memory Type	Description
Buffered memory	Modules that contain buffer logic chips that re-drive signals through memory chips and enable modules to include more memory chips. ECC, EDO, and FPM memory can be buffered.
Registered memory	A special type of buffered memory. Simply put, registered memory is the Synchronous DRAM (SDRAM) version of buffered memory. They have built-in registers, which are small temporary area (usually 64 bits) to store data on their address and control lines. In these memory modules, the buffer logic chip has been replaced by a registered logic chip. The registers delay data transferred to the chip. Registered memory is slightly slower than unregistered memory by 1 clock cycle, but it increases the 'reliability' of the data. Like buffered memory, registered memory doesn't allow the mixing of registered and unbuffered memory modules. ECC and SDRAM memory can be registered.
Unbuffered memory/ unregistered memory	Memory where no buffers or registers are included in the memory module. With this type of memory, the buffers or registers are located on the system board. The design of the computer's memory controller dictates whether memory must be buffered or unbuffered; however, in servers with more than 512 MB of RAM, it's often recommended that you use registered memory. SDRAM, EDO, and FPM memory can be unbuffered.

Memory and Processor Compatibility

The rate of developments taking place in microprocessor speed is far greater than that of developments in DRAM memory speed. Though both are improving exponentially, the growth of the microprocessor is substantially higher than that of DRAM. When planning to build a server, you need to be familiar with the various RAM types and their compatible motherboards. Some processors require specific types of RAM to be used. For example, certain versions of the Pentium 4 processor require Rambus RAM to be installed.

ACTIVITY 2-3
Exploring Server Memory

Scenario:
In this activity, you will explore server memory.

---

1. **Which of these is a characteristic of buffered memory?**

   a) It contains a register that delays incoming data.

   b) It holds data until it can be written to the disk drive.

   c) It helps to minimize the load of information transfer.

   d) It holds data in a secondary cache to speed up processes.

---

2. **What are the speed and cost differences between SRAM and DRAM?**

   a) SRAM memory is slower and less expensive than DRAM.

   b) DRAM memory is slower and more expensive than SRAM.

   c) SRAM memory is faster and more expensive than DRAM.

   d) DRAM memory is faster and less expensive than SRAM.

---

3. **True or False? RAMBUS is the fastest type of RAM available.**

   ___ True

   ___ False

---

4. **Match a RAM memory type to its description.**

___	DRAM	a. Runs at high clock speeds and is synchronized with the CPU bus.
___	EDO	b. A type of RAM that needs to be refreshed.
___	SDRAM	c. Memory access cycles overlap, saving about 10 nanoseconds per bit of data accessed.

---

5. **True or False? Memory interleaving provides for concurrent memory requests, so read and write operations can occur almost simultaneously.**

   ___ True

   ___ False

TOPIC D

Examine Server Cooling and Power Systems

In the previous topic, you examined the various types of memory used in servers. Besides the memory components, you also identified various other system board components. The life expectancy of these components will decline without proper system cooling and power supply. In this topic, you will examine the cooling and power supply systems installed in the server.

Underpowered systems and improper cooling systems, especially older systems with relatively small power supplies, can experience lockups, random reboots, and other quirky behavior. If you are upgrading server components, you might exceed the capacity of the current power supply. Replacing it with an adequate power supply can prevent system power problems and keep the number of support calls down. Also, because servers need to run all the time, you need to make sure that they do not become overheated.

Cooling Systems

Definition:

A *cooling system* is a system unit component that prevents damage to computer parts by dissipating the heat generated inside a computer chassis. The cooling system can consist of one or more fans and other components such as heat sinks or liquid coolants that service the entire computer as well as individual components such as the power supply and CPU.

Example:

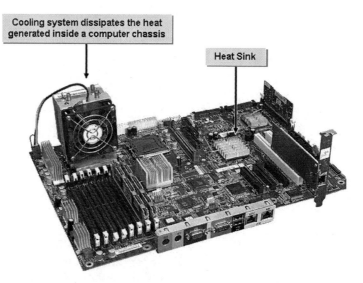

Figure 2-19: Cooling system prevents damage to computer parts.

Components that Require Cooling

Computer systems contain several components that require cooling:

- The server case
- The CPU
- The power supply

- Some adapter cards
- Some hard disk drives

Types of Cooling Systems

Various cooling systems are used to dissipate the heat produced and to safeguard components.

Cooling System	Description
Fans	Computer fans provide cooling by simply blowing regular air across heated components. It is common to see case fans, power supply fans, adapter card fans, and CPU fans.
Ducts	Normally, a CPU cooler cycles warm air from inside the case though the CPU cooler's fins. A CPU air duct draws cooler air from outside the case directly onto the CPU cooler, making it more efficient.
Redundant cooling	It is accomplished by appending extra Air Moving Devices (AMDs), either fans or blowers, so that if one AMD fails, adequate cooling is supplied by the remaining AMDs. Providing redundant cooling by exploiting more AMDs than is needed for a nonredundant case has several disadvantages. They include: • Cost of extra AMDs. • Cost of supplying extra power capacity to drive the extra AMDs. • Need for extra space to accommodate the extra AMDs. This is a serious concern because the room occupied by fans cannot be used for electronics. Due to these drawbacks redundant cooling is implemented only in servers.
Hot swappable	Enables to replace a malfunctioning fan without shutting down or throttling the system.
Active/Passive cooling	Active generally means that there is a power source, such as a cooling fan. Passive generally means that it does not use a power source, such as a heat sink and cooling fins that are used to cool the rising air.
Vents	Computer cases are designed with vents to facilitate airflow through the case and across all components. A common implementation is to include air vents near the bottom of the front of the case and to place a fan near the top of the rear of the case to pull cooler air through the system.
Shroud	A device that serves as a standoff between the fans and the radiator. Generally, fans produce a dead spot in the center of their surface, so a shroud is needed to produce even airflow across the fins to maximize efficiency.
Heat sinks	A device attached to a processor that addresses the problem of overheating processors. It has metal fins to increase its surface area to aid in heat dissipation. Cool air is blown past it by a fan, removing the heat from the processor.
Thermal compound	Thermal compounds are used to connect a heat sink to a CPU. At the microscopic level, when two solids touch, there are actually air gaps between them that act as insulation; the liquid thermally conductive compound gel fills these gaps to permit a more efficient transference of heat from the processor to the heat sink.

Cooling System	Description
Liquid	CPUs can also be kept cool using a device to circulate a liquid or liquefied gas, such as water or freon, past the CPU. Like an air conditioner, heat from the CPU is absorbed by the cooler liquid, and then the heated liquid is circulated away from the CPU so it can disperse the heat into the air outside the computer. Liquid cooling systems are not as prevalent as heat sinks in most server systems or low-end servers.

Dead Spots

Dead spots are particular areas of the server chassis that are deprived of air flow. By altering new components, the favored airflow through the chassis is disturbed and the air may stop flowing in particular areas of the chassis, thereby, causing dead spots.

Computer Cases and Cooling

Although it might seem to be a good idea to remove the chassis cover to provide additional cooling, it is not recommended. Most server cases have been designed to provide an airflow path, with fans positioned to keep the air moving and blow hot air away from heat-sensitive components. The server case must be closed for this airflow path to work properly. If the case cover is removed, the fans will be less efficient, blowing air around at random.

Power Supply System

Definition:

A *power supply* is an internal server component that converts line voltage AC power from an electrical outlet to low-voltage DC power for system components. It is a metal box at the rear of the computer chassis and is attached to the system board. Though not a part of the system board, the power supply component is required for system components to receive power. It contains a fan for cooling because of the heat generated. Some power supply components have a voltage selector switch to set the voltage configuration for the state used in different countries.

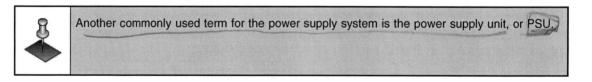

Another commonly used term for the power supply system is the power supply unit, or PSU.

Example:

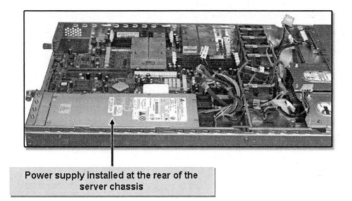

Power supply installed at the rear of the server chassis

Figure 2-20: A power supply converts AC power from an electrical outlet to DC power for system components.

Power Supply Wire Color Conventions

System components cannot use the 120-volt or 240 power coming directly from the electrical outlet. The power supply steps the voltages down to 3.3-, 5-, and 12-volt connections for system components. Wires are color-coded according to their voltages. The following table shows the wire color for each voltage connection.

Color or Component	Voltage
Yellow wire	+12
Blue wire	-12
Red wire	+5
White wire	-5
Motor	+/-12
Circuitry	+/-5
Processor	3.3

Server Power Requirements

Because server-class computers can be running multiple hard disks, as well as other internal peripheral components, their power requirements can be quite substantial. In addition, the types of applications that are running on a server machine can contribute to its power needs. Mission-critical servers can require specially conditioned power to ensure that any fluctuations in the current do not have an adverse affect on the server. Finally, the physical placement of a server can affect its power needs. A departmental server that is housed in a cubicle or a small server closet will have different power needs than one of several dozen servers housed in a larger data center.

Power Requirements

You can check the documentation for a component to determine how much power it actually will use. The following table shows the wattages needed for some of the common components in systems.

Component	Voltage and Power Requirements
ISA bus	• Voltage: 5 V • Power: 12.1 watts
PCI bus	• Voltage: 3.3 or 5 V • Power: 56.1 watts
AGP bus	• Voltage: 3.3 or 5 V • Power: 25, 50, or 110 watts
PCI card	• Voltage: 3.3 or 5 V • Power: 5 watts
AGP card	• Voltage: 3.3 or 5 V • Power: 20 to 30 watts
SCSI PCI card	• Voltage: 3.3 or 5 V • Power: 20 to 25 watts
Floppy drive	• Voltage: 5 V • Power: 5 watts
RAM	• Voltage: 3.3 V for Dual Inline Memory Modules (DIMMs) • Power: 10 watts for every 128 MB of RAM
7200 RPM hard drive	• Voltage: 5 V for logic, 12 V for motor • Power: 5 to 15 watts
1 GHz Pentium III CPU	• Voltage: 3.3 V • Power: 34 watts
1.7 GHz Pentium IV CPU	• Voltage: 3.3 V • Power: 65 watts
300 MHz Celeron CPU	• Voltage: 3.3 V • Power: 18 watts
600 MHz AMD Athlon CPU	• Voltage: 3.3 V • Power: 45 watts
1.4 GHz AMD Athlon CPU	• Voltage: 3.3 V • Power: 70 watts

 If you only have wattage measurements and want to obtain the equivalent British Thermal Unit (BTU) rating, multiply the total wattage by 3.41 to obtain the BTU/hr.

Calculating Power Needs

In order to calculate whether your power supply meets your power needs, you will need to add up the maximum power you might use at one time. A range of maximum power consumption for various components has been established. Most components use much less than the maximum. You can check the documentation for the component to determine how much power it actually will use.

To calculate the amount of power needed for your system:

1. Determine the number of watts used by each component. This should include the following components:

    - System board
    - CPU
    - RAM
    - Hard drives
    - CD drives
    - DVD drives
    - Floppy drives
    - Expansion cards

2. Add up all of the power needed by the system components.

3. Look at the label on the power supply to see what the maximum wattage output is.

AC Power for Peripherals

Although internal system components rely on the power supply, other devices such as printers and external modems require their own direct supply of AC power. In such a case, you must plug the device directly into a source of AC power such as a wall socket or power strip.

CPU Voltages

Even some of the most powerful current CPUs, such as the Intel® Core™2 Extreme and the AMD Opteron Dual Core, only use 1.1-1.3 V. Necessary voltage for CPU and RAM is usually detected by the motherboard (BIOS) and configured appropriately, but sometimes you have to manually configure it by accessing the BIOS and entering the appropriate values. The power supply will supply 3.3 V for the CPU, RAM, and other devices, but the motherboard regulates how much they actually get.

Power Phase

The three-phase power is a method of transmitting electric power using three wires. The deployment of three-phase power to servers is due to the increased power requirements of high-density servers, particularly blade servers. These high-density servers use various processors. There are several facts that contribute to the demand for three-phase power in server cabinets. They include:

- The standard server equipment is designed with universal power supplies that draw a wide range of input power and most commonly can support 208 V/230 V power. 208 V power is more efficient than 120 V power.

- The amount of power that a three-phase power can deliver, whether it is 20, 30 or 60 Amp. It is almost twice the power or (1.73 times) more than a single phase.

- Three-phase power provides power redundancy.

Server Power Connectors

Server *power connectors* are electrical connectors that carry electrical power from the power supply component to every server component. The server uses two types of connectors: the system board power connector that connects the power main to the motherboard, and the peripheral power connector, which includes two types of four-pin connectors to supply 5 volts and 3.3 volts of power to peripherals such as the floppy disk and hard disk drives.

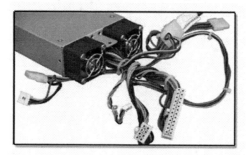

Figure 2-21: *Power connectors carry electrical power from the power supply component to every server component.*

There are various types of power connectors used in servers.

Type	Description ATX
System Board	The modern ATX power supply connection to the system board is a keyed connection that enables the power supply to provide power to the internal components of the system. Keyed connectors are designed such that the plug and socket have notches that must line up in order for the plug to fit into the socket.
	Older AT power supplies used two connectors, labeled P8 and P9. Be sure not to switch them when you plug them in or you could damage the system board. Most systems today have a single, keyed connector that is inserted only one way, which avoids damage to the system board.
	There are specific connectors, depending on the motherboard requirements, usually tied to the CPU type. There is the 20-pin (ATX), a 24-pin ATX connector, and the 20+4 combo (which you can separate, or not, depending on the motherboard). The 20+4 combo includes a 20-pin for the main power, plus a 4-pin connector for additional CPU power. This 4-pin is sometimes known as the Intel Pentium IV connector. There is also an 8-pin CPU connector that requires an ATX 2.02, or EPS12V, PSU.

Type	Description
Peripheral	There are various power connectors that supply power to various storage devices. They include: • **Berg connectors:** They are used to supply power to floppy disk drives and some tape drives. • **Molex connectors:** They are used to supply power to Parallel ATA drives, optical drives, and SCSI drives. It provides both 12-volt and 5-volt power. The Molex connector has two rounded corners and two sharp corners to ensure that it will be properly installed. • **SATA connectors:** They are used to supply power to Serial ATA drives.

Redundancy Power

Redundancy power is the ability of the power supply component to provide fault tolerance for the system's power and to prevent server shutdown due to a power supply failure. Redundancy power supply actually contains two or more individual power units, each of which is capable of powering the entire system. In case, there is a failure in one of the units, the other one will seamlessly supply power to the server. You can also replace the impaired unit without shutting down the server. To drive a load, the outputs of the two power supplies are transferred to an OR gate. In this way, power supplies can either share the load or have one active and the other in standby. A Field Effect Transistor (FET) ORing controller is a better practical solution because it eludes diode voltage drop, power loss, and heat dissipation.

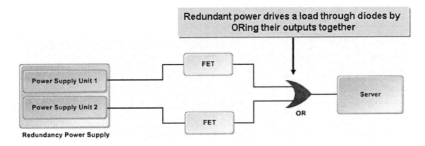

Figure 2-22: Redundancy power provides better fault tolerance.

Power Buttons, Shut Off Switches, and Reset Buttons

Most server cases have two or three common switches outside the chassis. These switches are used for controlling the basic level operation of the server, such as switching the server on or off, and resetting it.

Case Switch	Description
Power on/off	Usually round or square button that powers on and powers off a device. The power on/off switch for modern servers is on the front of the case.
Reset	A button that clears any pending tasks and drives the computer system to the initial start up routine state. Normally, it is an open switch that is connected to two pins on the system board. When the button is pressed, the switch is closed. When it is released, the system performs a hardware reset. Reset buttons are no longer seen is servers.
Shut off switch or chassis intrusion switch	The board supports a chassis security feature that detects if the chassis cover is removed. The security feature uses a mechanical switch on the chassis that attaches to the chassis intrusion header. When the chassis cover is removed, the mechanical switch is in the closed position.

Diagnostic LEDs

A Diagnostic Light Emitting Diode (LED) is an electronic device that lights up when electricity is passed through it and provides a quick visual notification of the status of the server for some of the Field Replaceable Units (FRUs). The LED indicates power on and hard disk drive activity. A control circuit drives the LED in on-off state to indicate diagnostic information.

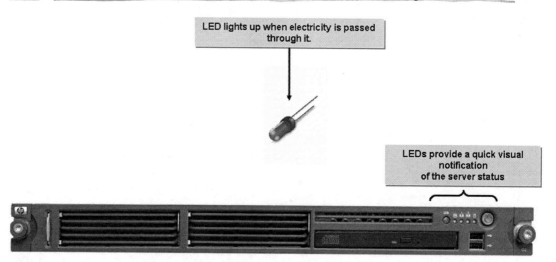

Figure 2-23: LEDs notifies the status of the server.

Field Replaceable Unit

Field Replaceable Unit (FRU) is a circuit board that can be quickly and easily removed from a computer and be replaced by the user or a technician. FRUs include motherboards, socketed microprocessors, primary storage modules (such as RAM), secondary storage devices (such as floppy drives, hard drives, and optical drives), bus devices (such as video cards and sound cards), power supply units, cooling fans, and peripherals (such as keyboards, mice, printers, and cables connecting them).

Front and Rear Panel LEDs

Six front panel LEDs are located in the upper left corner of the server chassis. Three of these LEDs are also provided on the rear panel.

 The following information on LEDs is generic. The location and types of LEDs vary based on the server manufacturer and its form factor.

LED	Color	Description
Locator LED/ button	Blue	This LED provides the following indications: • **Off:** Normal operating state. • **Fast blink:** The server received a signal as a result of one of the preceding methods and is indicating that it is operational.
Service Required	Amber	If on, indicates that service is required.
Power OK	Green	The LED provides the following indications: • **Off:** The server is unavailable. • **Steady on:** Indicates that the server is powered on and is running in its normal operating state. • **Standby blink:** Indicates that the service processor is running, while the server is running at a minimum level in standby mode and ready to be returned to its normal operating state. • **Slow blink:** Indicates that a normal transitory activity is taking place. Server diagnostics may be running, or the system may be powering on.

LED	Color	Description
Rear-FRU Fault	Amber	Provides the following indications: • **Off:** Indicates a steady state, no service action is required. • **Steady on:** Indicates a failure of a rear-access FRU (a power supply or the rear blower). Use the FRU LEDs to determine which FRU requires service.
OverTemp LED	Amber	Provides the following operational temperature indications: • **Off:** Indicates a steady state, no service action is required. • **Steady on:** Indicates that a temperature failure event has been acknowledged and a service action is required.

Hard Drive LEDs

Hard drive LEDs are located on the front of each hard drive that is installed in the server chassis.

LED	Color	Description
Power OK	Green	• **On:** Normal operation. DC output voltage is within normal limits. • **Off:** Power is off.
Failure	Amber	• **On:** Power supply has detected a failure. • **Off:** Normal operation.
AC OK	Green	• **On:** Normal operation. Input power is within normal limits. • **Off:** No input voltage, or input voltage is below limits.

Fan LED

Fan LEDs are located on the top of each fan unit and are visible when you open the top fan door.

LED	Color	Description
Fan	Amber	• **On:** The fan is faulty. • **Off:** Normal operation.

Blower Unit LED

The blower unit LED is located on the back of the blower unit and visible from the rear of the server.

LED	Color	Description
Blower unit	Amber	• **On:** The blower unit is faulty. • **Off:** Normal operation.

ACTIVITY 2-4
Examining Server Cooling and Power Systems

Scenario:
In this activity, you will examine server cooling and power systems.

---

1. **Which provides sufficient cooling even if an air moving device fails?**

    a) Vent cooling system

    b) Hot swappable cooling system

    c) Liquid cooling system

    d) Redundant cooling system

2. **True or False? A diagnostic LED is an electronic device that lights up when electricity is passed through it to provide a quick visual notification of the status of the server and FRUs.**

    ___ True

    ___ False

3. **Match a power connector to the peripheral devices that uses it.**

___	Berg	a.	Serial ATA drives
___	Molex	b.	SCSI drives
___	SATA	c.	Floppy disk drives

4. **What is the power required by the PCI bus?**

    a) 12.1 watts

    b) 56.1 watts

    c) 5 watts

    d) 20 to 25 watts

Lesson 2 Follow-up

In this lesson, you identified the main components that make up a server. The ability to identify various parts of a server helps you to perform installation and troubleshooting tasks.

1. **What types of processors are used in most of the servers on your network?**

2. **What expansion cards might you frequently use in your server?**

3 Introduction to Server Software

Lesson Time: 1 hour(s), 30 minutes

Lesson Objectives:

In this lesson, you will describe the features of server software.

You will:

- Describe the fundamentals of server software.

- Examine the important user management and resource management features present in server software.

- Identify the security features of a NOS.

- Examine some of the important networking essentials for TCP/IP based networks.

Introduction

You are familiar with the server hardware. The other important part of a server is the software that makes the hardware work. In this lesson, you will examine the fundamentals of server software and its various management and security features. You will also examine some essential networking concepts.

Servers perform more complex operations than personal computers and workstations. Therefore, the operating system present in servers is much more complex in design and comes with many advanced features. Understanding the server software and its features will help you to identify and implement the best configuration for your network.

This lesson covers all or part of the following CompTIA Server+ (2009) certification objectives:

- Topic A:
    - Objective 1.7: Install, update and configure appropriate firmware.
    - Objective 2.1: Install, deploy, configure and update NOS (Windows / *nix).
- Topic B:
    - Objective 2.2: Explain NOS security software and its features.
    - Objective 2.5: Summarize server virtualization concepts, features and considerations.
- Topic C:

- Objective 2.2: Explain NOS security software and its features.
- Objective 2.3: Given a scenario, implement and administer NOS management features based on procedure and guidelines.
- Topic D:
  - Objective 2.6: Describe common elements of networking essentials.

TOPIC A
Describe Server Software

You are familiar with the basic components that constitute server hardware. Like any computer, a server too has software that is specially designed to support its functions. In this topic, you will examine the fundamentals of server software.

A server needs software to act as an interface between the user, application, and hardware. Because the server software has to support multiple users, it comes with a lot of advanced resource management and security features. Knowing the fundamentals of server software is the first step in understanding the advanced concepts relating to resource management and security.

Network Operating System

Definition:

A *Network Operating System (NOS)* is an operating system that controls the functioning of various network components by implementing necessary protocol stacks and device drivers appropriate for the hardware. This aspect of the NOS differentiates it from a *standalone operating system*, which is designed for individual computers. Though a NOS is designed for servers, it can also be redesigned to service client computers for certain applications. Therefore, the distinction between a NOS and a standalone operating system is not always obvious. A NOS provides features such as printer sharing, file sharing, database sharing, application sharing, network security, data backup and replication services, and remote access services. It also offers a high degree of fault tolerance compared to a standalone operating system.

Example:

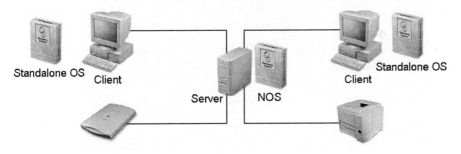

Figure 3-1: Different types of operating systems on a network. A NOS controls the functioning of various components on a network.

Common Network Operating Systems

Operating systems such as Novell's Open Enterprise Server, Linux-based Fedora, Google's Chrome and Microsoft's LAN Manager are examples of network operating systems. In addition, some multipurpose operating systems such as Microsoft's Windows NT, Windows Server 2003, and Windows Server 2008 come with capabilities that enable them to be classified as a NOS.

NOS Environment

The collection of all the NOSs running on various servers in a network is known as a NOS environment. Large networks often have more than one server in the network to provide different services to the users. For example an organization's network may use separate servers for each service such as DNS, DHCP, print and file sharing, and network security. In such cases, each server on the network is configured with a NOS that best suits its role.

The Basic Input Output Sequence

The *Basic Input Output Sequence (BIOS)* is the first program that is executed when you switch a computer on. When the system boots, the BIOS identifies, tests, and initializes system devices such as the video display card, hard disk, system clock, CD-ROM drive, and other hardware. The BIOS then prepares the machine into a known state by instructing the processor to load the operating system into the RAM.

There are different BIOS programs stored on BIOS chips located on the system boards. The BIOS chip on the motherboard contains the code for hardware components such as the keyboard, disk drives, hard disk controllers, and USB human interface devices. Devices such as SCSI controllers, RAID controllers, and video boards often include their own BIOS, complementing or replacing the system BIOS code for any given component.

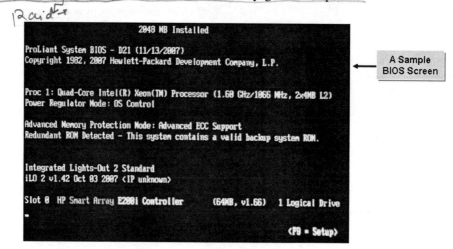

Figure 3-2: A sample BIOS program being executed during the boot up process.

Bootloader

A *bootloader* is a piece of code that is run before the operating system is loaded into the RAM. Each operating system has a predefined set of bootloaders specific to it. These bootloaders specify the ways to boot the operating system's kernel and also contain commands for debugging or modifying the kernel environment.

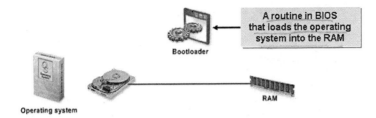

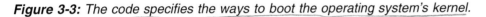

Figure 3-3: The code specifies the ways to boot the operating system's kernel.

> During the booting process, as soon as a storage medium containing the operating system is detected, the BIOS instructs the processor to execute the appropriate bootloader.

Boot Devices

A *boot device* is a device from which the operating system is loaded into the hard disk during the booting or installation process. The BIOS allows the user to configure the boot order. For example, if the boot order is set to read the DVD drive first and then the USB device drive, the BIOS will first try to boot from the DVD drive. If the BIOS fails to read the drive or if there is no DVD in the drive, only then the BIOS will try to boot from the USB device drive.

Hard Disk   USB Flash   DVD

Figure 3-4: Common boot devices.

Preboot Execution Environment

The *Preboot Execution Environment (PXE)*, or network share booting, is a booting or installation technique in which a computer loads the operating system from a connected network rather than from a boot device. This method of booting can be performed by routers, diskless workstations, and centrally managed computers such as public computers at libraries and schools. Any device that takes part in PXE booting is known as a PXE client, and the device that boots the PXE client is known as the PXE server.

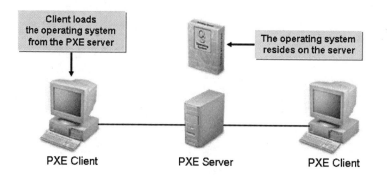

Figure 3-5: *A computer booting from a central server in the PXE environment.*

PXE booting centralizes the management of disk storage, which can result in reduced capital and maintenance costs. To locate a PXE server, the BIOS of the PXE client broadcasts or multicasts a DHCP request to which the PXE server can respond. On TCP/IP networks, the operating system is loaded from the PXE server using a protocol known as the *Trivial File Transfer Protocol (TFTP).* Due to security reasons, this method is normally discouraged except in trusted network environments.

Remote Installation Service / Windows Deployment Services

Windows Deployment Services (WDS) is a technology from Microsoft for network-based installation of Windows operating systems. It is the successor to the earlier Remote Installation Services (RIS) feature. WDS can be used for remotely installing Windows Server 2008, Windows Server 2003, Windows Vista, and Windows XP operating systems on remote client machines. To enable WDS on a network, the server role should be set to WDS in Windows Server 2008 and Windows Server 2003 operating systems.

File Systems

A *file system* is a database maintained by an operating system on a storage medium for the storage, organization, manipulation, and retrieval of data. The main objective of a file system is to organize data in such a way that it is easy for the operating system to search and access it. This shows that the operating system being used often influences the choice of a file system.

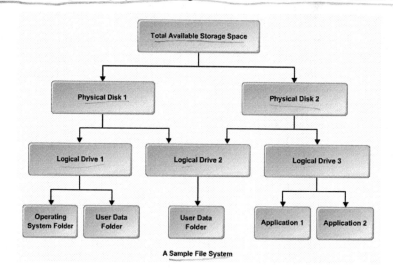

Figure 3-6: *A general file system layout.*

Types of File Systems

There are different types of file systems.

File System	Description
File Allocation Table (FAT)	It is an older file system that is best suited for use with drives less than 4 GB in size. The primary advantages of the FAT file system are its extremely low disk overhead (less than 1 MB), and its compatibility with different operating systems, including all versions of Windows and also MS-DOS and UNIX. The FAT file system can support dual-booting a computer between a version of Windows and another operating system. It is primarily used for formatting floppy disks.
FAT32	FAT32 is an enhanced version of the FAT file system. It scales better to large hard drives (up to 2 terabytes in size) and uses a smaller cluster size than FAT for more efficient space usage. The maximum possible size for a file on a FAT32 volume is 4 GB minus 1 byte (232-1 bytes). Video applications, large databases, and some other software easily exceed this limit.
NT File System (NTFS)	NTFS is the recommend file system for today's Windows-based computers. NTFS was introduced with the Windows NT operating system and is sometimes read as NT File System. NTFS provides many enhanced features over FAT or FAT32, including file-level and folder-level security, file encryption, disk compression, and scalability to very large drives and files.
Virtual Machine File System (VMFS)	VMware Inc.'s Virtual Machine File System (VMFS) is a proprietary cluster file management used by VMware ESX server and the company's flagship server virtualization suite "VMware Infrastructure." It is used to store disk images of various virtual machines. Multiple servers can read/write the same file system simultaneously, while individual virtual machine files are locked. VMFS volumes can be logically increased in size by spanning multiple VMFS volumes together.
Zettabyte File System (ZFS)	ZFS is a file system designed by Sun Microsystems for use with the Solaris operating system. The features of ZFS include support for high storage capacities, integration of filesystems and volume management, disk snapshots and copy-on-write clones, continuous integrity checking and automatic repair, and RAID-Z for supporting RAID implementations. ZFS is implemented as open-source software, licensed under the Common Development and Distribution License (CDDL).
Ext3	Ext3 or third extended file system is a journaling file system used only by Linux operating systems and is an evolution of Ext2, the previous file system. A journaling file system is a file system that logs changes to a journal (usually a circular log in a dedicated area of the file system) before committing them to the main file system. Such file systems are less likely to become corrupted in the event of a power failure or system crash.

Encryption

Encryption is a security technique that converts data from plain, or cleartext form, into coded, or ciphertext form. Only authorized parties with the necessary decryption information can decode and read the data. It includes the encryption algorithm and encryption key. Encryption algorithm is the rule, system, or mechanism used to encrypt data and Encryption key is specific piece of information that is used in conjunction with an algorithm to perform encryption and decryption. Most file systems use some encryption technique to encrypt the data into a suitable format.

Device Driver

A *device driver* is a program that acts as an interface between the operating system and a hardware device. When an application requires the use of a device, it invokes a routine in the device's driver. The driver then issues commands to the device. Once the device sends data to the driver, the driver may invoke routines in the application program. Drivers are hardware-dependent and operating system-specific; therefore, a piece of hardware may need a separate device driver for each operating system.

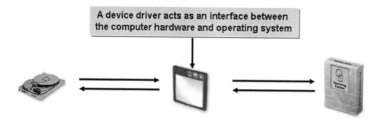

A device driver acts as an interface between the computer hardware and operating system

Figure 3-7: Device drivers are hardware-dependent and operating system-specific.

Patch Management

A *patch* is a small program designed to fix problems in an application or update a computer program or its supporting data. A patch may also be used for replacing graphics or audio and for improving the usability or performance of a program. The process of planning what patches should be applied to which systems at a specified time and developing an appropriate strategy is known as *patch management*. Software vendors usually distribute patches on a storage medium, such as a floppy drive or CD-ROM, or through email. Most vendors also allow end users to download patches from their sites. Though meant to fix problems, poorly designed patches can sometimes introduce new problems.

Some software applications are designed to automatically update themselves whenever an update is available on the Internet. In situations where system administrators control a number of computers, this automation helps to ensure consistency across a network.

ACTIVITY 3-1
Discussing Server Software Fundamentals

Scenario:
In this activity, you will discuss the fundamentals of server software.

---

1. **Which operating system is a NOS?**

   a) Microsoft Windows XP

   b) Microsoft Windows Server 2008

   c) Microsoft Windows 2000

   d) Microsoft Windows Vista

---

2. **Which file system is an example of the journaling file system?**

   a) FAT32

   b) FAT

   c) NTFS

   d) EXT3

---

3. **Which program acts as an interface between a hardware device and its operating system?**

   a) BIOS

   b) File system

   c) Device driver

   d) Patch

---

4. **Which file systems can be used with Windows-based computers?**

   a) FAT

   b) VMFS

   c) NTFS

   d) ZFS

---

5.   **Which of these require the implementation of PXE?**

   a) Personal computer

   b) Centralized network of a library

   c) Office networks

   d) Peer-to-peer network

TOPIC B

NOS → Network Operating System

NOS Management Features

You are familiar with the server software fundamentals. The server software comes with many features that help users and administrators to manage network resources in an efficient manner. In this topic, you will examine the important user management and resource management features present in server software.

Because resources on a network are shared with multiple users, it is essential to have some mechanism to ensure their sharing among all users in an efficient manner. All network operating systems have important user management and resource management features. Knowing these features is essential to managing users and resources efficiently.

User Management Features

The NOS provides network administrators the ability to centrally manage users and resources on a network. Some of its user management features include adding and removing users from the network, setting up individual and group-level permissions for accessing shared resources, setting up policies for users, and maintaining logon scripts consisting of the resource usage history.

Resource Management Features

Resource management allows network administrators to efficiently distribute shared resources among the users. Some of the resource management features supported by a NOS include Access Control Lists (ACLs), disk quotas, shadow copies, baselines, server virtualization, and Management Information Bases (MIBs).

Access Control Lists

An *Access Control List (ACL)* is a list of permissions set up by a user or an administrator. It is attached to a shared resource. The list specifies which users are allowed to access a resource and what operations are allowed on that resource. Each entry in the list specifies an object, such as a file or a device, and the permitted operation, such as read-only or read-and-write.

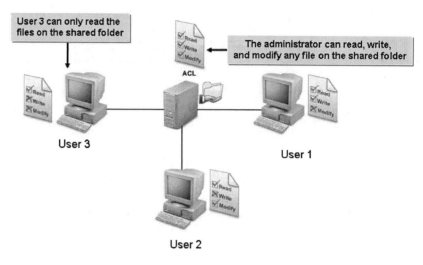

Figure 3-8: Access control lists set up for each user by the administrator.

Disk Quotas

Disk quotas are often used by network administrators to limit the utilization of shared disk space by a user. There are two basic types of disk quotas: usage quota and file quota. *Usage quota*, or block quota, limits the amount of disk space that can be used by a user. The *file quota* limits the number of files and directories that can be created by a user. In addition, administrators usually define a warning level, or *soft quota*, to inform users when they are nearing their effective limit, or *hard quota*. There may also be a small amount of *grace quota*, which allows users to temporarily violate their allotted limits by certain amounts if necessary.

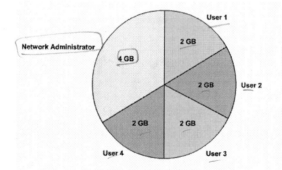

Total Disk Capacity : 12 GB

Figure 3-9: Division of available disk space among different users on a network.

Shadow Copy

Shadow copy is a feature that allows users to make manual or automatic backup copies or snapshots of a file or folder on a specific volume at a specific point in time. Snapshots are read-only copies of a volume, and they help users to access the version of a file or folder that existed when the snapshot was taken. This feature is used for retrieving an earlier version of a file or recovering a file deleted by mistake.

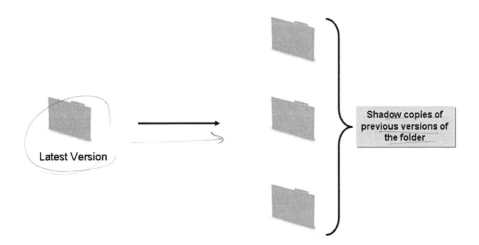

Figure 3-10: *Shadow copies of a file can be used to backup previous versions.*

Volume Snapshot Service and Shadow Volumes

The shadow copy feature is also known as *Volume Snapshot Service (VSS)* in Windows Server 2003 and all other subsequent releases of the Microsoft Windows server operating system. The shadow copies of a file or folder are known as shadow volumes in all Windows operating systems. The VSS feature requires the file system to be NTFS.

Server Baselining

Server baselining is a method of analyzing the performance of a sever by comparing its current performance level to a level before an upgrade or a modification is made. The historical data is used as the baseline. Some common server baselines include the CPU speed, CPU usage levels, and response times of various server components. Baselining is useful for many performance management tasks, including monitoring daily performance of a server, measuring trends in server performance, and assessing whether server performance is meeting the requirements laid out in the service agreement.

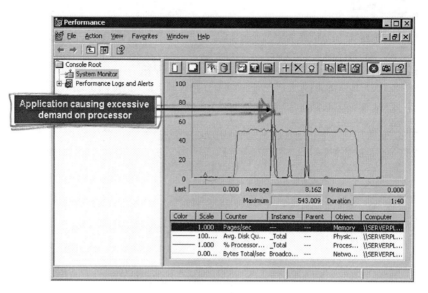

Figure 3-11: Measuring network performance using baselining.

Server Virtualization

Server virtualization is a resource management feature that allows a single physical server to run multiple virtual servers on it. Each virtual server is distinct, and it can run separate instances of an operating system or even different operating systems. The use of a single physical server leads to better utilization of costly hardware resources, which in most cases are not used to their full capacity.

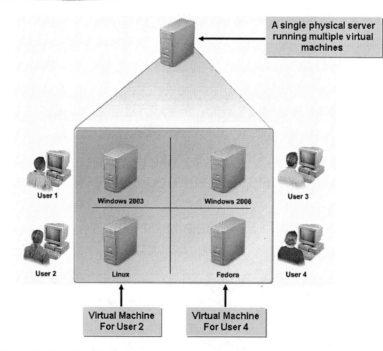

Figure 3-12: Multiple virtual servers running on a single server.

Virtualization using a single physical server offers many benefits. For instance:

- It leads to space consolidation.

- It is comparatively easy and reduces the cost of installation and maintenance.
- It reduces the power required for processing data and cooling devices.
- Newer technologies in server virtualization allow virtual machines to automatically restart on different host servers in case of any failure in the main server. This is achieved by running virtual machines inside a storage server that can be shared by all physical servers. This provides better redundancy of services.
- Because virtual machines in a single server are independent of each other, they can be used as sandbags for testing multiple applications at the same time on a single physical server.

Disaster Recovery and Server Virtualization

The server virtualization technique can be used for disaster recovery purposes as well. The use of some virtual machines as backup for other virtual machines on the same physical hardware reduces the amount of time required for backup when compared with the time required for backing up from external machines. This is because writing data from one virtual machine to another on the same hardware is comparatively faster than writing from an external tape drive.

Green Initiatives

Server virtualization reduces the hardware requirements of an organization, which in turn reduces the energy demand and helps in supporting the green initiative aspect of that organization.

As IT organizations face increasing pressure to become green, executives can implement green initiatives through following methods:

- Implementing server virtualization in data centers and workplaces.
- Reconfiguring the data center floor and ceiling layouts to eliminate energy leaks.
- Using innovative and more efficient cooling methods.
- Using alternative storage tactics.
- Exploring alternative energy sources.
- Encouraging adoption of energy-saving settings on computer monitors.
- Practicing proper disposal and recycling of IT assets.

Virtualization Requirements

Before planning to migrate a server from physical environment to virtual environment it is essential to ensure that the hardware intended to be virtualized meets the requirements of all virtual machines that are intended to be run on it. Also, the operating system running on the bare metal hardware should be capable of supporting the guest operating systems running on each virtual machine.

Configuring and Interconnecting Virtual Servers

Once the virtual servers have been created on a server, each virtual machine can be configured independent of another. Also each virtual machine must be provided with different IP addresses. The server hardware should have enough number of NICs to support multiple addresses. Once the IP address and network settings of a virtual machine are configured, it can be connected to other virtual machines on the same hardware or external hardware using the Internet or local domain network.

Management Server

A management server or virtual server console is a virtual machine that is used by network administrators for managing other virtual machines running on the server. The management server can be used for performing tasks such as adding or removing a virtual machine from the server and reallocating the resources between various virtual machines running on the server.

Limitations of Virtualization

While virtualization has many benefits, it is not a good choice for servers dedicated to applications requiring high processing power or storage capabilities. Because virtualization divides the server's processing power and storage capacity among many virtual servers, some applications may slow down or crash if the server's processing power cannot meet the application's requirement. Therefore, the network administrators should check the CPU usage and storage requirements of each user before dividing a physical server into multiple virtual machines.

Virtual Server Migration

An emerging trend in server virtualization is the ease of migrating a server environment from one physical device to another. Originally, this was possible only if both physical machines ran on the same hardware, operating system, and processor configuration. It's now possible to migrate virtual servers from one physical machine to another, even if both machines have different processor configurations. However, both processors must be of the same manufacturer.

Simple Network Management Protocol

Simple Network Management Protocol (SNMP) is a protocol used for exchanging management information among network devices. It is used by organizations, as part of network management, to monitor devices for conditions that warrant administrative attention. A part of the TCP/IP protocol suite, SNMP helps network administrators to monitor network performance and troubleshoot problems using the NOS.

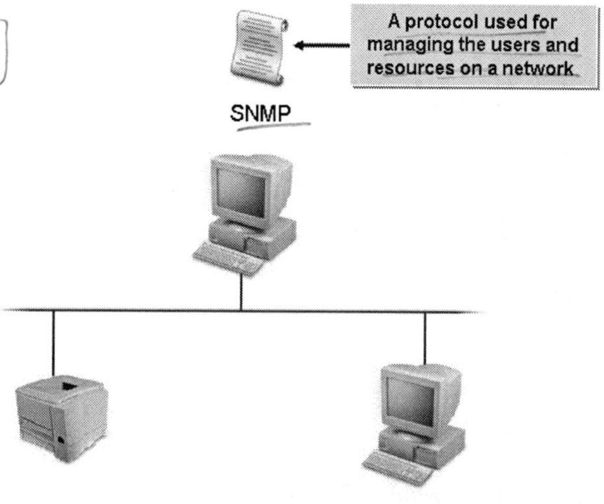

Figure 3-13: SNMP helps network administrators to monitor network performance.

Management Information Base

Management Information Base (MIB) is a type of database used to manage devices in a communications network. It comprises information on devices to be managed in a network and is frequently used by SNMP agents or clients and managers. The MIB associated with the agent is known as the agent MIB, and the one associated with a manager is known as the manager MIB. The manager MIB contains information about the different network components that it manages and the agent MIB is required to know just the local information relating to it.

Web-Based Enterprise Management

Web-Based Enterprise Management (WBEM) is a set of Internet-based technologies and standards that help a NOS to unify the management of distributed computing environments and to facilitate the exchange of data across otherwise different technologies and platforms. Because WBEM is an evolving technology, there are no major standards governing it, although the Desktop Management Task Force (DMTF) has been assigned the task of developing some specifications.

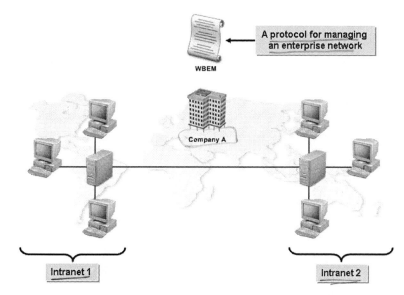

Figure 3-14: Managing an organization's network through WBEM.

WBEM Operation

In WBEM, the client and the operator are interfaced through a set of application program interfaces and graphical user interfaces. The clients find the WBEM server for the device being managed and construct an XML message with the request. The clients use the HTTP protocol to pass the request to the WBEM server. The WBEM server receives the incoming request, performs the necessary authentication and authorization checks, and then consults the previously created model of the device being managed to see how the request should be handled. WBEM is extensible, facilitating the development of platform-neutral, reusable infrastructure, tools and applications. In addition to its use by vendors, end users and the open source community, WBEM is enabling other industry organizations to build on its foundation in areas including web services, security, storage, grid and utility computing.

Windows Management Instrumentation

Windows Management Instrumentation (WMI) is Microsoft's implementation of WBEM on their products. WMI allows scripting languages such as VBScript or Windows PowerShell to manage personal computers and servers, both locally and remotely. WMI is preinstalled in Windows 2000 and newer OSs. It is available as a download for Windows 98. Microsoft also provides a command line interface (CLI) to WMI called Windows Management Instrumentation Command-line (WMIC).

ACTIVITY 3-2
Discussing the Features of NOS Management

Scenario:
In this activity, you will discuss the various features of NOS management.

1. **Which of these is a user management feature?**

   a) ACL

   b) Group level permission

   c) Disk quotas

   d) Shadow copy

2. **Which are the resource management features of a NOS?**

   a) Setting up permissions

   b) Virtualization support

   c) Shadow copy

   d) Maintaining logon scripts

3. **Which statements are valid for server virtualization?**

   a) Server virtualization leads to reduction in space, power, and cooling requirements.

   b) It is possible to use a single physical server as a sandbag for testing multiple applications at the same time.

   c) All virtual servers need to run the same operating system.

   d) Server virtualization reduces the cost.

4. **True or False? Virtual server migration is possible between physical hardware made by different manufacturers.**

   ___ True

   ___ False

5. **Which disk quota indicates the effective limit of the data that can be stored by a user on the shared disk?**

   a) Soft quota

   b) Hard quota

   c) Grace quota

   d) File quota

6. **In which operating system, the shadow volume copy is known as Volume Snapshot Service (VSS)?**

_____

TOPIC C
NOS Security Features

You are familiar with the various management features of a NOS. Besides providing management features, a NOS also provides various security features for securing the network and its resources. In this topic, you will identify the various security features of a NOS.

Because many users connect to a network and its resources, trusting all of them is simply not an option when it comes to securing the network from hackers. Most NOS come with advanced security features that can minimize the risk of potential attacks. Knowing the various security features provided by a NOS will help you to implement an appropriate level of security in your networks.

Share-Level Permissions

Share-level permissions are permissions set for network shares. A network share is a folder on a computer that can be remotely accessed from other computers through a local area network as if it were a resource in the local machine. By setting up a share-level permission, a user can prevent the remote users from accessing or modifying the files in the user's network share. Although share-level permissions work well across a network, they offer no protection against a user who's logged on locally to the computer or server containing the shared resource.

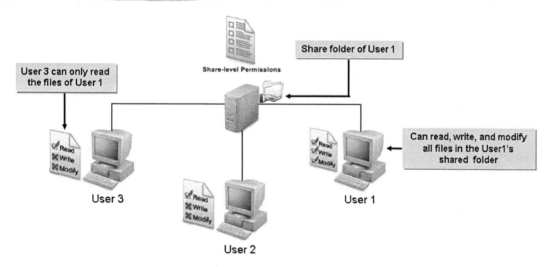

Figure 3-15: Share-level permissions on a network.

Drawbacks of Share-Level Permissions

A downside to share-level security is that the server may eventually contain so many shares that it's hard for users to remember their folders. If users want to search for information and they don't know which share it's contained in, they'll have to find the server and search each share on the server for the desired information.

File-Level Permissions

File-level permissions allow users to set access control to individual files and folders. File-level permissions will prevent any unauthorized access to a file or folder both across the network and locally by prompting all users, including the user who created the file, to enter the correct user name and password for access. In Windows operating systems, file-level permissions can be implemented only on those hard disks or partitions that use NTFS file systems.

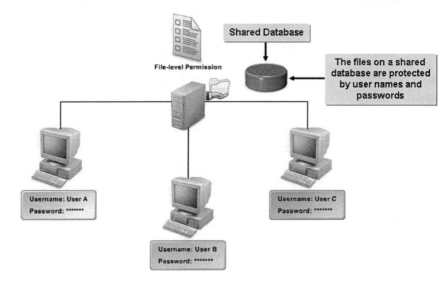

Figure 3-16: *File-level permission on a network.*

Separate Permissions at Share Level and File Level

The idea of separate permissions at share level and file level is unique to Windows environments. In Unix/Linux, the same set of read, write, and delete permissions are valid at both local level and across the network.

Firewall

A *firewall* is hardware or software that regulates data flow to a secured network by filtering data originating from unsecured or untrusted sources. The filtering of data is carried out on the basis of some parameters set by the network administrator or user.

Software Firewall Implementations

There are different ways of implementing the firewall using the operating system software.

Software Firewall Implementation	Description
Port blocking	Ports are the logical communication channels through which many computer programs can communicate over a network at the same time, with each program using a different port. The ports in a communication channel are identified by a unique number known as port number. Certain well-known ports can be exploited by viruses and Trojans and, therefore, the network administrator can block these ports to reduce the risk of a virus attack.
Application exception	It is a feature that allows the firewall to be configured to allow some restricted content in exceptional situations. To decrease the security risk, the application exception should be allowed only when it is needed and must be removed when it is no longer needed. Also, the best practice is not to allow exceptions for applications that are not recognized.
ACLs	By setting up a list of permissions attached to a shared resource, the administrators can specify which users are allowed to access the resources and what operations are allowed to be performed on that resource.

Antivirus Software

Antivirus software is software used for combating computer malware such as viruses, worms, and trojans. It employs a variety of strategies such as searching the executable code for patterns similar to malware and emulating a program in a simulated environment to check if it acts maliciously. However, antivirus software may not always recognize malware. For maximum security, antivirus software should be enabled at all times and it should be purchased from a reputable vendor. Also, it should always be updated to the latest version for better security.

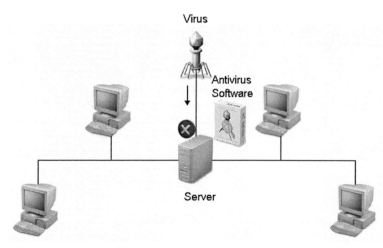

Figure 3-17: An antivirus software protects the network from attacks by viruses and other malware.

Antivirus Software Vendors

Symantec (**http://www.symantec.com**) and McAfee (**http://www.mcafee.com**) are two major antivirus software vendors.

Antispyware

Antispyware is software designed for removing or blocking spyware. Spyware is a type of software installed on personal computers to collect information about users, their browsing habits, and other sensitive information without their consent. In certain cases, spyware is used for supervision purposes. Hackers too may use spyware to obtain personal details about a user.

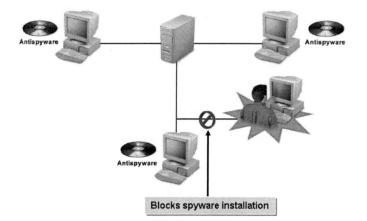

Figure 3-18: An antispyware software is deployed to block the spyware.

ACTIVITY 3-3
Discussing NOS Security Features

Scenario:
In this activity, you will discuss the security features of a NOS.

1. **Which statements are valid for antivirus software?**

   a) They cannot detect any spyware.

   b) An antivirus can remove any code that resembles a virus.

   c) Antivirus software is always deployed on gateway servers at the network perimeter.

   d) Antivirus software is capable of monitoring a system for activities common to virus programs.

2. **Which statements are valid for share-level permissions?**

   a) They prompt the user for user name and password each time the shared resource is accessed.

   b) Any user who logs into the user's computer can access the protected resources.

   c) They are more secure than file-level permissions.

   d) All shared files are stored on user's computer.

3. **The firewall implementation in which the communication channel used by the malware is blocked is known as ___ _____ .**

4. **What is the name of the folder that can be remotely accessed from other computers through a local area network as if it were a resource in the local machine?**

TOPIC D
Network Essentials for Servers

You are familiar with the various management and security features of a NOS. In addition to these features, there are some essential concepts of networking that a server professional must be familiar with. In this topic, you will examine some of the important networking essentials for TCP/IP based networks.

Because the most important function of a server is to control the resources on a network, it is essential for server professionals to be familiar with the type of network in which the server is being used. Most of the present day servers are being used in TCP/IP based networks, and therefore, knowledge of certain essential concepts related to TCP/IP will help you to properly configure the server on such networks.

Subnetting

Subnetting is the technique of dividing a large network into smaller interconnected domains to prevent excessive rates of packet collision. Such subnets can be arranged hierarchically, with the organization's network address space partitioned into a tree-like structure. Routers are used to manage traffic and function as borders between various subnets.

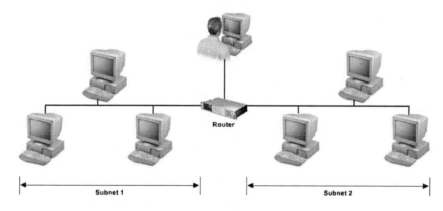

Figure 3-19: *Subnets of a large network.*

Domain Name System

The *Domain Name System (DNS)* is a TCP/IP name resolution service that translates a *Fully Qualified Domain Name (FQDN),* which is a domain name that denotes a specific location in the DNS hierarchy, into an IP address. For example, the FQDN server03.ourglobalcompany.com will be translated into the IP address 74.43.216.152. The *domain name space* holds information about the hierarchy of domains and the hosts under each domain. This domain name space is referenced by the name servers for mapping purposes.

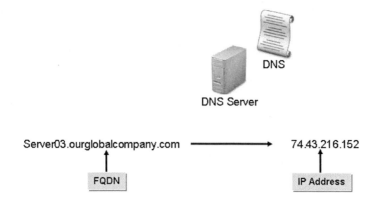

Figure 3-20: DNS translates the URLs or FQDNs into their corresponding IP addresses.

Static IP Address Assignment

Configuring TCP/IP addresses statically on a network requires an administrator to visit each node to manually enter IP address information for that node. If the node moves to a different subnet, the administrator must manually reconfigure the node's TCP/IP information for its new network location. In a large network, configuring TCP/IP statically on each node can be very time consuming, and can be prone to errors that disrupt communication. Static addresses are typically assigned only to systems with dedicated functionality, such as router interfaces, network-attached printers, or server systems that host network applications.

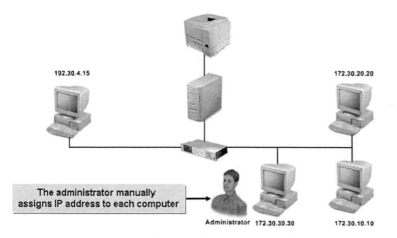

Figure 3-21: Static assignment of IP addresses.

> On Windows systems, static IP configuration information is entered in the Internet Protocol (TCP/IP) Properties dialog box for each network connection object.

Dynamic Host Configuration Protocol

Dynamic Host Configuration Protocol (DHCP) is a network protocol that provides automatic assignment of IP addresses and other TCP/IP configuration information to the network nodes that are configured as DHCP clients. DHCP requires a DHCP server configured with at least one DHCP scope. The scope contains a range of IP addresses and a subnet mask, and can contain other options such as a default gateway address. When the scope is enabled, it automatically leases TCP/IP information to DHCP clients for a defined lease period.

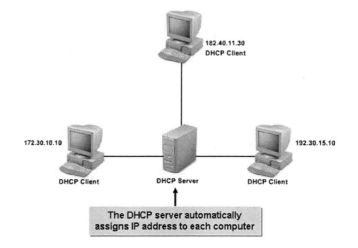

Figure 3-22: Automatic assignment of IP addresses.

IP Address Classes

There are five classes of IP addresses, which break up the IP address space into ranges that account for networks of different sizes.

Class	Address reuse
A	1.0.0.0 to 127.255.255.255
B	128.0.0.0 to 191.255.255.255
C	192.0.0.0 to 223.255.255.255
D	224.0.0.0 to 239.255.255.255
E	240.0.0.0 to 255.255.255.255

Figure 3-23: The various classes of IP addresses.

Address Class	Description
Class A	Class A addresses provide a small number of network addresses for networks with a large number of nodes per network. • Address range: 1.0.0.0 to 127.255.255.255 • Number of networks: 126 (The IP address 127.0.0.1 is reserved.) • Number of nodes per network: 16,777,214 • Network ID portion: First octet • Node ID portion: Last three octets
Class B	Class B addresses provide a balance between the number of network addresses and the number of nodes per network. • Address range: 128.0.0.0 to 191.255.255.255 • Number of networks: 16,382 • Number of nodes per network: 65,534 • Network ID portion: First two octets, excluding Class A addresses • Node ID portion: Last two octets
Class C	Class C addresses provide a large number of network addresses for networks with a small number of nodes per network. • Address range: 192.0.0.0 to 223.255.255.255 • Number of networks: 2,097,150 • Number of nodes per network: 254 • Network ID portion: First three octets, excluding Class A and Class B addresses • Node ID portion: Last octet
Class D	Class D addresses are set aside to support multicast transmissions. Any network can use them, regardless of the base network ID. A multicast server assigns a single Class D address to all members of a multicast session. Class D addresses are routable only with special support from the routers. • Address range: 224.0.0.0 to 239.255.255.255 • Number of networks: N/A • Number of nodes per network: N/A • Network ID portion: N/A • Node ID portion: N/A
Class E	Class E addresses are set aside for research and experimentation. • Address range: 240.0.0.0 to 255.255.255.255 • Number of networks: N/A • Number of nodes per network: N/A • Network ID portion: N/A • Node ID portion: N/A

Applications of Different Classes

Class A: Used only by extremely large networks, Class A addresses are far too big for most companies. Large telephone companies and ISPs leased most Class A network addresses.

Class B: Most companies leased Class B addresses for use on Internet-connected networks. In the beginning, there were plenty of Class B addresses to go around, but soon they were depleted.

Class C: Class C addresses are widely used in small organizations that require few IP addresses.

Class D: Because multicasting has limited use, the Class D address block is relatively small.

Class E: These addresses are not tightly defined. Set aside strictly for research and experimentation purposes, they are not available for use by network administrators.

Restricted IP Addresses

Some IP addresses have special uses and cannot be assigned to networks and hosts. For example, IP address 127.0.0.1 is reserved for testing. It identifies your network and host on the Internet. The following table describes IP addressing restrictions and the reasons behind them.

Restriction	Reason	Example
A network address of 0 is not permitted.	When the network address is set to 0, TCP/IP interprets the IP address as a "local" address, meaning that the data packet does not need to be transmitted through a router.	The 0.0.0.22. address identifies host 22 on the local network.
A host address of 0 is not permitted.	When the host address is set to 0, TCP/IP interprets the address as a network address and not a host address.	The address 122.0.0.0 identifies the network whose address is 122.
The network address of 127 is reserved.	Messages addressed to a network address of 127 are not transmitted out onto the network; instead, these messages are sent back to the transmitting node. The address of 127 is used to test the configuration of TCP/IP.	127.0.0.1 is referred to as the loopback address. It is a shorthand way for any host to refer to itself.
Neither the network address nor the host address can be 255.	The 255 address is reserved for broadcasts.	255.255.255.255 is a broadcast address. Data packets will be sent to all hosts on all networks. 187.205.255.255 is also a broadcast address and data packets will be sent to all hosts on network 187.205.
Network address 1.1.1.1 is not permitted.	TCP/IP identifies all hosts with that address.	1.1.1.1 refers to every host.

TCP Ports

A *TCP port* is an end-point to a logical connection in a TCP/IP based network and is generally application specific. A port is identified by its number, commonly known as the *port number*, a 16-bit nonnegative integer ranging from 0 to 65535. Ports 1 through 1023 are referred to as "well-known," and they correspond with different applications. These port numbers are assigned by IANA. When a client needs to connect to an application on a server, it uses one of these port numbers as the destination port to let the server know of the required application.

Ports 1024 through 49151 are known as "registered ports," and ports ranging from 49152 to 65535 are known as "dynamic" or "private" ports. All ports can be used by custom applications, but they are most often randomly used as source ports for client traffic. Therefore, a machine can have multiple connections to a server and still keep each connection uniquely identified. When traffic flows back from the server, the source and destination ports are reversed.

Common Port Numbers and Their Services

Most systems maintain a file of port numbers and their corresponding services that the operating system and applications refer to. Some of the common port numbers and their services are given in the following table.

Port Number	Service
20	File Transfer Protocol (FTP)-Data transmission
21	File Transfer Protocol-Control
23	Telnet
25	Simple Mail Transfer Protocol (SMTP)
53	Domain Name Server (DNS)
80	Hypertext Transfer Protocol (HTTP)
110	Post Office Protocol version 3 (POP3)
161	Simple Network Management Protocol (SNMP)

Ethernet

Ethernet is a family of LAN technologies developed to enable communication between different computers over a shared broadcasting medium. It was jointly developed by Xerox and Digital Equipment Corporation for use in their network products. After its standardization as IEEE 802.3, Ethernet became the most popular LAN technology. Ethernet LANs have evolved from supporting communication through only coaxial cables to using other mediums such as twisted pair cables and optical fibers. Today, Ethernet LANs support a data transfer rate of 10, 100, or 1000 megabits per second depending upon the network media used.

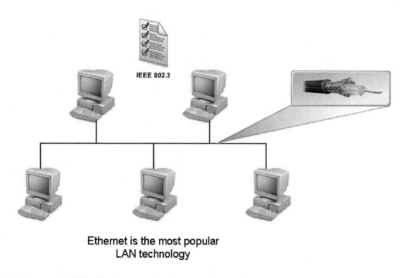

Ethernet is the most popular
LAN technology

Figure 3-24: Ethernet LANs have evolved to using other mediums such as twisted pair cables
and optical fibers.

Popular Ethernet Technologies

There are different types of Ethernet technologies, each of which is described in the following
table.

Ethernet Technology	Description
10 BASE 5 or Thick Ethernet	It is a bus topology LAN using thick coaxial cables. The common bus is divided into smaller segments of 500 meters each. The maximum number of segments allowed is five. Also, the maximum number of nodes per segment is limited to 200 to reduce the probability of collisions. The coaxial cable used is known as RG-8 cable. It provides a data rate of 10 Mbps.
10 BASE 2 or Thin Ethernet	It is a bus topology LAN similar to 10 BASE 5 but uses a much thinner and lightweight cable. The cable used is known as RG-58. Due to its thin structure, it is more flexible and cheaper than RG-8. However, the length of each segment is limited to 180 meters. The number of nodes per segment is less than 10 BASE 5.
10 BASE T	It is a star topology LAN in which each node is connected to the hub through a twisted pair cable known as RJ-45 cable. The data packet is transmitted by the hub to all nodes. However, the logic in the network ensures that only the node whose address is attached to the packet can open and read it. It provides a data rate of 10 Mbps and the maximum length of each RJ-45 cable is 100 meters.

Ethernet Technology	Description
Switched Ethernet	It is a variant of 10 BASE T network. In switched Ethernet, the hub is replaced by a switch which can recognize the destination address and routes the packet only to the destination node. Thus, the switch can route other packets as well to their destinations at the same time.
Fast Ethernet	It is a star topology LAN, which provides a data transfer rate of 100 Mbps. The maximum length of the cable is limited to 250 meters and can use either coaxial cables or optical fibers. It is used as a backbone network to interconnect several LANs.
Gigabit Ethernet	It provides a data transfer rate of 1000 Mbps and mainly uses optical fibers. It can be used for a distance ranging from 500 to 5000 meters depending on the type of optical fiber used. The hardware required for Gigabit Ethernet is very expensive as compared with other types.

Virtual Private Networks

A *Virtual Private Network (VPN)* is a network that uses a public telecommunication infrastructure, such as the Internet, to provide remote offices or individual users with secure access to their organization's network. VPNs contrast sharply with other expensive systems of owned or leased lines that can only be used by a single organization owning the network. However, the goal of a VPN is to provide the same capabilities for an organization, but at a much lower cost.

A VPN works by using the shared public infrastructure while maintaining privacy through security procedures and tunneling protocols such as the Layer Two Tunneling Protocol. In effect, the protocols, by encrypting data and addresses at the sending end and decrypting them at the receiving end, send data through a "tunnel." Data that is not properly encrypted cannot enter this tunnel.

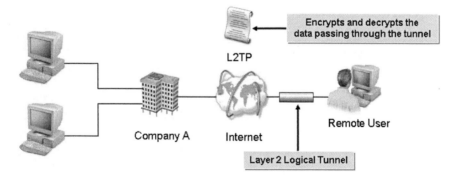

Figure 3-25: A VPN over a public network.

Virtual LANs

A *Virtual LAN (VLAN)* is a logical subgroup within a local area network. It is established using software rather than manually shifting cables in the wiring closet. Therefore, VLANs provide logical isolation instead of physical segregation. VLAN port assignments can be configured as either static or dynamic VLANs. In static VLANs, the administrator statically configures the VLAN port assignment: VLAN membership on switch ports is assigned on a port-by-port basis. In dynamic VLANs, the server dynamically assigns VLAN ports. By creating a VLAN, a set of nodes can be treated as one broadcast domain, and the nodes can share information only within the VLAN.

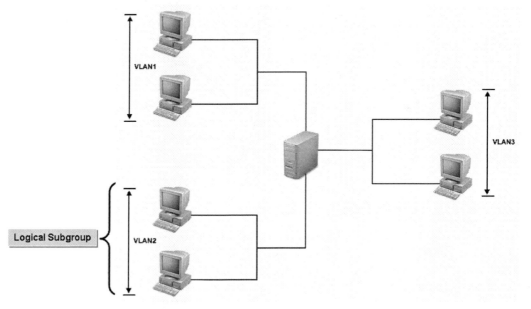

Figure 3-26: *A VLAN within a LAN.*

There are a few advantages to implementing a VLAN on a network.

Advantage of a VLAN	Description
Flexible network segmentation	Users and resources that communicate most frequently can be grouped into common VLANs, regardless of the physical location. Each group's traffic is efficiently controlled within the VLAN, and therefore, improves the efficiency of the whole network.
Simple management	The node addition, node removal, or node shifting can be dealt with quickly and conveniently from the management console rather than the wiring closet.
Increased performance	VLANs free up bandwidth by limiting the broadcast traffic throughout the network.
Enhanced network security	VLANs create virtual boundaries that can only be crossed through a router. So standard, router-based security measures can be used to restrict access to each VLAN as required.

Demilitarized Zones

Definition:

A *Demilitarized Zone (DMZ)* in a computer network is a small section of a private network that is made available for public access. A DMZ enables external clients to access data on private systems without compromising the security of the internal network as a whole. The external firewall enables public clients to access the service; the internal firewall prevents them from connecting to protected internal hosts.

Example:

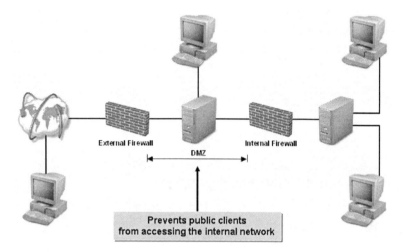

Figure 3-27: A DMZ protects the internal network of an organization from external clients.

ACTIVITY 3-4
Discussing Networking Essentials for Servers
Scenario:
In this activity, you will discuss the networking essentials for servers.

1. **Which class of IP address is set aside for research and experimentation purpose?**

   a) Class A

   b) Class B

   c) Class D

   d) Class E

2. **Match the classes of IP addresses to their range.**

   ___ Class A   a. 1.0.0.0 to 127.255.255.255

   ___ Class B   b. 240.0.0.0 to 255.255.255.255

   ___ Class C   c. 128.0.0.0 to 191.255.255.255

   ___ Class D   d. 224.0.0.0 to 239.255.255.255

   ___ Class E   e. 192.0.0.0 to 223.255.255.255

3. **Match the TCP port types to their range.**

   ___ Well known ports   a. 1024 through 49151

   ___ Registered ports   b. 49152 through 65535

   ___ Dynamic ports   c. 1 through 1023

4. **True or False? A VPN network infrastructure is owned by a single organization.**

   ___ True

   ___ False

5. **Which utility of TCP/IP provides dynamic configuration of IP addresses?**

   a) Subnetting

   b) DNS

   c) DHCP

   d) FQDN

6. **Which Ethernet types use the star topology?**

   a) 10 BASE 5

   b) 10 BASE 2

   c) 10 BASE T

   d) Switched Ethernet

Lesson 3 Follow-up

In this lesson, you examined the fundamentals of server software and the various management and security features provided by the server software. You also examined some essential concepts related to networking using TCP/IP. This knowledge is essential to implement a configuration that best suits your network.

1. **What are the various factors that will influence your choice of a network operating system?**

2. **What are the various factors that you will take into account before implementing virtualization on a server?**

4 Exploring the Server Storage System

Lesson Time: 3 hour(s)

Lesson Objectives:

In this lesson, you will examine the various types of storage systems used in servers.

You will:

- Identify the various types of storage devices used in servers.
- Explore the various types of hard disk drives used in servers.
- Describe a RAID system.
- Explore NAS implementations.
- Explore SAN implementations.

Introduction

Previously, you examined the fundamentals of server software and the system board components of a server. Another important general component supporting the data storage needs of your organization is the storage system. In this lesson, you will identify data storage technologies and implementations.

You can implement a variety of storage solutions for a server—from simple external storage devices and internal hard drives to advanced methods of data storage. You should be able to compare and contrast the various storage technologies and specifications to decide upon the best high performance storage solution.

This lesson covers all or part of the following CompTIA Server+ (2009) certification objectives:

- Topic A:
  - Objective 3.3: Install and configure different internal storage technologies.
  - Objective 3.4: Summarize the purpose of external storage technologies.
- Topic B:
  - Objective 3.3: Install and configure different internal storage technologies.
  - Objective 1.1: Differentiate between system board types, features, components and their purposes.
- Topic C:

- Objective 3.1: Describe RAID technologies and its features and benefits.
- Objective 3.2: Given a scenario, select the appropriate RAID level.
- Topic D:
  - Objective 3.4: Summarize the purpose of external storage technologies.
- Topic E:
  - Objective 3.4: Summarize the purpose of external storage technologies.

TOPIC A
Examine Storage Devices Used for Servers

In the earlier lessons, you identified the main components of a server. Among the important server components is the storage device. In this topic, you will identify the various types of storage devices used in servers.

As a server technician, your responsibilities include installing and maintaining different types of internal and external computer components, including storage devices. The ability to identify the types of storage devices found in most servers will be very useful when you are asked to work on a server.

Storage Devices

A *storage device* is a hardware device for storing data. Computers have many types of data storage devices, both internal and external.

Data Storage Device	Description
Internal storage	
	Internal storage devices are installed inside the system chassis. Apart from their speed and cheaper price, internal storage devices need not be charged or plugged into a power source to function. Because it is inside the server, it receives its power from the server power supply. Moreover, internal storage devices are free from external threats because the server chassis casings will protect the internal devices as well as the data that resides in it. Examples of internal storage devices include floppy drives, optical drives, SCSI, SATA, hard drives, and RAID.

Data Storage Device	Description
External storage	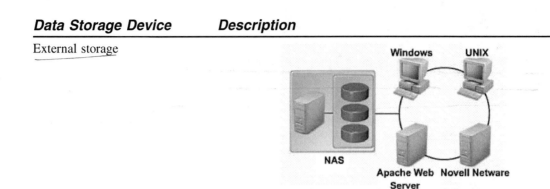 External storage devices provide auxiliary storage for data. They reside outside the server chassis and are connected to the server by means of cables and connectors. External storage devices are easier to set up. In most cases, you only need to plug in the proper power source and USB cables and then install the proper drivers. In addition, external storage devices are much easier to share between different users. However, external storage devices are slower and more expensive than internal storage devices. Examples of external storage devices include tape library, Write Once Read Many (WORM), optical jukebox, Network Attached Storage (NAS), and Storage Area Network (SAN).

Internal Storage Device Installation Considerations

There are several factors to be considered when attempting to install an internal storage device.

Factor	Description
Placement	Make sure you place the storage device where it will get proper air flow to avoid overheating the device. Consider the placement of drives inside bays with cable configuration. You may need to adjust the placement of drives to match the order of cable connectors.
Total air flow	Make sure there is sufficient total air flow to handle whatever heat the new storage device will add to the computer.
Power	Make sure that the storage device will not cause the computer to exceed the capacity of its power supply.
Device drivers	Make sure that you have the appropriate device drivers for the operating system of the computer on which you plan to install the new storage device. If necessary, download the device drivers from the device manufacturer's website.

Floppy Disk Drives

Definition:

A *Floppy Disk Drive (FDD)* is a storage device that reads data from and writes data to removable disks made of flexible Mylar plastic with magnetic coating, inside stiff, protective plastic cases. The vast majority of floppy drives are internal devices that connect to the system board and draw power from the computer's power supply. Today, these drives are not used much and are considered to be a legacy technology.

 Although 3.5 inches is the most recent standard for floppy disks and drives, 5.25-inch floppy disks and drives were once a standard, and before that, 8-inch disks and drives. You will probably never encounter either of these, and even 3.5-inch models are becoming obsolete.

Example:

Mylar plastic with magnetic coating

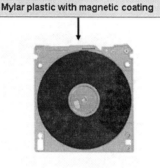

Floppy Disk

Figure 4-1: An FDD reads from and writes data to removable floppy disks.

Floppy Disk Drive Connector

Floppy disk drives are connected to the motherboard by means of a 34-conductor ribbon cable, which has a twist at the end of the cable that attaches to the drives. Each cable may have two to five connectors: one to attach to the motherboard and the others to the drive. Each floppy drive connector contains 34-pin holes.

Floppy USB

Servers nowadays do not include a floppy drive. Therefore, a USB floppy drive provides a simple way to add an external floppy drive to the server. This cost-effective, universal drive is removable, compact, and easy to use. The USB floppy drive serves as a perfect solution for small data exchanges, mini backups, or archiving.

Write Protection

Floppy disks can be protected so that you cannot write over data on the disk. On the back side of the floppy disk, there is a slider in the upper-left corner. If the slider blocks the write-protect hole, it enables you to write to the floppy disk. If the write-protect hole is visible, you will not be able to write to the disk.

Hard Disk Drives

Definition:

A *hard disk drive (HDD)* is a storage device that uses fixed media. In other words, the disk is built into a drive that remains in the computer until an upgrade or a repair is underway. Hard drives connect directly to the system board via at least one cable for data and another for power. The hard disk itself consists of several metal or hard plastic platters with a magnetic surface coating. Data, which is stored magnetically, can be accessed directly.

Example:

Figure 4-2: Hard drives are directly connected directly to the system board.

Internal hard disk drives are mounted inside the computer case and are connected directly to the system board. External hard disk drives are standalone portable units connected to the system using a number of connections, including USB and IEEE 1394. There are many types of hard disks. For example:

● Parallel Advanced Technology Attachment (PATA—it is also known as Integrated Development Environment (IDE), Enhanced IDE (EIDE), Ultra Direct Memory Access (UDMA), and ATA.)

● Small Computer Systems Interface (SCSI)

● Serial Advanced Technology Attachment (SATA)

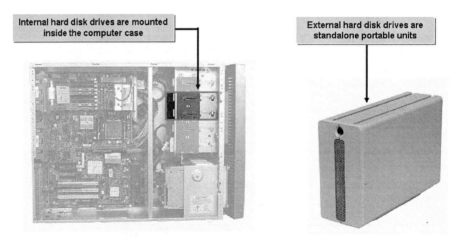

Figure 4-3: Internal and external hard drive components.

Hard Drive Firmware

Hard drive firmware is located in a flash memory chip on the hard drive. To ensure the correct functioning of the hard drive, the firmware will access various drive unique parameters from the hard disk during operation. The firmware controls various hard drive operations. It includes:

- When the hard drive is powered on, the firmware configures the hardware and allows the server to load the OS.

- During the hard drive operation, the firmware allows the hard disk to interact with other components on the system.

- When the hard drive is powered down, the firmware executes a shutdown sequence and ensures the hard drive powers down correctly.

Optical Disks

Definition:

An *optical disk* is an internal storage device, such as a CD or DVD, that stores data optically rather than magnetically. Removable plastic disks have a reflective coating and require an optical drive to read them. In optical storage, data is written by either pressing or burning the reflective surface of the disk with a laser to create pits (recessed areas) or lands (raised areas). An optical drive laser then reads the data off the disk.

Example:

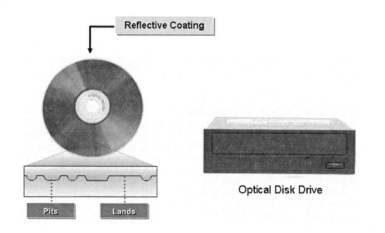

Figure 4-4: Optical disks store data optically, rather than magnetically.

Types of Optical Disks

There are several types of optical disks.

Type	Description
CD-ROM	Compact Disk Read-Only Memory. Data is permanently burned onto the disk during its manufacture.
CD-R	CD-Recordable. Data can be written to the disk only once.
CD-RW	CD-Rewritable. Data can be written to the disk multiple times.

Type	Description
DVD-ROM	Digital Versatile Disk Read-Only Memory. Data is permanently burned onto the disk during its manufacture.
DVD-R	DVD-Recordable. Data can be written to the disk only once.
DVD+R	Another format of DVD Recordable. Data can be written to the disk only once.
DVD+R DL	A higher-capacity double layer format of DVD Recordable Double Layer. Data can be written to the disk only once.
DVD-RW	DVD-Rewritable. Data can be written to the disk multiple times.
DVD+RW	Another format of DVD Rewritable. Data can be written to the disk multiple times.
DVD-RAM	DVD-Random Access Memory. Data can be written to the disk multiple times.
BD-ROM	Blu-ray disks are intended for high-density storage of high-definition video as well as data storage. They use blue laser light to read and store data. The blue laser has a shorter wavelength than existing CD and DVD laser technologies, which enables the system to store more data in the same amount of physical space. Current Blu-ray disks can hold up to 200 GB.

DVD Plus or DVD Dash

There are several competing DVD formats. DVD-ROM, DVD-R, DVD-RW, and DVD-RAM are approved by the DVD Forum, while DVD+R, DVD+R DL, DVD+RW are not. Because some of the competing formats are incompatible, many hybrid DVD drives have been developed. These hybrid drives are often labeled DVD±RW.

Tape Drives

Definition:

A *tape drive* is an internal storage device that stores data on a magnetic tape inside a removable cartridge. Data on any such magnetic devices is read sequentially. The size of external tape drives varies, but internal drives have a 5.25-inch form factor. Tape drives are most commonly used for storing data backups.

Example:

Tape Drive

Cartridge

Figure 4-5: Tape drive stores data magnetically on a tape enclosed in a removable tape cartridge.

Types of Tape Drives

There are several types of tape drives.

Type	Specification
Quarter-inch cartridge (QIC)	The Quarter-inch cartridge (QIC) technology is among the oldest, most standardized, and most reliable of the tape technologies. QIC drives are used for backing up servers or small networks. QIC cartridges are available in 60 MB/s to 4 GB/s with a data transfer rate of up to 0.3 MB/s. Most of the drives designed to read the higher capacity cartridges can also read the lower capacity cartridges. The original width was 0.25-inch, but the drives are also available in 3.5-inch (Travan) and 5.25-inch cartridges.
	Two of the biggest detractions to QIC technology are cost and speed. QIC drives are inexpensive; however, the cartridges are expensive when cost per megabyte is considered. Quarter-inch cartridge drives are slow, having about the slowest transfer rates of any of the tape technologies.
4 mm Digital Audio Tape	Originally adapted from the audio market, the 4 mm DAT tape format offers higher storage capacities at a lower cost than does QIC technology. DAT cartridges are about the size of an audio tape, so they are quite small compared with QIC cartridges, and therefore, are much easier to store and use. Capacities for 4 mm tapes range from 1 GB to 12 GB with a transfer rate of 4 MB/s.
	DAT tapes are considered to be less reliable than QIC tapes. They are especially vulnerable to heat and moisture. Because the tape is pulled out of the cartridge during operation, to be wrapped around the spinning read/write head, the tapes wear more quickly than do QIC tapes. Due to lack of strict standards, 4 mm tape drives are not always compatible: tapes from one drive might not be readable in another drive.
Stationary Digital Audio Tape or SDAT	Shuttles the tape back and forth over a head that uses several individual tracks. Native capacity is 300 GB with a transfer rate of 36 MB/s.
8 mm tape (Exabyte)	The 8 mm tape format was originally developed by Exabyte, which continues to be the only manufacturer of 8 mm drives. Many other manufacturers purchase raw drives from Exabyte and integrate them into internal or external 8 mm tape drives. This arrangement ensures compatibility between 8 mm drives. These 8 mm tape drives offer storage capabilities between 2.2 GB and 10 GB per cartridge. The tape cartridges are only slightly larger than DAT tapes. They are often considered more reliable than 4 mm drives; however, the drives and tapes are more expensive than 4 mm units. The 8 mm tape drives are popular in the UNIX and workstation industry.
Digital linear tape	Digital Linear Tape (DLT) was developed by DEC, who sold this technology to Quantum. The tape is a half-inch cartridge with a single hub and is used mainly in mid- to large-sized networks for network backups. There are 128 or 208 linear tracks, holding 10 to 35 GB of data. Another DLT format, Super DLT, holds up to 600 GB. Currently, DLT transfer rates are in the 1.25 MB/s to 72 MB/s range. The forecast is for DLT to soon hold up to 1500 GB with up to 100 MB/s transfer rates.
Super Digital Linear Tape or SDLT	SDLT provides a current native capacity of 300 GB and native transfer rate of 40 MB/s and is backwards compatible with several DLT formats.

Type	Specification
Linear Tape Open	Linear Tape Open (LTO) was developed by IBM, HP, and Seagate. LTO's primary format is called Ultrium. The newest version, Ultrium-3, has a maximum capacity of 800 GB on a single tape with a transfer rate of 160 MB/s.

How Tape Drives Work

While hard drives, floppy drives, and removable cartridge drives are direct-access devices, tape drives are sequential access devices. Rather than being able to go to a specific file directly, with a tape, you have to read past every file on the tape until you get to the one you want. For this reason, tape drives are typically used to store backup copies of information, as opposed to for live data access. When you insert a tape cartridge in a tape drive and perform a backup of files from your hard drive:

1. The computer reads the file system table on the hard drive, locates the files that you want to back up, and begins reading file data into the RAM.
2. Data is then dumped from the RAM to the tape drive controller buffer as memory fills.
3. The controller sends commands to the drive to start spooling the tape.
4. The capstan in the center of the supply reel turns the rollers in the cartridge. The belt around the tape and the rollers provide resistance and keep the tape taut and tight to the drive heads.
5. Data is sent from the controller to the read/write heads.

Flash Storage

Definition:

Flash storage, also known as solid state storage, is an internal storage device that stores data using flash memory. Flash memory gets its name because its microchip is organized in such a way that a section of its memory cells can be erased in a single action or "flash." In flash storage devices, data can be erased and reprogrammed in units of memory called blocks. Common types of flash storage devices include USB drives, commonly known as jump drives or thumb drives; flash memory cards; and secure digital (SD) memory cards.

Example:

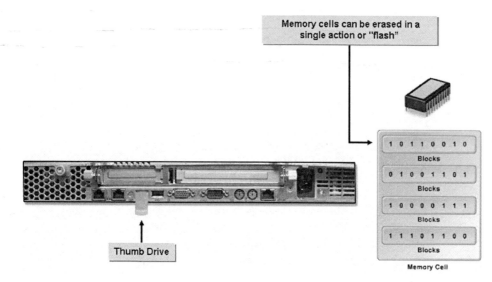

Figure 4-6: Solid state storage stores data in special types of memory instead of on disks or tapes.

Solid State vs. Magnetic Storage

Storage devices typically store data in either solid-state or magnetic form. Solid state devices, such as flash drives, contain no moving parts and tend to be more reliable than magnetic drives. Magnetic drives, such as hard drives, store information on a magnetic coated media that is rotated underneath a read/write head.

Types of Flash Storage

There are various types of flash storage devices, many of which are used in external devices such as digital cameras and cell phones.

Device Type	Specification
USB flash drives	USB flash drives come in several form factors, including thumb drives and pen drives. Thumb drives can be small, from 50 to 70 mm long, 17 to 20 mm wide, and 10 to 12 mm tall. Data-storage capacities vary, from 128 MB up to 128 GB. Data-transfer rates also vary, from 700 KB/s to 28 MB/s for read operations, and from 350 KB/s to 15 MB/s for write operations.
Solid State Drives (SSD)	Flash memory-based disks do not need batteries, allowing makers to replicate standard disk drive form factors (2.5-inch and 3.5-inch). Flash SSDs are extremely fast since these devices have no moving parts, eliminating seek time, latency, and other electromechanical delays inherent in conventional disk drives.
Compact flash cards	Compact Flash cards are flash memory cards that are 43 mm long x 36 mm wide. Type I is 3.3 mm thick and Type II is 5 mm thick. They hold up to 100 GB or more and have a 50-pin contact. Transfer speeds up to 66 MB/s are possible.

Device Type	Specification
Smart media cards	Smart media cards are flash memory cards that are 45 mm long x 37 mm wide x 0.76 mm thick. They can hold up to 128 MB and can transfer data at speeds up to 8 MB/s.
xD-Picture Cards	xD-Picture Cards (xD) are flash memory cards that are 20 mm long x 25 mm wide x 1.7 mm thick. They can hold up to 2 GB with plans for up to 8 GB. Data transfer rates range from 4 to 15 MB/s for read operations and from 1.3 to 9 MB/s for write operations.
Memory Sticks (MS)	Memory sticks are flash memory cards that are 50 mm long x 21.5 mm wide x 2.8 mm thick. They can hold up to 16 GB and are used extensively in Sony products. Data transfer rates are 2.5 MB/s for read operations and 1.8 MB/s for write operations.
Secure Digital (SD) cards	The original SD Memory Card is 32 mm long, 24 mm wide, and 2.1 mm tall. The miniSD Card measures 21.5 mm by 20 mm by 1.4 mm, and the microSD/TransFlash Card measures 15 mm by 11 mm by 1 mm. SD Memory Cards are currently available in several capacities, up to 2 TB. Data transfer rates range from 10 MB/s to 20 MB/s.
Multi Media Cards (MMC)	Multi Media Cards are 32 mm long by 24 mm wide by 1.5 mm tall. Reduced Size MMCs (RS-MMCs) and MMCmobile cards are 16 mm by 24 mm by 1.5 mm. MMCmini cards are 21.5 mm by 20 mm by 1.4 mm, and MMCmicro cards are 12 mm by 14 mm by 1.1 mm. These cards can hold up to 8 GB, and data transfer rates can reach 52 MB/s. MMC cards are generally also compatible with Secure Digital (SD) card readers.

Tape Libraries

A *tape library* is an external storage device that stores, retrieves, writes, and reads data from multiple magnetic tape cartridges. Tape libraries incorporate two important hardware components, the tape drive and the robotic autoloader. The robotic autoloader provides the required tape cartridge by selecting the appropriate tape cartridges from the built-in storage racks, loading them into the drive as required, removing them when the data is packed, and storing them until they are needed. Although tape library devices are not as fast as online hard disks, they do have their data readily available at all times and are, therefore, referred to as "near-line" devices.

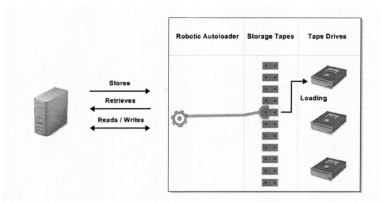

Figure 4-7: *Tape libraries incorporate two important hardware components, the tape drive and the robotic autoloader.*

Write Once Read Many

Write Once Read Many (WORM) is an external storage system that allows information to be written once on a storage medium; however, the data can be read several times. The basic property of WORM storage is to not allow updates on the data inserted. The WORM disk incorporates cheap disk arrays such as ATA to create large economical online storage arrays; ATA-based storage arrays deliver up to a capacity of terabytes (TBs).

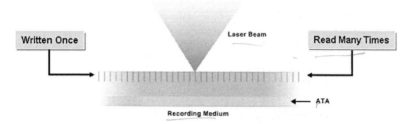

Figure 4-8: *WORM allows information to be written once on a storage medium but the data can be read several times.*

ROM vs. WORM

ROM is an internal storage unit with a storage capacity of 64 to 256 KB, whereas WORM is an external storage device with a storage capacity of a few TBs.

Optical Jukebox

An *optical jukebox,* also referred to as an optical disk library, is an automated external storage system that houses many optical disks with multiple read/write drives to archive and store data. Optical jukebox devices may have up to 2,000 slots for disks, and usually have a picking device, called the robotic arm, that traverses the slots and drives. The arrangement of the slots and robotic arm affects the storage and retrieval performance, which depends on the space between a disk and the robotic arm. The loaded optical disk can be a CD, DVD, Ultra Density Optical disk, or Blu-ray disk. Jukeboxes are used in high-capacity archive storage environments such as imaging, medical, and video applications.

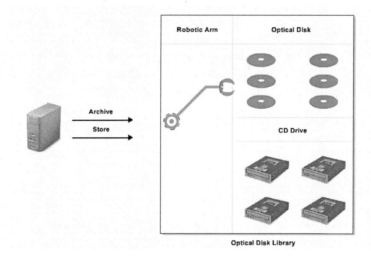

Figure 4-9: *Optical jukebox houses many optical disks with multiple read/write drives to archive and store data.*

ACTIVITY 4-1
Identifying Storage Devices
Scenario:
In this activity, you will identify storage devices.

---

1. **Which storage system does not involve any moving parts to read and write data?**

   a) Flash storage

   b) Optical jukebox

   c) Optical storage

   d) Tape libraries

---

2. **Match the storage device to its appropriate description.**

   ___ Floppy disk drive   a. Records data magnetically; most often used for backups.

   ___ Hard disk drive   b. Records and reads data by using a laser.

   ___ Optical disk drive   c. Records data magnetically on removable disks.

   ___ Tape drive   d. Records data magnetically on nonremovable disks.

   ___ Flash drive   e. Records data in nonvolatile memory.

---

3. **Which optical drive media types enable you to write to an optical disk only once?**

   a) CD-RW

   b) DVD-RW

   c) CD-R

   d) DVD-RAM

---

4. **Which tape drive provides the maximum storage capacity of 800 GB on a single tape with a transfer rate of 160 MB/s?**

   a) QIC

   b) DLT

   c) 4 mm digital audio tape

   d) Ultrium-3

---

5. **A user wants to transfer several megabytes of data between two computers that are not connected by a network. What storage device would you recommend?**

    a) A USB thumb drive

    b) A floppy disk

    c) An external tape drive

    d) A CD-ROM or DVD-ROM drive

TOPIC B
Explore IDE and SCSI

You examined the various types of internal and external storage devices. Internal hard drives are connected to the system memory with the help of SCSI and IDE interfaces. In this topic, you will explore the SCSI and IDE.

Understanding the various types of hard disk drives is important to a server technician because most storage drives fall under these two categories—SCSI and IDE/ATA. Their wide use makes it critical for server specialists to have a thorough understanding of their characteristics.

Integrated Drive Electronics/ATA

The term Integrated Drive Electronics (IDE) refers to a disk drive interface based on the ISA bus. Its specifications are a subset of the AT Attachment (ATA) specifications. A basic ATA or IDE drive has an on-board controller and connects to other IDE devices. The major advantages of using an IDE drive are its low cost and ease of use. The ATA specifications have been revised several times, making the original specifications obsolete. Other versions of ATA include ATAPI (which defines IDE standards for CD-ROM and tape drives), ATA-3, ATA-4, ATA-5, and ATA-6.

ATA has an on-board controller and connects to other IDE devices

IDE/ATA

Figure 4-10: IDE is a disk drive interface based on the ISA bus.

The features of an IDE drive include:

- A built-in controller.
- Two channels, each with up to two devices.
- Automatic detection of drives. Earlier drives came in "types" that corresponded to a particular internal geometry, and the drive type had to be set in the system BIOS.
- Manual configuration of the drive type in the system BIOS is allowed only if the automatic detection fails.
- Several revisions to the standard, each supporting different data transfer rates.
- A Cable Select preset that allows the BIOS to configure itself as needed. Earlier, when you installed PATA drives, you used jumpers to set the master/slave or Cable Select configuration.

IDE Standards

The original IDE specification predated CD-ROM drives and did not support hard drives larger than 504 MB. However, revisions to the specifications over the years have extended the capabilities of the IDE to provide support for faster and larger hard drives and other devices.

IDE Standard	Description
IDE, ATA, ATA-1, or PATA	The original PATA specification supported one channel, with two drives configured in a master/slave arrangement. A second channel was added later.
EIDE, Fast ATA, ATA-2, or Fast ATA-2	Also known as ATA Interface with Extensions ATA-2, Western Digital called its implementation Enhanced IDE (EIDE). Seagate's was called Fast ATA or Fast ATA-2. You could implement power-saving mode features if desired.
ATA-3	Minor enhancement to ATA-2. Improved reliability for high-speed data transfer modes. Self Monitoring Analysis And Reporting Technology (SMART) was introduced. This is logic in the drives that warns of impending drive problems. Password protection available as a security feature of the drives.
ATA/ATAPI-4, ATA-4, Ultra ATA/33, Ultra DMA, UDMA, UDMA/33	Doubled data transfer rates. ATA Packet Interface (ATAPI) is an EIDE interface enhancement that includes commands used to control tape, CD-ROM, and other removable drives.
ATA/ATAPI-5, ATA-5, Ultra ATA/66, UDMA/66	The ATA-5 specification introduced Ultra DMA modes 3 and 4, as well as mandatory use of the 80-conductor (40 pin), high-performance IDE cable with Ultra DMA modes higher than 2. Additional changes to the command set were also part of this specification. Supports drives up to 137 GB.
ATA/ATAPI-6, ATA-6, Ultra ATA/100, UDMA/100	Supports data transfers at up to 100 MB/s. Supports drives as large as 144 PB (petabytes), which is approximately 144 million GB or 144 quadrillion bytes.
PIO	Programmed Input/Output is a data transfer method that includes the CPU in the data path. It has been replaced by DMA and Ultra DMA.
DMA	Direct Memory Access is a data transfer method that moves data directly from the drive to main memory. Ultra DMA transfers data in burst mode at a rate of 33.3 MB/s. The speed is two times faster than DMA.
Serial ATA (SATA)	Uses serial instead of parallel signaling technology for ATA and ATAPI devices. Serial ATA employs serial connectors and serial cables, which are smaller, thinner, and more flexible than traditional parallel ATA cables. Data transfer rates are 150 MB/s or greater.
SATA II, SATA2, SATA 3 Gb/s	Provides data transfer rates of 300 MB/s.
SATA 6 Gb/s	Doubled data transfer rates, designed to support the latest (and future) solid state drives.

SATA Connectors

SATA cables are used to connect high-speed SATA drives to the motherboard. SATA cables have only seven connectors and are, therefore, much thinner than ribbon-type IDE cables, a feature which improves airflow and makes them easier to route inside the case. SATA cables can be as long as one meter in length and are more rugged than IDE cables, which provides for more flexibility in choosing where to mount hard drives. They're also capable of very high data transfer rates as high as 300 MB/sec.

PIO Mode

The original IDE/ATA transfer method used programmed I/O (PIO), wherein the system's CPU controls the transfer of data between the system memory and the hard disk. PIO can work at several speeds, so *PIO modes* are used to distinguish between the speeds. But even with increased speeds in PIO modes 3, 4, and 5, performance was an issue. Performance suffered because the CPU had to execute all of the instructions for every data transfer, consuming processing time that could be used for other processes.

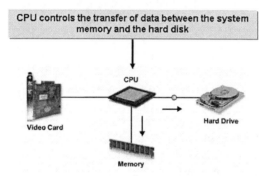

Figure 4-11: In PIO mode, CPU executes all of the instructions for every data transfer.

Direct Memory Access

A better alternative to using the PIO mode is to take the CPU entirely out of the picture and have the hard disk and system memory communicate directly. *Direct Memory Access (DMA)* refers to any transfer protocol that allows a peripheral device to transfer information directly to the memory or read from it, without the system processor being required to perform the transaction. Several *DMA modes* that have been defined for the IDE/ATA interface are grouped into two categories: single-word and multi-word. Single-word transfers two bytes of data, while multi-word transfers data in bursts.

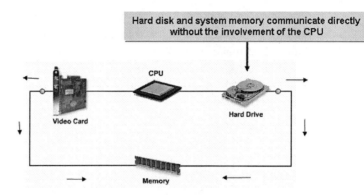

Figure 4-12: *In DMA mode, the CPU is out of the picture.*

Single-Word DMA

Three single-word DMA modes were defined in the original ATA standard, but they provided relatively low transfer rates. Performing transfers of a single word at a time is very inefficient; each transfer requires overhead for setup. Single-word mode has been removed from the ATA specification.

Multi-Word DMA

Today, multi-word DMA is used exclusively, to the point where single-word DMA has been removed from the ATA specifications, and the distinction isn't even made between single-word and multi-word. For even better performance, the combination of bus mastering and DMA on the PCI bus became commonplace. In addition, later technological advances made Ultra DMA possible. Instead of increasing the speed of the interface, as the earlier DMA modes did, Ultra DMA improved the efficiency of the interface, thus allowing performance enhancements never seen before with IDE/ATA interfaces. To accomplish this, Ultra DMA uses double-transition clocking, which enables data transfers to take place twice in one clock cycle—both on the rising and falling edges of the clock. To ensure data integrity, Ultra DMA also uses Cyclical Redundancy Checking or CRC at the interface.

IDE/ATA Cables and Connectors

There are several cables and connectors associated with an IDE device.

Cable Type	Description
40-conductor	The standard cable that was originally used with virtually all IDE devices. It's a flat ribbon cable, usually gray with a red stripe along one edge. The cable contains 40 wires and 40 pins, and usually has three identical female connectors: one for the IDE controller (or system board header for PCs with built-in PCI ATA controllers) and the other two for the master and slave devices on the interface. Use the red stripe to line up pin 1 on the controller (or system board) with pin 1 on the devices being connected, since the techniques used for keying the cables are not standardized. In many ways, the cable is the weak link in the IDE/ATA interface. It was originally designed for very slow hard disks that transferred less than 5 MB/s, not the high-speed devices of today. Flat ribbon cables are either not insulated or do not have protection from electromagnetic interference. These are the main reasons why the 80-conductor cable was developed for Ultra DMA. Even with slower transfer modes, there are limitations to how the cable can be used, mainly dealing with the cable length. The longer the cable, the higher the chance of data corruption due to interference on the cable and uneven signal propagation, so you should try to keep the cable as short as possible. According to the ATA standards, the official maximum length is 18 inches, but if you suspect problems with your hard disk, try using a shorter cable. Sometimes, moving the disks physically in the system case will let you use a shorter cable. As long as the cable you select isn't being used, any connector on a standard 40-conductor cable can go to any device, because all 40 wires are connected straight through to all three connectors. Usually, two of the connectors are closer to each other than the third, and the most distant connector is attached to the system board (or hard disk controller card). The other two devices can be used for either the master or the slave, and it doesn't matter which is which as long as the jumper settings are configured accordingly. If you're using a single device, attach it to the connector at the end of the cable, and leave the connector in the middle of the cable unattached. Using the middle connector and leaving the end connector unattached is technically allowed for regular PIO and DMA transfer modes, but it leaves part of the cable dangling. Other potential problems with the 40-conductor cable include the possibility of inserting the cable the wrong way (by not using the stripe to line up the various pin 1s) and the possibility of the cable coming loose (since there aren't any latching mechanisms as there are with SCSI cables). Neither of these issues will ruin the hard drive, but until you correct them the hard drive won't work either. If all else fails when you're using a standard 40-conductor cable, try replacing it with one of the 80-conductor cables; they're backward-compatible.

Cable Type	Description
40-conductor CS	A special cable used to implement Cable Select that has the master connector in the middle of the cable and the slave connector as the device at the end of the cable, farthest from the host. If you have two devices on the channel, that isn't much of a problem, but if you have just one device on the channel, connecting it to the master connector creates a stub condition, and connecting it to the slave connector creates a condition where you have a slave with no master, which isn't a valid configuration.
Y-shaped 40-conductor CS	To get around problems with stub conditions, a second type of cable was created—the Y-shaped cable. On this cable, the host connector is in the middle, and the slave and master connectors are on the two opposite ends of the cable. Although this cable design solved some of the problems with the original CS cable, it caused others. For instance, because IDE/ATA cables are subject to stringent length limitations, the Y-shaped cable was hard to implement in large tower systems. All drives have to be mounted very close to the system board or controller card so the cable can reach.
80-conductor	The ATA-4 standard introduced a new cable for use with the new Ultra DMA modes. Although there are 80 wires, there are still 40 pins on the connectors, making these cables compatible with older drives. The extra 40 wires are connected to ground, enabling them to absorb much of the interference and other signaling problems that can arise with the higher transfer rates.
	Because this cable is required for all Ultra DMA modes above mode 2, there has to be a way for the system to make sure the cable is indeed an 80-conductor cable. This is accomplished by having the /PDIAG /CBLID signal, which is carried on pin 34 of the interface, grounded in the connector that attaches to the system board. Because the older 40-conductor cable wouldn't have this pin grounded, the host can determine if an 80-conductor cable is present by looking for the grounding on this pin at startup. The 80-conductor cables also support Cable Select by default.
	In addition, consistent connector assignments and color coding was implemented with this cable. Blue connectors attach to the host system board or controller, gray connectors are in the middle of the cable and attach to any slave device, and black connectors are at the far end of the cable and attach to the master or a single device. These cables are the same width as the standard 40-conductor cables, and are subject to the same length restrictions.

Master and Slave Designations

IDE drives are configured in a master/slave hierarchy, usually by setting jumpers. Each IDE/ATA channel can support either one or two devices. Because each IDE/ATA device contains its own integrated controller, you need to have some way of differentiating between the two devices. This is done by configuring a device to assign master and slave designations, and then having the controller address commands and data to either one or the other.

There are two ways in which the devices are configured.

Configuration	Description
Master/slave	In the master/slave configuration scheme, the drive that is the target of the command responds to it, and the other one ignores the command, remaining silent. Each manufacturer uses a different combination of jumpers for specifying whether its drive is master or slave on the channel, though they're all similar. Some manufacturers put this information right on the top label of the drive itself, while others don't. Jumpering information is available in the hard disk's documentation, or by checking the manufacturer's website and searching for the model number.

If you are using two drives on a channel, you must make sure that they are jumpered correctly. Making both drives the master, or both the slave, will likely result in a very confused system. It doesn't make any difference which connector on the standard IDE cable is used in a standard IDE setup, because the jumpers control master and slave, not the cable; however, this doesn't apply when the Cable Select feature is used. Also, there can be electrical signaling issues, particularly with Ultra DMA modes, if you connect a single drive to only the middle connector on a cable, leaving the end connector unattached. |

Configuration	Description
Cable Select	With Cable Select, you don't have to set jumpers to designate which device is master and which is slave. The connectors that are connected to the devices take care of the configuration.
	To set up Cable Select, you need to use a special jumper to set both devices on the channel to the Cable Select (CS) setting, along with a special cable. This cable is similar in most respects to the regular IDE/ATA cable, except for the CSEL signal. CSEL is carried on wire 28 of the standard IDE/ATA cable, and is grounded at the host's connector (the one that attaches to the system board or controller). On a Cable Select cable, one of the connectors (the master connector) has pin 28 connected through to the cable, but the other (the slave connector) has an open circuit on that pin (no connection).
	Cable Select was never widely accepted in the industry, so most drives come with the drive jumpered as a master (or single) drive. This means that to enable Cable Select, you have to change a jumper anyway, which negates some of the advantage of using it. In addition, standard 40-conductor cables don't support Cable Select, which contributed to it not being widely accepted in the marketplace.

SCSI Specification

There are different types of SCSI devices and drives. Some servers will have SCSI controllers right on the system board. In other types of servers, you will need to install a SCSI adapter into one of the expansion slots to be able to implement SCSI solutions in that server. If you need to install a SCSI adapter, be sure to select one that is compatible with the system bus. In most cases— at least with newer servers— you'll have to select a SCSI adapter capable of working with PCI systems.

Limitations of Using an ISA SCSI Adapter

If you do need to use an ISA-compatible SCSI adapter, you will lose a lot of the potential throughput of SCSI because the system bus itself can handle only about 8 MB/s of throughput.

System Bus Throughput Limitations

No matter which type of system bus the computer has, if the throughput of the system bus is less than the potential maximum throughput of the SCSI channel, the actual maximum throughput of the SCSI channel will be limited to the maximum throughput of the system bus.

IDs and LUNs

All SCSI devices must be uniquely identified. SCSI ID numbers run from 00 to 07 on an 8-bit SCSI bus, 00 to 15 on a 16-bit bus, and 00 to 31 on a 32-bit bus. The host bus adapter is usually assigned ID number 07 and has the highest priority on the bus. Each SCSI ID can also support additional logical devices, so *Logical Unit Numbers (LUNs)* were developed as another means of identifying these devices. On an 8-bit bus, LUNs can run from 00 to 07, and on a 16-bit bus, LUNs can run from 00 to 15. Dividing a device into logical units is useful if the device is a controller supporting multiple sub-units (certain RAID subsystems, for example) or if the target also supports a separate control or management interface. In practice, most SCSI-1 tape drives and a large number of disk devices support only a single LUN (LUN 0). Some devices can require more than one ID or LUN.

SCSI Signaling

There are three types of SCSI signaling.

Type of SCSI Signaling	Description
Single-Ended (SE) SCSI	Enables you to attach devices to a total cable length of 6 meters for SCSI I and II, and a length of 3 meters for Fast, Wide, and Ultra SCSI. SE SCSI is not defined for Ultra2 SCSI and higher. Most devices use SE signaling; in fact, unless a device is labeled otherwise, it's safe to assume it's an SE device. Single-ended SCSI uses one data line and a ground wire. SE SCSI is also susceptible to noise interference.
Differential SCSI, or High Voltage Differential (HVD) SCSI	Used when devices are spread across a room, because it's less susceptible to noise than SE SCSI and the total cable length is 25 meters. Differential devices cost more than their SE counterparts. HVD SCSI uses data low and data high lines to increase transmission distances. You can't mix HVD and SE SCSI devices; the signaling schemes are incompatible. In addition, you can't mix HVD and LVD SCSI devices because the voltages are incompatible. Unless a SCSI device, controller, or cable adapter is labeled "differential" or "HVD," it will probably not work with other differential SCSI devices. Because of the benefits of LVD SCSI, differential SCSI is becoming less popular. This scheme was defined in SCSI-2 and made obsolete with SCSI-3. Not compatible with SE or LVD devices unless a SCSI converter is added.

Type of SCSI Signaling	Description
Low Voltage Differential signaling (LVD or LVDS)	Supports cable lengths up to 12 meters. Like HVD SCSI, LVD SCSI uses data low and data high lines to increase transmission distance; however, LVD uses less power and is less expensive because the transceivers are built into the controller chips. LVD SCSI also offers legacy support in devices labeled LVD/SE, which means that you can run them either in LVD mode or in SE mode. Most LVD SCSI devices are LVD/SE, but you must run only one mode. If one device on your SCSI bus is SE, all devices will be limited to the SE limitations; in other words, all devices must be set to LVD to achieve the distance and speed capabilities of LVD. For LVD SCSI cabling, you need to use a Twist and Flat ribbon cable and an LVD/SE terminator or a Twist and Flat ribbon cable with built-in LVD termination. If you're operating in SE mode, you need to use only an active terminator.

Multitasking and Multithreading

The factor that makes SCSI beneficial for servers when compared to IDE is its ability to handle overlapping processes and threads, which enables the system to operate and access data on multiple devices simultaneously. IDE does not enable multiple drives to work at the same time—they must "take turns."

The ability to perform multiple tasks is possible because of disconnect/reconnect. This allows a device to release control of the SCSI bus while performing a task and then reconnect to complete the task. While disconnected, the bus goes into Bus Free phase, which indicates that no SCSI device is actively using the bus and it is available for other users. Disconnect/reconnect optimizes the use of bus bandwidth, therefore speeding up overall rate of data transfer.

SCSI Standards

SCSI standards have been revised repeatedly over the years.

SCSI Standard	Description
SCSI-1	Features an 8-bit parallel bus (with parity), running asynchronously at 3.5 MB/s or 5 MB/s in synchronous mode, and a maximum bus cable length of 6 meters, compared to the 0.45-meter limit of the Parallel ATA interface. A variation on the original standard included a *high-voltage differential (HVD)* implementation with a maximum cable length of 25 meters.
SCSI-2	Introduced the Fast SCSI and Wide SCSI variants. Fast SCSI doubled the maximum transfer rate to 10 MB/s, and Wide SCSI doubled the bus width to 16 bits to reach 20 MB/s. Maximum cable length was reduced to 3 meters.
SCSI-3	The first parallel SCSI devices that exceeded the SCSI-2 capabilities were simply designated SCSI-3. These devices were also known as Ultra SCSI and Fast-20 SCSI. The bus speed doubled again to 20 MB/s for narrow (8-bit) systems and 40 MB/s for wide (16-bit). The maximum cable length stayed at 3 meters.

SCSI Standard	Description
Ultra-2 SCSI	This standard featured a *low-voltage differential (LVD)* bus. For this reason Ultra-2 SCSI is sometimes referred to as LVD SCSI. LVD's greater immunity to noise allowed a maximum bus cable length of 12 meters. At the same time, the data transfer rate was increased to 80 MB/s.
Ultra-3 SCSI	Also known as Ultra-160 SCSI, this version was basically an improvement on the Ultra-2 SCSI standard, in that the transfer rate was doubled once more to 160 MB/s. Ultra-160 SCSI offered new features such as cyclic redundancy check (CRC), an error correcting process, and domain validation.
Ultra-320 SCSI	This standard doubled the data transfer rate to 320 MB/s. Ultra 320 is the latest evolution in SCSI, it is backwards compatible with other SCSI types of the same connection, but with reduced date transfer. Ultra requires LVD signaling, the maximum allowable cable length is 12Mts (with more than two active SCSI devices).
Ultra-640 SCSI	Also known as Fast-320 SCSI, Ultra-640 doubles the interface speed yet again, this time to 640 MB/s. Ultra-640 pushes the limits of LVD signaling; the speed limits cable lengths drastically, making it impractical for more than one or two devices.
Serial SCSI	Four versions of SCSI (*SSA*, *FC-AL*, IEEE 1394, and *Serial Attached SCSI*, or SAS) perform data transfer via serial communications. SAS is a point-to-point architecture that uses a disk controller with four or more channels operating simultaneously. SAS also supports serial ATA (SATA) drives, which can be mixed with SAS drives in a variety of configurations. Serial SCSI supports faster data rates than traditional SCSI implementations, hot swapping, and improved fault isolation. Serial SCSI devices are generally more expensive than the equivalent parallel SCSI devices.
iSCSI	*iSCSI* provides connectivity between SCSI storage networks over an IP-based network without the need for installing Fiber Channel.

SCSI Cables and Connectors

There are many SCSI connectors and cables that meet the specific electrical requirements associated with different SCSI signaling speeds and methods.

Cable Type	Description
Internal	

Used to connect SCSI devices that are installed in the computer. Internal cables tend to be less expensive because they don't have to be designed to protect the data from electromagnetic and radio frequency noise and other types of interference. Generally, internal devices use unshielded cables, which are flat ribbon cables similar to those used for floppy drives and other internal devices. Although internal cables are easier and cheaper to make than external cables, there are differences in construction (beyond the obvious width issue, 50 wires for narrow SCSI and 68 wires for wide SCSI). One issue is the thickness of the wires used; another is the insulation that goes over the wires. Better cables generally use Teflon as a wire insulation material, while cheaper ones may use PVC (polyvinyl chloride). Regular flat cables are typically used for SE SCSI applications up to Ultra speeds (20 MHz). Internal cables use the following connectors:

- 50-pin Regular Density
- 50- and 68-pin High Density (HD)
- 80-pin Single Connector Attachment (SCA)

Cable Type	Description

External

Used to connect SCSI devices that aren't installed in the computer. External cables are round shielded cables that protect the data they carry from interference. The wires in the cable are divided into pairs, consisting of a data signal paired with its complement. For SE signaling, each signal is paired with a signal return, or ground, wire. For differential signaling, each positive signal is paired with its corresponding negative signal. The two wires in each pair are then twisted together to improve signal integrity, compared to running all the wires in parallel to each other. This means that an external narrow cable with 50 wires actually contains 25 pairs and a 68-wire cable contains 34 pairs. External cables use the following connectors:

- 50-pin D-Shell
- 50-pin Centronics
- 50- and 68-pin High Density (HD)
- 68-pin Very High Density Cable Interconnect (VHDCI)

External Cable Layer Construction

The wire pairs in an external cable are placed in a specific layered structure to create the cable. The core layer of the cable contains the pairs carrying the most important control signals: REQ and ACK (request and acknowledge). Around the core, pairs of other control signals are arranged in a middle layer. The outer layer of the cable contains the data and other signals. The purpose of this three-layer structure is to further insulate the most important signals to improve data integrity. Finally, the cable is wrapped with a metallic shield such as copper braiding to block out noise and other interference.

Twist and Flat Cables

For Ultra2 or faster internal cables using LVD signaling, the poor electrical characteristics of cheaper flat ribbon cables affected signal integrity even within the computer case, so a new type of internal ribbon cable was created. The new design combines some of the characteristics of regular internal and external cables. With these ribbon cables, pairs are twisted between the connectors on the cable, just like in external cables, but the ribbon remains flat near the connectors for easier attachment. The pair twisting improves performance for high-speed SCSI applications. The cost of these cables is higher than regular internal cables, but they are still less expensive than external cables. This technology is sometimes called Twist and Flat cable, since it is partially flat and partially twisted-pair.

Termination

SCSI buses require proper termination to prevent signals from traveling back along the bus. However, Ultra 320 termination is defined by the manufacturer and therefore, it cannot be changed. Special components are used that make the bus seem as if it is infinite in length. Any signals sent along the bus appear to go to all devices and then disappear, with no reflections. There are several different kinds of termination used on SCSI buses. They differ in the electrical circuitry used to terminate the bus. Better forms of termination make for more reliable SCSI chains; the better the termination, the fewer problems (all else being equal) with the bus, though cost is usually higher, too. In general, slower buses are less particular about the kind of termination used, while faster ones have more demanding requirements. In addition, buses using differential signaling (either HVD or LVD) require special termination.

- *Passive termination* is the oldest and simplest, but least reliable, type of termination. It uses simple resistors to terminate the bus, similar to how terminators are used on coaxial Ethernet networks. Although passive termination works for short, low-speed SE SCSI-1 buses, it isn't suitable for modern SCSI speeds.

- *Active termination* adds voltage regulators to the resistors used in passive termination to allow for more reliable and consistent termination of the bus. Active termination is the minimum required for faster-speed SE SCSI buses.

- *Forced Perfect Termination (FPT)* is a more advanced form of active termination, where diode clamps are added to the circuitry to force the termination to the correct voltage. This eliminates virtually any signal reflections or other problems and provides for the best form of termination of an SE SCSI bus.

- For buses using HVD signaling, you need to use special HVD terminators.

- For buses using LVD signaling, you also need to use special LVD terminators. In addition, there are special LVD/SE terminators designed for use with multimode LVD devices that can function in either LVD or SE modes; when the bus is running in SE mode, these behave like active terminators.

ACTIVITY 4-2
Discussing IDE and SCSI Devices

Scenario:

In this activity, you will discuss IDE and SCSI devices.

---

1. **What is the bus speed of the first SCSI standard?**

   a) 8 bits wide at 7 MB/s

   b) 16 bits wide at 5 MB/s

   c) 8 bits wide at 5 MB/s

   d) 8 bits wide at 8 MB/s

---

2. **Which is the common name for an ATA-4 device that uses Ultra DMA mode 2?**

   a) ATA/ATAPI

   b) Ultra ATA 33

   c) Ultra ATA 66

   d) EIDE

---

3. **Why was performance an issue in the PIO transfer mode?**

---

4. **True or False? IDs identify physical devices and LUNs identify logical devices.**

   ___ True

   ___ False

---

5. **For each SCSI ID, what is the maximum number of LUNs that you can have on a 16-bit bus?**

   a) 7

   b) 8

   c) 16

   d) 32

---

6. **True or False? You cannot connect two ATA devices with an 80-conductor cable and still implement the Cable Select feature.**

___ True

___ False

7. **Which SCSI type supports a data transfer rate of 80 MB/s?**

   a) Wide SCSI

   b) Ultra-320

   c) Wide Ultra-2

   d) Ultra-160

8. **Match each type of SCSI termination to its appropriate characteristic.**

___	Active	a.	Special terminators needed.
___	Forced Perfect	b.	Uses diode clamps.
___	HVD	c.	Simplest form of termination.
___	Passive	d.	Uses voltage regulators.

TOPIC C
Describe RAID

You examined two ubiquitous storage specifications—SCSI and IDE/ATA. RAID is a storage implementation that is capable of making use of either of these storage technologies. In this topic, you will describe the role played by RAID in the storage realm.

What if a drive failed and you never knew the difference because another drive just took over? What if you could replace that failed drive without needing to power down the system? Both of these things can be a reality if you implement RAID on the computer system.

Redundant Array of Independent Disks

A *Redundant Array of Independent Disks (RAID)* is a term that refers to the technique used for spreading and storing a same set of data across multiple hard disks to provide data redundancy. Systems using this technology also retrieve data at higher speeds. RAID can be implemented through the operating system, but hardware-based RAID implementations are more efficient and are widely deployed.

A hardware-based RAID implementation will require a card, or a controller, to show all its disks as a single drive to the computer. These cards, usually PCI or PCI-e cards, can also be built into the motherboard. There are several RAID levels, each with a different combination of features and efficiencies. In many servers, a RAID subsystem provides increased performance and fault-tolerance.

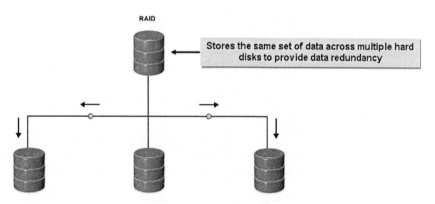

Figure 4-13: *RAID spreads the same data across multiple hard disks.*

> The original RAID specifications were titled Redundant Array of Inexpensive Disks. As the disk cost of RAID implementations has become less of a factor, the term "Independent" disks has been widely adopted instead.

Just a Bunch of Disks or JBOD

Just a Bunch of Disks or JBOD, also referred to as spanning, is a storage method that uses a number of external physical hard drives organized into a single logical drive to store data. JBOD is a simple storage technology that allows a server to write to a large storage medium comprising multiple smaller drives. Unlike RAID, JBOD does not provide any advantages in terms of redundancy or performance.

Hardware RAID Controllers

With hardware RAID, you use a dedicated hardware device called a RAID controller to control the disk array. There are two main types of RAID controllers: Bus-based RAID and External RAID.

 Do not confuse external RAID controllers with external RAID enclosures. The enclosures typically provide only power and a physical infrastructure, while the external controller also provides high-end processing and array management.

Type	Description
Bus-based RAID	 In bus-based hardware RAID, the RAID controller takes the place of the SCSI host bus adapter or IDE/ATA controller that would normally provide the interface between the hard disks and the system bus. Some server system boards include integrated, onboard RAID controllers, but if your system board does not have one of these, you can use a RAID controller card, which is an expansion board. Bus-based hardware RAID is cheaper and easier to implement than external RAID controllers.
External RAID	 External RAID controllers are considered higher-end designs, because they contain a dedicated processor. An external RAID controller manages the disk array from a separate enclosure, usually by using a form of SCSI. It presents the logical drives from the array to the server via a standard interface (again, usually SCSI), and the server interprets the array as one or more hard disks. Compared to bus-based hardware RAID, external RAID controllers are more flexible, offer more features, and tend to be more expandable, but they are also more expensive.

Controller Firmware Levels

Hardware controllers are generally very expensive. This led to the introduction of controller chips with special drivers and firmware. With these firmware controllers, the entire storage processing is processed by the CPU and not the controller chips. It is essential that all firmware controllers used in the hard drives should be of the same version or level.

RAID Interface Issues

Some system boards specify what expansion slot should be used for RAID controllers. Consequently, it is recommended that you consult the documentation for your specific board and controller.

Because both types of hardware RAID use SCSI or IDE/ATA interfaces, they are subjected to the same issues as single hard drives that use those interfaces. Data-transfer rates with IDE-based RAID are not affected by the RAID implementation because IDE can handle only one transfer at a time, but when you start using large numbers of SCSI drives in a RAID solution, throughput can become affected since multiple drives can simultaneously transfer data on a SCSI bus. To alleviate this potential problem, some SCSI RAID controllers support the use of multiple channels, so that you can split the load between two or more SCSI buses.

Another issue to consider when you are dealing with high transfer rates is the bandwidth of the bus. The standard PCI bus is 32 bits wide and runs at 33 MHz, providing a total maximum theoretical bandwidth of about 127 MB/s, which is not enough to handle multiple-channel SCSI RAID. So, high-end cards with multiple channels often use the enhanced 64-bit, 66 MHz PCI bus. This version of PCI has a theoretical bandwidth of over 500 MB/s, but it requires a server system board that has a matching high-speed PCI slot.

RAID Cache

A *RAID cache* is a form of disk or peripheral cache. Although implementing RAID can increase fault-tolerance and availability of data, performance can suffer. RAID controllers often include cache memory that is used to store the most recently accessed files, thus decreasing access time if those files are needed again by the system. With a RAID cache, I/O occurs at the speed of the PCI bus, not at the speed of the hard disks.

RAID Cache Issues

A RAID cache can help provide increased performance and fault-tolerance. Performance is enhanced through the use of read cache (holding data that is anticipated to be read) and write cache (holding data that is to be written to disk). However, fault-tolerance is enhanced only by the read cache and is actually decreased by the use of write cache. This is because when data is placed in cache prior to the disk write, the only copy of the current data resides in the write cache until the write operation is completed. If a power outage occurs prior to the write operation, the data in the write cache is lost. Disabling the write cache will ensure that all data is written to disk.

In addition, some NOS manufacturers recommend that the RAID cache be disabled. Consult your NOS documentation to determine whether or not the use of a RAID cache is recommended for your installation.

RAID Controller Batteries

RAID level 5 (or any other level involving parity calculations) is notoriously slow when it comes to writing data to the array. RAID controllers sometimes use substantial amounts of RAM to reduce performance bottlenecks caused by writing data to the disk array. Data is not written directly to the drive array but to a dedicated memory module or other discrete component from which it is processed and forwarded to the individual drives. Using RAM for RAID cache can have an adverse affect on data reliability, because this type of memory is volatile—if a sudden loss of power occurs, data that has not yet been written to the array can be lost. Some controllers include a battery to keep SDRAM in autorefresh mode to prevent data loss due to power losses.

Software RAID

Software RAID implementations do not require extra hardware (other than the disk array, of course). In this type of implementation, the system processor uses special software routines to take over the functions handled by a hardware RAID controller. Because array management is a low-level activity that must be performed before any other software activity, software RAID is usually implemented at the operating system level.

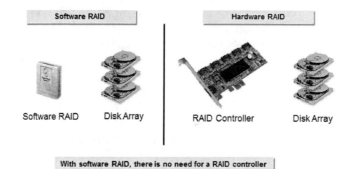

Figure 4-14: Software RAID does not require extra hardware.

 Most of the major NOS support some of the RAID levels.

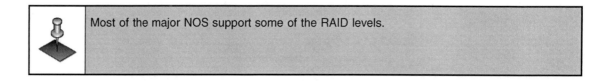 Although extra hardware is not required, you will probably want to increase the memory in any server on which you plan to implement a software RAID solution.

Software RAID Benefits and Limitations

Software RAID is inexpensive (support comes with the operating system) and is easy to implement (no extra controller to install, configure, and manage), but these benefits can be offset by the limitations of software RAID:

● Server performance can be severely affected, since the CPU is doing the work of the server and of the RAID controller. With lower levels like RAID 1, the effect might not be too noticeable, but when you get to the levels that include striping and parity, like RAID 5, the performance hit can be substantial.

● Because the NOS has to be running to enable the array to operate, the NOS itself cannot reside on the array. A separate partition must be created for the NOS, which can affect the capacity of the RAID array unless a separate hard disk is used, and the NOS cannot benefit from the performance gains of running on the array.

- In addition to limiting the levels of RAID that can be implemented, using software RAID limits the accessibility of the array to only those systems that are running the same NOS. In single-NOS systems, this is not much of an issue, but many networks contain a combination of Windows 2000/2003/2008 servers, Linux, and UNIX servers. In mixed systems like these, the NOS limitation can become quite important.

- With software RAID solutions, you are also limited in the advanced RAID features you can implement. For instance, software RAID cannot support hot-swapping or hot spares.

- Some software utilities, particularly disk-partitioning and formatting tools, can conflict with software-based RAID.

RAID Levels

There are several RAID levels with varying functions.

RAID Level	Description
RAID level 0	 RAID level 0 is *disk striping* only, which interleaves, or distributes, data across multiple disks for better performance. However, despite the high data-transfer rate and the high maximum I/O rate for disk reads and writes, this level is not recommended for most applications because it does not provide any safeguards against disk failure. In fact, if one of the drives fails, all of the data on all of the drives becomes inaccessible. This actually makes RAID level 0 less reliable than a single hard disk. At least two hard disks for the RAID array are needed at this level.

RAID Level	Description
RAID level 1	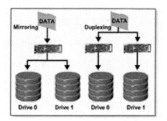

RAID level 1 uses *disk mirroring*, which provides complete duplication of the data on two separate drives. This level of RAID offers the highest reliability, but it doubles storage cost because you need two hard disks to store one disk's worth of data. Disk mirroring does not prevent against writing bad blocks to both drives, either. Data-transfer rates for disk reads can be substantially higher than with a single hard disk, but is about the same or slightly lower for disk writes. As for maximum I/O rates, disk reads can occur at up to twice the speed as with a single disk, while disk writes occur at about the same rate or slightly lower as with a single disk. This level of RAID requires an even number of hard disks for the RAID array. |
| RAID level 2 | RAID level 2 is similar to RAID level 0 in that data is interleaved across several disks, but the difference is that bits, instead of bytes or groups of bytes, are interleaved across multiple disks. In addition, extra disks provide parity by way of Hamming code ECC. This technique is used mainly with large computer systems, but this is a rare method. Reliability is much higher than with a single disk, and is comparable to RAID levels 3, 4, and 5. This level also provides the highest data-transfer rates, and maximum I/O rates. |

RAID Level	Description
RAID level 3	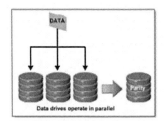

RAID level 3 also uses disk striping, but data is striped across three or more drives. This technique provides the highest data-transfer rates, because all drives operate in parallel. Parity bits are stored on separate, dedicated drives. This technique can be useful with imaging systems. Reliability is much higher than with a single disk, and is comparable to RAID levels 2, 4, and 5. This level also provides the highest data-transfer rates, and maximum I/O rates tend to be about twice that of a single disk. RAID level 3 requires a minimum of four hard disks per array (at least three for data, and one for the parity disk).

RAID level 4

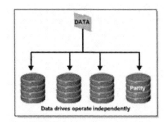

RAID level 4 is similar to Level 3, but it manages the disks independently, instead of in unison. It isn't often used. Reliability is much higher than with a single disk, and is comparable to RAID levels 2, 3, and 5. Data-transfer rates and maximum I/O rates are similar to disk striping for disk reads, but are much lower than a single disk for disk writes. Like RAID level 3, Level 4 requires a minimum of four hard disks per array (at least three for data, and one for the parity disk).

RAID Level	Description

RAID level 5

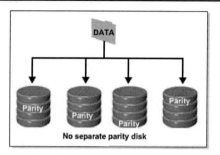

RAID level 5 is probably the most widely used level. Data is striped across three or more drives for performance, and parity bits are used for fault-tolerance. The parity bits from two drives are stored on a third drive in the array, instead of on a separate hard drive like in RAID levels 2, 3, and 4. Reliability is much higher than with a single disk, and is comparable to RAID levels 2, 3, and 4. Data transfer rates and maximum I/O rates are similar to disk striping for disk reads, but are generally lower than a single disk for disk writes. This level of RAID requires at least three hard disks per array.

RAID level 6

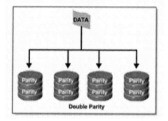

RAID level 6 is the term applied to extensions of RAID 5 in which two different levels of parity calculations are spread across the disks along with the data. This is also called double-parity RAID. RAID 6 offers another level of protection that has been in existence for some time, but has, until recently, been available almost exclusively in proprietary devices. By using additional parity calculations, RAID 6 can protect mission-critical data from two concurrent disk drive failures. With the growth of disk array sizes, increasing disk densities, and the introduction of Serial ATA (SATA) drives into the storage market, the likelihood for two concurrent failures are high and so RAID level 6 implementations are catching up fast.

Additional RAID Levels

Because single RAID levels do not always address the administrator's specific server requirement, combinations evolved to support more comprehensive protection and greater performance. Dual level RAID operations are complicated. RAID combinations are often referred to using only numerical digits such as RAID 10. RAID 50, or by using a '+' sign between the numbers such as RAID 1+0, RAID 5+0. Although RAID 0+1 is slightly different from RAID 1+0, they are the most commonly found combinations in use and they both require at least four drives to implement. The following table describes the various dual level RAID levels.

RAID Level	Description
RAID level 01 or RAID 0+1	RAID 01 is a combination that utilizes RAID 0 for its high performance and RAID 1 for its high fault tolerance. A server running eight hard drives is split into two arrays of four drives each. Then, RAID 0 is applied to each array, resulting in two striped arrays. RAID 1 pertains to the two striped arrays with one array mirrored on the other. The major pitfall of RAID 01 is that when a hard drive in one striped array fails, the entire array is lost. Although the other striped array remains, it contains no fault tolerance for protection against the failure of one of its drives.
RAID level 10 or RAID 1+0	RAID level 10 is actually RAID 1,0. You might also see it referred to as 1+0 or 0+1. This technique is a combination of RAIDs 1 and 0 (mirroring and striping). For this RAID level, a minimum of four hard disks per array is required, and the number of disks must be even. RAID 10 applies RAID 1 first, after splitting the eight drives into four sets of two drives each. Now each set is individually mirrored with duplicate information. RAID 0 is now applied by individually striping across all four sets.
	This combination has better fault tolerance than RAID 0+1 because as long as one drive in a mirrored set remains active, the array still functions properly. Theoretically, up to half the drives can fail before everything is lost, as opposed to RAID 0+1, where the failure of two drives can lead to the loss of the entire array.
RAID level 30 or RAID 3+0	It combines RAID level 3 and RAID level 0 and provides high data transfer rates, along with high data reliability. RAID 30 is best implemented on two RAID 3 disk arrays with data striped across both disk arrays.
RAID level 50 or RAID 5+0	It combines striping independent data disks with distributed parity. It stripes data across at least two Level 5 arrays. RAID 5+0 offers the same fault tolerance as RAID 3; therefore, it might be a good solution for those who would have otherwise gone with RAID 3 but need additional performance provided by striping.

RAID Level	Description
RAID level 51 or RAID 5+1	It employs both redundancy methods by mirroring entire RAID 5 arrays. It can be used for critical applications requiring very high fault tolerance, but it is an uncommon solution because performance and storage efficiency is not as high as other nested RAID levels—especially when cost is considered.

Performance Benefits and Trade-off of RAID Levels

RAID is capable of performing multiple independent, simultaneous I/O activity to the disk drives. The performance improvement of a RAID array trades off to some extent with the cost of the RAID array. Each RAID level contains unique cost, performance, and fault-tolerance characteristics to meet the various storage needs.

RAID Level	Redundancy	Read Performance	Write Performance	Data Reconstruction Performance
RAID 0	Not available	Excellent	Excellent	Not allowed
RAID 1	Excellent	Excellent	Good	Good
RAID 2	Good	Excellent	Good	Good
RAID 3	Good	Sequential: Good Transactional: Poor	Sequential: Good Transactional: Poor	Average
RAID 4	Good	Sequential: Good Transactional: Good	Sequential: Good Transactional: Poor	Average
RAID 5	Good	Sequential: Good Transactional: Good	Average	Poor
RAID 6	Excellent	Good	Poor	Poor
RAID 0+1, RAID 1+0	Excellent	Good	Average	Good
RAID 30	Excellent	Good	Average	Average
RAID 50	Excellent	Good	Average	Average
RAID 51	Excellent	Good	Average	Good

Zero Channel RAID

Zero Channel RAID (ZCR) provides entry-level RAID that is ideal for 1U and 2U servers in which a PCI RAID controller is designed to use the on-board SCSI channels of a motherboard to implement a cost-effective hardware RAID solution.

RAIDIOS

RAID I/O Steering (RAIDIOS) is an Intel specification that enables an I/O controller (either embedded on the system board or on an add-in card) to be used as just an I/O controller or as the I/O component of a hardware RAID subsystem. It is compatible with PCI and PCI-X.

Hot Spares

A *hot spare* is an extra drive configured in your system. If one of your working disks fails, you can enable the hot spare by making it online and adding it to the array. The new disk automatically takes over the data storage, enabling you to fix or replace the failed drive at your convenience.

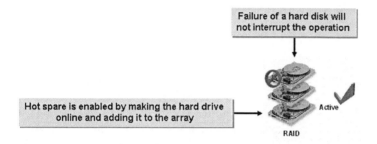

Figure 4-15: Hot spare is an extra drive configured in a system.

Hot Swapping

Hot-swapping is the ability to exchange computer hardware "on the fly" without interrupting the computer's service or, at least, minimizing the interruption. It prevents you from having to power off the system while you switch an old or faulty part for a new one, which, in turn, enables users to keep working while you are fixing the problem.

Hot-Swap Hardware

There are a few things to keep in mind—namely, preserving the integrity of your system's data and preventing damage to any hardware parts involved. Having hot swap capabilities is not good if your hardware is ruined during an exchange. To ensure that all goes smoothly when you hot-swap components, there are a couple of things you can do. First, make sure the new component, which is unpowered, will not be damaged when you connect it to the "live" (powered) system. Also, make sure the component has features that let you disable the "power-off" command and partially power it down and that its outputs stay in a high-impedance state during power-up or power-down. This will keep the system from getting bogged down by the component's input and output pins when you connect the component.

These steps help protect your system's circuitry and ultimately your data. When swapping components, such as a new network card, you need to make sure the ground pins on the card make contact first with the pins on the connector. Current is flowing, and you do not want it flowing from the "live" board through unexpected return paths in the new board.

Online Capacity Expansion

Online capacity expansion (OCE) is a technique to improve the availability by allowing you to increase the capacity of an array by adding hot-pluggable drives without needing to recreate the array or interrupt service.

Hot-Swap Software

Anytime you introduce a new hardware component to an existing system, software running on the computer needs to "detect and accept" it. The same is true when you hot-swap components. Hot-swapping requires additional software at three levels: device driver, applications, and services. The software takes care of allocating card resources; it configures new cards and redistributes the old card's resources. It detects when a new card is present, reconfigures the address space and system memory to accommodate it, and makes the system aware of the changes, preventing damage to both the system itself and its applications. The beauty of it all is that users are oblivious to everything.

The problem is that a lot of big operating systems, such as Windows, Solaris, and Linux, do not have the necessary additional software layers that the latest hot-swapping capability requires so they have to forgo using these capabilities. Also, since some aspects of the hot swap standard itself are hazy in regard to software, system board manufacturers provide different implementations of hot swap mechanisms, which require different drivers.

Warm Swap

A *warm swap* is middle ground between a hot swap and cold swap. You can keep your system powered on, but the component you are swapping must not be in use. For example, when warm-swapping a hard drive, the array might require you to stop I/O transactions while you swap the failed drive, but you do not have to completely power off the system. It is a compromise; you are stopping I/O requests, but preventing drive spin-up, controller boot-up, and host negotiation delays. As soon as the drive is swapped, you can resume I/O requests. Typically, this is the only type of component exchange that PCI-based RAID systems offer.

Cold Swap

A *cold swap* simply refers to the way exchanges used to take place—by powering off a system before doing repairs or maintenance, such as replacing memory in a server.

Hardware RAID Implementation Considerations

After determining the type of RAID controller you want to use, you must keep in mind that any successful implementation of the controller will depend upon several considerations.

Consideration	Description
Hard drive interfaces	Must match the RAID controller interface.
Capacity and storage efficiency	Depends on the number and size of drives used in the array, as well as the RAID level you implement.
Drive size	Think of both physical size (volume) and the storage size (number of GB), as both will affect your implementation. Using large-capacity drives provides more array capacity. You should ensure that all drives in the array have the same capacity so that no storage space will be wasted. In addition, think about the future; if you implement a RAID controller that can handle six drives and you use smaller hard drives to fill the available slots, you will probably have to replace the drives if you end up needing more space later on.

Consideration	Description
Array performance	The more disks you have in the array, the better performance you will get from the array. Stripe width is the number of drives in the array. This should not be confused with stripe (or block) size, which is a parameter that is set by the user.
Array reliability	Increasing the number of drives can decrease reliability, simply because there are more hardware components with the potential for failure.
Potential cost	More disks cost more money, even when the array size is the same. For instance, ten 20 GB hard drives will cost more than five 40 GB hard drives. Plus, each hard disk has associated support costs, such as power consumption, space and cooling considerations, and the potential for having to buy a separate enclosure for the disks.

Physical Drive Sizes

Most RAID systems use 3.5" form-factor drives, but some are 1" high (often referred to as slimline or low-profile drives) and others are 1.6" high (often referred to as half-height). If you determine that you want to use half-height drives, make sure your server case is designed to support that size, to ensure proper cooling and power for the drives.

Storage Capacity Determination

There are a few calculations involved in determining the storage capacity of a RAID level.

RAID Level	Calculation
0	(Size of Smallest Drive * Number of Drives)
1	Size of the Smaller Drive
3	(Size of Smallest Drive) * (Number of Drives - 1)
5	(Size of Smallest Drive) * (Number of Drives - 1)
0+5	(Size of Smallest Drive) * (Number of Drives In Each RAID 0 Set) * (Number of RAID 0 Sets - 1)
5+0	(Size of Smallest Drive) * (Number of Drives In Each RAID 5 Set - 1) * (Number of RAID 5 Sets)
1+5 and 5+1	(Size of Smallest Drive) * ((Number of Drives / 2) - 1)
0+1 and 1+0	(Size of Smallest Drive) * (Number of Drives) / 2

RAID Management

All RAID controllers come with configuration and management software.

 Software RAID's management utilities will be bundled with the NOS.

Function	Description
Controller configuration	At the hardware level, you can set how the controller's internal cache (if any) works, manage how alarms and warnings are communicated, whether to use manual or automatic rebuild for failed drives, and disable the BIOS, if necessary.
Array configuration	You can define and configure disk arrays, and assign specific drives to specific arrays when more than one array has been set up.
Physical device management	You can check the status of the drives that are connected to the controller, format drives, and designate drives as hot spares.
Logical device management	You can create logical drive volumes from an array, and format the logical volumes.
SCSI channel management	When the RAID controller offers multiple SCSI channels, you can control the settings and parameters for each channel, including the SCSI termination.
Remote management	When the controller supports remote management, you can monitor the status and operation of the array from any location on the physical network (LAN), and sometimes even over the Internet.

RAID Management Software for Hardware RAID

For hardware RAID, the RAID management software is incorporated in two main components:

- The controller BIOS setup program, which enables you to set up and configure the array before the NOS is running.

- The RAID management utility, which is a regular software package that runs after the NOS is up and running on the array.

Controller BIOS Setup and Management Utility

Like the system BIOS setup program, you run the controller BIOS setup when you boot the server. This enables you to set up the RAID system even before the NOS is installed, so that you can install the NOS right on the RAID array.

The management utility is similar to the BIOS setup program in some respects, but it also enables you to check the status of the array, change normal operating parameters, and set up the system so that operations can continue while some rebuilds occur on a fault-tolerant array.

RAID Alarms and Warnings

RAID controller software usually contains a feature that can issue immediate alarms and warnings when there is trouble with the array, or with the controller itself. By default, the alarms are audible, but you might also be able to be notified remotely or over a LAN connection. The following table describes some of the more common types of alarms and warnings.

 For RAID level 0, only one drive has to fail to compromise the array, while for Levels 1, 3, 4, and 5, the failure of at least two drives will compromise the array. When you have implemented nested RAID levels, such as 0+1, the failure of any sub-array will compromise the array.

Alarm and Warning Type	Description
Array Failure	You will receive this alarm when an array connected to the controller has actually failed. Generally, this means that enough drives in the array fail that the entire array is compromised. Sometimes this alarm uses the terminology "array offline."
Degraded Mode Operation	You will get this alarm when a hardware fault causes decreased performance but is not severe enough to take down the entire array. This most often occurs when a redundant RAID level has been implemented and a drive fails. Performance continues to be degraded until the failed drive is rebuilt.
Rebuild Completion	When auto rebuild is enabled at the controller, the controller will signal when it finishes a rebuild. What this tells you is that the array is not running in degraded mode anymore, and if you have set up the system to include a hot spare, then you should check to see which disk was used for the rebuild. If the hot spare was used, replace the failed drive and designate it as the new hot spare.
Controller Hardware Fault	You will receive this message if the controller is self-monitoring and has detected an internal problem, such as a temperature increase.

Partitioning with RAID

With RAID, the array is treated as an enormous virtual hard disk, which can be partitioned just like any physical hard disk. Theoretically, hardware RAID should be transparent to any application running on it, including the NOS (except that you might need to use a NOS-specific driver for the controller). So you should be able to use any partitioning utility you like, but some manufacturers will tell you not to use any third-party partitioning utilities with their controllers. Another issue to consider with regard to partitioning the array is the size of the array. Some partitioning utilities cannot handle the massive size of some arrays, but usually applying a NOS update or patch can help alleviate this problem. Finally, some file systems lend themselves better to RAID than others do. For instance, the NTFS and UNIX file systems tend to work better than the FAT file systems.

Advanced RAID Features
The following table lists advanced RAID features.

Feature	Description
Onboard caching	Some controllers include a slot that you can use to add cache memory by inserting a regular memory module. Doing this can increase performance, but like regular system cache, the performance increase might not be as large as you expect. With RAID, read and write-back caches tend to be more important, because some RAID levels are more write-intensive than others. It depends on the amount of redundancy provided by the RAID level you have implemented.
Drive-swapping	It is also referred to as hot swap. This feature enables you to change a hard drive without powering down the server, and has no effect on other components or applications running on the server. It lets you pull out a failed hard drive, replace it with a good one, and rebuild the drive immediately.
Hot spare	In RAID arrays that provide redundancy, which include all levels except RAID 0, when a drive fails, you want to replace it as soon as you can to regain performance and fault-tolerance levels. With hot spare, extra drives are attached to the controller, but are in a standby mode. If a drive in the array fails, the controller can use the spare to replace the bad drive by doing an automatic rebuild of the data from the failed drive onto the hot spare drive.
Array expansion	Some controllers support the expansion of existing arrays. This is a combination of physical expansion and logical expansion. To perform a physical expansion, you add drives to the system, by either adding an external enclosure or replacing the existing drives with larger ones. For the logical expansion, you need to get the controller to add the drives to the existing array, increasing the overall array size. This depends on the level of RAID implemented and whether or not the controller supports array expansion. If the controller supports expansion, you add the drives and the controller reconfigures the array. If expansion is not supported, you have to tear down and rebuild the array manually. This method does cause data to be lost, so if you need to tear down and rebuild an array, make sure that you have a valid backup of the data on the array. If you are thinking about taking advantage of logical expansion, you need to remember that most RAID arrays are limited in size by the smallest drive on the array, and that older drives tend to be slower than newer drives and are more likely to fail. To counter these issues, you might want to go ahead and use all of the drive slots when you set up the array; then, when you need to expand, just replace all the drives. Or you can set up a second array, either in the original server or in another server, then designate the older array to act as a backup or secondary array that handles older or less-critical data.

Some hardware RAID solutions require not only the same size drive, but the same manufacturer and firmware as well.

ACTIVITY 4-3
Examining the RAID System

Scenario:

In this activity, you will examine the RAID system.

---

1. A user wants some fault tolerance on her workstation. She has two physical disk drives available. Which level of RAID could she employ?

   a) RAID 0

   b) RAID 1

   c) RAID 2

   d) RAID 5

---

2. What is the minimum hardware requirement for a hardware-based RAID 5 implementation?

   a) Two disks and a RAID controller

   b) Three disks and a RAID controller

   c) Four disks and a RAID controller

   d) Six disks and a RAID controller

---

3. True or False? Software RAID provides the same reliability and performance as hardware RAID.

   ___ True

   ___ False

---

4. What is the role of a hot spare drive in a RAID configuration after a primary drive has failed?

   a) To continually be idle in the array.

   b) To return the system to its normal operational mode.

   c) To reconstruct lost data.

   d) To assume the role of the failed drive.

---

5. **What is the total available disk space for seven 10 GB drives running in a RAID 5 array?**

    a) 20 GB

    b) 40 GB

    c) 60 GB

    d) 80 GB

TOPIC D
Explore NAS Implementations

You described an advanced method of data storage called RAID. In addition to RAID, there exists other advanced ways to implement data storage. In this topic, you will explore NAS implementations.

Network-attached storage is a versatile and efficient system that is an attractive data storage solution for many organizations. So, there is a good chance that you will work with or evaluate a NAS system at some point in your career. NAS systems have specific software, hardware, and configuration requirements that you should understand if you find yourself evaluating, implementing, or supporting a NAS in your environment.

Network-Attached Storage

Definition:

A *Network-Attached Storage (NAS)* system is a specialized file server designed and dedicated to support only data storage needs. There is no mouse, keyboard, or monitor present in the NAS server, which runs a streamlined operating system. The server can, however, contain a variety of storage devices such as large hard disk arrays or tape drives, or it can simply be a hard drive with an Ethernet port. A NAS server can be accessed over the network by clients and servers running different operating systems.

 Generally speaking, NAS systems are considered to work at the file level.

Example:

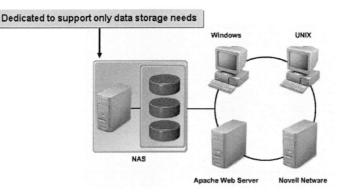

Figure 4-16: NAS server can be accessed over the network by clients and servers running different operating systems.

NAS Addressing

The NAS system has a TCP/IP address and is commonly attached to a high-performance network such as FDDI or ATM.

Advantages of a NAS

It can be expensive to implement a specially designed and dedicated NAS server to replace or supplement existing general-purpose file servers. However, there are several advantages to implementing a NAS:

● NAS system is often more reliable and less prone to downtime than a traditional file server, which improves data availability.

● NAS system can scale efficiently because it is relatively inexpensive to add additional storage devices once the NAS is implemented.

● Because the NAS system is dedicated to storage management, data storage and retrieval performance is very high.

● NAS systems are easier to secure than traditional file systems because there are fewer points of access to the device. For example, without a keyboard and monitor, no one can log on directly to the system console.

● NAS facilitates data backups because the data can be backed up over a local bus system inside the NAS while it continues to serve client requests. Or, a separate high-performance network link can be created between the NAS and a backup server.

● NAS improves administrative efficiencies because it turns an entire company's storage into a single management entity. Data can be managed and reconfigured without affecting clients or their ability to access the data.

NAS Operating Systems and Protocols

All NAS systems have a specially modified operating system. Some NAS appliances use a custom microkernel written specifically to control the storage hardware; others use modified network operating systems such as Windows Server 2008 or Linux. Because unnecessary operating system functions are removed, a NAS operating system can be very efficient and provide a level of storage performance unattainable on traditional file servers. To access a NAS over a network, clients use a file access application protocol such as the Network File System (NFS) or Server Message Block (SMB) protocol.

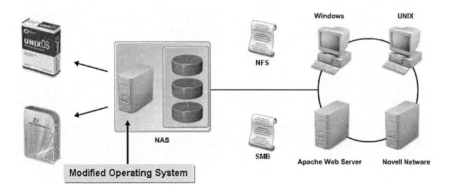

Figure 4-17: To access a NAS over a network, clients use a file access application protocol such as NFS or SMB.

NAS Connection Options

Clients can access a NAS either directly or through a server. When users connect directly, it is like connecting to any other server or share. When a server provides connectivity, it either acts as a gateway to the NAS, or hosts a distributed file system that provides the client with access to the data on the NAS. In either case, the client is unaware of the NAS as a separate device. The client does not need to be reconfigured if the data structure on the NAS changes.

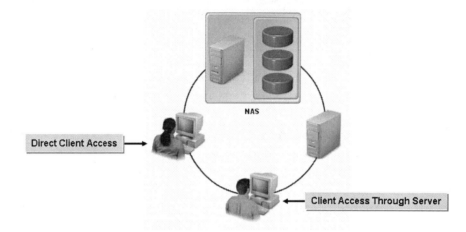

Figure 4-18: Options for connecting NAS.

> In a NAS implementation where a server provides connectivity, the server can be considered a single point of failure. In other words, if the server crashes, the NAS is no longer accessible.

NAS Connectivity Options

When a server acts as a gateway for the NAS appliance, it connects to the NAS on behalf of the client and retrieves its data. One big advantage to using a gateway to connect to a NAS is that the network media containing the NAS doesn't have to be compatible with the client. As long as the server has a connection on both networks, the NAS can be on almost any type of high-performance network media. The client might not even know that the NAS is on the network. However, many times a server must run special client or gateway software to make the connection to the NAS data. This software isn't available to clients, but even if a client discovered where the NAS is on the network, it can't attach to it without proper configuration.

When a server distributes a share on a NAS, it provides a point to which the client can map, but the drives the client connects to are actually aliases for drives on the NAS or other machines. When the client connects to the share, the server redirects it to the NAS for the actual data. In this case, the distributing server can possibly provide added security and functionality features not available on the NAS. Also, because the server does not handle the data directly, its equipment requirements might be less.

ACTIVITY 4-4
Exploring NAS Implementations

Scenario:
In this activity, you will test your knowledge of network-attached storage systems.

1. **What protocols are commonly used with NAS systems?**
   a) TCP/IP
   b) HTTP
   c) NFS
   d) SMB

2. **True or False? Implementing a NAS system is a cost-effective alternative to traditional file servers.**
   ___ True
   ___ False

3. **What are the options for connecting a NAS?**

4. **What are the benefits of using a NAS?**

TOPIC E
Explore SAN Implementations

You examined NAS implementations. A SAN is similar to a NAS, but with its own set of advantages and drawbacks. In this topic, you will explore SAN implementations.

Implementing a SAN is an intriguing possibility for organizations that need extremely high performance storage solutions. But it is important to weigh the cost, complexity, and tradeoffs of selecting this type of solution over a NAS, a traditional server cluster, or even basic file servers. You'll need to understand these and other technical issues if you ever support an organization that considers a SAN implementation.

SAN Implementations

Definition:

A *Storage Area Network (SAN)* is a special purpose high-speed network dedicated to data storage. The SAN contains servers that share access to data storage devices such as disk arrays and tape drives. The servers and devices within the SAN interconnect using a high-speed networking technology such as Fiber Channel, FDDI, ATM, or high-speed Ethernet. Data can be stored and accessed quickly, and because the servers and storage devices all have redundant connections, data remains available during a server failure. The direct data traffic between servers and storage appliances on the SAN is separated from the traffic on the production network.

> Generally speaking, SAN systems are considered to work at the block level.

Example:

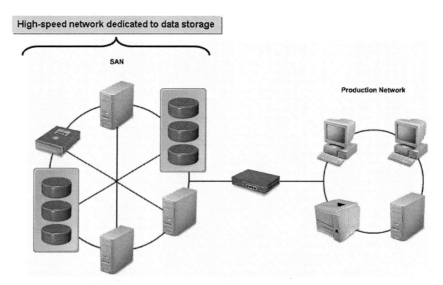

Figure 4-19: A SAN connected to an organization's network.

SANs vs. NAS with SCSI

SANs overcome some of the technical limitations of network-attached storage. Typically, the NAS servers attach to drive arrays using parallel SCSI buses. This can create system bottle-necks as the high-speed data rate of multiple SCSI controllers has to interface with the slower data rate of the server's internal PCI bus. Also, SCSI limits the number of drives per channel. Finally, network-attached SCSI drives must be in close proximity to NAS servers. SANs enable the arrays to be distributed throughout the network.

The SAN uses a high-speed network connection to replace the SCSI communications channel between the drive controller in the server and the data controller on the disk array. This removes the drive limit, data rate limits, and separation distance limits of NAS and SCSI.

Advantages of a SAN

SANs can be used when it is important to have flexibility in the placement of storage devices. Data centers can be set up with servers on one side and storage on the other, or custom laser-powered, single-mode fiber optic links can be used for separation distances of up to 100 kilometers. This greater distance enables companies to separate their data mirrors and provide security from local disasters.

SANs have become an integral part of clustering and other high-availability solutions. Because a SAN can support multiple servers accessing the same data and because the data is separate from any server, it makes sense to use a SAN as the shared data storage solution in a cluster. The drives appear local to the individual nodes in the cluster. If the active server fails, the passive server can access the same data that the active server was accessing on the SAN.

Disadvantages of a SAN

SANs can be complex to implement, and the required redundancies mean they are quite expensive.

SAN Connectivity

TCP/IP networks provide a viable low-cost solution for small- and medium-sized networks, especially when the extremely high data-transfer speeds of Fiber Channel are not a requirement. Lower cost is not the only advantage: in organizations with a fully routed network and TCP/IP infrastructure, a network storage device can easily be placed at a remote site for a hot backup. Also, separate servers can be placed in remote offices with a common data storage location. All these steps will help you to keep distributed data synchronized.

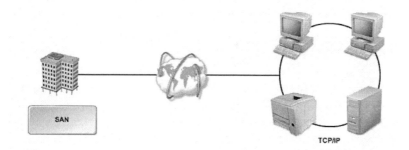

Figure 4-20: *In organizations with a fully routed network and TCP/IP infrastructure, a network storage device can easily be placed at a remote site for a hot backup.*

Fiber Channel

Fiber Channel is a reliable high-speed transmission technology originally developed for connecting mainframe computers to various peripheral and storage devices. It enables concurrent communications among workstations, mainframes, servers, data-storage systems, and other peripherals that use the SCSI and IP protocols. It is also scalable to the total system bandwidth of up to one terabit per second. Fiber Channel can use either a copper or fiber-optic cable. Its bandwidth may range from 100 Mbps to 2 Gbps, though there are plans to expand the bandwidth to 10 Gbps.

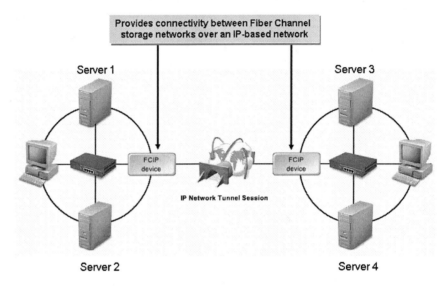

Figure 4-21: Fiber Channel is a reliable high-speed transmission technology.

Fiber Channel Topologies

The following table describes three topologies used for Fiber Channel implementations.

Topology	*Description*
Point-to-point	Two devices are connected together directly.
Switched fabric	Devices are connected to switches, which manage their connections.
Arbitrated loop	Devices are connected in a ring topology.

Fiber Channel Implementations

Switches, hubs, storage systems, storage devices, and adapters are among the products that are on the market today, providing the ability to implement a total system solution. Although mainly implemented with fiber optic cable, you can also implement Fiber Channel with copper wire. Fiber Channel is the next generation of storage interfaces for enterprise systems and is an emerging choice for RAID systems and Storage Area Networks (SANs) because of its scalability, interoperability, and support for legacy systems. It was introduced as part of the SCSI-3 specifications.

Fiber Channel Specification Table

The following table summarizes the specifications for Fiber Channel arbitrated loop solutions.

Interface	Bus Width (bits)	Max. No. of Devices	Max. Band-width (MB/s)	Bus Length for Copper (meters)	Bus Length for Fiber Optic (meters)
FC-AL (single loop)	16	127	100	30	2000-10000
FC-AL (dual loop)	16	127	200	30	2000-10000

FCIP and iSCSI

Fiber Channel over IP (FCIP) provides connectivity between Fiber Channel storage networks over an IP-based network. This technology extends the relatively small distances of a Fiber Channel network to include the greater distances available over an IP network; therefore, making it possible to create a unified storage network between remote locations. The FCIP throughput is currently limited to the 2 GB limit of Fiber Channel.

Another network storage protocol, called the iSCSI, was developed to serve the same purpose, but without requiring the implementation of Fiber Channel on both ends. iSCSI can be used over already ubiquitous Ethernet connections, theoretically reducing the Total Cost of Ownership (TCO). iSCSI can run on 1-Gigabit Ethernet and 10-Gigabit Ethernet networks.

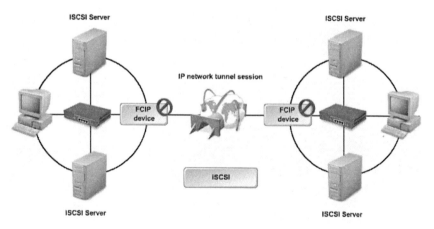

Figure 4-22: iSCSI does not require the implementation of Fiber Channel.

ACTIVITY 4-5
Exploring SAN Implementations
Scenario:
In this activity, you will test your knowledge of SAN technologies and implementations.

1. How does a SAN differ from a NAS implementation?

   a) SANs are dedicated to data storage.

   b) SAN devices use high-speed network connections.

   c) SAN devices have redundant connections for high reliability.

   d) SAN data traffic is separated from the production network traffic.

2. True or False? Unlike SCSI NAS devices, SAN arrays can be distributed throughout the network.

   ___ True

   ___ False

3. With which SCSI specification was Fiber Channel introduced?

   a) SCSI-2

   b) SCSI-3

   c) Ultra 2

   d) Ultra 160

4. Where can iSCSI be implemented?

5. What are the drawbacks of a SAN?

Lesson 4 Follow-up

In this lesson, you identified the different types of storage devices used in servers. Understanding the different storage devices and their features is critical to selecting the right type of storage device required for specific needs.

1. **Do you have a RAID implementation in your environment? If yes, what RAID level do you use?**

2. **Do you have any NAS or SAN implementations in your environment? If yes, what are they used for?**

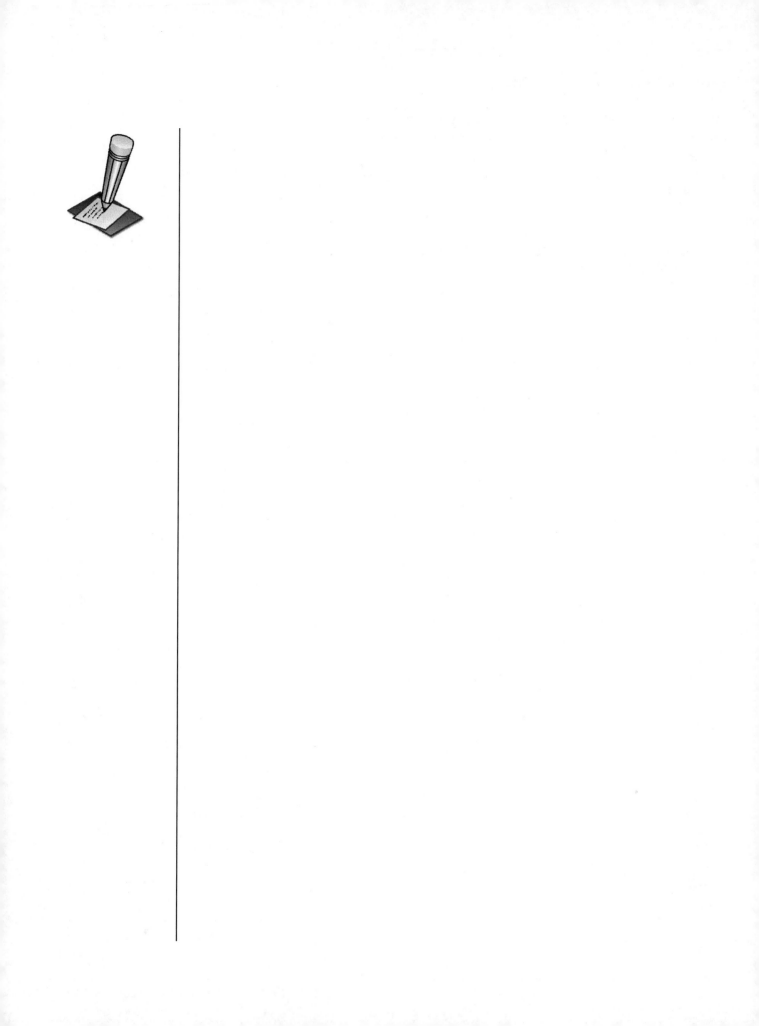

5 | Installing the Server Hardware

Lesson Time: 5 hour(s)

Lesson Objectives:

In this lesson, you will install hardware components on a server.

You will:

- Identify the best practices for installing server hardware.

- Install hardware components on a server.

- Verify the server installation.

- Describe the various considerations that should be followed when installing a server into their environments.

Introduction

You explored the various components of a server. Now you can apply this knowledge to the process of physical server installation. In this lesson, you will install hardware components on a server.

Installing a server can be both commonplace and complex. Being knowledgeable in all areas of server subsystems will help you to correctly install a server in any network environment—an exceptionally challenging task under stressful circumstances, but one that can go smoothly if you plan and prepare appropriately.

This lesson covers all or part of the following CompTIA Server+ (2009) certification objectives:

- Topic B:
    - Objective 1.2: Deploy different chassis types and the appropriate components.
    - Objective 3.2: Given a scenario, select the appropriate RAID level.
    - Objective 3.3: Install and configure different internal storage technologies.
- Topic C:
    - Objective 1.2: Deploy different chassis types and the appropriate components.

TOPIC A

Identify the Best Practices in Server Hardware Installation

Previously, you examined the various components of a server. As a server technician it is essential to know how to install the server components. However, before installing any server component, it will help if you are familiar with the best practices to be followed. In this topic, you will identify the best practices for installing server hardware.

Server installation and configuration is a serious but simple task, only if you know the tips and tricks and the standard procedures that need to be followed when installing the server hardware. Otherwise you might perform steps that cannot only be harmful to the server but to you as well. Being familiar with the best practices for installing hardware into a server will ensure proper and safe installation of the server components.

System Board and System Board Components Installation Best Practices

Follow these best practices for installing a system board or any system board components:

- Before you attempt any hardware installation, but particularly for internal system components, verify that the system is powered down and all power sources have been disconnected from the server.
- For any internal components, follow all ESD safety precautions.
- If possible, install the processor, heat sink, internal fan, and memory onto the system board before installing the board into the chassis.
- Verify that all standoff screws are fastened correctly to prevent short-circuiting the system board.

Drive Installation Best Practices

Follow these best practices for installing a drive:

- Check the hard drive's documentation for proper jumper configuration; newer drives may be auto-sensing and won't require any configuration.
- Ensure that the hard drive is positioned where it will get proper ventilation; it is one of the few moving parts in the server.
- Check the BIOS to ensure that the drive size is supported and drive detection is set to Auto.
- Verify SCSI IDs and termination for SCSI installation.

Processors and Power Supply Best Practices

Follow these best practices for installing a processor and power supply unit:

● Avoid making contact with the processor's pins and verify that none of the pins are bent.

● When installing a single processor into a dual processor system board, install the processor in the CPU 0 slot.

● Make any necessary BIOS configuration changes.

● Take special care to disconnect the power cord before you start work on the power supply. Servers continue to have a high-voltage supply even if the power is turned off.

● If there are two power supply connectors, ensure that both are switched off when you plug them in, otherwise you could damage the system board.

Sometimes you may wish to have a dual processor in the system. Follow these best practices for installing a second processor:

● Avoid making immediate contact with the heat sink of the existing processor if it is operational. The heat sink should be cooled for a short period of time with the cover off.

● Ensure that the cache size is identical for each of the processors, otherwise it will cause system failure.

● Ensure that the processors are rated for use at the same speed. Failure to follow this rule will result in performance degradation.

Memory Installation Best Practices

Follow these best practices for installing the system memory:

● Verify that the memory is supported by the system board manufacturer.

● Verify that the system board will support the size of the module to be installed.

● Ensure that module sizes within a single bank (pair of slots) are matching. Dissimilar sizes are acceptable, but they should not be in the same bank.

● When inserting the module into a slot, avoid applying too much pressure on it or else you run the risk of damaging the socket.

● The clips should snap into place on their own. If you have to move the clips by hand, then the module isn't installed correctly.

● Fill the lowest numbered slot first.

Internal Cable Installation Best Practices

Follow these best practices for installing internal cables:

● Provide enough cable length so that there is enough slack to allow clearance for accessing components that might require replacement.

● Label wires and connectors as you detach them, and make sure you plug them back into their sockets in proper order.

● When you replace the server's case, make sure all wires are inside. The case may have sharp edges that can cut through exposed cables.

External Device Installation Best Practices

Follow these best practices for installing external devices, such as the keyboard, monitor, and mouse:

- For a single server installation, install the keyboard, monitor, and mouse directly in the server chassis. For multiple server installations, consider using a KVM switch to save space and power.

- For any external subsystems that rely on the server for power, verify that the server's power supply can handle the increased load.

- For any external subsystems that connect to an expansion card, verify that the expansion card is correctly installed.

- For modem rack subsystems, verify that the phone or leased lines are of sufficient length to reach the rack system, and that you have a COM port available on the server.

- Use multi-channel SCSI controllers or multiple controllers to avoid mixing device types such as hard disk subsystems, tape drives, and scanners. Where possible, do not place external and internal devices on the same channel.

- For SCSI subsystems, verify that you have the correct cabling, that all SCSI IDs are set correctly, and that proper termination is applied at the end of any daisy chains you create.

ACTIVITY 5-1
Examining Server Hardware Installation Best Practices

Scenario:
In this activity, you will examine best practices to follow when installing hardware into a server.

1. Match the hardware component with the appropriate installation recommendation.

   ___ System board   a. Ensure length provides for slack to allow for clearance.

   ___ Hard drive   b. When possible, attach it before installing the system board.

   ___ Processor   c. Make sure that cache sizes match.

   ___ Memory   d. Attach heat sink before installation.

   ___ Internal cable   e. Fill the slots in order from lowest to highest number.

   ___ Internal fan   f. If needed, set jumpers.

   ___ External device   g. If needed, verify that the power supply can handle the additional load.

2. What are the most important overall best practices when installing any internal system hardware components?

3. When you are installing a system board, which part can cause the board to short circuit if not properly installed?

   a) Standoff screws

   b) Management software

   c) RAID controller card

   d) DVD drive

4. What specific safety precautions are recommended for installing a power supply?

   a) Ensure that both of the power supply connectors are switched off when you plug them in.

   b) Place the power supply in the top rack of a rackmount system.

   c) Unplug the power cord from the power supply before you do any other work on it.

   d) Remove any unused power supply connectors.

5. **True or False? When installing memory, you must use the same size memory sticks in all slots in the server.**

___ True

___ False

6. **In which CPU slot should a single processor be installed in a dual processor system board?**

TOPIC B

Install Hardware Components on a Server

You have identified the best practices to be followed by server technicians while installing server hardware components. Now that you have a solid base of background information, it is time to install and configure some hardware components on the server. In this topic, you will install internal system components such as storage devices, power supplies, memory, processors, and system boards.

Much of the work that you will perform as a server technician will involve installing and configuring various hardware components. Adopting a systematic approach for efficient installation will enable you to ensure that you have a server that performs optimally and also prevent potentially crippling problems that might be caused by inappropriate or wrong ways of installing server hardware components.

Installing a Power Supply Unit

Installing a power supply unit for a rackmount server requires you to follow a sequence of steps.

Step	*Information*
Prepare to work inside the server's chassis.	Before you begin installing a power supply, you need to prepare for the installation. You can do this by gathering the tools and equipment you will need, including an ESD kit, the power supply, and a Phillips-head screwdriver, and by establishing an ESD-free work area. Verify that the server is powered off. Unplug the power cord, monitor, and any other peripherals from the server. Open the server's chassis enclosure. Depending on the server you might need to remove screws, unhook latches, or loosen sliders before you can open the chassis.
Identify the location of the power supply	Identify the location of the power supply in relation to the chassis opening, and remove any brackets or components that are in the way of your reaching the power supply. Often, the power supply is located in the back of the machine, surrounded by brackets or other components.
Remove the power supply	Unscrew the screws holding the power supply in place. Disconnect the power leads from the system board and all peripherals. As you perform this step, you might want to make a note of where each connector is attached, so that you can connect the new power supply correctly. Lift the power supply out of the chassis, and set it aside.

Step	Information
Install the new power supply	Use the screws to anchor the new power supply in place. Reconnect the power leads in the proper order. Replace any brackets or components that were removed to access the power supply. Close the chassis enclosure, plug the power, and other peripheral cables and turn on the system.

Installing Power Supply Unit in a Tower Server

This is the sequence of steps to be followed while installing a power supply unit on a tower server:

- Turn off the system.
- Unplug the electrical power cord from the electric outlet.
- Unplug the power and other peripheral cables from the server.
- Determine where the power supply is in relation to the chassis. Often, in tower servers, the power supply with an external lever is located at the back of the machine.
- Press the lever of the power supply and simultaneously pull the power supply unit out of the chassis.
- Insert the new power supply into the power supply bay.
- Connect the power cord from the power supply to the electrical outlet.
- Plug the power and other peripheral cables, and turn on the system.

Power Supply Unit

ACTIVITY 5-2

Installing a Power Supply Unit in a Server

Scenario:

You've been asked to install and replace some hardware components in a departmental server. First, you will replace the power supply in the server.

 There is a simulated version of this activity available on the CD-ROM shipped with this course. You can run this simulation on any Windows computer to review the activity after class, or as an alternative to performing the activity as a group in class. The activity simulation can be launched either directly from the CD-ROM by clicking the Interactives link and navigating to the appropriate one, or from the installed data file location by opening the C:\ServerPlus\Data\Simulations\Lesson 5\5-b folder and double-clicking the executable Installing a Power Supply Unit.exe file.

What You Do	How You Do It
1. Establish an ESD-free work area.  These setup instructions are geared to ESD kits that include work surface mats. If your ESD kit has a floor mat, you will need to alter the setup steps accordingly.	a. Gather the tools and equipment you will need, including an ESD kit, the power supply, and a Phillips-head screwdriver.
	b. Install an antistatic work surface mat in your work area. The mat can be partially under the system chassis, but you should leave enough room to place any components to be added to or removed from the system.
	c. To ground the antistatic mat, clip a ground wire to the mat and to an unpainted section of the system chassis.
	d. If necessary, use antistatic spray to counteract any static electricity in your clothes.
	e. Place the strap on your wrist and attach the ground wire to the system chassis or the mat.
	f. Use a multimeter to verify that the resistance of the antistatic mats is less than 1 ohm.

2.	Remove the existing power supply.	a.	Turn off the system.
		b.	Unplug the power cord from the electrical outlet.
		c.	Unplug the peripherals connected to the server.
		d.	Open the server's chassis enclosure.
		e.	Locate the power supply in relation to the chassis opening.
		f.	Unscrew the screws holding the power supply in place.
		g.	Disconnect the power leads from the system board and all peripherals.
		h.	Lift the power supply out of the chassis, and set it aside.
3.	Install the replacement power supply.	a.	Use the screws to anchor the new power supply in place.
		b.	Reconnect the power leads in the proper order.
		c.	Plug the power cord from the power supply to the electrical outlet.
		d.	Close the server's chassis enclosure.
		e.	Plug the power and peripherals cables to the server.
		f.	Plug the power cord to the electrical outlet.
		g.	Turn on the system.

Installing a Network Interface Card

Installing a network interface card on the rackmount server involves a sequence of steps.

Step	Description
Prepare to work inside the server's case	Verify that the server is powered off. Unplug the power cord, monitor, and any other peripherals from the server. Open the server's chassis enclosure. Depending on the server, you might need to remove screws, unhook latches, or loosen sliders before you can open the chassis.
Remove the riser card	Depending on the server type, either unscrew or lift to remove the riser card from the chassis.
Remove the NIC card	Hold the NIC card firmly by the upper edge and pull it gently to remove the NIC card that has to be replaced.
Install the NIC card into the riser card	Pick up the card by the upper edge. Firmly press the card into the riser card slot.
Replace the riser card	Anchor the riser card along with the NIC and secure the NIC card to the chassis. Close the chassis enclosure, plug the power and other peripheral cables, and turn on the system.

Installing a NIC in a Tower Server

This is the sequence of steps to be followed while installing a NIC in a tower server:

- Turn off the system.
- Unplug the electrical power cord from the electric outlet.
- Unplug the power and other peripheral cables from the server.
- Open the server chassis enclosure.
- Determine whether the new network card is an ISA or a PCI card. Identify an open slot on the ISA or PCI bus. Remove the slot cover from the open slot.
- Pick up the card by the upper edge.
- Align the connectors with the slot openings on the system board. Firmly press the card into the slot.
- Anchor the card either with the screw from the slot cover or by whatever mechanism available on the server.
- Close the server chassis enclosure.
- Connect the power cord from the power supply to the electrical outlet.
- Plug the power and other peripheral cables, and turn on the system.

ACTIVITY 5-3

Installing a Network Interface Card in a Server

Before You Begin

Verify that you have all tools and equipment needed and that your work area is ESD-free.

Scenario:

You've been asked to replace the NIC card in a departmental server.

 To use more than one NIC to provide fault-tolerance and load balancing, additional configuration is required beyond the physical installation of the NIC. Consult the NIC manufacturer's website for specific details and setup steps beyond those listed here.

 There is a simulated version of this activity available on the CD-ROM shipped with this course. You can run this simulation on any Windows computer to review the activity after class, or as an alternative to performing the activity as a group in class. The activity simulation can be launched either directly from the CD-ROM by clicking the Interactives link and navigating to the appropriate one, or from the installed data file location by opening the C:\ServerPlus\Data\Simulations\Lesson 5\5-b folder and double-clicking the executable Installing a Network Interface Card.exe file.

What You Do	How You Do It
1. Open the system cover to access the slots.	a. Turn off the system power.
	b. Unplug the server from the electrical outlet.
	c. Unplug power and other peripheral cables from the system.
	d. Open the server's chassis enclosure.
	e. Locate the riser card.

2. Install the network interface card.

 Do not rock the card side to side when installing or removing it.

a. Remove the riser card form the chassis.

b. Remove the NIC card that has to be replaced.

c. Install the new NIC card into the riser card slot.

d. Replace the riser card into the chassis.

e. Secure the NIC card to the chassis.

f. Close the server's chassis enclosure.

g. Plug the power and peripherals cables to the server.

h. Plug the power cord to the electrical outlet.

i. Turn on the system.

Installing a CPU and a Cooling System Unit

Installing a CPU and a cooling system on a rackmount server involves a sequence of steps.

Step	Description
Prepare to work inside the server's case	Verify that the server is powered off. Unplug the power cord, monitor, and any other peripherals from the server. Open the server's chassis enclosure. Depending on the server, you might need to remove screws, unhook latches, or loosen sliders before you can open the chassis.
Remove the CPU	Remove the heat sink by unscrewing the screws. Pull up the lever on the side of the ZIF-socket. If you have a different style CPU, refer to the system documentation on how to remove it. Pick the CPU straight up so that you do not bend any pins. Place the old CPU in a safe location in an appropriate container to prevent damage to the CPU should you need or want to reinstall it later.
Install the new CPU	Align the pins on the CPU with the holes in the ZIF socket on the system board. Press the CPU lever back down to lock the CPU in place. Apply thermally-conductive gel to the CPU and fix the heat sink onto it by screwing it back into the motherboard. Close the chassis enclosure, plug the power, and other peripheral cables and turn on the system.

Installing a CPU and a Cooling System in a Tower Server

This is the sequence of steps to be followed while installing a CPU and a cooling system in a tower server:

- Turn off the system.
- Unplug the electrical power cord from the electric outlet.
- Unplug the power and other peripheral cables from the server.
- Open the server chassis enclosure.
- Unplug the cooling fan and remove it with the heat sink.
- Pull up the lever on the side of the ZIF-socket.
- Pick the CPU straight up so that you do not bend any pins.
- Place the old CPU in an appropriate container to prevent any damage, for you may want to reinstall it later.
- Align the pins of the new CPU with the holes in the ZIF socket on the system board.
- Apply thermally-conductive gel to the CPU, and install the heat sink and cooling fan onto it.
- Press the CPU lever back down to lock the CPU in place.
- Connect all the required power connectors.
- Close the server chassis enclosure.
- Connect the power cord from the power supply to the electrical outlet.
- Plug the power, and other peripheral cables and turn on the system.

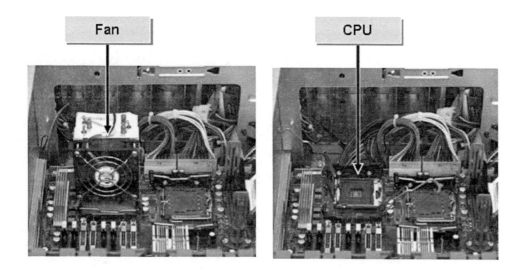

ACTIVITY 5-4

Installing a CPU and a Cooling System Unit in a Server

Before You Begin

Verify that you have all tools and equipment needed and that your work area is ESD-free.

Scenario:

One of your clients has an older server that needs to be upgraded. The CPU in the server does not meet the requirements for the application the client needs to run. The client has purchased a CPU upgrade and would like you to install it.

 There is a simulated version of this activity available on the CD-ROM shipped with this course. You can run this simulation on any Windows computer to review the activity after class, or as an alternative to performing the activity as a group in class. The activity simulation can be launched either directly from the CD-ROM by clicking the Interactives link and navigating to the appropriate one, or from the installed data file location by opening the C:\ServerPlus\Data\Simulations\Lesson 5\5-b folder and double-clicking the executable Installing a CPU and Cooling System Unit.exe file.

What You Do	How You Do It
1. Remove the existing CPU.	a. Turn off the system.
	b. Unplug the power cord from the electrical outlet.
	c. Unplug the peripherals connected to the server.
	d. Open the server's chassis enclosure.
	e. Determine where the CPU is in relation to the chassis opening.
	f. Remove the heat sink by unscrewing the screws.
	g. Pull up the lever on the side of the ZIF-socket.
	h. Pick the CPU straight up so as not to bend any pins and place it in a safe location.

2. Install the new CPU.	a. Align the pins on the CPU with the holes in the ZIF socket on the system board.
	b. Press the CPU lever back down to lock the CPU in place.
	c. Apply thermally-conductive gel to the CPU and fix the heat sink onto it by screwing it back into the motherboard.
	d. Close the server's chassis enclosure.
	e. Plug the power and peripherals cables to the server.
	f. Plug the power cord to the electrical outlet.
	g. Turn on the system.

Installing RAM

Installing RAM on a rackmount server involves a sequence of steps.

Step	Description
Prepare to work inside the server's case	Verify that the server is powered off. Unplug the power cord, monitor, and any other peripherals from the server. Open the server's chassis enclosure. Depending on the server, you might need to remove screws, unhook latches, or loosen sliders before you can open the chassis.
Remove the RAM	Locate the RAM modules to be removed. Push the ejector tabs on each end of the memory pair modules out to release the memory pair modules, and then remove the memory pair modules. In servers, memory cards are inserted in pairs into the slots. Press down on the ejection tabs. Then, firmly grasp the memory module and pull it out of the slot.
Install the new RAM	Align the notches in the connector edge of the memory module with the notches in the memory expansion socket, and then firmly press the memory module down into the socket. If the ejection tabs did not lock into the notches on the ends of the memory module, the module may not be properly seated. You should first try to remove and reinsert the module, but if all else fails, you may need to push the ejection tabs up until they lock. Close the chassis enclosure, plug the power and other peripheral cables, and turn on the system.

Installing RAM in a Tower Server

The steps involved in installing RAM in a tower server are similar to that of installing it in a rackmount server.

ACTIVITY 5-5

Installing RAM in a Server

Before You Begin

Verify that you have all tools and equipment needed and that your work area is ESD-free.

Scenario:

The departmental server is performing sluggishly, so additional RAM has been purchased for this server.

 There is a simulated version of this activity available on the CD-ROM shipped with this course. You can run this simulation on any Windows computer to review the activity after class, or as an alternative to performing the activity as a group in class. The activity simulation can be launched either directly from the CD-ROM by clicking the Interactives link and navigating to the appropriate one, or from the installed data file location by opening the C:\ServerPlus\Data\Simulations\Lesson 5\5-b folder and double-clicking the executable Installing a RAM.exe file.

What You Do	How You Do It
1. Open the system cover to access the slots.	a. Turn off the system power.
	b. Unplug the server from the electrical outlet.
	c. Unplug power and peripherals cables from the system.
	d. Open the server's chassis enclosure.
2. Remove the RAM modules.	a. Locate the memory modules that have to be replaced.
	b. Press down on the ejection tabs.
	c. Firmly grasp the memory module and remove it out of the slot.

3. Install the new memory in the system.

   a. Align the notched edge of the new memory pair modules with the memory expansion slot, and then firmly press the module down into the socket.

   b. Close the server's chassis enclosure.

   c. Plug the power and peripherals cables to the server.

   d. Plug the power cord to the electrical outlet.

   e. Turn on the system.

Installing a System Board

Today's system boards are highly integrated and generally not repairable. You'll have to follow a series of steps to replace a motherboard on a rackmount server.

Step	Description
Prepare to work inside the server's case	Verify that the server is powered off. Unplug the power cord, monitor, and any other peripherals from the server. Open the server's chassis enclosure. Depending on the server, you might need to remove screws, unhook latches, or loosen sliders before you can open the chassis. Remove the RAM and CPU from the motherboard.
Remove the system board	Disconnect cables from the system board, marking each cable as to what it connects and where it goes. Unscrew the system board from the case and lift it out of the case. On some systems, after lifting the system board over the pins, you will need to slide it out of the case.
Install the new system board	Place the new system board into the case and align the mounting holes. Secure the system board to the case. Install RAM and processor on the new system board. Close the chassis, plug the power, and other peripheral cables and turn on the system.

Installing a System Board in a Tower Server

The steps involved in installing a system board in a tower server are similar to those of a rackmount server.

ACTIVITY 5-6

Installing a System Board in a Server

Before You Begin
Verify that you have all tools and equipment needed and that your work area is ESD-free.

Scenario:
The system board of the departmental server has been rendered ineffective by an unexpected power surge. You've been asked to install and replace the system board. While doing so, the customer would like you to put in an upgraded system board to improve system performance.

 There is a simulated version of this activity available on the CD-ROM shipped with this course. You can run this simulation on any Windows computer to review the activity after class, or as an alternative to performing the activity as a group in class. The activity simulation can be launched either directly from the CD-ROM by clicking the Interactives link and navigating to the appropriate one, or from the installed data file location by opening the C:\ServerPlus\Data\Simulations\Lesson 5\5-b folder and double-clicking the executable Installing a System Board.exe file.

What You Do	How You Do It
1. Open the system cover to access the slots.	a. Turn off the system power.
	b. Unplug the server from the electrical outlet.
	c. Unplug power and peripherals cables from the system.
	d. Open the server's chassis enclosure.

 You may find it helpful at this point to take a picture of the inside of the server to use as a reference later.

2. Remove cards and cables.	a. Remove the CPU and RAM from the system board.
	b. Disconnect cables from the system board.

3.	Remove the existing system board.	a.	Unscrew the system board from the case. Be sure to set the screws aside to use in mounting the new system board.
		b.	Lift the system board.
4.	Install the new system board.	a.	Slide the new system board into the case, aligning the mounting holes.
	Be sure not to screw the system board too tightly to avoid damaging the system board.	b.	Secure the system board to the case using the screws you removed from the old system board.
5.	Install the RAM and processor on the new system board.	a.	Install the memory modules beginning with the first memory slot (Bank 0).
		b.	Install the CPU according to the manufacturer's directions.
6.	Reinstall the cards and cables.	a.	Reconnect all cables to the new motherboard.
		b.	Reconnect the power supply to the system board.
		c.	Close the server's chassis enclosure.
		d.	Plug the power and peripherals cables to the server.
		e.	Plug the power cord to the electrical outlet.
		f.	Turn on the system.

Installing an Optical Drive

There are various steps involved in installing an optical drive on a rackmount server.

Step	Description
Prepare to work inside the server's chassis.	Power down the server. Unplug the power cord, monitor, and any other peripherals from the server. Open the server's chassis enclosure.
Remove the optical drive	Locate the optical drive. Disconnect the power cables and data cables from the rear of the optical drive. If necessary, remove the screws, brackets, or clips that mount the optical drive in the chassis bay and then slide the optical drive out of its bay.

Step	Description
Install the optical drive.	Insert the new optical drive into its bay. Connect the power cables and data cables to the rear of the optical drive. Close the chassis enclosure, plug the power, and other peripheral cables and turn on the system.

Installing an Optical Drive on a Tower Server

The steps involved in installing an optical drive on a tower server are similar to those of a rackmount server.

ACTIVITY 5-7

Installing an Optical Drive in a Server

Before You Begin

Verify that you have all tools and equipment needed and that your work area is ESD-free.

Scenario:

You have been assigned the task of refurbishing a server for a user. This computer has an optical drive that needs to be replaced with a new optical drive.

There is a simulated version of this activity available on the CD-ROM shipped with this course. You can run this simulation on any Windows computer to review the activity after class, or as an alternative to performing the activity as a group in class. The activity simulation can be launched either directly from the CD-ROM by clicking the Interactives link and navigating to the appropriate one, or from the installed data file location by opening the C:\ServerPlus\Data\Simulations\Lesson 5\5-b folder and double-clicking the executable Installing an Optical Drive.exe file.

What You Do	How You Do It
1. Open the system cover to access the slots.	a. Turn off the system power.
	b. Unplug the server from the electrical outlet.
	c. Unplug the power and peripherals' cables from the system.
	d. Open the server's chassis enclosure.
2. Remove the old optical drive from the computer.	a. Disconnect the power and data connector from the rear of the optical drive.
	b. If necessary, remove the screws, brackets, or clips that mount the optical drive in the chassis bay.
	c. Slide the optical drive out of its bay.

3. Install the new optical drive in the computer.

    a. Insert the new optical drive into its bay.

    b. Mount the optical drive to the chassis using the appropriate screws, brackets, or clips.

    c. Connect the power and data connector to the rear of the optical drive.

    d. Close the server's chassis enclosure.

    e. Plug the power and peripherals cables to the server.

    f. Plug the power cord to the electrical outlet.

    g. Turn on the system.

Configuring RAID

There are various steps involved in configuring RAID.

Step	Description
Prepare to work inside the server's chassis.	Power down the server, unplug the power cord, monitor and any other peripherals from the server, and open the server's chassis enclosure.
Install additional hard drives into the server.	Determine how many hard drives are already installed in the server. If your server has only one hard drive installed, you will need to add at least one more to implement hardware RAID. Determine what RAID level you want to implement. If you have only one additional hard drive available, you will be able to implement RAID 0 or RAID 1; if you have two additional hard drives available, you will be able to implement RAID 5. Install the extra hard drive or drives into the server.

To install a hard drive:
- Locate an available drive bay.
- Insert the drive in an available drive bay.
- Connect the data and power cables to the drive.

Step	Description
Install the RAID controller.	If your server contains an onboard RAID controller, you need to perform the following steps: ● Identify an open expansion slot that will hold the RAID controller. ● Remove the slot cover. ● Insert the RAID controller into the slot. ● Use the screw from the slot cover to anchor the RAID controller to the chassis.
Enter the RAID controller's BIOS setup program.	Replace the chassis cover and reconnect the power cord, monitor, and peripherals. Power up the server. When prompted, enter the controller BIOS setup program. The specific keystrokes can vary depending on the RAID controller.
Define the RAID level for the new array.	Follow the menu prompts to create a new array. Define the array level as determined earlier in the process. For instance, if you added one hard drive, you can define RAID level 0 or 1; if you installed two hard drives, you can define RAID level 5. If necessary, initialize the array. Exit the controller BIOS setup program.
Verify that the array has been set up correctly.	Restart the server. If necessary, troubleshoot any problems that you encounter.

Configuring RAID in a Tower Server

The steps involved in configuring RAID in a tower server are similar to those of a rackmount server.

ACTIVITY 5-8
Configuring RAID

Before You Begin:

Verify that you have all tools and equipment needed and that your work area is ESD-free.

To complete this activity, you will need the following hardware:

- A RAID controller, either onboard or an expansion card.
- At least one additional hard drive. Two additional hard drives will be needed if you plan to implement RAID level 5.

Scenario:

You've been asked to implement RAID on a departmental server.

> There is a simulated version of this activity available on the CD-ROM shipped with this course. You can run this simulation on any Windows computer to review the activity after class, or as an alternative to performing the activity as a group in class. The activity simulation can be launched either directly from the CD-ROM by clicking the Interactives link and navigating to the appropriate one, or from the installed data file location by opening the C:\ServerPlus\Data\Simulations\Lesson 5\5-b folder and double-clicking the executable Configuring RAID.exe file.

What You Do	How You Do It
1. Open the system cover to access the slots.	a. Turn off the system power.
	b. Unplug the server from the electrical outlet.
	c. Unplug power and peripherals cables from the system.
	d. Open the server's chassis enclosure.
	e. Identify the hard drive location in relation to the server chassis.

2. Install additional hard drives into the server.

   a. Determine how many hard drives are already installed in the server. If your server has only one hard drive installed, you will need to add at least one more to implement hardware RAID.

   b. Determine what RAID level you want to implement. If you have only one additional hard drive available, you will be able to implement RAID 0 or RAID 1; if you have two additional hard drives available, you will be able to implement RAID 5.

   c. Locate an available drive bay.

   d. Insert the drive in the drive bay.

   e. Connect the data and power cables to the drive.

3. Reassemble and restart the server, and enter the RAID controller's BIOS setup program.

   a. Replace the chassis cover and reconnect the power cord, keyboard, monitor, and mouse.

   b. Power up the server.

   c. When prompted, enter the controller BIOS setup program. The specific keystrokes can vary depending on the RAID controller.

4. Define the RAID level for the new array. (Remember, the specific keystrokes can vary depending on the RAID controller.)

   a. Follow the menu prompts to create a new array.

   b. Define the array level as determined earlier in the activity.

   c. If necessary, initialize the array.

   d. Exit the controller BIOS setup program.

   e. Restart the server. If necessary, troubleshoot any problems that you encounter.

OPTIONAL ACTIVITY 5-9
Examining Server Hardware Installation

Scenario:
In this activity, you will examine the server hardware installation.

---

1. **True or False? When examining a system board, you will often find that very few components on the board are repairable.**

   __ True

   __ False

---

2. **When installing or upgrading a system board, what should you do while disconnecting cables from the board?**

   a) Remove them completely from the case, so they are out of the way.

   b) Mark each cable as you go, so you can easily reconnect them later.

   c) Unscrew the system board from the case.

   d) Disconnect all external devices.

---

3. **True or False? When installing a CPU, you need to verify that you have an appropriate and compatible cooling system to cool the new processor.**

   __ True

   __ False

---

4. **When installing and configuring a power supply, what step should you complete first?**

   a) Unplug the power supply from the system board.

   b) Unplug the electrical power cord from the electric outlet and from the power supply.

   c) Toggle the power switch on the computer on and off to discharge any remaining electricity stored in the computer's capacitors.

   d) Shut down and turn off the system.

TOPIC C
Verify Server Installation

You have installed all internal hardware components in the server. Before loading all servers in their racks, you need to verify that the server boots and recognizes the hardware properly. In this topic, you will verify the server hardware installation.

Imagine putting a server together and then installing it on a production network without even flipping the switch on. Verifying that the installed hardware works or not is important, so that you don't have to spend time installing software on a malfunctioning machine.

Power-On Self Test

The *Power-On Self Test (POST)* is a built-in diagnostic program that is run every time a server starts up. The POST checks your hardware to ensure that everything is present and functioning properly, before the system BIOS begins the operating system boot process.

Power-On Self Test (POST) makes hardware verification an easy task. All you need to do is observe the power-on sequence when the server's power is turned on.

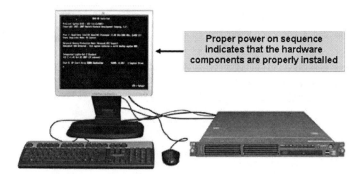

Proper power on sequence indicates that the hardware components are properly installed

Figure 5-1: Post is a built-in diagnostic program that is run every time a server starts up.

Common POST Codes
The following table lists some common POST codes and their meanings.

Audio Error Code	Video Output	Problem	Solution
One or more short beeps	DOS prompt	None; (normal startup beep)	None.
None	None	Power	Check power cords, wall voltage, server's power supply.
None	Cursor	Power	Check the server's power supply; check for sufficient wall voltage.
None	DOS prompt	Audio	May be a defective speaker.
One short, one long beep	None	Display	Check for monitor power; check video cable; check display adapter.

Audio Error Code	Video Output	Problem	Solution
Two short beeps	None or incorrect display (garbage)	Display	Check for monitor power; check video cable; check display adapter.
Two short beeps	Error code number	Refer to a list of error codes and their interpretations.	Refer to a list of error codes and their interpretations.
Repeating short beeps	Probably none	Power	Check the server's power supply; check for sufficient wall voltage.
Continuous tone	Probably none	Power	Check the server's power supply; check for sufficient wall voltage.
One long, one short beep	Probably none	System board	Check to see that all adapters, memory, and chips are seated firmly; check for proper power connections to the system board; use diagnostics software or hardware to further troubleshoot the system board.
One long, two short beeps	Probably none	Display	Check for monitor power; check video cable; check display adapter.
One long, three short beeps	Probably none	Display	Check for monitor power; check video cable; check display adapter.

Wall Voltage

Wall voltage is the voltage measured as the root mean squared value (RMS), between two slots or holes in an electrical outlet which is mounted on a wall.

POST Error Code Numbers

The following table lists some error code numbers and their meanings.

POST Error Code	Problem
02#	Power
01##	System board
0104	Interrupt controller
0106	System board
0151	Real-time clock or CMOS RAM
0162	CMOS checksum error
0163	Time and date (clock not updating)
164 or 0164	System memory configuration incorrect
199 or 0199	User-indicated device list incorrect
02##	Memory
201 or 0201	Memory error (may give memory address)
0202	Memory address error

POST Error Code	Problem
03##	Keyboard
0301	Stuck key (scan code of the key may be indicated)
0302	Keyboard locked
06##	Floppy disk driver or controller
0601	Floppy disk adapter failure
0602	Disk failure
17##	Hard disk or adapter
1701	Drive not ready or fails tests
1704	Hard drive controller failure
1707	Track 0 failure
1714	Drive not ready
1730-1732	Drive adapter failure

The POST process contains several steps to ensure that the system meets the necessary requirements to operate properly. There are various criteria for which each hardware component is tested during POST.

Hardware Component	POST Test Criteria
Power supply	Must be turned on and must supply its "power good" signal.
CPU	Must exit the Reset status mode and must be able to execute instructions.
BIOS	Must be readable.
BIOS memory	Must be readable.
Memory	Must be read by the CPU and the first 64 KB of memory must hold the POST code.
I/O bus or I/O controller	Must be accessible and be able to communicate with the video subsystem.

Verifying Server Installation

You need to follow a sequence of steps to verify server hardware installation.

Step	Description
Connect the peripherals	Replace the chassis cover and the power cord, and connect the keyboard, monitor, and mouse.
Power up the server	Plug the server and monitor into a power strip or UPS and power up the server.

Step	Description
Perform a POST test	Watch the screen as the server works through the power-on sequence.

ACTIVITY 5-10
Verifying the Server Installation

Scenario:

You have replaced the various hardware components of a server and before you move on to installing the server software, you want to ensure that the hardware components are configured properly.

 There is a simulated version of this activity available on the CD-ROM shipped with this course. You can run this simulation on any Windows computer to review the activity after class, or as an alternative to performing the activity as a group in class. The activity simulation can be launched either directly from the CD-ROM by clicking the Interactives link and navigating to the appropriate one, or from the installed data file location by opening the C:\ServerPlus\Data\Simulations\Lesson 5\5-c folder and double-clicking the executable Verifying the Server Installation.exe file.

What You Do	How You Do It
1. Verify the server hardware installation.	a. Replace the chassis cover and power cord, and connect the keyboard, monitor, and mouse
	b. Plug the server and monitor into a power strip or UPS.
	c. Power up the server and monitor, and watch the screen as the server works through the power-on sequence.
	d. If necessary, power down the server and troubleshoot any POST or other errors that occur, and then start the server again to verify that no errors remain.

ACTIVITY 5-11
Discussing the POST Routine

Scenario:
In this activity, you will discuss the POST routine.

---

1. **What is the audio error code and video output for a system board failure?**

   a) Continuous tone without any display.

   b) One long, one short beep without any display.

   c) Two short beeps without any display.

   d) One or more short beeps with DOS prompt on the display.

---

2. **Match a POST error code with its problem.**

___	0106	a.	Memory error
___	0602	b.	System board
___	0201	c.	Disk failure

---

3. **True or False? 1714 indicates drive not ready.**

   ___ True

   ___ False

TOPIC D
Install a Server in a Network Environment

You have verified that all the server components are properly installed. Once the server is built, the next step is to install the server in a network environment. In this topic, you will describe the various considerations that should be followed when installing a server into their environments.

As a server technician, you must know the various considerations for the installation of servers into an environment. These considerations include keeping them safe from physical harm, using space efficiently, and preventing a maze of tangled cables and cords, so that they can be easily accessed. This will enable you to establish a safe and secure server network.

Tower Installation Considerations

Tower servers are the most economical solution for small businesses that do not usually dedicate an entire room to store their servers. To prevent issues with heat, EMI, and stability, do not stack towers directly on top of each other. They should be stored on steel racks or shelving units wherever there is available space. Even though they frequently come with foot pedestals, it is good practice to get the towers off the floor to curtail flood damage.

There are some more considerations to be followed when setting up a tower server.

Tower Consideration	Description
Power	In situations where several towers are to be installed in close proximity to each other, consider the power requirements for each system, as well as any peripheral systems such as UPSs or KVM switches that will need to be installed, in addition to the power requirements for any systems that are already installed in the area. If you are approaching the upper limits of the available power supply to the area, you might need to consider installing additional circuitry to handle the increased power load.
KVM	In situations where several towers are to be installed in close proximity to each other, consider installing a KVM switch to minimize the space and power required by multiple monitors.
Cable Organization	Provide an appropriate amount of cable clearance for easy maintenance. To maintain a neat appearance, yet allow you to easily maneuver a tower, leave some slack in the cable and coil it up with a fastener. Installing cables of standard length saves installation cost. If you implement KVM switches to control several servers, consider using combination cables or IP-based devices to minimize the impact of the additional cabling needed.

Rackmount Installation Considerations

Rackmount server systems often provide sliding rails and hinged cases for easy access. Many rackmount server components, such as hard drives, power supplies, expansion cards, and fans, are hot-swappable, enabling you to replace faulty parts without downing the server. Implementing server racks and rackmount servers can save considerable space, but rackmount servers can cost up to 15 percent more than their tower counterparts.

There are some more considerations to be followed when setting up a rackmount server.

Rackmount Consideration	Description
Dimensional standards	The Electronic Industries Association (EIA) sets dimensional standards for all rackmount components and for the cases that hold them. In the rackmount world, height is measured in rack units (U), where 1 U is 1.75 inches. The maximum height for a rackmount server is defined as 42 U (73.5 inches). Width is standardized at 19 inches (at the face panel), and depth can be up to 32 inches.
Ventilation	Rackmount servers are designed to be stacked, unlike conventional tower machines. In fact, many rackmount servers need less than one inch of headroom for cross-ventilation, which is often provided by the overhang on the server faceplate. Because rackmount servers are designed to draw in air from the front and vent from the back of the server, the vertical space savings might be offset by the amount of room needed in front of and behind the server rack itself. Again, depending on the configuration of the rack (such as the rack's thermal efficiency, the presence of front and back door panels, and the presence of built-in air-conditioning) and the overall heat-dissipation ability of the air-conditioning units in the server room, you might need to provide one to three feet of space at the front and back of the rack unit.
	Although some racks come with locking doors and shelves, enclosing the rack units causes you to have to provide for ventilation inside the rack case. If the rack system isn't in a climate-controlled server room, this doesn't matter much because you would have to provide for airflow inside the rack anyhow. But if the rack is in a server room for which you've already provided air-conditioning, cooling the inside of the rack is redundant, so it might be better to leave the rack open and rely on the security measures for the server room itself.

Rackmount Consideration	Description
Power	With rackmount systems, unless you want to live in a forest of extension cords, you'll need one or more power strips. Some cabinets come with power strips built in, but if you need to order them, consider which kind will be best for your installation. Rackmount power strips come in versions that mount either vertically or horizontally. Some have outlets that are widely spaced to accommodate transformer blocks—a useful feature if your equipment uses bulky power transformers. Surge protection is another important issue. Some power strips have built-in surge protection; others don't. To protect the investment you've made in rackmount equipment, you'll want to make sure it's as protected as possible. Any mission-critical equipment should also be connected to an Uninterruptible Power Supply (UPS), to keep your equipment from crashing during a brief blackout or brownout and to give you enough time to shut everything down properly in an extended power outage. You can choose a rackmount UPS for the most critical equipment, or you can plug the whole rack into a stand-alone UPS.
KVM	Racked server setups are an ideal place to use KVM switches, and the additional space savings provided can be an added benefit. For simple tower-rack installations, place the switch so that the cables from each server, and the cables from the switch to the console station, can reach the switch without being completely taut. Some rackmount systems lend themselves to KVM implementation better than others do, so check with the server or rack manufacturer's documentation to see whether or not additional hardware or software will be needed to implement KVM switches. Other systems might provide for network-based KVM implementations, which would allow you to access the connected servers from a workstation that is outside the server room, or any place on the network.

Rackmount Consideration	Description
Cable Organization	As you can imagine, placing several servers in a rack can result in a fairly impressive tangle of cables, unless you take steps to neatly organize the cables. Proper placement of cables can help prevent problems such as having cables and cords catch on sliding rack components. Some racks include special enclosures for storing cables, and separate rackmount cable and patch cord managers are available for a relatively low price.
	Planning cable connections in advance helps you to decide how to organize the cables. Examine the position of the connectors on your equipment; they can help you determine where it's most efficient to run cables horizontally and where it's better to run them vertically. Many network problems are caused by the cabling, so if you let your cables get away from you now, it's likely you'll pay for it later on.

When you're installing rackmount servers into a server rack, make sure that the rack is in the correct position *before* you load it up with equipment. Weight is a concern when mounting on the higher levels of the rack. Trying to move a loaded rack can cause the rack to tip over or collapse, endangering both you and the server equipment stored in the rack. Likewise, if you ever need to move a loaded rack, unload it before trying to move it.

Brownouts refers to reduced electrical availability due to a voltage drop, whereas blackout refers to total unavailability of electricity to a given area.

Blade Installation Considerations

For the most part, blade servers are chosen by companies that need a lot of servers and have a limited amount of space. The simplified wiring and plug-and-play nature of blades makes them relatively easy to deploy. The single backplane makes them easier to manage and troubleshoot.

Blade servers are installed in the same type of chassis as rackmounts. It is important to keep connections clean and not force the blades into the chassis. Use blanks to fill in the empty slots.

There are some more considerations to be followed when setting up a blade server.

Blade Consideration	Description
Power and Ventilation	Because blade servers are normally deployed into existing rackmount-type environments, the power and ventilation issues to be considered are quite similar to those in rackmount installations. However, you should be aware that the increased density of blade servers can have a serious impact on power and cooling issues, and you should carefully calculate the power and cooling needs of the new blade server installation prior to attempting an actual installation.
KVM	Because blade servers are normally deployed into existing rackmount-type environments, the KVM issues to be considered are quite similar to those in rackmount installations.
Cable Organization	Because blade servers are normally deployed into existing rackmount-type environments, the cabling issues to be considered are quite similar to those in rackmount installations. The good news is that because the server blades all plug into one backplane, there are fewer cables to deal with than with tower or rackmount installations.

ACTIVITY 5-12
Examining Server Installation in an Environment

Scenario:

In this activity, you will examine the issues that can affect server installations.

---

1. **What is the main benefit of implementing tower servers?**

   a) Cost savings

   b) Space savings

   c) Energy savings

   d) Best performance

---

2. **What issues should you consider when implementing a tower server setup?**

   a) Airflow

   b) Cable management

   c) Number of slots on the backplane

   d) Power

---

3. **What is the main benefit of implementing blade servers?**

   a) Cost savings

   b) Space savings

   c) Energy savings

   d) Easy implementation

---

4. **Your company has purchased a new server rack with locking doors. The plan is to install the rack in the main server room, which has a security system and environmental controls already in place. A colleague asks you if you would lock the rack. What would be your response and reasoning?**

   a) Lock the rack, because there is no such thing as too much security.

   b) Lock the rack, but fans might need to be installed inside the rack to ensure proper airflow and cooling.

   c) No, the server room environment provides adequate security, and airflow should not be an issue.

   d) No, because it will be easier to work on the system if it is unlocked.

---

5. You've been asked to install a new tower server into an existing small business environment. The three existing servers are situated in a locked utility closet. To have enough room for the UPS, monitors, keyboards, and mice, the servers are stacked on the floor. Each server is also connected to an Ethernet switch via a short cable that needs to be unplugged when the server needs to be moved. What recommendations would you make to improve this installation environment?

   a) Place the servers and the UPS on metal racks or shelves.

   b) Implement a KVM switch.

   c) Use longer network cables, and organize all cables with ties or fasteners.

   d) Remove all input and output devices, and implement remote console management for the servers.

   e) Provide sliding rails and hinged cases for easy access.

Lesson 5 Follow-up

In this lesson, you installed server components. The ability to successfully install and configure server components is integral to a server technician's job.

1. **What are the basic precautionary steps that you would take when installing server components?**

2. **Have you encountered any problems while installing and configuring a server component?**

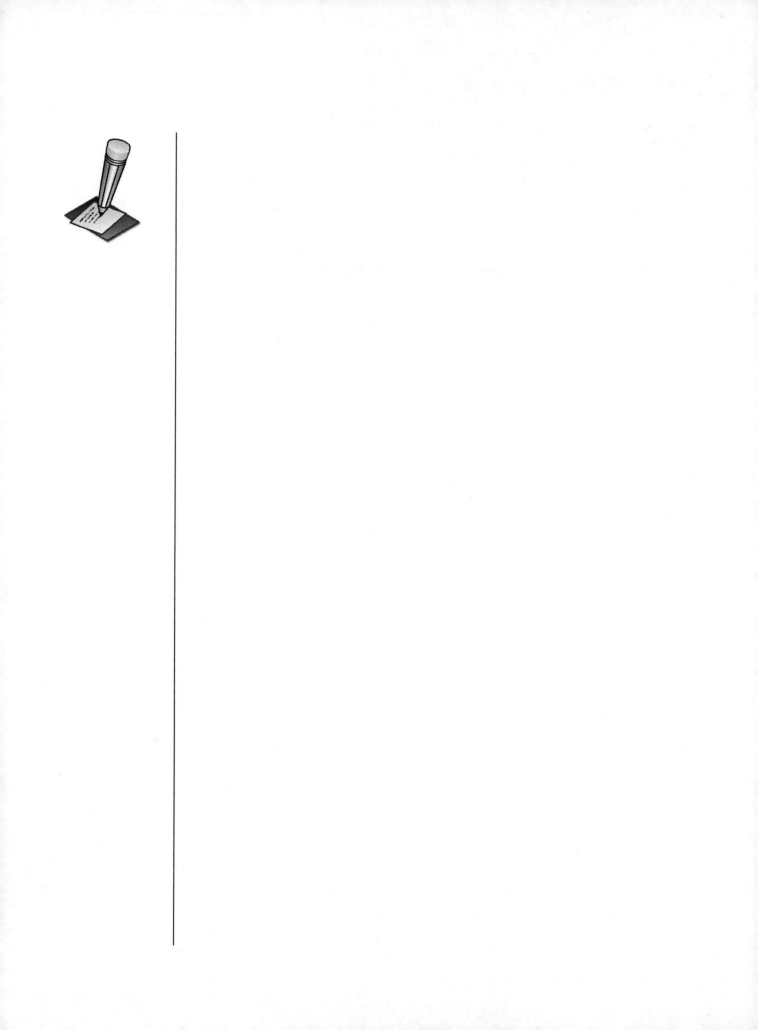

6 | Configuring Servers

Lesson Time: 4 hour(s)

Lesson Objectives:

In this lesson, you will configure servers.

You will:

● Install and configure a NOS and test the installation.

● Enable SNMP on a server computer.

● Identify the various types of information that should be included in a server's configuration documentation.

Introduction

You are familiar with installing hardware components on a server. Once server hardware has been fully installed, the next step is to install the software and configure the machine for operation. In this lesson, you will configure server software and enable some system management tools.

A server that is physically installed on a network without being configured for daily operation is not a useful asset. You need to install appropriate software and configure it to set up reliable server that can be easily managed and maintained by network administrators and hardware specialists.

This lesson covers all or part of the following CompTIA Server+ (2009) certification objectives:

● Topic A:

   ■ Objective 2.1: Install, deploy, configure and update NOS (Windows / *nix).

   ■ Objective 2.4: Explain different server roles, their purpose and how they interact.

● Topic B:

   ■ Objective 2.3: Given a scenario, implement and administer NOS management features based on procedures and guidelines.

● Topic C:

   ■ Objective 4.1: Write, utilize and maintain documentation, diagrams and procedures.

TOPIC A
NOS Installation and Verification

Once the server hardware is set up, the next logical step would be to install the NOS that can act as an interface between the user and the server hardware. In this topic, you will examine some of the issues surrounding the installation of a NOS.

Because there are multiple vendors, each specific NOS may have its own unique installation procedures. There are certain things you need to take care of as part of the overall software installation procedure. A server specialist's main area of concern will be to configure the server hardware to work with the installed NOS so that users can get proper access to network resources.

NOS Installation Considerations

Although each NOS may have its own unique installation procedures, there are some issues that must be taken care of as part of the overall software installation procedure. One of these issues is preparing the network for the new server. The user or administrator needs to determine the IP addresses and subnet masks to be assigned for each NIC on the server. Other information that might be required for choosing a particular NOS over others include the various features and functionality required on the network; the protocol to be used for name resolution such as DNS or WINS; whether the IP addresses are to be configured statically or dynamically; and the network, gateway, or broadcast addresses to be used on the network segment that will contain the new server.

Hardware Compatibility List for Windows Operating Systems

Hardware Compatibility List (HCL) is a list that provides the hardware components that are compatible with a particular OS. You should check all your hardware to ensure that it is compatible with the version of Windows you plan to install. Starting with Windows XP Professional, you can run the Microsoft Windows Upgrade Advisor from the product compact disc to generate compatibility reports. Microsoft also maintains a list of all supported hardware for Microsoft Windows in their HCL.

Hardware Compatibility List for Macintosh Operating System

If your Macintosh computer meets the minimum requirements for Mac OS installation, the hardware should all be compatible with the operating system. You can verify that your hardware is supported by examining the product specifications for your preferred version of the Mac OS at **http://www.apple.com**.

Hardware Compatibility List for Linux Operating System

Because Linux is a portable operating system, it is compatible with a wide range of hardware. You will need to check with the vendor or provider of your Linux distribution to verify if your particular system hardware is supported by that distribution.

One web resource you can use to research general Linux hardware support is the Linux Hardware Compatibility HOWTO site at **http://tldp.org/HOWTO/Hardware-HOWTO/index.html**. You can find additional Linux hardware compatibility lists at **http://www.linux-drivers.org**.

Device Driver Acquisition

The user or administrator should review the installation procedures for the NOS being installed to ensure that all the necessary information and driver files are collected before actually attempting to start the installation. For instance, although most newer NOS installation routines detect hardware during the installation process and enable the user to confirm which device drivers to use, the way that each NOS handles different device drivers is quite unique. With NetWare and some distributions of Linux, users are prompted for or are able to provide different device drivers during the installation process. With Windows servers, users need to press F6 near the beginning of the setup routine to be able to provide device drivers other than those that shipped with the NOS.

NOS Installation Verification

Once the NOS is installed, the functionality of the installation can be verified by:

- Writing data to the hard drive.
- Accessing the server from another computer on the network.
- Successfully pinging the default gateway.
- Checking the event or setup logs for errors.

Shutting Down and Rebooting a Server

While shutting down a server, it is important to protect the integrity of the data stored on it. Rather than just powering down the server computer to be able to add hardware components or perform other tasks, each NOS has recommended procedures for properly shutting down the operating system software. Following these procedures can ensure that the server software will reload properly without data corruption or error messages. In addition, there are many instances where configuration changes require you to restart or reboot the server for the new parameters to take effect.

Shutdown and Reboot Procedures

The following table describes the shutdown and reboot procedures for some popular NOSs.

NOS	Shutdown Routine	Reboot Routine
Windows Server 2003/2008	1. From the **Start** menu, choose **Shut Down.** 2. Enter a comment in the **Comment** text box and click **OK.**	1. From the **Start** menu, choose **Shut Down** and, from the **What Do You Want The Computer To Do** drop-down list, select **Restart.** 2. Enter a comment in the **Comment** text box and click **OK.**
Windows 2000 Server	1. From the **Start** menu, choose **Shut Down.** 2. Enter a comment in the **Comment** text box and click **OK.**	1. From the **Start** menu, choose **Shut Down.** 2. Select **Restart** and click**OK.**

NOS	Shutdown Routine	Reboot Routine
Novell Open Enterprise Server 2 (OES2)	1. At the console prompt, enter down 2. When the DOS prompt is displayed, press the **Power** button.	At the console prompt, enter restart server
UNIX	At the command prompt, enter shutdown with the options or arguments needed for the version of UNIX you're using. For instance, to shut down immediately on a BSD-based system, you would enter shutdown -h now	At the command prompt, enter shutdown with the options or arguments needed for the version of UNIX you're using. For instance, to reboot a BSD-based system, you would enter shutdown -r now
Linux	At the command prompt, enter shutdown with the options or arguments needed for the version of Linux you're using. For instance, to shut down immediately on a Red Hat Linux system, you would enter shutdown -h now	At the command prompt, enter shutdown with the options or arguments needed for the version of Linux you're using. For instance, to reboot immediately on a Red Hat Linux system, you would enter shutdown -r now
OS/2 Warp Server	From the Workplace Shell GUI, click **Shutdown** on the LaunchPad. Or, from the command prompt, enter shutdown	Shut down the server, and then press the **Power** button to reboot.

Shutting Down Multiple Servers

While shutting down multiple servers, it is essential to ensure that servers providing least critical services are shut down first and servers providing most critical services are shut down in the end. For example, while shutting down the servers in organization's office, administrators may shut down the file and print servers first and the domain controller server in the end. While starting multiple servers, it is essential to start the domain controller first because no network connection will be possible without the domain controller being powered on. Because shutting down a server affects all services provided by a server, it is essential that the administrators inform all users or clients about the scheduled shut down.

Shutting Down the Attached Components and Peripherals

While shutting down an entire network, it is essential to shut down all the client computers and connected peripherals first and then the server computer. Shutting down the server computer in the end is essential to ensure that all the services and applications running on the server are terminated properly before the entire network is shut down.

Implementing Peripheral Accessibility

While installing a peripheral device on the server, the user or administrator needs to make the new device available to network users if it is intended for shared access. Each NOS has specific procedures for accomplishing this, and the documentation for the NOS installed should be checked for the peripheral to determine the best course of action for providing the needed levels of accessibility. In general, the administrators will most likely need to configure the NOS to set access rights, define shares, or set permissions for users to access the new device.

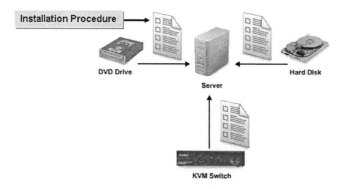

Figure 6-1: Checking the accessibility considerations is an essential task in the installation of a peripheral device on the server.

System Cloning

System cloning or *imaging* is the process of copying the contents of one computer hard disk to another hard disk of identical configuration so as to create an identical clone of the source disk. Unlike plain file copying—which can be done from a hard disk to any hard disk or storage media, independent of the configuration of either of them—cloning requires both the hard disks to be of the same configuration and from the same manufacturer. System cloning copies all contents of the source disk, such as the installed operating system and applications, user data, and even disk partitions to an image file, known as the ghost image as an intermediate step, and then creates an identical image of the source disk on the destination disk.

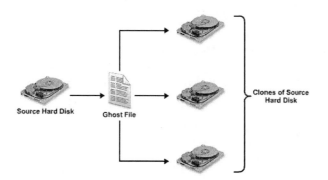

Figure 6-2: Creation of multiple clone hard disks from a single source hard disk.

Due to the popularity of the Norton's imaging software "Ghost," the system cloning or imaging process is also referred to as "ghosting."

System cloning is generally used for configuring a large number of computers with identical hardware. System cloning consumes less time than configuring each computer individually in a repetitive manner. The disk clones can also be used as back up tools in case the original disks get corrupted. However, the settings such as IP addresses must be manually changed for each cloned system to avoid conflicts on the network. Some of the popular imaging software include Norton's Ghost and Symantec's Altris.

Virtualization Templates

A virtualization template is a set of hard disk drive image files that represent a single virtual machine, and its operating system and can be used to deploy a similar virtual machine on the same hardware through cloning. Virtualization templates help in reducing the task of creating an image on each virtual hard disk to simple file copying, thereby saving time. Thus, the image creation is done only for a single template, which is known as the base template, and the files are copied to all virtual hard disks. Each virtual machine is created by the combination of a base template and a virtual hard disk. A server supporting three virtual machines will require four virtual templates: one base template and one template for each virtual machine.

How to Install and Configure a NOS

Procedure Reference: Install and Configure Windows Server 2008

To install the Windows Server 2008 operating system on the server and configure the network settings:

1. Verify that all the hardware is properly set up by performing a power-on self test.
2. Configure the BIOS of the server to boot from the DVD drive.
3. Insert the DVD containing the NOS software into the DVD drive and reboot the system.
4. Press any key when prompted to begin the installation of NOS from the DVD disc and follow the on-screen instructions to begin the installation.
5. If necessary, create as many logical partitions on the hard disk as desired by specifying the size of each logical drive and accepting it.
6. Follow the on-screen instructions in the Install Windows dialog box to complete the installation.
7. Wait for the server to restart and enter and confirm the password for the administrator's login.
8. Use the server manager tools of the NOS to configure a name for the server computer and define a workgroup.
9. Use the Server Manager tool to configure the network settings such as TCP/IPv4 address, the subnet mask, and the default gateway.
10. Connect the server to a network.
11. Test the network settings of the server.
    - Open the **Administrator: Command Prompt** window and type `ipconfig` to verify the IP address of the server.
    - Test the connectivity to another computer on the network by typing `ping` followed by the IP address of the other computer and pressing **Enter.** If zero packets are lost, then the network connectivity is established.

12. If necessary, view the list of all installed hardware resources in the System Properties window.

13. Close all the open windows.

Procedure Reference: Create and Add Users to a Domain Using Windows Server 2008

To create a domain on the server and add users to the domain:

1. In the server computer, using the Server Manager tool, open the list of services and features available for installation.

2. Select the Active Directory Domain Services (ADDS) utility for installation.

3. Follow the on-screen instructions to finish the installation of ADDS utility.

4. Allow the server to restart and then log in as administrator.

5. Run the domain configuration file, dcpromo.exe for Windows Server 2008, to configure a domain name and its password.

6. From the options listed in the **Domain Configuration** dialog box, define a new user profile.

7. Enter the details of the user such as the first name, last name, user name, and password and confirm the same.

8. Create as many user profiles as required.

9. Configure a client computer with a compatible operating system and connect it to the server using the Ethernet bridge.

10. Configure the network settings of the client computer to accept the server computer as the default gateway.

11. In the client computer, set your organization's domain as the domain of the client computer.

12. Wait for the welcome screen to appear on the client computer and then log in to the domain from the client computer as an administrator to complete the setting up of trust relationship between the server and the client computer.

13. Allow the client computer to restart and then log in as a user.

14. If necessary, open the system properties on the client computer and try to modify the network settings. The computer will prompt you to enter an administrator user name and password for making any change, which indicates that the computer is in the domain and the user cannot make any changes to the system settings without the administrator rights.

15. Close all the open windows.

Procedure Reference: Create a Computer Clone Through System Cloning/Imaging

To configure multiple computers through system cloning or imaging software:

1. Install the operating system and configure the necessary settings on one computer. This computer will be the source computer and all other computers will be known as destination computers.

2. Verify that the source and destination computer's CPU, system board, hard disks, and RAM are identical to each other and come from the same manufacturer.

3. Remove the destination computer's hard disk from the chassis and connect it to the source computer's chassis using any available serial SATA or IDE connector port.

4. Restart the source computer and insert a bootable CD-ROM or DVD containing the disk cloning or imaging software into the optical drive.

5. Configure the system BIOS to boot from the optical disc drive and restart the computer.

6. During restart, if necessary, choose the option corresponding to the imaging software to run the disk cloning utility. Most of the system cloning software comes along with some other software utilities.

7. Verify the details of the source hard disk and the destination hard disk, and confirm the same to begin the process of disk cloning.

8. After the disk cloning process is over, a message will be displayed confirming the same. Accept the message and exit the disk cloning utility.

9. Restart the computer and configure the system BIOS to boot from the destination hard disk. If the computer boots normally from the destination hard disk, it indicates that the disk cloning is successful.

ACTIVITY 6-1

Installing a Network Operating System

There is a simulated version of this activity available on the CD-ROM shipped with this course. You can run this simulation on any Windows computer to review the activity after class, or as an alternative to performing the activity as a group in class. The activity simulation can be launched either directly from the CD-ROM by clicking the Interactives link and navigating to the appropriate one, or from the installed data file location by opening the C:\ServerPlus\Data\Simulations\Lesson 6\6-1 folder and double-clicking the executable Installing a Network Operating System_guided.exe file.

Before You Begin:

1. Power on the server if necessary.

2. Configure the system BIOS to boot from the DVD drive first and then from the hard disk and save the changes.

3. Insert the Windows Server 2008 installation DVD into the DVD drive of the server.

4. Using the power button of the server, power off the server and then again power it on.

Scenario:

You have assembled the necessary hardware and now wish to install the Windows Server 2008 operating system on your server. You have decided to configure the server with the following settings:

- Computer name: deptserver##

- Administrator's password: !Pass1234

- IP address and subnet mask for the server: 192.168.1.1## and 255.255.255.0

- Default gateway for the server should be the same as the IP address

What You Do	How You Do It
Server Computer	
1. Start the NOS installation.	a. In the **Install Windows** dialog box, click **Next** and on the next page of the **Install Windows** dialog box, click **Install now.**
	b. In the **Select the operating system you want to install** list box, verify that the **Windows Server 2008 Standard (Full Installation)** option is selected by default and click **Next.**
	c. On the **Please read the license terms** page, check the **I accept the license terms** check box to accept the license terms for installation and click **Next.**
	d. On the **Which type of installation do you want?** page, double-click the **Custom (advanced)** option and on the **Where do you want to install Windows?** page, click the **Drive options (advanced)** link.

Server Computer

2. Create logical partitions on the unallocated hard disk space and complete the installation.

a. Select **Disk 0 Unallocated Space** and click the **New** link to create a logical partition on the unallocated disk space.

b. In the **Size** text box, double-click, type half the size of the available unallocated space for the first partition and click **Apply.**

c. Verify that the first partition is created and its details are displayed.

d. Select **Disk 0 Unallocated Space** and click the **New** link to create another logical disk partition on the remaining unallocated space.

e. In the **Size** text box, double-click and type the desired partition size of the second partition and click **Apply.**

f. Verify that the second partition is created and its details are displayed.

g. Select **Disk 0 Partition 1** to install the Windows Server 2008 on the first partition and click **Next** to continue with the installation and allow the computer to restart.

 The Installation process will take some time depending on the speed of the server system; the server will automatically restart after the installation.

Server Computer

3. Configure the administrator password and name for the server.

a. During the restart, when prompted for a password, click **OK** and in the **New password** text box, click and type *!Pass1234* as the password for the administrator login.

b. In the **Confirm password** text box, click and type *!Pass1234* and click the **Go** button.

c. In the **Your password has been changed** screen, click **OK.**

d. In the **Initial Configuration Tasks** window, in the **Provide Computer Information** section, click the **Provide computer name and domain** link.

e. In the **System Properties** dialog box, verify that the **Full computer name** and **Workgroup** fields are set to default values.

f. Click **Change** to change the computer name and workgroup name.

g. In the **Computer Name/Domain Changes** dialog box, in the **Computer name** text box, delete the default name and type *deptserver##*, where ## corresponds to the student number provided to each student by the instructor. The instructor should have the number 00.

h. In the **Member of** section, verify that the **Workgroup** option is selected by default.

i. In the **Workgroup** text box, double-click and type *ACCOUNTS*

j. Click **OK** and in the **Computer Name/ Domain Changes** message box, click **OK.**

k. Verify that a message box asking you to restart the computer is displayed. Click **OK**, close the **System Properties** dialog box, and in the **Microsoft Windows** message box, click **Restart Now** to restart the computer.

l. Log on to the computer with the administrator password and, in the **Initial Configuration Tasks** window, in the **Provide Computer Information** section, verify that the **Full computer name** and

Workgroup are displayed as configured.

Server Computer

4. Configure the TCP/IP address for the server.

a. In the **Initial Configuration Tasks** window, in the **Provide Computer Information** section, click the **Configure networking** link.

b. In the **Network Connections** window, double-click **Local Area Connection.**

c. In the **Local Area Connection Status** dialog box, click **Properties.**

d. In the **Local Area Connection Properties** dialog box, select **Internet Protocol Version 4 (TCP/IPv4)** and click **Properties.**

e. In the **Internet Protocol Version 4 (TCP/IPv4) Properties** dialog box, select **Use the following IP address.**

f. In the **IP address** text box, click and type *192.168.1.1##*, where ## corresponds to the number provided to each student by the instructor. The instructor should type *00* in the place of ##.

g. Click the **Subnet mask** text box and verify that the subnet mask value of *255.255.255.0* is displayed by default.

h. In the **Default gateway** text box, click and type *192.168.1.1##*

i. Click the **Preferred DNS Server** text box and type *192.168.1.1##*, where ## is the value typed in the IP address text box.

j. Click **OK** to close the **Internet Protocol Version 4 (TCP/IPv4) Properties** dialog box and close the **Local Area Connection Properties** dialog box.

k. Close the **Local Area Connection Status** dialog box.

l. Close the **Network Connections** window.

ACTIVITY 6-2
Verifying the Server Installation

 There is a simulated version of this activity available on the CD-ROM shipped with this course. You can run this simulation on any Windows computer to review the activity after class, or as an alternative to performing the activity as a group in class. The activity simulation can be launched either directly from the CD-ROM by clicking the Interactives link and navigating to the appropriate one, or from the installed data file location by opening the C:\ServerPlus\Data\Simulations\Lesson 6\6-2 folder and double-clicking the executable Verifying the Server Installation_guided.exe file.

Before You Begin:

1. Ensure that all the server and client computers in a group are connected to a common Ethernet hub using Ethernet cables.

2. Ensure that the Ethernet hub is powered on.

 In case of any issues with the network setup, seek help from the network administrator.

3. If any of the computer gets locked due to inactivity, press **Ctrl+Alt+Delete** and enter the administrator password to unlock it.

4. Minimize the **Initial Configuration Tasks** window.

Scenario:

Now that you have installed NOS on your server and configured the network settings, you decide to verify the same.

What You Do	How You Do It
Server Computer	
1. Turn off the firewall on the server computer.	a. Choose **Start→Control Panel** and in the **Control Panel** window, double-click **Network and Sharing Center**.
	b. In the **Network and Sharing Center** window, in the **See also** section, click the **Windows Firewall** link.
	c. In the **Windows Firewall** window, in the **Windows Firewall is helping to protect your computer** section, click the **Change settings** link.
	d. In the **Windows Firewall Settings** dialog box, verify that the option **On** is selected by default and select **Off**.
	e. Click **Apply** and then click **OK**.
	f. Close the **Windows Firewall** window and the **Network and Sharing Center** window.
Server Computer	
2. Test the networking functionality of the server.	a. Choose **Start→Command Prompt**.
	b. In the **Administrator: Command Prompt** window, type *ipconfig* and press **Enter**.
	c. Verify that the IP address displayed matches the IP address configured earlier for the computer.
	d. Type *ping 192.168.1.1##*, where ## is the next highest number than the one allotted to you.
	If your IP address is 192.168.1.101, then type ping 192.168.1.102, and so forth. If you have the highest IP address on the network, then ping 192.168.1.101.
	e. Observe that the number of packets lost is indicated as 0. This indicates that the network connectivity between the computers is configured properly.
	f. Close the **Administrator: Command Prompt** window.

Server Computer

3. Verify the server installation of the hard disk, RAM, and CPU.

a. Choose **Start→Computer** to open the **Computer** window.

b. Observe the details of all the partitions created during the installation process.

c. In the **Standard** tool bar, click **System properties.**

d. In the **System** window, observe the details of the operating system, processor, and memory installed on the server.

e. Close the **System** window.

ACTIVITY 6-3
Configuring Roles and Features on the Server

 There is a simulated version of this activity available on the CD-ROM shipped with this course. You can run this simulation on any Windows computer to review the activity after class, or as an alternative to performing the activity as a group in class. The activity simulation can be launched either directly from the CD-ROM by clicking the Interactives link and navigating to the appropriate one, or from the installed data file location by opening the C:\ServerPlus\Data\Simulations\Lesson 6\6-3 folder and double-clicking the executable Configuring Roles and Features on the Server_guided.exe file.

Before You Begin:

1. Ensure that the server and client computers in a group are connected to different ports of a common Ethernet hub using Ethernet cables.

2. Ensure that the Ethernet hub is powered on.

 In case of any issues with the network setup, seek help from the network administrator.

3. If any of the computer gets locked due to inactivity, press **Ctrl+Alt+Delete** and enter the password to unlock it.

4. Maximize the **Initial Configuration Tasks** window and check the **Do not show this window at logon** check box and click **Close**.

5. Observe that the **Server Manager** window opens automatically.

Scenario:

Now that the NOS has been installed and the network connectivity tested, you want to create a domain, deptsrv.com, for the departmental server and clients, add users to the domain, and connect a client computer to the domain.

What You Do	How You Do It
Server Computer	
1. Install the **Active Directory Domain Services** utility on the server.	a. In the **Server Manager** window, in the left pane, right-click **Roles** and select **Add Roles.**
	b. In the **Add Roles Wizard**, on the **Before You Begin** page, click **Next.**
	c. On the **Select Server Roles** page, in the **Roles** list, check the **Active Directory Domain Services** check box and click **Next.**
	d. On the **Active Directory Domain Services** page, click **Next** and, on the **Confirm Installation Selections** page, click **Install** to start the installation.
	e. On the **Installation Results** page, view the result of the installation and click **Close** to close the **Add Roles Wizard.**
	f. Close the **Server Manager** window.

Server Computer

2. Create a new domain on the server.

a. Click **Start** and in the **Start Search** text box, click and type **dcpromo.exe** and press **Enter**.

b. In the **Active Directory Domain Services Installation Wizard**, click **Next**, and then on the **Operating System Compatibility** page, click **Next**.

c. On the **Choose a Deployment Configuration** page, select **Create a new domain in a new forest** and click **Next**.

d. On the **Name the Forest Root Domain** page, in the **FQDN of the forest root domain** text box, type *deptsrv.com* and click **Next** to create the **deptsrv.com** domain.

e. On the **Set Forest Functional Level** page, from the **Forest functional level** drop-down list, select **Windows Server 2008** and click **Next**.

f. On the **Additional Domain Controller Options** page, verify that the **DNS server** option is selected by default and click **Next** to install the DNS utility along with Active Directory Domain Services.

g. In the **Static IP assignment** message box, select **Yes, the computer will use a dynamically assigned IP address (not recommended)**.

h. In the **Active Directory Domain Services Installation Wizard** message box, click **Yes**.

i. On the **Location for Database, Log Files, and SYSVOL** page, view the default location of all files and click **Next**.

j. On the **Directory Services Restore Mode Administrator Password** page, in the **Password** text box, type *!Pass1234* as the password of the deptsrv.com domain.

k. In the **Confirm password** text box, click and type *!Pass1234* and click **Next**.

l. On the **Summary** page, view the domain creation summary and click **Next**.

m. In the **Active Directory Domain Services**

Installation Wizard message box, check the **Reboot on completion** check box.

Server Computer

3. Create user profiles on the server for the deptsrv.com domain.

a. After restart, log into the deptsrv.com domain as administrator by typing the domain password *!Pass1234*

b. Close the **Server Manager** window.

c. Choose **Start→Administrative Tools→ Active Directory Users and Computers.**

d. In the **Active Directory Users and Computers** window, in the left pane, right-click **deptsrv.com** and choose **New→User** to create a new user profile.

e. In the **New Object - User** dialog box, in the **First name** text box, type *student1*

f. In the **User logon name** text box, click and type *user1* and click **Next.**

g. In the **New Object - User** dialog box, in the **Password** text box, type the password for user1 as *!Pass##1234*

h. In the **Confirm password** text box, click and type the password *!Pass##1234*, and then uncheck the **User must change password at next logon** check box.

i. Check the **User cannot change password** and **Password never expires** check boxes and click **Next.**

j. Click **Finish** to finish creating the first user.

k. Similarly, create the user profile for student2.

Configure the user logon name for student 2 as *user2* and password as *!Pass###1234*

l. In the left pane, select **deptsrv.com.**

m. Verify that **student1** and **student2** are listed in the right pane of the window.

n. Close the **Active Directory Users and Computers** window.

Client Computer

4. Connect user1's computer to the server.

a. Choose **Start→All Programs→ Accessories→Command Prompt.**

b. In the **Administrator: Command Prompt** window, type **Ping 192.168.1.100** and press **Enter** to test the network connectivity with the server.

c. In the **Ping statistics for 192.168.1.100** message, verify that the number of packets lost is displayed as 0.

d. Close the **Administrator: Command Prompt** window.

e. Choose **Start**, right-click **My Computer** and select **Properties.**

f. In the **System Properties** dialog box, click the **Computer Name** tab and, in the **Windows uses the following information to identify your computer on the network** page, click **Change.**

g. In the **Computer Name Changes** dialog box, verify that the **Computer name** is displayed as clientsys##, where ## corresponds to the number provided to each client computer.

h. In the **Member of** section, select **Domain**, and in the text box, click and type **deptsrv**

i. Click **OK** to add the computer into the deptsrv.com domain.

j. In the **Computer Name Changes** dialog box, in the **User name** text box, type **administrator**.

k. In the **Password** text box, click and type **!Pass1234** and press **OK.**

l. In the **Computer Name Changes** message box, click **OK** and, in the **You must restart this computer for the changes to take effect** page, click **OK.**

m. Close the **System Properties** dialog box.

n. Choose **Start→Turn Off Computer** and, in the **Shut Down Windows** dialog box, from the **What do you want the computer to do** drop-down list, select **Restart.**

           o. Click **OK** to restart the computer.

Client Computer

5. From the client computer, log in to the deptsrv domain as user1.

a. During restart, when prompted by the **Welcome to Windows** message box, press **Ctrl+Alt+Delete**.

b. In the **Log On to Windows** dialog box, click **Options** and from the **Log on to** drop down list, select **DEPTSRV**.

c. In the **User name** text box, double-click and type *user1*

d. In the **Password** text box, click and type **!Pass##1234** as the password for user1, and press **Enter** to view the desktop.

e. Click **Start** and, in the **Start** menu, observe that the full name of user1 is displayed at the top indicating that user1 has successfully logged in.

f. In the **Start** menu, right-click **My Computer** and select **Properties.**

g. In the **System Properties** dialog box, click the **Computer Name** tab.

h. In the **Windows uses the following information to identify your computer on the network** section, verify that the **Network ID** and **Change** buttons are disabled and a note stating **Only Administrators can change the identification of this computer** is displayed at the bottom.

i. Click **Cancel** to close the **System Properties** dialog box.

Server Computer

6. Remove student2 from the **deptsrv.com** domain.

    a. Choose **Start**→**Administrative Tools**→ **Active Directory Users and Computers.**

    b. In the right pane of the **Active Directory Users and Computers** window, right-click **Student 2** and select **Delete** to remove student2 from the domain.

    c. In the **Active Directory Domain Services** message box, click **Yes** to confirm the deletion of student2.

    d. Close the **Active Directory Users and Computers** window.

DISCOVERY ACTIVITY 6-4

Discussing Issues Related to NOS Installation and Verification

Scenario:

In this activity, you will discuss issues relating to the installation of network operating systems.

---

1. **Match each shutdown procedure to its appropriate NOS.**

   ___ Choose Start→Shut Down, type a comment in the Comment text box, and click OK.

   a. OS/2 Warp Server

   ___ Switch to the console prompt, type down, press Enter, and power down the computer.

   b. Linux

   ___ Switch to the Workplace Shell GUI and click Shutdown.

   c. Windows Server 2008

---

2. **True or False? One way to verify a NOS installation is to ping the newly set up server from another computer.**

   ___ True

   ___ False

---

3. **True or False? Using the proper shutdown procedure for a NOS can help prevent data corruption.**

   ___ True

   ___ False

---

4. **True or False? Any peripheral connected to the main server is automatically accessible to all users.**

   ___ True

   ___ False

5. **You've been asked to help set up a dedicated remote access server for the company. What external peripheral devices would you install on this server?**

   a) Printer

   b) Drive array

   c) Modem subsystem

   d) UPS

TOPIC B

Install System Monitoring Agents and Service Tools

You are familiar with the installation of a NOS and configuring some of the user management and resource management features of the NOS. Most NOSs also provide some built-in management features that can be used to monitor the performance and functioning of various components of the network domain. In this topic, you'll examine some common service and monitoring utilities, and install one of them.

Installing system monitoring agents and service tools helps you to monitor the performance of various components of the network domain. The reports generated by system monitoring tools in response to each event taking place on the network are an important source of information for detecting the cause of any faults in the server setup. Also, in the absence of these features, the user or administrator has to monitor the network resources manually, a task that may become tiring and inefficient if the number of users are very large.

Server Management

Most NOSs, and some server-class computers, ship with several utilities designed specifically for managing the server and the network. These utilities include backup software, system monitors, and event or error logs. Some servers even ship with a hardware management layer that enables users to monitor and troubleshoot hardware problems, whether or not a NOS is installed or running. In addition, many third-party tools and utilities are also available.

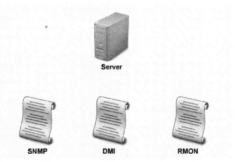

Figure 6-3: The various server management protocols used by a NOS.

When the TCP/IP protocol stack is installed on an IP-based network, some management protocols are automatically installed.

Management Protocol	Description
SNMP	Stands for Simple Network Management Protocol. SNMP Managers (or management systems) request information from SNMP Agents regarding current configuration, network activity, and performance statistics. This information is stored in a Management Information Base (MIB) on each host (or Agent). Agents can send alarms or traps to the Manager when certain conditions occur, such as network errors or when network traffic exceeds a set threshold value.

Management Protocol	Description
DMI	Stands for Desktop Management Interface. This protocol provides a bi-directional path to interrogate all hardware and software components in a host. When a computer is DMI-enabled, you can monitor the hardware and software configuration from a central station in the network. A background agent runs on DMI-enabled computers, so whenever you use a management console to query the agent, the agent returns the requested data in a Management Information File (MIF) or activates a MIF routine, if that was part of the query. Although DMI is a complete management system, it can coexist with SNMP and other management protocols using the MIF information to satisfy queries from SNMP Managers.
RMON	Stands for Remote Monitoring. This is an extension to SNMP and is intended to provide additional functionality over and above that provided by standard SNMP. While SNMP requires the SNMP Manager to request information from SNMP Agents, RMON is more proactive and provides for enhanced monitoring of network traffic. RMON uses probes to provide information about network traffic that might not otherwise get reported to the management system, particularly for network segments that don't have a direct connection to the management console.

System-Monitoring Tools and Utilities

Although each NOS provides the SNMP protocol and system monitoring agents, the user may normally be required to purchase the management console software separately to fully implement SNMP, DMI, and RMON.

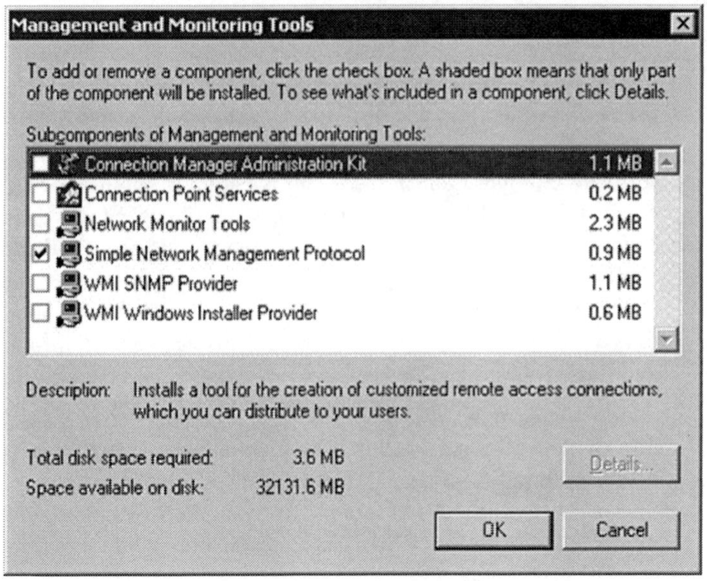

Figure 6-4: The various system monitoring tools in Windows Server 2008 operating system.

Examples of Management Tools and Utilities

Some of these products include HP's OpenView, Cabletron's Spectrum, Nortel/Bay Networks' Optivity, Tivoli NetView, Seagate ManageExec, LANDesk Server Manager, Red Hat Network, Google's Chrome, and Novell's ZENworks for servers.

System Monitoring and Service Tools and Utilities

The following table lists a few of the built-in system monitoring and service tools and utilities for each of the major NOSs. Refer to your NOS documentation for a more complete listing.

NOS	Tool	Description
Windows NT Server	Systems Management Server	Part of the BackOffice suite, SMS enables you to manage hardware and software inventories, automated software distribution, remote systems, and applications.
	Event Viewer	Enables you to monitor the events recorded in the Application, Security, and System logs.
	Network Monitor	Enables you to view information about the LAN holding the NT Server by capturing, filtering, and displaying packets sent to the server over the LAN.
	Performance Monitor	Enables you to track many counters and settings on the server, and on other servers on the same network. Four views are available: Alert, Log, Chart, and Report.
	WinMSD	Enables you to gather diagnostic information from an NT server. Categories include Version, System, Display, Drives, Memory, Services, Resources, Environment, and Network.

NOS	Tool	Description
Windows 2000 Server and Windows Server 2003	Microsoft Management Console	Central point for using various consoles such as Event Viewer, Network Monitor, Disk Defragmenter, etc.
Windows Server 2008	Server Manager	The management console feature is known as Server Manager in Windows Server 2008.
Novell OES2	MONITOR.NLM	Enables you to view dozens of performance statistics for a NetWare server. You can view server statistics and activity, RAM and processor usage, and set values for server parameters.
	NetWare Management Portal (Novell OES2)	A browser-based management tool that enables you to monitor and manage NetWare servers from any TCP/IP client with a web browser. Other features include the ability to check the general health status of the server; view the status and memory usage of all loaded modules; view information about all hardware adapters, hardware resources, and processor data; and monitor the health of various server processes and resources.
	config command	Enables you to view the configuration of all network parameters for the server, including configuration for each NIC in the server.
	display servers command	Lists all IPX servers as well as all services advertised by the SAP protocol, such as file and print services, NDS (tree information), Storage Management (backup) Services, and any services for SQL servers. It also displays the metrics to reach them from the local server. Because display servers show information about so many services, many servers will be listed twice (or more), depending on what services the server provides.
	display networks command	Lists all the IPX external network numbers recognized by the NetWare server's internal router and the metrics to reach them from the local server.
	protocol command	Enables you to see all of the network protocols running on the local server, along with the frame type.
UNIX	ifconfig command	Enables you to view communication information for each network interface. You can also use this command to configure network interfaces.
	statnet command	Provides an instant, dynamic snapshot of network traffic conditions, but has no way of producing trend or cumulative data.
	ps command	Shows a detailed list of all processes currently running on the server.
	top command	Displays system information in real time.
	free command	Displays free RAM and virtual memory.
	df command	Displays information about the hard disk, such as free space and partition information.

NOS	Tool	Description
Linux	`ifconfig` command	Enables you to view communication information for each network interface. You can also use this command to configure network interfaces.
	`ps` command	Shows a detailed list of all processes currently running on the server.
	`top` command	Displays system information in real time.
	`free` command	Displays free RAM and virtual memory.
	`df` command	Displays information about the hard disk, such as free space and partition information.
	`linuxconfig` command	A system-wide configuration tool that exists for Red Hat Linux and many other Linux distributions.

Event Logs

Event logs are files generated by the NOS to record the events that have taken place in the server or the domain network. There are five types of events recorded in the log files.

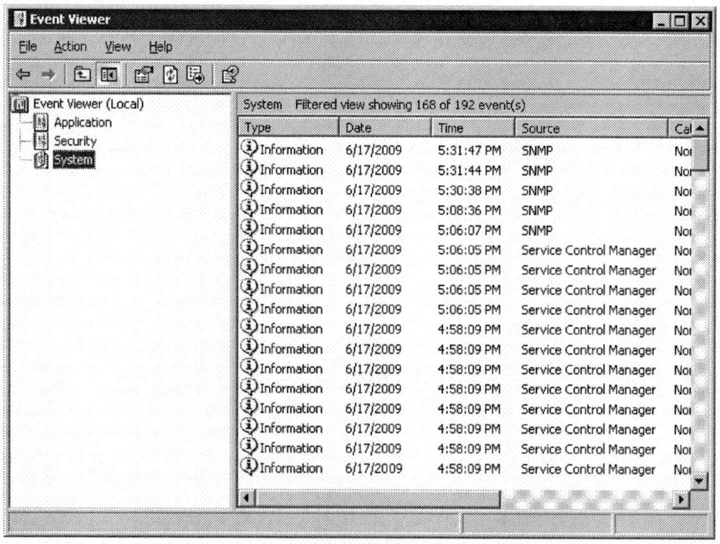

Figure 6-5: The Windows Event Viewer displaying the reported events.

Event Type	Description
Information	Infrequent and moderately significant events describing the successful operations of major services. For example, a database program that loads successfully might log an Information event.
Warning	Events that aren't necessarily significant but might indicate possible future problems. For example, a warning event might be logged if disk space is low.

Event Type	Description
Error	Events with highest significance of all types, such as loss of data or functions. For example, an error event might be logged if a service didn't load when the server was booted.
Success audit	Audited security access attempts that were successful. For example, a user's successful attempt to log on to the system might be logged as a success audit event.
Failure audit	Audited security access attempts that failed. For example, if a user tried to access the server and failed, the attempt might be logged as a failure audit event.

Different NOSs may have different types of log files.

NOS	Description
Novell OES2	NetWare log files include the console log (SYS:\ETC\CONSOLE.LOG), the abend log (SYS:\SYSTEM\ABEND.LOG), and the server and volume logs (SYS:\SYSTEM\SYS$LOG.ERR and SYS:\SYSTEM\VOL$LOG.ERR). ● The console.log is a copy of everything—error messages and other system information that were displayed on the server console during that session. (Console logging isn't enabled by default, but you can enable it.) ● The abend.log is a recording of any abnormal ends or abends on a NetWare server, along with other information that can help you determine the abend's cause. ● The server.log file is a text file containing all system messages and alerts displayed on the server console. ● The volume.log file is a text file containing all messages and alerts pertaining to the server volume. You should view these files periodically to see what kinds of errors your server is incurring. Novell OES2 security violations are also recorded in the SYS$LOG.ERR file. Check this file daily if you're concerned about security at your site.

NOS	Description
Windows	Windows log files include the system, security, and application logs. You can display the contents of these log files by using the Windows Event Viewer. Each event log entry contains a header, a description of the event (based on the event type), and optionally, additional data.

- The system.log is similar to the NetWare SYS$LOG.ERR file in that it records system messages and alerts; however, it focuses on three main types of events: Information, Warning, and Error. For example, the failure of a driver or other system component to load during server startup is recorded in the system log.

- The security.log records security events. This log helps track changes to the security system and identifies any attempts to breach security. It's also used for system-wide auditing. The types of events logged in this file are Success Audit and Failure Audit. The security log can contain valid and invalid logon attempts as well as events related to resource use, such as creating, opening, or deleting files or other objects.

- The application.log contains events logged by applications. Event types logged in the application log include Information, Warning, and Error. For example, a database program might record a file error in the application log. Application developers decide which events to monitor. Application logs often contain additional data generated by the application that was the source of the event record. Because the data appears in hexadecimal format, you'll probably need the assistance of a support technician who's familiar with the source application to be able to interpret the data.

 Operating systems allow you to filter log events and define the size of the event log files.

Event Icons

Each type of event on a Windows server has a corresponding icon associated with it and includes fields like Time, Source, Category, Event, User, and Computer, so you can tell when an event occurred, which process caused the event, the event category (used primarily in the security log), which user—if any—initiated the process, and which computer the event occurred on.

Wake-on-LAN

Jointly developed by Intel and IBM, *Wake-on-LAN* technology lets users to remotely access and update their network computers any time of the day. This is done by issuing a special trigger packet over the network to a computer.

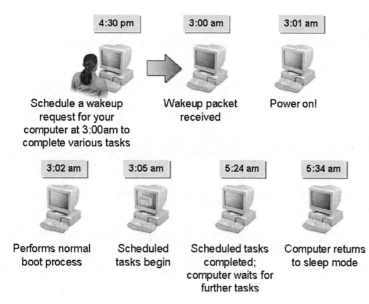

Figure 6-6: A LAN using the wake-on LAN technology.

Remote Alerts

Definition:

A *remote alert* is a message that apprises you of a problem when your operating system is in the sleep mode, hasn't booted yet, or freezes up. Remote alerts are extremely helpful because they can minimize the effects of problems on your system. You can configure remote alerts to be triggered by any common (but serious) computer problem, such as a wrong password, an open chassis, or a critical component failure, or by exceeded thresholds, such as the fan speed and internal temperature.

Example:

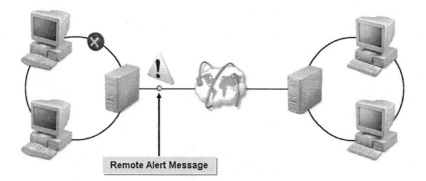

Figure 6-7: Remote alerts are used to indicate faults in the network.

NOS Default Remote Alert

Systems sometimes come with remote alert capability already installed that you can either disable or enable them. Sometimes it's in the form of software that you need to install on your server.

Catastrophic Events

Remote alert is an excellent mechanism for reporting potential show-stopping problems, but unfortunately not all of them will function in the midst of a catastrophic event. Most remote alert capabilities are useless when the computer is in the middle of a disaster.

How to Enable SNMP on a Server Computer

Procedure Reference: Enable the SNMP Feature on the Windows Server 2008 NOS

To enable the SNMP feature in a server running on Windows Server 2008 operating system:

1. Open the **Server Manager** window.

2. In the **Features Summary** section, click the **Add features** link to open **Add Features Wizard.**

3. On the **Select Features** page, in the **Features** list, scroll down and check the **SNMP services** check box.

4. On the **Confirm Installation Selection** page, click **Install** and on the **Installation Results** page, verify that the **Installation succeeded** message is displayed.

5. Close all the open windows and dialog boxes.

Procedure Reference: View Event Logs in Windows Server 2008

To view the event logs in Windows Server 2008:

1. Choose **Start→Administrative Tools→Event Viewer**.

2. Expand **Windows Logs** and select **System** to open the **System Event Log** list.

3. In the right pane of the **Event Viewer**, verify that all events related to the system are listed in the reverse chronological order.

4. Double-click the most recent SNMP event and in the **Event Properties** message box, view its description.

5. Close all the open windows.

Configure SNMP for Novell OES2

SNMP configuration varies according to the operating system running on the server. To configure SNMP for Novell OES 2:

1. At the console prompt, load INETCFG.

2. If necessary, transfer settings from the startup files.

    a. Choose **Yes** to transfer LAN drivers, protocols, and remote access commands.

    b. When prompted, reboot the server.

    c. Reload INETCFG.

3. Choose **Manage Configuration→Configure SNMP Parameters.**

4. Configure the **Monitor Community** information.

    a. Set the **Monitor State** to the appropriate setting.

    • **Any Community May Read**

    • **Leave As Default Setting**

    • **No Community May Read**

- **Specified Community May Read**

b. If necessary, change the **Monitor Community Name.**

c. Press **Esc** to return to the **Configure SNMP Parameters** menu.

5. Configure the **Control Community** information.

a. Set the **Control State** to the appropriate setting.

- **Any Community May Read**
- **Leave As Default Setting**
- **No Community May Read**
- **Specified Community May Read**

b. If necessary, change the **Control Community Name.**

c. Press **Esc** to return to the **Configure SNMP Parameters** menu.

6. Configure the **Trap Community** information.

a. Set the **Monitor State** to the appropriate setting.

- **Do Not Send Traps**
- **Leave As Default Setting**
- **Send Traps To Specified Community**

b. If necessary, change the **Trap Community Name.**

c. Press **Esc** to return to the **Configure SNMP Parameters** menu.

7. Press **Esc** to return to the **Manage Configuration** menu.

8. When prompted, choose **Yes** to save changes.

9. Press **Esc** to return to the **Internetworking Configuration** menu.

10. Choose **Protocols→TCP/IP→SNMP Manager Table.**

- To add SNMP trap destinations, press **Insert**, enter the destinations, and press **Esc.**
- To modify SNMP trap destinations, press **Enter**, modify the destinations, and press **Esc.**
- To delete SNMP trap destinations, press **Delete**, and then press **Esc.**

11. To return to the **TCP/IP** menu, press **Esc.**

12. When prompted to save changes, choose **Yes.**

13. Press **Esc** twice to return to the **Internetworking Configuration** menu.

14. Choose **Reinitialize System**, press **Esc**, and choose **Yes.**

Configure SNMP on Linux with the snmpconf Utility

SNMP configuration varies according to the operating system running on the server. For instance, using the snmpconf command with the -g and basic_setup arguments enables you to start configuring SNMP by answering a series of questions. To configure SNMP on Linux versions that use net-snmp:

1. Verify that net-snmp is installed on the system.

2. At a command prompt, enter snmpconf -g basic_setup.

3. When prompted to configure the information returned in the system MIB group, press **Enter** to accept the default of **Yes.**

4. When prompted, enter the physical location of the system.

5. When prompted, enter the name and contact information for the contact person.

6. When prompted to set the value of the **sysServices.0 OID**, type n and press **Enter** to accept the default values.

7. When prompted, specify whether or not you want to allow read-write user access. If read-write user access is not necessary, type n, press **Enter** and proceed to the next step.

   a. Press **Enter** to accept the default of **Yes.**

   b. Enter the read-write user name.

   c. Enter the minimum security level for the read-write user.

   d. If necessary, enter the OID associated with the read-write user.

   e. When prompted, add other read-write users, or proceed to the next section of the configuration utility.

      ● If you do not need to add any other read-write users, type n and press **Enter**.

      ● If you need to add other read-write users, press **Enter** and enter the user name, security level, and OID information. Repeat as needed to include all read-write users.

8. When prompted, specify whether or not you want to allow read-only user access. If read-only user access is not necessary, type n, press **Enter** and proceed to the next step.

   a. Press **Enter** to accept the default of **Yes.**

   b. Enter the read-only user name.

   c. Enter the minimum security level for the read-only user.

   d. If necessary, enter the OID associated with the read-only user.

   e. When prompted, add other read-only users, or proceed to the next section of the configuration utility.

      ● If you do not need to add any other read-only users, type n and press **Enter.**

      ● If you need to add other read-only users, press **Enter** and enter the user name, security level, and OID information. Repeat as needed to include all read-only users.

9. When prompted, specify whether or not you want to allow read-write community access. If read-write community access is not necessary, type n, press **Enter** and proceed to the next step.

   a. Press **Enter** to accept the default of **Yes.**

   b. Enter the read-write community name.

   c. Enter the host name or IP address to accept this community name from or press **Enter** to include all hosts or addresses.

   d. If necessary, enter the OID associated with the read-write community.

   e. When prompted, add other read-write communities or proceed to the next section of the configuration utility.

      ● If you do not need to add any other read-write communities, type n and press **Enter.**

      ● If you need to add other read-write communities, press **Enter** and enter the community name, host names or IP addresses, and OID information. Repeat as needed to include all read-write communities.

10. When prompted, specify whether or not you want to allow read-only community access. If read-only community access is not necessary, type n, press **Enter** and proceed to the next step.

    a.   Press **Enter** to accept the default of **Yes.**

    b.   Enter the read-only community name.

    c.   Enter the host name or IP address from which to accept this community name, or press **Enter** to include all hosts or addresses.

    d.   If necessary, enter the OID associated with the read-only community.

    e.   When prompted, add other read-only communities, or proceed to the next section of the configuration utility.

        ●   If you do not need to add any other read-only communities, type n and press **Enter.**

        ●   If you need to add other read-only communities, press **Enter** and enter the community name, host names or IP addresses, and OID information. Repeat as needed to include all read-only communities.

11. When prompted that the snmpd.conf file was written, copy the file to the proper location, such as /usr/local/share/snmp.

12. If necessary, set up SNMP users by using the command `snmpusm create user clonefrom-user`. See the man pages for complete instructions on using this command.

13. To implement the changes, at the command prompt, enter `service snmpd restart`.

ACTIVITY 6-5
Enabling SNMP on the Server

> There is a simulated version of this activity available on the CD-ROM shipped with this course. You can run this simulation on any Windows computer to review the activity after class, or as an alternative to performing the activity as a group in class. The activity simulation can be launched either directly from the CD-ROM by clicking the Interactives link and navigating to the appropriate one, or from the installed data file location by opening the C:\ServerPlus\Data\Simulations\Lesson 6\6-5 folder and double-clicking the executable Enabling SNMP on the Server_guided.exe file.

Before You Begin:
If any of the computer gets locked due to inactivity, press **Ctrl+Alt+Delete** and enter the password to unlock it.

Scenario:
In this activity, you will enable the SNMP feature on your server.

What You Do	How You Do It
1. Open the **Add Features Wizard** and start the installation of SNMP.	a. On the **taskbar**, click the **Server Manager** icon.
	b. In the **Server Manager** window, in the right pane, scroll down and in the **Features Summary** section, click the **Add Features** link to open **Add Features Wizard.**
	c. On the **Select Features** page, in the **Features** list box, scroll down and check the **SNMP Services** check box to install SNMP service and SNMP WMI features and then click **Next.**
	d. On the **Confirm Installation Selections** page, click **Install.**

2. Verify the installation and close the window.

    a. On the **Installation Results** page, verify that the **Installation succeeded** message is displayed.

    b. Click **Close** to close the **Add Features Wizard** dialog box.

    c. Close the **Server Manager** window.

ACTIVITY 6-6
Viewing Event Logs

 There is a simulated version of this activity available on the CD-ROM shipped with this course. You can run this simulation on any Windows computer to review the activity after class, or as an alternative to performing the activity as a group in class. The activity simulation can be launched either directly from the CD-ROM by clicking the Interactives link and navigating to the appropriate one, or from the installed data file location by opening the C:\ServerPlus\Data\Simulations\Lesson 6\6-6 folder and double-clicking the executable Viewing Event Logs_guided.exe file.

Before You Begin:

If any of the computer gets locked due to inactivity, press **Ctrl+Alt+Delete** and enter the password to unlock it.

Scenario:

In this activity, you will view the event logs for any events that might have been reported.

What You Do	How You Do It
Server Computer	
1. Open **Event Viewer** and view the system event log.	a. Choose **Start→Administrative Tools→ Event Viewer**.
	b. In the **Event Viewer** window, in the left pane, expand **Windows Logs** and select **System**.
	c. In the middle pane of the **Event Viewer**, verify that recent events related to the system are listed in the reverse chronological order.
	d. Double-click the SNMP event and in the **Event Properties - Event 1001, SNMP** message box, view its description.

You can scroll down the list and verify that an event corresponding to the successful installation of SNMP service in the previous activity has been logged in the event log. You can also verify the time when the event was logged.

     e. Click **Close** to close the **Event Properties - Event 1001, SNMP** message box.

     f. Close the **Event Viewer** window.

2. **Which event type is of the highest significance to the user?**

    a) Information

    b) Warning

    c) Error

    d) Success audit

3. **Which log files are present in Windows operating systems?**

    a) system.log

    b) console.log

    c) security.log

    d) application.log

TOPIC C
Server Configuration Documentation

You are familiar with the basics of installing and configuring a NOS on the server. The last step in server configuration is to document all information related to the hardware and software configuration for future use. In this topic, you'll identify the various types of information that should be included in a server's documentation.

Proper documentation can be a priceless asset for the troubleshooter. Searching for configuration related information at the time of servicing is a waste of time. Striking a balance between recording information beforehand and rediscovering the information when you need it eases both the creation and use of server documentation.

Server Documentation

The documentation related to a server's configuration is specific to each organization or user. Generally, a server supporting a large network requires more documentation.

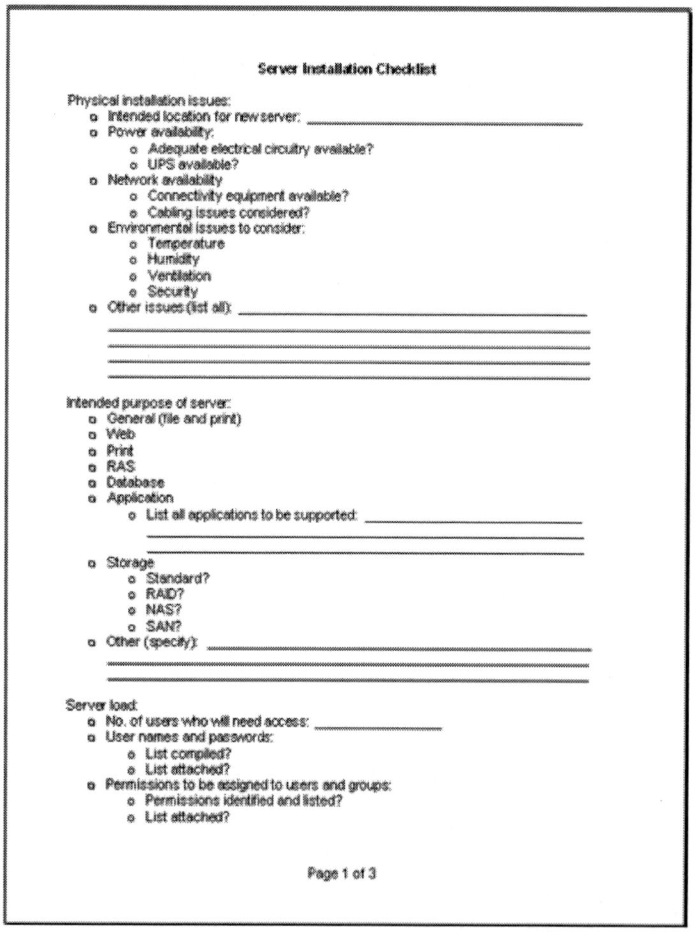

Figure 6-8: The general documentation for a server.

Server Documentation Type	Description
High-priority server documentation	It includes all the documentation that is frequently required by the administrators. • Server name and location • Server brand, model, and hardware configuration information • Network operating system type, version, and serial number information • Network configuration information, such as the server's IP addresses and subnet masks, gateways, DNS information, and protocols
Low-priority server documentation	It includes all the documentation that is not used frequently. • Warranty information of the product and expiration dates for the warranty agreement • Asset management documentation consisting of service tags and serial numbers for each component • Manufacturer or technical-support phone numbers or service providers' phone numbers

Gathering Server Information

There are software packages available that will query your devices for much of the information you need. You can also print the server configuration files as part of your information-gathering routine. Once you have all of the information, consider creating a log book, in a three-ring binder, to hold the information you gathered. The contents should be arranged logically; maybe you could divide the information into different server and network categories. Each server on a network should have its own log book, conveniently located near the server or the management station, and updated as needed to provide an accurate description of the server.

 Although it might be somewhat convenient to keep the server information on a computer, would you be able to access it if the network is down? The use of a log book would provide a documented version of the information.

Documentation Best Practices

However you decide to organize it, your log book should contain not only configuration information but also a complete record of problems encountered and their solutions. Also, consider including information describing any preventative maintenance performed on the server. Either with the server documentation or separately, you should also record pertinent network information, such as cabling diagrams and topology maps, to aid you in determining if a reported problem is due to the server itself or due to the network or segment it resides on.

Documentation Storage

It's a good idea to store the hardware and software documentation nearby, so that you can access it easily when the need arises. A separate copy of the log book should be stored and maintained off-site for disaster recovery purposes.

Problem-History Information

Problem-history information will be most helpful if it's included in the log book in the same location as the device it's referring to. For example, including records of the problems and resolutions encountered with a server immediately following the server's configuration information makes it easier to review the history of problems you've faced with that server, and you can also review its configuration by turning to only one section of your book.

Server Management Plan

A server management plan is a plan that is used as a road map for monitoring and servicing both OS-dependent and OS-independent server components efficiently. A server management plan includes procedures for managing software installation, availability of service providers, change requirements, security requirements, and remote management. Server management plans also identify the person or persons responsible for carrying out each management task.

In-Band and Out-of-Band Management

Server management plans should also outline the means by which the servers can be managed. In-band management refers to server management tasks that are accomplished through live production network connections and pathways, while out-of-band (OOB) management refers to server management tasks that are accomplished without using the production network. Managing a server from your cubicle via a wireless connection to the LAN is an example of in-band management.

Examples of OOB management include direct connection to the server via a crossover cable or a console connection, or the use of an additional network card configured with an IP address that is not on the organizational LAN.

In-band management primarily provides ease of use, while OOB management provides fault-tolerance. If a switch or even the entire network fails, you will still be able to manage the server, if you have included OOB management strategies in your server management plan.

Documentation of Server Management Plans

Once information has been captured in the form of a server management plan, the plan is implemented by developing quantifiable performance expectations and by collecting and documenting baseline statistics. It is a good practice to regularly document the performance statistics and compare the server event logs with the baseline expectations.

Server Component	Baseline Expectations	Before the Upgrade	After the Upgrade
CPU Usage	70%	80%	50%
Disk Space Usage	90%	95%	60%
Memory Usage	70%	80%	50%

Figure 6-9: A sample report collected for server management plan.

ACTIVITY 6-7
Documenting the Server Configuration

Scenario:

In this activity, you will examine the common practices used for documenting server configuration.

---

1. **Which information could be considered for high-priority server documentation?**

   a) IP address

   b) Warranty information

   c) Phone list

   d) NOS version

   e) Hardware configuration

---

2. **Your company's server documentation practices require a copy of the server management plan to be included with each server's documentation. What management-related documentation should also be included?**

   a) Hardware manuals

   b) Server baseline information

   c) BIOS information

   d) Support phone numbers

---

3. **True or False? It is a good practice to maintain more than one copy of server documentation.**

   ___ True

   ___ False

---

4. **True or False? It is essential to have a description of the various problems encountered and their solutions in the logs.**

   ___ True

   ___ False

Lesson 6 Follow-up

In this lesson, you installed and configured server software. A proper configuration is essential to set up a reliable machine that can be easily managed and maintained by network administrators and hardware specialists.

1. **What types of peripheral devices have you implemented to enhance the functions and services of your current network environment?**

2. **What types of system monitoring agents might be required in your network environment?**

7 | Examining the Issues in Upgrading Server Components

Lesson Time: 2 hour(s)

Lesson Objectives:

In this lesson, you will examine the issues in upgrading server components.

You will:

- Examine the issues that should be included in the upgrade checklist.
- Examine the issues in upgrading server hardware and collect server performance data.
- Examine server software upgrades.

Introduction

You are familiar with configuring the server hardware and software. Even under the strictest maintenance planning and attention, server hardware and software will experience complications, or worse, complete failures. In other cases, you may need to upgrade a component to provide improved functionality or additional services. In this lesson, you will prepare yourself for such situations by examining the issues in upgrading server hardware and software.

The server infrastructure needs to be upgraded from time to time as users needs change. Upgrading the server hardware and software is an important job carried out by a server technician. Hardware and software upgrades enable you to provide improved functionality and additional network services to users without completely replacing expensive servers.

This lesson covers all or part of the following CompTIA Server+ (2009) certification objectives:

- Topic C:
  - Objective 1.7: Install, update and configure appropriate firmware.

TOPIC A
Examine an Upgrade Checklist

In this topic, you will examine issues associated with the upgrade of server hardware and software components. Because the task of upgrading server hardware or software requires careful planning, a typical first step is to have a checklist that can guide you during the upgrade. In this topic, you will examine the various issues that should be included on upgrade checklists.

While upgrading the network infrastructure, server professionals may need to upgrade or replace some components of the server. Adding hardware and software to an existing server will have different ramifications than when adding them while the server is standalone. Documenting these issues on an upgrade checklist provides a standard framework for future upgrades.

Upgrade Checklists

An upgrade checklist helps users and administrators to upgrade server components. This checklist:

- Provides a visual reminder of the steps needed to complete a task.
- Helps prevent errors during an upgrade.
- Helps develop a consistent method of implementation.
- Makes it easier to train other users to perform an upgrade.
- Provides more information relating to upgrading a server.

Basic Upgrade Checklist Items

Upgrading a server involves a series of steps.

 Before adding or replacing hardware or software on a server, it is best practice to back up all data on that server so that the data can be restored in case of a failed upgrade.

Step	Description
Find up-to-date software components	Even if you are upgrading server hardware, you should find the most up-to-date software components. This includes device drivers, NOS updates, and other software. Check the hardware and software manufacturers' websites for updates to download.

Step	Description
Research the upgraded components	Research the component you're upgrading by reviewing any documentation or instructions that shipped with the component. Search for related FAQs and technical documents with the information on streamlining the upgrade process. Discuss potential problems that you could run into by performing the upgrade in question. Don't forget to look for specific upgrade checklists that might be provided by the hardware or software manufacturer. As with hardware installations on a new server, make sure that any hardware you're planning to add to the server is supported by both the server and the NOS.
Test the upgrade in a non-production environment	This is especially important when you're upgrading software because sometimes the upgrade can cause issues with other software or hardware. If the upgrade is one that will be rolled out to many servers on the network, such as a NOS update, you should also consider running a pilot implementation after the non-production test, but before rolling out the upgrade across the network. For instance, if you have a Windows server that is accessed only by the IT personnel, you could install a NOS update and have the IT group use the server as they normally would, to see if they encounter any issues that might adversely affect the network if the update was implemented on every Windows server.

Step	Description
Schedule the necessary downtime	Discuss with the affected departments or personnel to schedule the necessary downtime to be able to perform the upgrade. This may take some negotiation, particularly if mission-critical applications or functions will be affected by the downtime. Try to balance the needs of the users and the company with the need for the upgrade.
Perform and test the upgrade	Make sure that you follow ESD precautions and other best practices, such as backing up the data on the server to be upgraded, as well as any others described in the information you researched earlier in the process. When you've completed the upgrade, verify that the server and the network recognize the upgrade and that the upgraded components work as expected. This should be fairly straightforward, if you tested and piloted the upgrade as described above. Also check the server event logs for errors.
Revisit the upgrade after a short time	Review the operation of the server after the upgrade has been in place for a short time. Also, make sure that every time you change a server or network component, you create a new baseline for that server.
Document the upgrade	Include this information with the server documentation. Be sure to include a completed copy of the upgrade checklist, along with any comments, problems, and solutions you encountered during the upgrade process. As with all other forms of server documentation, the more information you include, the more helpful that information will be if there is any trouble with that server or component.

Checklist Customization

As you develop the upgrade checklists, include anything that you feel is important or might be forgotten. For instance, some people might make following ESD precautions an entirely separate step in the process, to stress the importance of it.

ACTIVITY 7-1
Examining the Upgrade Checklist

Scenario:

In this activity, you will examine the upgrade checklist.

---

1. **What are the benefits of using upgrade checklists?**

   a) They act as a visual reminder. ✓

   b) They ensure consistent methodology across the organization.

   c) They improve server performance.

   d) They act as a training tool. ✓

---

2. **You have been assigned to perform a hardware upgrade. What types of software might you need to accomplish this assignment?**

   a) None. It's a hardware upgrade.

   b) Device drivers

   c) NOS updates

   d) User applications

---

3. **What types of information should always be documented with each upgrade that you perform?**

   a) A completed upgrade checklist.

   b) A description of problems encountered and their solutions.

   c) Data relating to return on investment (ROI) resulting from the upgrade.

   d) An updated server baseline.

---

4. **You need to upgrade a mission-critical database application that is installed on several servers across the network. You decide to test the implementation on some servers in a non production environment. What should you do before you implement the upgrade?**

   a) Baseline the performance of each server in the test bed.

   b) Research issues and guidelines that can have an impact on the upgrade's success.

   c) Nothing. Testing the upgrade in a non-production environment is sufficient preparation.

   d) Schedule downtime.

TOPIC B

Examine the Issues in Upgrading Server Hardware

You are familiar with the issues to be included in a hardware upgrade checklist. Once these issues are accounted for, then the next logical step is to perform the upgrade. In this topic, you will examine the issues with adding or replacing server hardware.

Because the server requirements of an organization are bound to change as time progresses, no hardware configuration lasts forever. A major part of the server specialist's job function is to replace hardware that has either failed or has been targeted for upgrade or replacement. Knowing the various issues related to upgrading the hardware will help you to proceed in an effective manner.

Issues in Processor Upgrade

When replacing or adding a CPU to a server, you need to consider a few points aside from those mentioned in the upgrade checklist. You must:

- Verify that the new CPU is compatible with the server's system board and chipset.
- Check the processor stepping, CPU speed, and available cache.
- Upgrade or modify the BIOS so that the new processor is properly recognized by the system.
- Ensure that the case, heat sink, and cooling fan provide proper ventilation.
- Ensure that the server processor is not overclocked.

Issues in Hard Drive Upgrade

Similar to replacing or adding a CPU to a server, replacing the hard drives of a server requires you to consider a few points, too. For instance, you must:

- Make sure that the hard-disk drives to be added are of the right type.
- Double check the termination and cabling needs, especially for SCSI and IDE/ATA drives.
- Verify the Serial ATA's connection to Windows computers by restarting the computer.
- Ensure that the new drives added to RAID systems are of the same brand as the existing drives in the array.
- Integrate the new drives into the storage solution and make it available to the NOS.
- Verify that the RAID controller can support additions.

RAID and Operating System Partitions

When you are upgrading hard drives, be sure you have a complete understanding of the disk configurations. The NOS may only see one or two logical partitions while, in actuality, RAID is writing data to partitions on several physical drives.

Issues in Memory Hardware Upgrade

In addition to the general upgrade checklist items, there are a few issues that must be taken care of when upgrading the memory modules of a server. You must:

- Verify that both the hardware and NOS will support additional RAM or memory.
- Make sure that the RAM you plan to add has been validated by the hardware manufacturer.
- Make sure that the RAM sticks in the memory bank are compatible with the hardware being used.
- Configure the BIOS to optimize the server and make good use of the additional memory.

Memory Pins and Pairings

Following are the differences between memory pins:

- SIMMs have 72 pins and must be installed in pairs.
- DIMMs have 168 pins and can be installed individually.
- RIMMs have 184 pins and up to three RIMMs can be installed on a direct RAMBUS channel.

Issues in Upgrading Adapters and Peripheral Devices

Adapters and peripheral devices that might require upgrades include NICs, SCSI cards, RAID controllers, modems, KVM devices, and removable media devices.

Device Issue	Description
Implications to consider	Consider the implications of adding adapters and peripherals to an existing system. In some cases, adding equipment requires additional power and other resources that can adversely affect overall system performance.
Proper system resources	Make sure that the server has the proper system resources available for the adapter you want to install. System resources include physical expansion slots, IRQs, and DMAs. Keep in mind, though, that most server-class computers have more than 16 IRQs available, and that IRQ routing can help prevent IRQ conflicts.
Installing the adapter	Make sure that you install the adapter into a slot of matching size. Even though it's possible to use a 64-bit card in a 32-bit slot, you will not get the expected performance from the adapter. And using a 32-bit adapter in a 64-bit slot can crash every slot in the group.

Device Issue	Description
Voltage (signaling) level	Make sure that the voltage (signaling) level of any new PCI card matches the voltage level of the PCI chipset. PCI chipsets can be 3.3V or 5V. PCI cards are keyed so that you can't accidentally insert a 3.3 V card into a 5 V slot, but some cards are designed to support both voltage levels. These cards can fit into either type of connector and select the correct voltage by using special Voltage Input/Output (VIO) pins.
Balancing the expansion cards	When possible, balance expansion cards across all available buses to help avoid unnecessary bus saturation. Remember, with PCI, the system bandwidth depends on the transfer widths supported and the transfer speed of the bus.
Upgrading data storage	For any adapter or peripheral upgrades that deal with data storage, make sure that you back up any data stored on the server.
For RAID configurations	For RAID configurations, consider the potential effects of changing a RAID controller before you attempt the upgrade. In some instances, the array might need to be rebuilt or reconfigured if a different controller is used.

Maximum and Sustained Throughput

The formula for calculating the maximum bus throughput is ((bus width of target device)/8)*(maximum bus speed). The following table shows the basic calculations for 32-bit and 64-bit transfers on 33 MHz and 66 MHz buses.

 The bus width of a device indicates how many bits per cycle it can transfer. You can divide this number by eight to get the number of bytes per cycle.

Device Width (bits)	Bus Speed (MHz)	Calculation	Maximum Throughput (MB/s)
32	33	(32/8)*33	132
32	66	(32/8)*66	264
64	33	(64/8)*33	264
64	66	(64/8)*66	528

Maximum throughput is sometimes referred to as burst rate or maximum bandwidth, or the highest speed at which you can push data across the bus. This rate can usually be maintained for only a short period of time. Sustained throughput is the highest constant data-transfer rate for a device, from the device into its buffer.

To maximize your investment in adapters, you need to compare the combined sustained throughput of all devices on a bus channel to the maximum throughput for the device. For instance, a 32-bit, two-channel SCSI controller that supports 100 MB/s on each channel supports a total of 200 MB/s. On a 33 MHz PCI bus, the possible sustained burst rate of 200 MB/s is limited by the maximum throughput of the PCI bus, so both the maximum and sustained throughput for this device is 132 MB/s. Adding another adapter to this bus would further decrease the sustained throughput for the SCSI controller. On a 66 MHz bus, however, the maximum throughput is 264 MB/s and the sustained throughput is 200 MB/s. Adding another adapter to this bus might not affect the sustained throughput for the SCSI controller; for instance, a 100 Mbps, 32-bit, 66 MHz NIC added to the bus would have a sustained throughput of 12.5 MB/s, which would not adversely affect the SCSI controller's throughput.

Issues in Upgrading a UPS

You may decide to replace a hot-swappable battery in the UPS or replace the entire unit. In any of these cases, upgrading a UPS involves a series of steps.

 Some vendor websites provide online tools that can help you determine the proper upgrade strategy for your needs.

Step	Description
Determining the current capabilities of the UPS	Identify physical and load requirements, as well as support for features such as hot-swappable batteries and Smart Cabling. You should be able to get this information from your server documentation set.
Determining any changes to the system or the environment	Identify any changes in physical or load requirements that would have an effect on the scope of the upgrade. For instance, if there are very few modifications to the original server hardware and the UPS is only a few years old, the upgrade might be as simple as replacing the battery.
Identifying the need for new or enhanced features	If you want to take advantage of new features, or provide support for additional devices, you need to verify that your UPS will support the changes. For example, to provide support for Smart Cabling (where sensors identify power problems and automatically send signals that assist devices in making graceful shutdowns), you might need to upgrade the UPS's firmware and other management tools such as MIBs and management cards, or you might need to completely replace the unit.
Determining the effect of the proposed upgrade	Any modification that can't be hot-swapped will likely require the server to be shut down and will need to be scheduled. This necessary downtime makes having a UPS with a hot-swappable battery tremendously valuable. To dispose of old batteries, some companies sell replacement batteries in a reusable container so that you can ship the old ones to a recycling center or back to the manufacturer.

Reasons for an Upgrade

Reasons for an upgrade may include growth in the amount of equipment supported by the UPS, the need to replace an older battery, or the addition of new features. Because of the variety of reasons for upgrading, and the different ways to upgrade, it's imperative to identify the scope of the upgrade before you do anything else.

Need of Creating Baselines

Network administrators and server technicians often record the performance data of various server components under normal operating conditions in a baseline. The baselines document the current performance level of the server components and provide a quantitative basis for identifying abnormal or unacceptable performance. They also reveal the bottlenecks that may be impeding system performance, and provide evidence for upgrading systems to improve performance.

The success of an upgrade can be verified by comparing the baseline performance data of various server components before and after the upgrade. A successful upgrade always results in better performance. The set of objects or components selected for baselining is known as the *data collector set* and each performance parameter associated with an object is known as a performance *counter*. For example, the object CPU can have performance counters such as CPU speed and CPU utilization.

The Baseline Process

Creating a baseline is a cyclical process.

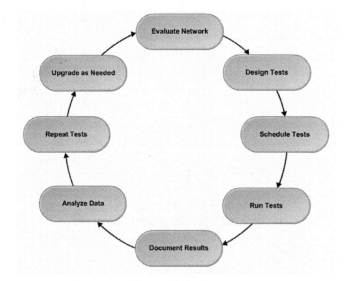

Figure 7-1: *The various steps involved in the baseline process.*

Step	Description
Evaluate network	To decide what statistics to measure, evaluate the network's purpose. You will monitor differently on a network that primarily provides file access than you would on one that hosts web servers.

Step	Description
Design tests	Develop a suite of tests that reveals the network's performance level. Make the tests consistent and yield scalable results, speed times, percentages, and other ratings. Avoid tests that do not show improvement or degradation.
Schedule tests	Determine when to run the tests. The tests should include a sampling of different network usage levels, including peak and off-peak usages, and should be run over a period of time to present a realistic profile.
Run tests	Run the tests.
Document results	Document the test results. Record the data in a way that can be saved and compared with future tests.
Analyze data	Analyze the data to identify *bottlenecks*, which are parts of the system that perform poorly compared to other components and reduce overall system performance.
Repeat tests	Repeat the tests at regular intervals or when network performance seems low. If the performance data compares unfavorably to the baseline, try to identify the cause and troubleshoot the problem.
Upgrade as needed	On an ongoing basis, upgrade or reconfigure components to remove bottlenecks, and then repeat the tests to establish new baseline values.

Customizing the Baseline

The number, type, and frequency of tests performed and recorded in the baseline will vary depending upon the systems and the needs of the organization. The organization must also decide how often to establish a new baseline to reflect current performance.

Baseline Logging

Typically, you will record baseline measurements to a log file that you can review later, rather than examining the measurements in real time. Most performance or network monitoring systems enable you to save log data. For example, in Windows Server 2008, the Reliability and Performance Monitor enables you to save each capture to a log, and gives you the option to record data directly to log format.

How to Collect Server Performance Data

Procedure Reference: Create a Data Collector Set for Collecting Performance Related Data of a Server in Windows Server 2008

To create a data collector set and collect the performance related statistics of a server :

1. Choose **Start→Administrative Tools→Reliability and Performance Monitor** to open the **Reliability and Performance Monitor** window.

2. In the **Reliability and Performance Monitor** window, expand **Data Collector Sets.**

3. Right-click **User Defined** and select **New→Data Collector Set** and in the **Name** text box, type the name of the data collector set being defined.

4. Select a location for storing the data collector set and verify that the data collector set is displayed under the **User Defined** option.

5. Configure the properties of the data collector set to include only the required parameters or performance counters by removing all the unnecessary performance counters and save the changes.

6. Right-click the data collector set's icon and select **Start** to start the data collection.

7. Open the folder containing the data collector set and double click the **Performance Counter** to view the performance statistics data collected at regular intervals of time.

ACTIVITY 7-2
Collecting Data for Baselining

There is a simulated version of this activity available on the CD-ROM shipped with this course. You can run this simulation on any Windows computer to review the activity after class, or as an alternative to performing the activity as a group in class. The activity simulation can be launched either directly from the CD-ROM by clicking the Interactives link and navigating to the appropriate one, or from the installed data file location by opening the C:\ServerPlus\Data\Simulations\Lesson 7\7-2 folder and double-clicking the executable Collecting Data for Baselining_guided.exe file.

Before You Begin:
If any of the computer gets locked due to inactivity, press **Ctrl+Alt+Delete** and enter the password to unlock it.

Scenario:
You are planning to upgrade your server, and your manager has asked you to collect the baseline data for the physical disk utilization and memory utilization on the departmental server before and after the upgrade. You decide to create a data collector set named baseline to collect the current performance data related to only these two parameters before performing the upgrade.

What You Do	How You Do It
Server Computer	
1. Create a user defined data collector set.	a. Choose **Start→Administrative Tools→Reliability and Performance Monitor** to open the **Reliability and Performance Monitor** window.
	b. Verify that the statistics for CPU, physical disk, network, and memory are displayed by default.
	c. In the left pane of the **Reliability and Performance Monitor** window, expand **Data Collector Sets.**
	d. Right-click **User Defined** and choose **New→Data Collector Set.**
	e. In the **Create new Data Collector Set** dialog box, in the **Name** text box, type *baseline* to name the data collector set as baseline.
	f. Verify that **Create from a template (Recommended)** option is selected by default and click **Next.**
	g. In the **Which template would you like to use?** page, in the **Template Data Collector Set** list box, verify that the **System Performance** option is selected by default and click **Next.**
	h. In the **Where would you like the data to be saved?** page, click **Browse**, and in the **Browse For Folder** dialog box, select the **Admin** folder and click **OK.**
	i. Verify that the **Root directory** is set to **C:\PerfLogs\Admin** and click **Next.**
	j. In the **Create the data collector set?** page, verify that the **Save and close** option is selected by default and click **Finish** to close the **Create new Data Collector Set** dialog box.
	k. Verify that the newly created baseline data collector set is displayed in the right pane of the **Reliability and Performance Monitor** window.

Server Computer

2. Choose the performance counters to be viewed in the output.

   a. In the **Reliability and Performance Monitor** window, in the right pane, double-click **baseline.**

   b. Double-click **Performance Counter** to open the **Performance Counter Properties** dialog box.

   c. In the **Performance counters** list box, verify that all the performance counter options are displayed by default.

   d. Verify that the **\Process(*)*** option is selected by default and click **Remove** to remove the data related to processing from the output of the log file.

   e. Similarly remove all other performance counters except **\PhysicalDisk(*)*** and **\Memory*.**

   f. Click **Apply** and then click **OK.**

Server Computer

3. View the output file.

    a. In the **Reliability and Performance Monitor** window, in the left pane, right-click **baseline** and choose **Start** to start collecting the data.

    b. Minimize the **Reliability and Performance Monitor** window.

    c. Choose **Start→Computer** and in the **Computer** window, double-click **Local Disk (C:).**

    d. In the **Local Disk (C:)** window, double-click the **PerfLogs** folder and in the **PerfLogs** window, double-click the **Admin** folder.

    e. Double-click the folder with the latest date and time to view the **Performance Counter** icon.

    f. Double-click the **Performance Counter** icon to view the data related to the physical disk and memory.

    g. Observe the graph indicating the data related to the utilization of memory and physical disk space on the server.

    h. Close all open windows.

    i. On the task bar, right-click the **Reliability and Performance Monitor** window and choose **Close.**

DISCOVERY ACTIVITY 7-3
Discussing the Issues Related to Upgrading Hardware

Scenario:
In this activity, you will discuss the issues that you might face while adding or replacing server hardware.

1. One of the processors in a multiprocessor server appears to be failing, so you want to replace it immediately. What compatibility issues do you face?

    a) Stepping

    b) CPU speed

    c) Cache size

    d) External ventilation

2. True or False? Before upgrading RAM with additional capacity, it is recommended to test its compatibility with the older version.

    ___ True

    ___ False

3. Your office has recently experienced several lengthy power outages during business hours. During a couple of these outages, the UPS battery was completely drained. What UPS component could you upgrade to minimize downtime and data loss?

    a) User application management software

    b) Battery

    c) Cabling

    d) NOS

4. A departmental server contains a RAID 5 array with eight 73 GB SCSI drives and one 73 GB hot spare. The controller supports up to 15 hard drives. The department has grown dramatically and now needs this array to hold twice as much data. You decide to replace the existing drives with identical 146 GB drives. What issues should you consider?

    a) Termination and cabling

    b) Brand compatibility

    c) Master/slave reconfiguration

    d) Array reconfiguration

TOPIC C
Examine the Issues in Upgrading Server Software

In the previous topic, you described the issues in adding and replacing server hardware. However, hardware isn't the only thing that can be upgraded to improve a server. In this topic, you will examine the issues related to upgrading the server software.

Upgrading server software is just as much a part of a server technician's job as upgrading hardware. Because a single fault in the server may lead to disruption of services to clients, it is essential to ensure that all upgrades are carried out in a well planned manner. Upgrading the software on a server requires good knowledge of the various issues that can arise during the upgrade and their possible solutions.

Reasons to Upgrade the BIOS and Firmware

There are a few reasons why you should consider upgrading the BIOS and firmware. The reasons include:

● To provide support for new hardware, such as a large hard drive or removable storage device.
● To fix bugs that prevent the operating system from installing or running properly.
● To enable advanced Plug-and-Play or advanced power management features.

Implications of a Failed BIOS and Firmware Upgrade

The temptation to upgrade the BIOS and firmware simply because a newer revision is available should be avoided. Upgrading the system BIOS or other firmware can be damaging to your server if it is not done correctly. If you improperly flash the system BIOS, or if the flash process is interrupted by a power failure, or even if you use the wrong BIOS image to flash the system BIOS, you can corrupt the BIOS chip so that the system will no longer boot. Often, your recovery options will be limited, but they should be listed on the manufacturer's support website.

Issues in Upgrading the BIOS and Firmware

There can be more than one BIOS in a server-class computer. The system BIOS is the one that includes the bootstrap routine, while video and RAID controllers, and even hard drives, can have their associated BIOS. A server manufacturer may add or modify the standard BIOS and firmware features to support unique capabilities, or to fit the particular requirements of their product lines. Therefore, the Original Equipment Manufacturer (OEM) is the best source for general assistance and information on BIOS and firmware upgrades. OEMs often package these updates into self-installing applications that can help reduce installation problems. Several third-party developers may also offer BIOS and firmware upgrades, which can be helpful if the OEM is no longer supporting the system board or other component.

BIOS Versions

Each BIOS has a serial and version number, which you'll need to know to determine if you need an upgrade, and if you do, which upgrade you should apply. The identification numbers of some BIOS contain information about the supported chipset and the manufacturer. This information is displayed at the bottom of the screen after power on and during memory count. Depending upon the system, you can press the Pause key to read and record the ID number, the BIOS date, and the version.

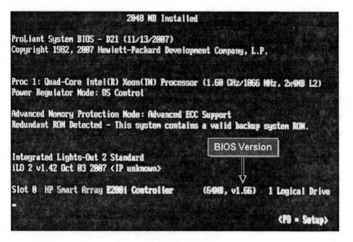

```
                        2048 MB Installed

ProLiant System BIOS - D21 (11/13/2007)
Copyright 1982, 2007 Hewlett-Packard Development Company, L.P.


Proc 1: Quad-Core Intel(R) Xeon(TM) Processor (1.60 GHz/1066 MHz, 2x4MB L2)
Power Regulator Mode: OS Control

Advanced Memory Protection Mode: Advanced ECC Support
Redundant ROM Detected - This system contains a valid backup system ROM.


                                         ┌──────────────┐
                                         │ BIOS Version │
Integrated Lights-Out 2 Standard         └──────────────┘
iLO 2 v1.42 Oct 03 2007 <IP unknown>            │
                                                ▼
Slot 0  HP Smart Array E200i Controller     (64MB, v1.66)   1 Logical Drive
-

                                                       <F9 = Setup>
```

Figure 7-2: A BIOS screen displaying the BIOS version.

Version Information

On other systems, you might need to enter the BIOS setup program to access version information. Record the BIOS ID string exactly as it appears on your screen. Then use this information to search for possible upgrades on the manufacturer's or other websites. In some instances, you can also use NOS utilities to check BIOS and other firmware levels.

Printing BIOS Information

You can also send BIOS information to the printer using the Print Screen key.

NOS Upgrade

As with the other types of software upgrades, upgrading the NOS can provide additional functionality or support for new products, in addition to solving problems that have been identified by the NOS developer.

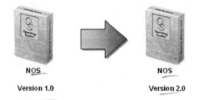

NOS   NOS
Version 1.0   Version 2.0

Figure 7-3: Upgrading a NOS to the latest version provides additional functionality.

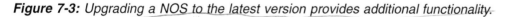

NOS Updates

It doesn't matter if they're called hotfixes, patches, service packs, support packs, or updates, the main idea behind NOS updates is the same — changing parts of the core operating system code or other code that was supplied with the original NOS.

Each NOS supplier has its own way of packaging and delivering updates. Consult the NOS manufacturer's website for specific information pertinent to your NOS, and for information that can help you decide if a particular update is needed for your server environment.

Device Driver Upgrade

Hardware manufacturers often provide updated device drivers to solve known problems or to increase performance and functionality. Ensuring that the server is using the most up-to-date drivers for the hardware installed on it can help prevent many problems from affecting its performance and reliability. Corrupt drivers are often a reason why you should update your server's device drivers.

Figure 7-4: Upgrading a device driver to the latest version enhances the performance of the hardware.

Upgrading System Monitoring Agents and Service Tools

When a server or other hardware manufacturer provides management and service software for a system, it's likely that this software will need to be upgraded occasionally, similar to the NOS and device drivers. Periodically consult the websites for updates to tools and utilities that you use often. In addition, if you upgrade a hardware component that is being managed by a system-monitoring agent that uses the SNMP or the DMI protocol, you will probably also need to upgrade MIBs or MIFs.

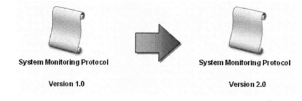

Figure 7-5: Upgrading the system monitoring protocol to the latest version leads to better performance.

Intelligent Platform Management Interface

Another upgrade that you might need to consider is the upgrade from IPMI version 1.5 to IPMI version 2.0. Intelligent Platform Management Interface (IPMI) is an instrumentation interface developed by Intel to provide a common interface for various types of server hardware platforms and management solutions. It provides interoperable, extensible, and scalable Plug-and-Play management of server hardware and monitoring instruments. Version 1.0 was the original specification released in 1998, version 1.5 was released in 2001, and version 2.0 was released in 2005. For detailed information about IPMI, consult the IPMI website **www.intel.com/design/servers/ipmi/ipmi.htm**.

How to Upgrade the Server Software

Procedure Reference: Upgrade the Server Software

To upgrade the server software:

1. Back up all data on the server onto an external hard disk to compensate for any loss of data during failed upgrade attempts. Get or keep copies of old device drivers that can be reinstalled in case the upgrade needs to be rolled back.

2. Obtain the latest version of software or update patch from the vendor. Some vendors may allow the upgrade software or patches to be downloaded through Internet.

3. Follow the on-screen instructions for installing the update.

4. If necessary, allow the server to restart after the upgrade.

5. Monitor the performance of the server to test whether the update was successful or not.

Procedure Reference: Deploy Upgrades in the Network

To deploy upgrades in the network environment:

1. Install the upgrades in a test bed consisting of only few client machines and the server.

2. Collect feedback from the clients connected in the test bed and assess the performance of upgraded hardware or software.

3. If the feedback is satisfactory, create an upgrade plan for adding all the client machines to the upgraded environment.

4. Request the required downtime from the clients.

5. Connect all the client machines to the upgraded server.

Procedure Reference: View the BIOS Firmware Version on Windows Operating Systems

To view the BIOS firmware version on Windows operating systems:

1. Open the **Start Search** text box or **Run** dialog box.

2. Type **msinfo32.exe** and press **Enter**.

3. In the **System Information** window, observe the information related to the BIOS version.

4. Close the **System Information** window.

ACTIVITY 7-4

Discussing the Issues in Upgrading Server Software

 There is a simulated version of this activity available on the CD-ROM shipped with this course. You can run this simulation on any Windows computer to review the activity after class, or as an alternative to performing the activity as a group in class. The activity simulation can be launched either directly from the CD-ROM by clicking the Interactives link and navigating to the appropriate one, or from the installed data file location by opening the C:\ServerPlus\Data\Simulations\Lesson 7\7-4 folder and double-clicking the executable Discussing the Issues in Upgrading Server Software_guided.exe file.

This activity can be performed on the client systems running Windows Vista or Windows XP as well by following the PR steps.

Before You Begin:

If any of the computer gets locked due to inactivity, press **Ctrl+Alt+Delete** and enter the password to unlock it.

Scenario:

In this activity, you will check the BIOS version and discuss the issues related to server software upgrade.

What You Do	How You Do It
1. View the BIOS level information of the server.	a. On the task bar, click **Start** and in the **Start Search** text box, click and type **msinfo32.exe** and press **Enter.**
	b. In the **System Information** window, observe the details of the BIOS version and date.
	c. Close the **System Information** window.

2. **True or False? Each time you receive a notice that there is a BIOS upgrade for a server's system board, you should immediately implement the upgrade.**

___ True

___ False

3. **What are the reasons to upgrade device drivers?**

   a) To solve known hardware problems or problems with corrupted driver files.

   b) To increase the performance and functionality of peripherals.

   c) To avoid flashing the BIOS.

   d) To increase NIC throughput.

4. **True or False? While upgrading a device driver, it is advisable to retain a copy of the old device driver.**

   __ True

   __ False

5. **True or False? A server computer can have only a single BIOS.**

   __ True

   __ False

Lesson 7 Follow-up

In this lesson, you examined the issues in upgrading server hardware and software. Upgrades provide improved functionality and services without needing to purchase additional server hardware or software.

1. **What hardware components do you need to upgrade or replace in your network environment?**

2. **What are the various software updates that you might need to upgrade your server?**

8 | Examining Servers in an IT Environment

Lesson Time: 1 hour(s), 30 minutes

Lesson Objectives:

In this lesson, you will identify some of the industry's best practices for deploying a server and the various strategies of securing, accessing, and remotely managing the server hardware.

You will:

● Identify some of the industry's best practices for installing, maintaining, and upgrading a server.

● Describe the strategies for physically securing the server and implement remote access to the server.

Introduction

You are familiar with the installation and upgrade of server components. A few of the industry defined best practices are followed widely for deploying a server in the IT environment. In this lesson, you will identify some of the industry's best practices for deploying a server and the various strategies of securing, accessing, and remotely managing the server hardware.

Because the maintenance of server components may sometimes adversely impact the services provided to end users, it is important to ensure that all changes to the server are implemented according to the industry's best practices. Network administrators and server specialists are also responsible for ensuring the physical security of the server hardware and the information it contains. Therefore, knowing the various methods of securing and accessing the server hardware is very important.

This lesson covers all or part of the following CompTIA Server+ (2009) certification objectives:

● Topic A:

■ Objective 1.7: Install, update and configure appropriate firmware.

■ Objective 4.1: Write, utilize and maintain documentation, diagrams and procedures.

■ Objective 4.2: Given a scenario, explain the purpose of the following industry best practices.

- Objective 4.3: Determine an appropriate physical environment for the server location.
- Topic B:
    - Objective 4.4: Implement and configure different methods of server access.
    - Objective 4.5: Given a scenario, classify physical security measures for a server location.

TOPIC A
Industry Best Practices for Server Installation and Maintenance

You are familiar with the installation, configuration, and upgrade of server components. There are a set of good practices to be followed while deploying a server in an IT environment. In this topic, you will learn the industry best practices for installing and maintaining a server.

Because a server is the most critical component of a network, any upgrade or maintenance of the server components may lead to disruption of essential services on the network, causing inconvenience to end users and affecting the productivity of the organization. Knowing the industry best practices for implementing a change will help the network administrators and server technicians to bring about a smooth transition with the least impact on end users.

Environmental Issues Affecting Server Hardware

If you can properly control environmental factors, such as temperature, humidity, dust, and power surge you can help ensure optimal performance and extend the life of your device.

Environmental Factor	Description
Temperature	Exposure to high temperatures can cause expansion within computing devices and compromise circuitry. High temperature can also lead to the failure of cooling systems to maintain adequate operating temperatures, leading to the overheating and failure of internal components such as the processor, video processor, and hard drive.
	Rapid changes in temperature, such as those seen when transporting a device from one climate to another, could result in condensation within the device. Devices should be allowed to come to room temperature before being powered on after a temperature change.
High humidity	Avoid operating in high humidity as condensation within the device may occur and promote corrosion. All manufacturers specify operating humidity levels. It is important to follow manufacturer operating procedures/guidelines at all times. Most systems can operate at high humidity without a problem, as long as there is no condensation (5 to 95 percent relative humidity, non-condensing).
	Be extra cautious as Electro Static Discharge (ESD) is more likely to occur in low humidity environments.

Environmental Factor	Description
Dust	Dust can be a more subtle hazard. Buildup of dust particles over time can cause problems with different types of equipment. Dust buildup causes resistance in moving parts, such as fans, drives, and printer motors. Dust buildup on circuit boards, heat sinks, and vents creates insulation that reduces heat dissipation. Dusting equipment often can prevent these types of issues. Make sure that printers and paper products are kept in a separate area from server equipment to prevent paper dust from getting into the server equipment.
Power surge	The common reasons for power surge include: lightning strikes, electrical power lines down, overload of electrical power needs. Use a power protection system such as an uninterruptible power supply (UPS) or surge suppressor to protect each server's power supply (and thus the server) from power failures, brownouts, surges, and spikes. You should also make sure that the server's power cord is plugged into a properly grounded electrical outlet. (Three-pronged outlets include grounding; never use an adapter to plug a server's power cord into a two-pronged electrical outlet.) You can buy a socket tester (available at hardware stores) to test your outlets if you suspect that they are not properly grounded.

Server Room Location and Design

There are several factors to consider when planning the location and design of the server room.

Factor	Description
Proximity	Locate the server room near the center of the building if possible. This is usually the most solid part of the building and the least vulnerable to attack. Limit access to the room by having IT employee cubes and security close to the server room. This makes it more difficult for unauthorized persons to access the server room undetected.
Waterproofing	Ensure the room has adequate waterproofing. This is necessary not only for flooding due to natural causes, but also from burst pipes and other water disasters. The server room should not have plumbing in the ceiling. The server room should not be in the basement either, as basements tend to be wet with high humidity. Locate servers at least one foot from the floor; this way if water does get into the room, you'll have a little time to rectify the situation before water gets to the systems. Also, consider installing a monitoring device to alert you to water in the room.
Fire protection	When you install fire protection, avoid the use of water-based fire extinguishers. They should be either aerosol based or dry chemical, nonreactive, and noncorrosive extinguishers such as Halon, carbon dioxide, or FM-200.

Factor	Description
ESD practices	As you design the server room, keep in mind safe ESD practices. This includes having static-resistant flooring and work surfaces. Additionally, users should follow ESD safety precautions. A difference in safe ESD practices between working on desktops and working on servers is related to standby power. You must unplug the server box from the electrical supply to disable the 5V standby for the system board.
Electrical and UPS	Monitor the electrical power to the server room. Consider using line conditioners and UPSs to prevent outages from sags, brownouts, and blackouts. The power should be as clean as possible to the server room, with no other power consumption on the circuit serving the server room. Before installing a UPS, ensure that it is sufficiently charged. Serial cables can be used to communicate with the UPS. Most network operating systems include a feature to automatically perform a clean shutdown when the UPS is activated. You can usually determine how long after the UPS kicks in before the shutdown is activated. If the power comes back on and the UPS goes back to standby, then the shutdown won't happen. Many UPSs use software to provide reporting and can be monitored from a console.
Temperature fluctuation	Carefully monitor the temperature in the server room. The room needs adequate ventilation, and should be maintained at a constant temperature. Computer components prefer a temperature in the 50s or 60s, whereas humans prefer upper 60s or low 70s for office temperatures. Try to reach a compromise between the two extremes, and maintain it as close as possible. Temperature fluctuation leads to problems such as *chip creep* and damage to components. Consider installing a monitor that will alert you when the temperature is outside of a set range.
Active monitoring	Alarms and monitors are available to alert you to many of the environmental factors. Monitor as many as possible, and be alerted to their change. Monitors can be installed for heat, humidity, fire, and power problems to name a few. Among the options you have available, the alerts can be sent via alarms, email, phone, or to pagers.

Environmental Considerations for Ceilings and Floors

The following table lists the environmental considerations for ceilings and floors.

Consideration	Description
Moisture	Check ceiling tiles for discoloration. This could indicate moisture problems that should be resolved before they cause a server room catastrophe.
Cable access	Cables are often run through these spaces leaving the floor clear. You need to be able to access the areas above the ceiling and below the floor so you can make repairs and updates as easily as possible.
Trim condition	Be sure that the trim around the tiles is kept in place and in good repair. The raised floor is usually made of special materials to reduce ESD problems and help maintain a clean operating environment for your equipment. If the trim is damaged, dirt and debris can get caught in between the tiles more easily.

Consideration	Description
Airborne particles	Try not to sweep floors, but use special non-ESD vacuum devices to remove dust and dirt. These devices use a filter to remove static from dust and are designed for this purpose. Sweeping has a tendency to make the particles airborne and easier for them to invade your systems. You should also consider using compressed air to blow dust out of and out from around systems.

Server Rack Diagrams

A *server rack diagram* is a graphical representation of the location of individual server racks, electrical power connections, and network connections of a server. Creating a rack diagram with proper labels is an essential task when you are planning to install a server and design the overall network topology. Information on the location of various server components can be useful during their upgrade, maintenance, or replacement. While rack diagrams are drawn manually, there are also a few proprietary software applications to help you draw them.

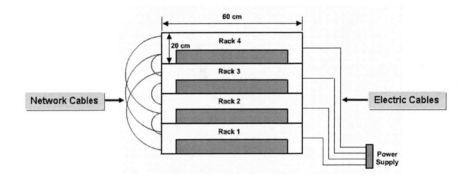

Figure 8-1: *A sample server rack diagram with labels.*

Environment Topology Diagrams

Network components can be connected in many physical topologies such as bus, star, ring, and mesh, depending on the requirements of the users. It is a good practice to have a labeled diagram for each segment of the network. Some of the details to be included in the environment topology diagram include the location of various components in the network, the length each connecting wire or cable, and the location of connecting points for the cables and wires.

Server Room Power Requirements

The server room should have provision for adequate power supply as required by the server hardware and its cooling equipment. Before installing the server, it is essential to ensure that there are a sufficient number of dedicated power supply ports with proper amperage and voltage rating. Also, the load capacity of the UPS should be checked before the installation and at regular intervals.

Documenting UPS Specifications

The documentation on UPS specifications must include the following:

● The maximum runtime for the UPS for a certain amount of electrical load.

● The maximum electrical load and the number of devices that can be supported by the UPS.

- Bypass procedures to be followed while changing the UPS. Before replacing the UPS, it is essential to provide an alternate source of power to ensure that the power supply to the server is not interrupted.

- The procedure for interfacing the UPS with the server.

- The various shutdown and monitoring procedures to be followed.

Server Room Cooling Requirements

Because servers generate a lot of heat, which can reduce the performance of electrical circuits, it is essential to provide adequate cooling and ventilation inside the server room. The cooling mechanism should conform to the industrial Heating Ventilating and Air Conditioning (HVAC) standards. In the case of rack mounted servers, it is good practice to ensure that there is sufficient space between each individual rack for proper ventilation. Also, the cooling system should be designed to provide adequate cooling to each individual rack. Besides providing cooling and ventilation, the HVAC standards require that the cooling system be capable of maintaining the humidity at an optimum level.

Server Room Cleaning

It is a good practice to schedule some time to clean the server room or the area where servers are situated. Use this time to perform the following tasks, along with any other tasks applicable to your specific situation:

- Clear away any accumulated clutter from server components and racks.

- Use compressed air or a vacuum to remove dust from both the exterior and interior of the server and related components.

- Verify that the clearances around servers and other components are maintained, and move away any objects that threaten the air flow to server components.

- Check the external and internal fans, ventilation ducts, and air-conditioning ducts for dust accumulation and clean them if required.

- Examine the cables to make sure they are ordered, properly labeled, not interfering with access to the equipment, and not placed where they pose a hazard.

Cable Management in the Server Room

Maintaining orderly network cables isn't just for aesthetic benefits. Tangled server room cables are much more likely to cause connectivity issues by coming loose due to the weight of the cables. The problem then compounds itself while doing emergency troubleshooting if you can't identify the source of the issue because of the unruly mess. Labeling the ends of cables can also be beneficial.

Generally, it is good practice to reduce the number of network cables in a server room to a bare minimum. In many cases, this can be accomplished through simple observation and a few KVM switches. Then, once you have reduced the number of cables, take extra steps to minimize the visible exposure of cables by consolidating cables into plastic conduit, cabinets, and floor runners. There are multitudes of available cabinet and rack accessories to simplify organization.

Service Level Agreements

Definition:

A *Service Level Agreement (SLA)* is a legally binding service contract in which the level of service is formally defined. SLAs are negotiated between an organization having a server and a vendor who performs the post-installation servicing and maintenance of server components.

Example:

Vendor   Service Level   Customer
Agreement

Figure 8-2: A service level agreement is negotiated between a customer and a service provider.

Common Service Level Agreements

Different organizations may have different SLAs with their vendors.

SLA	Description
Point of contact	This agreement involves assigning a system administrator and a backup system administrator for the servicing and maintenance of the organizations network.
Maintenance schedule	This agreement involves negotiating the provision of security updates, operating system updates and latest service packs, application updates, hardware updates, and client specific application updates.
Network security	This agreement involves negotiating the provision of security features for the network such as latest version of antivirus software and activation and deactivation of hardware ports as required by the organization.
Consultation	This agreement involves negotiating the provision of hardware consultation, capacity planning, consultation, and troubleshooting and problem resolution.
Migration	This agreement involves the provision for migrating user accounts and groups from the current domain to a new domain.
Hours of service	This agreement involves negotiating the hours of service. Most of the server components require 24*7 hours of service to ensure minimal disruption of services.

SLA	Description
Termination and renewal	These agreements include clauses related to termination and renewal of the contract such as notice period for the termination of service contract and charges for renewal of service agreements.
Scope of service	This agreement lists the various platforms, events, operating systems, and hardware for which the service will be provided. The vendors or service providers will not provide any service for the products other than those listed in the scope of service.

Vendor Specific Documentation

All hardware and software vendors provide some documentation, reference manuals, and links to websites containing useful information on their products. It is a good practice to go through all vendor specified information before planning to install, upgrade, or replace any hardware or software. Most of the vendor information includes details such as the power and cooling requirements for the hardware, device drivers required for the hardware, system requirements for an application, starting and shutdown procedures, upgrade procedures, upgrade patches, and compatibility with other vendors' products. Some vendors may also provide a list of third party service providers or support channels approved for servicing their products.

Change Control Procedures

A change control procedure is a sequence of steps to implement a change in the server system. Though not always necessary, change control procedures are followed to ensure a smooth transition during any upgrade or replacement of server components. Before implementing any change, the impact of the change on the organization must be determined by conducting a pilot implementation of the change on a limited number of end users and collecting their feedback.

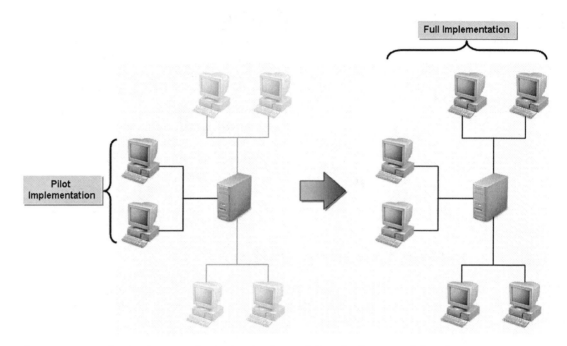

Figure 8-3: A pilot implementation helps in determining the impact of the change.

Based on the feedback, the administrator can proceed with the upgrading process by preparing a schedule. Because the server may not be available during the upgrading process and end users cannot access any of its services, the administrator must inform all clients about the required downtime. Once the upgrade is complete, the administrator must obtain feedback on the upgrade from all end users.

Local Laws and Regulations

The laws and industrial regulations related to the installation and maintenance of server equipment might vary from one region to another, and organizations located in any particular region must comply with the prevailing local laws. The scope of local laws may include maintaining certain standards for the safety of equipment and persons, purchasing or leasing hardware and software from vendors, and safe disposal of electronic waste. For example, the industrial laws in an area may allow certain electrical equipment to be imported without paying any customs duty because they are classified as customs bonded equipment. An organization must ensure that all customs bonded equipment is placed only at its registered office or warehouse and that no equipment is taken outside the premises by any employee. The local laws make it illegal to sell any customs bonded equipment to other organizations or individuals.

Disposing of a component requires you to follow all the procedures mentioned by the vendor in their documentation. The methods of disposal may vary for each component. For example, components such as used UPS batteries and silicon chips containing hazardous chemicals may have complex disposal procedures compared to circuit boards. The local laws may also permit certain equipment such as copper wires to be sold as scrap.

ACTIVITY 8-1
Discussing the Industry Best Practices for Server Installation and Maintenance

Scenario:
In this activity, you will discuss some of the best practices to be followed for installing and maintaining servers.

1. Which statements are valid for server rack diagrams?

    a) Server rack diagrams are pictorial representation of the rack locations.

    b) All server rack diagrams are prepared using software tools.

    c) Server rack diagrams help in planning the network topology.

    d) Server rack diagrams do not indicate the location of electrical power outlets.

2. Which statements are valid for service level agreements?

    a) SLAs can vary from one organization to another.

    b) SLAs may require the service provider to allot a system administrator for the organization's network.

    c) Service providers can be expected to provide services for products that are out of the scope of SLA.

    d) SLAs involve discussion on the maintenance schedule routine.

3. Which statement is not a best practice for server installation?

    a) Ensuring adequate power supply and backup for server components.

    b) Installing individual servers racks very close to each other to reduce the utilization of space.

    c) Installing cooling mechanisms for each individual rack of the server.

    d) Following all vendor specified installation procedures.

4. True or False? Administrators must inform end users about any down time required for the upgrading process.

    ___ True

    ___ False

TOPIC B
Server Security and Access Methods

You are familiar with some of the best practices of installing and deploying a server in the IT environment. Before deploying the server, it is essential to ensure that there are enough physical security measures to prevent the theft of costly hardware and data. In this topic, you will examine and employ some of the various strategies for physically securing the server and various methods of accessing the server.

Because a server may contain all sensitive information related to the organization, physically securing the server hardware is as important as securing the information on it. After all, if someone walks out the door with your server's hard disk, it could not only mean loss of data but also considerable financial loss, in terms of the lost equipment and proprietary and confidential information. Knowing the various methods of accessing the server remotely can help you to manage it from any location on your network with ease.

Need for Physical Security

Because the server contains important information, such as network configuration, security settings, data base access information, and user account information, it is essential to secure the server and its components from hackers. Though firewalls may offer protection, they are ineffective against physical theft of the server hardware. Hackers may steal hardware such as hard disks to access the data stored on them. Therefore, securing the server hardware through physical means is as important as securing the information it contains through a firewall.

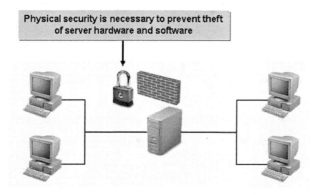

Figure 8-4: *Securing the server components through physical means is as essential as securing the information stored on it through firewalls.*

Physical Server Security

There are various methods of physically securing a server. This include:

- Locking the server room to prevent unauthorized persons from entering it. Administrators should retain the keys or access passwords and should not share them with others unless required.

- Using a door with a lock for each rack of a rack mounted server.

- Installing CCTVs inside the server room to help the administrator to monitor the activities inside the server room. The CCTVs should be installed in such a way that they capture the maximum possible view of the server room from their location with good resolution.

- Setting up mantraps that can physically trap any person trying to access the server room using unauthorized access keys or passwords. Most modern mantrap mechanisms consist of alarms that are activated whenever a person is trapped.

- Deploying adequate security personnel for securing the server room.

Server Room Locks

There are many types of locking devices to secure a server room. These include key locks, combination locks, cipher locks, swipe pads and keycards, biometrics, smart cards, and other locks. The door should also automatically close and remain locked. If the door is propped open, an alarm should sound. If you use keys, make sure you know who has a key; also, you should use a lock with keys that aren't able to be duplicated just anywhere—use ones that require special, controlled duplication.

Mantraps

Most modern mantraps consist of a small space having two sets of interlocking doors such that the first set of doors must close before the second set opens. Identification may be required for each door and possibly different measures for each door. For example, a key may open the first door, but a personal identification number entered on a number pad opens the second. Other methods of opening doors include proximity cards or biometric devices such as fingerprint readers or iris recognition scans. Certain mantraps that use deadly force or can cause serious injuries may be illegal for industrial use.

Anti-Theft Devices

There are many anti-theft devices available, each with its own set of advantages and disadvantages. Be sure to choose the right device for your environment.

Device	Description
Cable locks	Anchors are super-glued to the system and a locking steel cable is wrapped around a desk leg or other stationary object. Some systems, such as laptops, have a built-in receptacle for attaching a locking cable rather than gluing the anchors to the equipment.
Lockdown pads	A metal pad is secured to the work surface with strong adhesive or one-way screws. A lock device is fastened to the device being protected, and then the device and pad are locked together.

Device	Description
Cages	A metal box that encloses the component. Models are available with top, bottom, and side panels; others include front and/or back panels.
Alarm notifications	Devices are available to alert someone when a component is moved—possibly being stolen. Some of these devices include Ethernet cables that send an alert if the system is removed from the network; wireless transmitters attached to power cords that send an alert when the power cord is removed from the outlet or the component; and fiber-optic cables that send an alert if the cable is broken.
Other ideas	Stickers or paint that make the components unique and difficult to sell after being stolen. Lock up small components such as keyboard, mice, and portable devices in a desk or cabinet.

Access Control Devices

In addition to manual control, access to the server room can be restricted through the use of some electronic devices known as access control devices. Access control devices are linked to a centralized database and log information related to each access attempt. The information includes details such as the user ID used for gaining access, time of access, number of attempts made, and whether the attempt was successful or not.

There are many types of access control devices available.

Access Control Device	Description
RFID tags	An RFID tag can be incorporated into each component of the server for the purpose of identifying and tracking it. RFID tags emit radio waves that can be read from several meters away.
Keypad locks	These devices consist of a digital keypad that allows the user to enter the correct data required for accessing the server room. The data may include the user's name, employee number, and password. Users entering incorrect data will not be allowed to access the server.
Biometric sensors	These devices can distinguish between different persons on the basis of their fingerprints, facial features, DNA, hand and palm geometry, iris, and odor or scent. Most of the popular biometric identification devices use fingerprint scanning and retina scanning.

Access Control Device	Description
PIN pad	An access control PIN pad is an electronic device similar to the PIN pad used in a debit or smart card based transaction to input and encrypt the cardholder's PIN. The access control PIN pad allows only the users with authorized PIN number to enter the server room.

Manual Security Procedures

While it is important to keep the server room out of bounds to persons other than administrators, there may be situations where even non-administrators may require access to the server. For example, the maintenance personnel from a vendor required for replacing the UPS batteries or any other hardware. In such cases, there are security procedures to be followed to ensure the safety of the server components. Some of the widely used security procedures include limiting the access to the required personnel only, physically monitoring the tasks performed by each person at regular intervals and recording them in an access log, and limiting the access time for each person accessing the server.

Defense-in-Depth Strategy

Defense-in-depth is a security strategy in which multiple layers of physical security are used to help reduce the risk of compromising or circumventing a layer of defense mechanism. For example, an organization may choose to implement the first layer of defense to the server room by using physical locks for the outermost door; the second layer of defense by using mantraps to trap persons who manage to breach the first layer; and, the third layer of defense by adding RFID tags to each hardware component so that it can be detected while being removed from the premises.

In addition to securing physical components, the defense-in-depth strategy can be used for securing information on the organization's network. For example, an antivirus software application could be installed on each individual workstation as a second layer of defense—this is in addition to an existing virus protection feature enabled on the default gateway server.

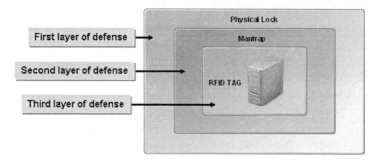

Figure 8-5: A three layer defense-in-depth security mechanism.

Levels of Importance

While you should attempt to implement as many security measures as possible, it is not always a realistic proposition. Prioritizing security measures determines which ones are the most important to your organization. Implement the highest priority ones and then, if the budget and other hindrances are removed, implement any additional security measures.

Securing Security Related Documentation

In addition to securing the server hardware, physical security should also be extended to secure any security related documentation prepared by the administrator. The security documentation might include information such as the user name and password for each individual user, the system configuration and security settings for each workstation and server, and various maintenance and access logs. Hackers might use this information to break into the network and alter the settings, thereby making the network more vulnerable to attacks.

Server Access Types

There are two types of server access methods: direct access and remote access. In direct access, the administrator accesses the server through a directly connected keyboard, video, and mouse console. In remote access, the administrator accesses the server from a remote location using a remote console. Servers located within an organization's premises are usually accessed through direct access, and servers located at remote locations—such as backup servers—are accessed using remote access.

Direct Access

Remote Access

Figure 8-6: Types of server access.

KVM Switch

Definition:

The *KVM switch* is a hardware device that allows the user or administrator to control multiple server computers from a single Keyboard, Video and Mouse (KVM) unit. Although multiple computers can be connected to the KVM, a smaller number of computers can be controlled at any given time. Modern devices have the ability to share USB devices and speakers with multiple computers. Some KVM switches also allow a single PC to be connected to multiple monitors, keyboards, and pointing devices. While not as common as the former access methods, this type of configuration is useful when the operator wants to access a single computer from more than one location.

Example:

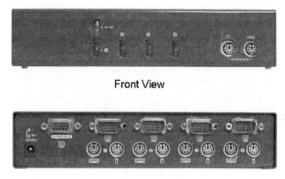

Front View

Back View

Figure 8-7: A 5-port KVM switch.

Types of KVM Switches

There are two types of KVM switches: local KVM and IP-based KVM.

KVM Device Type	Description
Local KVM	Allows users to control computers located up to 1000 feet away from the KVM console. It includes support for standard category 5 cabling between computers and users interconnected by the switch device. Category 5 based KVM device communication uses proprietary protocols across what can be considered a "closed loop" local area network infrastructure. Local KVM devices can support over 256 access points with access to over 8000 computers.
IP based KVM	Allows users to access servers located at remote locations through Internet using the IP addresses of the servers. Most of the access to remote servers is done with the help of a web browser but proprietary software can also be used for better performance. IP based KVMs are usually slower than local KVMs.

Remote Management

Remote management is a feature of NOS that allows the server hardware and its applications to be managed from any remote location on the network. To enable remote management, the server should be configured to accept management commands originating from the IP address of the remote workstation.

To enable remote connection, the operating systems of both the server and client computers should be compatible with each other and must be from the same vendor. Once the remote connection is enabled, the user or administrator can view the desktop or command prompt of the server from the remote workstation. Administrators usually configure some network ports as dedicated ports that cannot be used for any purpose other than remote access. Remote management can be used for deploying software or patches into all the remote workstations from a single server.

 The term remote management is also known as remote control.

How to Implement Remote Access

Procedure Reference: Implement Remote Access on a Windows 2008 Server

As a network administrator, you may require access to a server located remotely from your location. To set up a remote access connection between a client computer and a Windows 2008 server:

1. Configure the server's network settings and firewall settings to allow remote connections.

   a. Choose **Start,** right-click **Computer** and choose **Properties.**

   b. In the **System** window, click the **Remote Settings** link, and in the **System Properties** dialog box, select **Allow connections from computers running any version of Remote desktop (less secure).**

   c. Click **Apply** and click **OK.**

2. In the client machine, click **Start** and open the **Start Search** or **Run** text box.

3. In the **Start** or **Start Search** text box, type **mstsc** and press **Enter** to open the **Remote Access Wizard** dialog box.

4. Type the IP address of the server computer and press **Enter** to view the desktop of the server computer on the client machine.

5. From the server desktop, you can view or delete files stored on the server and shutdown or restart the server.

6. Close the remote login session and return to the client computer's desktop.

ACTIVITY 8-2

Implementing Remote Access

There is a simulated version of this activity available on the CD-ROM shipped with this course. You can run this simulation on any Windows computer to review the activity after class, or as an alternative to performing the activity as a group in class. The activity simulation can be launched either directly from the CD-ROM by clicking the Interactives link and navigating to the appropriate one, or from the installed data file location by opening the C:\ServerPlus\Data\Simulations\Lesson 8\8-2 folder and double-clicking the executable Implementing Remote Access_guided.exe file.

Before You Begin:

1. Ensure that all server and client computers in a group are connected to a common Ethernet hub using Ethernet cables.

2. Ensure that the Ethernet hub is powered on.

3. If any of the computer gets locked due to inactivity, press **Ctrl+Alt+Delete** and enter the administrator password to unlock it.

Scenario:

The network administrator requires frequent access to one of the servers located in a remote location. You have been asked to implement remote access to the server from one of the client machines located in the organization's premises.

What You Do	How You Do It
Server Computer	
1. Configure the server to facilitate remote connection.	a. On the desktop, click **Start,** right-click **Computer** and choose **Properties.**
	b. In the **System** window, click the **Remote settings** link and, in the **System Properties** dialog box, select **Allow connections from computers running any version of Remote Desktop (less secure).**
	c. In the **Remote Desktop** message box, click **OK.**
	d. In the **System Properties** dialog box, click **Apply** and click **OK.**
	e. Close the **System** window.

Client Computer

2. Access the server's desktop through the client machine.

 This step should be performed on the client computer by the students.

a. Choose **Start→Run** to open the **Run** dialog box and, in the **Open** text box, type *mstsc* and press **Enter.**

b. In the **Remote Desktop Connection** window, in the **Computer** text box, type the IP address of the server computer as *192.168.1.100* and click **Connect.**

c. In the **User name** text box, type *DEPTSRV\administrator*

d. In the **Password** text box, click and type *!Pass1234* and press **Enter** to view the desktop of the server computer's desktop.

e. Choose **Start→Computer** to open the **Computer** window of the server computer.

f. Right-click the **DVD Drive (E:)** and choose **Eject.**

g. Observe that the DVD drive tray of the server computer opens.

h. Manually close the drive tray of the server computer.

i. Close the **Computer** window of the server computer.

j. On the client computer, close the remote login session.

k. In the **Disconnect Windows session** message box, click **OK** to end the remote login session and return to your desktop.

DISCOVERY ACTIVITY 8-3

Discussing Server Room Security and Access Control Mechanisms

Scenario:

In this activity, you will discuss the issues related to server room security.

1. Which devices can be classified as biometric sensors?

   a) RFID tags

   b) Fingerprint scanners

   c) Retina scanners

   d) Keypad locks

2. Which statement is not valid for the defense-in-depth mechanism?

   a) It involves more than one layer of security around the server location.

   b) It is expensive to implement.

   c) It is impossible to break through the security layers.

   d) There is no limit on the maximum number of layers that an organization can have.

3. Which access control device emits radio waves for its detection and identification?

   a) RFID tag

   b) Keypad locks

   c) Biometric Sensors

   d) PIN pads

4. Which statements are valid for remote management of a server?

   a) Remote management is performed using KVM switches.

   b) Remote management should be enabled on both the client and server computers.

   c) It is possible to remotely manage a server running on Windows Server 2008 from a workstation running on Windows XP.

   d) It is possible to deploy some software on the workstation through remote management.

Lesson 8 Follow-up

In this lesson, you identified the various industry defined best practices of installing and maintaining server components. You also examined some methods of physically securing the server hardware and accessing the server from a remote location. This knowledge is essential for network administrators and server technicians to ensure uninterrupted and dependable service to end users.

1. **What are the various organizational practices that may be influenced by the local laws?**

2. **What are the various factors that influence the choice of a server location?**

9 | Troubleshooting Servers

Lesson Time: 4 hour(s)

Lesson Objectives:

In this lesson, you will troubleshoot servers.

You will:

● List the components of a troubleshooting process.

● Troubleshoot server hardware.

● Troubleshoot software related issues.

● Troubleshoot common network problems.

● Troubleshoot storage issues.

Introduction

You explored environmental issues surrounding servers. Despite it being in a physically secure and safe environment, every server will experience downtime at some point. In this lesson, you will identify the major issues, tools, and techniques for troubleshooting servers.

A server is not a system that can be simply rebooted in case of a problem. Troubleshooting a server is a step-by-step process. There are also several types of specialty hardware and software tools used in server maintenance and repair. In short, troubleshooting a server is a complex task that requires a systematic approach.

This lesson covers all or part of the following CompTIA A+ (2009) certification objectives:

● Topic A:

   ■ Objective 6.1: Explain troubleshooting theory and methodologies.

● Topic B:

   ■ Objective 6.2: Given a scenario, effectively troubleshoot hardware problems, selecting the appropriate tools and methods.

● Topic C:

   ■ Objective 6.3: Given a scenario, effectively troubleshoot software problems, selecting the appropriate tools and methods.

● Topic D:

   ■ Objective 6.4: Given a scenario, effectively diagnose network problems, selecting the appropriate tools and methods.

- Topic E:
    - Objective 6.5: Given a scenario, effectively trouble shoot storage problems, selecting the appropriate tools and methods.

TOPIC A

Examine the Troubleshooting Theory and Methodologies

There are various approaches to troubleshooting. You need to select a suitable troubleshooting process. In this topic, you will list the components of a troubleshooting process.

Because troubleshooting server problems is a vital part of a server technician's job, you should always use a systematic approach to problem-solving. Learning and using an effective troubleshooting process will help you to resolve problems efficiently and painlessly.

Troubleshooting a Server

Troubleshooting is the recognition, diagnosis, and resolution of problems affecting a server to restore it to its normal operation. You can troubleshoot a server in many ways, but all approaches have the same goal: solving a problem efficiently with a minimal interruption of service.

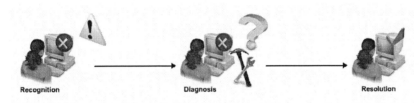

Figure 9-1: *The parameters of troubleshooting.*

Troubleshooting Model

Definition:

A *troubleshooting model* is any standardized step-by-step approach to the troubleshooting process. The model serves as a framework for correcting a problem efficiently without introducing further problems or making unnecessary modifications to the system. Models can vary in the sequence, number, and name of the steps, but all models have the same goal: to move in a methodical and repeatable manner through the troubleshooting process.

Example:

Figure 9-2: *The troubleshooting model provides a framework for correcting problems.*

Steps in the Troubleshooting Process

There are nine steps in the troubleshooting process. Of these steps, five are for establishing the cause of a problem and the remaining four for resolving the problem.

1. Gather information.

2. Identify the affected area.

3. Determine what has changed.

4. Establish a theory of the most probable cause.

5. Test the theory to determine the cause.

6. Create an action plan and solution, identifying potential effects.

7. Implement and test the solution.

8. Identify the results and effects of the solution.

9. Document the process and solution.

Standard Troubleshooting Process

Another simplified troubleshooting process that is followed across some organizations consists of four steps. These fours steps in the process can be illustrated with the example of broken network connection. The steps involved in troubleshooting the broken network connection includes:

- **Step:1 Identify symptoms**: Failure to reach remote host.

- **Step:2 Isolate the cause of the symptom**: Several possible causes for the identified symptoms include:

  - Local router is misconfigured.

  - Intermediate router is misconfigured.

  - Remote router is misconfigured.

  - No path to the remote router in the local routing table

- **Step:3 Take action**: The appropriate actions that are taken for this issue include:

  - Check the local router's configuration and edit if appropriate.

  - Troubleshoot intermediate router.

  - Troubleshoot routing protocols.

  - Identify additional possible causes.

- **Step:4 Evaluate solution**: If the problem is solved, you are done. If the problem remains or a new problem is identified, start the process over again.

Step 1: Gather Information; Identify Symptoms and Problems

To identify the symptoms and potential causes of a server problem, start by gathering as much information as you can.

- Ask the user to describe what happened. Ask open-ended questions instead of yes/no questions to get as much information as you can.

- And, look for error messages on the screen or in system and software log files.

Next, re-create the problem. A repeatable problem is easier to solve than an intermittent one.

- Have the user try the procedure again, recording all actions taken and all results received. Verify that the procedure is correct.

- Try to perform the task yourself at the user's workstation and at your workstation.

- Or, have another user try the task at the user's workstation and on an equivalent workstation.

Perform backups before making changes. Before troubleshooting the problem it is always recommended to take a backup of the current status of the system. This will enables you to restore the required data or system status incase any disaster occurs during the troubleshooting process.

While you gather the information, make a list of possible causes that could have the same symptoms.

Example: Establishing the Symptoms for a Logon Problem

For instance, if a user cannot log on to the network, have the user try once again. This time ask the user to observe exactly what happens and what is displayed onscreen. Think about the possible causes: a user who suddenly cannot log on could indicate a problem with the network cable or adapter, local DHCP server, local network connection, or authentication server.

Step 2: Identify the Affected Area

Determine if the problem is limited to one workstation, several workstations, one server, one segment, or the entire network. If only one person is experiencing a certain problem, the problem is most likely at the workstation. If groups of users are affected, the problem might lie at a part of the network or service shared by users, such as a particular software application or database, a server, the network segment, or the network configuration.

Example: Identifying the Affected Area for a Logon Problem

For instance, a logon problem can affect one or many users.

- When one user cannot log on to the network, try logging on as that user from another workstation belonging to the same group of users. If the logon is successful, start by checking the workstation's NIC and cabling, and then move on to more detailed workstation troubleshooting.

- When several users cannot log on, find out what they have in common. If all affected users use the same server, verify that the server is up and running smoothly, and check user connections and security levels. If several network segments appear to be affected, check for network address conflicts. If all users are having problems, check any components (such as servers, routers, and hubs) that they access. Also, remember to check WAN connections by verifying that stations on both sides of the WAN link can communicate; if they cannot, you will need to check the WAN hardware along with other devices between the sending and receiving stations.

- And, do not forget to check system and software logs for errors or alerts that may provide clues on what the problem is.

Step 3: Determine What Has Changed

To determine what has changed, ask questions such as:

● Were you able to do this task earlier? If this is a new task, perhaps the user needs different system permissions, or additional hardware or software.

● If you could do the task before, when did you first notice that you could not do it anymore? Try to discover what happened immediately before the problem arose, or at least pinpoint the time, since the source of the problem might be related to other changes elsewhere on the network.

● What has changed since the last time you were able to do this task? Users can give you information about events that might affect their local systems. You can help them with leading questions such as, "Did someone add something to the server?" or "Did you do something differently this time?" Be sure not to be judgmental or imply that the user is to blame; it will be harder for him to report his conditions accurately if you do so.

● Also, check all system and software log files to see if there are any records of recent activities.

Example: Determining What Has Changed for a Logon Problem

If a user cannot log on, ask him if he is aware of anything that has changed since the last log on, even if it is as simple as restarting the server that morning.

Step 4: Establish the Theory of the Most Probable Cause

To establish the theory of most probable cause, use a systematic approach. Eliminate possible causes, starting with the most obvious and simplest one and working back through other causes. Do not overlook straightforward and simple corrections that can fix a range of problems and do not cost much time or effort to try. You may find that you can resolve the issue on the spot.

Example: Selecting the Most Probable Cause for a Connectivity Problem

If a user has lost Internet connectivity, check to make sure that the network cable is plugged in and that the user's IP configuration is correct, then check the router settings or connection to the ISP.

Step 5: Test the Theory to Determine the Cause

Once you establish the most probable cause, determine the steps to resolve them. However, while troubleshooting a problem, you may find the cause of the problem is not an issue that can be resolved over the phone or at the user's desktop. It may be necessary to contact a fellow employee who has specialized knowledge, or a more senior administrator with the appropriate permissions and authorization. In these cases, the problem should be escalated to the appropriate personnel to be resolved as quickly as possible.

Example: Determining if a Connectivity Problem Needs To Be Escalated

Some users in the finance department have lost connectivity to a workgroup server. It has been determined that there are no problems with the software or hardware at the user end. Error logs on user machines indicate that there may be a configuration problem on the server side. Because the server in question contains company financial information and only a few highly trusted administrators have the ability to log onto the server, this issue will have to be escalated to one of them.

Step 6: Create an Action Plan and Solution

After you have determined the probable cause, you should create an action plan before you start making changes, detailing each step that you will take while attempting to resolve the issue. You should also make sure that you will able to restore the system to the condition it existed before the troubleshooting, in case things do not go as planned. You also need to think about how the action plan will affect the user or other aspects of the network. If you think ahead, you can help ensure that productivity does not suffer and that downtime is minimized.

Example: Implementing an Action Plan for a Workstation Problem

For example, if you are rebuilding a user's workstation, think about how this might affect the user's productivity in the interim. You might need to provide another workstation to the user, and you would need to transfer user data to a safe location before working on the old system. A rule of thumb is to back up data before working on a user's machine.

Step 7: Implement and Test the Solution

Implement the action plan step-by-step to fix the problem. If you make multiple changes at once, you will be unable to verify exactly what effect each adjustment had. Be sure to document each step, because you can lose sight of what you have tried in complex troubleshooting scenarios.

Test the solution. Make sure that the solution you have implemented actually solved the problem and did not cause any new ones. Use several options and situations to conduct your tests. For instance, try the task yourself, and then have the user try it while you observe the process, or test the workstation both before and after it is connected to the network. Sometimes, you will need to test over time to ensure that your solution is the correct one.

Example: Testing a Solution to a Switch Problem

Some users have all lost Internet connectivity, and all have their desktop workstations connected to the same switch. While the problem could be with the switch, the problem might also have been due to a faulty cable that connects the switch to a router. After replacing the cable that attaches the switch to the router, you should attempt to access the Internet from all the affected machines to check if they work fine.

Step 8: Identify the Results and Effects of the Solution

Verify that the user agrees that the problem is solved before you proceed with final documentation and closing the request. Additionally, even if the problem is solved and your solution was well thought-out and documented, there might be cascading effects elsewhere on the local system or on the network. Think about those potential effects and test for them before you close out the issue. Monitoring system and software logs throughout the testing and monitoring phase can provide additional visibility into the effects of the solution. If a major change was made, it may be advisable to continue monitoring and testing the system and network for several days or even weeks after implementing the solution.

Example: Identifying the Results for a Software Problem

If you reinstall a software application, you might find that the newly installed application makes changes that affect other applications, such as changing file associations on the system. You should have identified this potential effect before reinstalling the application and taken steps to ensure that all applications are functioning the way the user desires.

Step 9: Document the Process and Solution

Document the problem and process you used to arrive at the solution. Maintain records as part of your overall network documentation plan. Not only will this provide you with an ever-growing database of information specific to your network, but it will also be valuable reference material for use in future troubleshooting instances—especially, if the problem is specific to the organization. You might even want to create a troubleshooting template so that you can be sure that necessary information is included in all reports, and that all reports are consistent, no matter which support person completes them.

Troubleshooting Documentation

Some of the things you might want to include in a troubleshooting documentation template are:

● A description of the initial trouble call, including date, time, who is experiencing the problem, and who is reporting the problem.

● A description of the conditions surrounding the problem, including the type of server, the type of NIC, any peripherals, the desktop operating system and version, the network operating system and version, the version of any applications mentioned in the problem report, and whether or not the user was logged on when the problem occurred.

● Whether or not you could reproduce the problem consistently.

● The possible cause or causes you isolated.

● The exact issue you identified.

● The correction or corrections you formulated.

● The results of implementing each correction you tried.

● The results of testing the solution.

● Any external resources you used, such as vendor documentation, addresses for vendor and other support websites, names and phone numbers for support personnel, and names and phone numbers for third-party service providers.

ACTIVITY 9-1
Discussing the Troubleshooting Theory and Methodologies

Scenario:
In this activity, you will discuss the troubleshooting theory and methodologies.

1. **Users on the third floor cannot connect to the Internet, but they can log on to the local network. What should you check first?**

   a) Router configuration tables

   b) If viruses exist

   c) If the power cable to the hub is connected

   d) If users on other floors are having similar problems

2. **Which techniques will help you to identify an affected area for a logon problem?**

   a) Ask the user open-ended questions about the problem.

   b) Try to replicate the problem on another workstation nearby.

   c) Make a list of problems that can all cause the same symptoms.

   d) Find out if users in other parts of the building are having the same problem.

3. **A user calls to say that his server will not boot. He mentions that everything was fine until a brief power outage occurred on his floor. What stage of the troubleshooting process can this information help you with most directly?**

   a) Selecting the most probable cause.

   b) Implementing an action plan and solution, including recognizing potential effects.

   c) Documenting the solution and process.

   d) Establishing what has changed.

4. **What are the steps you will follow to identify the results and effects of a solution?**

5. **What are some of the steps you will follow in the process of implementing an action plan and solution?**

6. **A user calls the help desk and says that he cannot open a file. What are some of the questions you should ask?**

TOPIC B
Troubleshoot Server Hardware Problems

In the previous topic, you familiarized yourself with the troubleshooting process. One of the important tasks of a server technician would be to handle various types of server hardware issues and troubleshoot them. In this topic, you will explore common server hardware issues and the techniques used to troubleshoot them.

There will be time when the server's internal system components experience problems that cannot be fixed by users. As a server technician, many of the service calls that you respond to will involve troubleshooting system components. Therefore, your ability to quickly and effectively diagnose and solve the problems will be essential in maintaining the satisfaction level of the users you support.

Common Hardware Problems

There are some common problems you might encounter when troubleshooting server hardware components.

Hardware Problem	Possible Causes and Solutions
Failed POST	**Possible Causes:** Improperly seated or faulty internal components. Faulty KVM device. Improper connections. **Possible Solutions:** Visually inspect the internal hardware components and reinstall them, if required. Replace the KVM device. Visually inspect the internal components and their connections, and replace them.
Overheating of the CPU	**Possible Causes:** Failure of the CPU cooling system. Inadequate cooling of the CPU. **Possible Solutions:** Replace the existing cooling system unit. Add additional cooling units to prevent the CPU from getting overheated.

Hardware Problem	Possible Causes and Solutions
Memory failure	**Possible Causes:** Mismatched components, which may be due to the installation of incompatible memory installation. For instance, installing a non-parity memory instead of a ECC memory will result in memory failure. Improper insertion of the memory module into the slot. ESD or other power-related problems. **Possible Solutions:** Check for memory compatibility and replace the appropriate memory module. Visually inspect the memory components and replace them. Visually inspect the power supply component and its connections, and replace them.
Onboard component failure	**Possible Causes:** Improper power supply to the server onboard components. Overheating of the components due to the lack of adequate cooling system. Backplane failure, which may be due to voltage drops, installation of faulty components, or improper installation of the components on the backplane. **Possible Solutions:** Repair or replace the power supply to provide adequate power to the onboard components. Add additional cooling units to prevent the overheating of the components. Check the installation of all the components and replace the backplane, if required.
Processor failure	**Possible Cause:** Overheating of the processor. **Possible Solution:** Add more cooling devices, upgrade to more efficient devices, or clean or replace failed devices.
Power supply failure	**Possible Causes:** Electrical power lines down. UPS failure. Overload of electrical power needs. **Possible Solutions:** Visually inspect the main power supply source components and their connections and replace them if they are damaged. Check the power backup source. Remove the unnecessary components that are not currently in use.

Hardware Problem	Possible Causes and Solutions
Incorrect boot sequence	**Possible Causes:** Drive disconnected, damaged, or not recognized by the BIOS. Incorrect BIOS startup settings. **Possible Solutions:** Visually inspect and reconnect drive. Enable drive in CMOS setup utility and check startup settings.
Expansion card failure	**Possible Causes:** Third-party components or incompatible components, which is not detected by the OS. Improper installation of the expansion card. Installation of improper drivers for the expansion card. **Possible Solutions:** Replace the card with the appropriate expansion card that is compatible with system board. Visually inspect and reconnect expansion card. Install an appropriate driver for the expansion card.
OS not found	**Possible Causes:** BIOS does not detect the hard disk. The hard disk is damaged. Sector 0 of the physical hard disk drive has an incorrect Master Boot Record (MBR). **Possible Solutions:** Verify the BIOS settings and use the recovery console. Repair or replace the hard disk. Reformat the hard disk.
Hard drive failure	**Possible Causes:** Mismatched components, which may be due to the installation of different size hard disks. Hard drive is damaged. Hard drive is not configured for Master or Cable Select as appropriate to the system. Data cable is not connected or incorrectly connected to the drive. **Possible Solutions:** Ensure that the size of the hard disks is similar. Replace the hard drive. Visually inspect the hard drive and its connections, and connect them properly. Visually inspect the cables and connect them properly.

Hardware Problem	Possible Causes and Solutions
I/O failure	**Possible Cause:** Application settings stored in the registry are damaged. **Possible Solution:** Reinstall the OS.

Master Boot Record

Master Boot Record (MBR) is a small program that is read into memory and is executed after the BIOS bootup. The MBR tries to locate a bootable partition in the partition table. The boot sector of the partition is then loaded and executed. The MBR is located in the first sector of the first hard disk.

Hardware Troubleshooting Tools

Because of the complexity of server architecture, there are several types of specialty hardware tools used in server maintenance and repair.

Hardware Troubleshooting Tool	Description
Compressed air canister	A canister with a nozzle that can be aimed at components to blow dust out. This is often used when removing dust from the interior of a server. Be sure to blow the dust away from the power supply and drives. It can also be used to blow dust out of the power supply fan area, from keyboards, and from the ventilation holes on other peripherals. Use caution when working with compressed air. Read the instructions on the can and follow them carefully. Tipping the can too much, something easy to do when trying to maneuver the can into place, can cause the propellant to leave the can in liquid form and at sub-freezing temperatures. The freezing could easily damage components, particularly those which may still be hot from use. There is also the issue of the corrosiveness of the chemical damaging components later on. Also, some delicate components on the motherboard can be damaged (literally blown off the board) if used too close to a component. If you use compressed air, take the equipment to a different location, preferably outside, so that the dust does not simply disperse into the air in the work area and settle back on the server equipment or other devices.
Power supply tester or multimeter	An electronic measuring instrument that takes a wide variety of electronic measurements including voltage, current, and resistance. A multimeter also known as a volt/ohm meter, can be a handheld device for field service work or a bench-top process for in-house troubleshooting. Multimeters, like voltmeters, come in both analog and digital (DMM or DVOM) process.

Hardware Troubleshooting Tool	Description
System board tester	An electrical instrument that verifies if there is a proper flow of electrical pulses in a system board.
ESD equipment	Some people who work on server equipment never use a single piece of ESD safety equipment. They discharge themselves by touching an unpainted metal part of the server case before touching any components. In other instances, the company policy might require that you use a properly equipped ESD-free work area. The minimum equipment in this case would be a grounded wrist strap.
	Other ESD-protection equipment includes leg straps, anti-static pads to cover the work surface, and grounded floor mats to stand on. The mats contain a snap that you connect to the wrist or leg strap. Anti-static bags for storing components can also be included in an ESD toolkit. If the technician's clothing has the potential to produce static charges, an ESD smock, which covers from the waist up, can be helpful. To ensure that the ESD equipment remains effective, you should test it frequently. A minor shock that you cannot feel can compromise the ESD sensitive equipment.

ACTIVITY 9-2
Troubleshooting Server Hardware Problems

Scenario:

In this activity, you will troubleshoot server hardware issues.

1. **What are the possible causes for the 'OS not found' problem?**

   a) Data cable is not connected or incorrectly connected to the drive.

   b) The hard disk is damaged.

   c) Overheating of the processor.

   d) Sector 0 of the physical hard disk drive has an incorrect Master Boot Record (MBR).

2. **What are the main causes for onboard component failure?**

   a) Improper power supply to the server onboard components.

   b) Incorrect BIOS startup settings.

   c) Overheating of the components due to the lack of adequate cooling system.

   d) Backplane failure.

3. **Match a hardware problem to its causes.**

___	Failed POST	a.	Incompatible memory installation.
___	Overheating	b.	UPS failure.
___	Memory failure	c.	Improperly seated or faulty internal component.
___	Power failure	d.	Dust on the internal components.

4. **What is the possible cause for incorrect boot sequence?**

   a) Improper power supply to the server onboard components.

   b) Improper installation of the expansion card.

   c) Overheating of the processor.

   d) Drive disconnected, damaged, or not recognized by the BIOS.

5. **What is the application of compressed air canister?**

TOPIC C
Troubleshoot Server Software Problems

You identified the ways to troubleshoot the hardware issues of a server. Apart form hardware issues, servers also encounter problems related to the software. In this topic, you will describe the various software issues and troubleshoot them.

It would be best if you could install a system, configure it, verify it, and walk away without ever touching it again. But systems need attention. You need to look at ongoing maintenance tasks as well as resolve software problems that can, unfortunately, arise. To resolve software issues, you should have be familiar with the common software problems and also have knowledge on the software tools used for troubleshooting.

Common Software Problems

There are many software problems you might encounter while working with a server.

Software Problem	Possible Causes and Solutions
User unable to logon	**Possible Causes:** Incorrect password or improper User account Control (UAC) configuration. Improper values for the Superuser do (SUDO) command attributes. The system is not configured to a specific domain or work group. Failure of the encryption service on the system. **Possible Solutions:** Enter the correct password or reconfigure the UAC or the authentication parameters. Ensure that the correct values are entered for the SUDO command attributes. Reconfigure the system to the specific domain. Enable or configure the encryption service properly to provide the key for the encrypted password.
User cannot access resources	**Possible Causes:** Improper or insufficient permissions to access the resources. Unavailability or lack of the target system resources. **Possible Solutions:** Enable sufficient permissions to the user. Check and make sure that the resources and the sever are connected to the network.

Software Problem	Possible Causes and Solutions
Memory leak or unintentional memory consumption	**Possible Cause:** A bug in an application that prevents the application from releasing the memory when it is no longer required. **Possible Solution:** Repair / debug the application using appropriate tools or uninstall and reinstall the application.
Blue Screen of Death (BSOD) / stop	**Possible Causes:** Corruption of system files. If the OS detects an unauthorized device software, which are explicitly not permitted to be installed on systems. **Possible Solutions:** Reinstall the OS. Remove the unauthorized device software.
OS boot failure	**Possible Cause:** Corrupted boot files which may be due to the corruption of Master File Table (MFT) in the NTFS volumes. **Possible Solution:** Reinstall the OS.
Driver issues	**Possible Causes:** Incompatible driver software installation. Corrupted driver. **Possible Solution:** Install/reinstall the appropriate driver software.
Runaway process	**Possible Cause:** 100% usage of the CPU. **Possible Solutions:** Identify the application that has maximum CPU utilization and terminate the application or set a low priority to the application that utilizes maximum CPU capability.
Cannot mount drive	**Possible Cause:** Improper system shutdown. Corrupted files in hard disk. **Possible Solutions:** Ensure your system is shut down properly. Repair the corrupted files by using the checkdisk utility.

Software Problem	Possible Causes and Solutions
Cannot write to system log	**Possible Cause:** Complete usage of the event log viewer. Insufficient permissions or permissions denied to write event logs which may be due to a particular feature being disabled. **Possible Solutions:** Make a backup of the existing log files into another location and clear the log files in the event log viewer. Provide sufficient permissions to write event logs by enabling the particular feature.
Slow OS performance	**Possible Causes:** Fragmentation of the disk. Insufficient RAM capacity. Malware such as Trojans and spyware affecting the system. **Possible Solutions:** Defragment the disk. Install the additional RAM modules as per the requirement. Use an antivirus program and quarantine the virus.
Patch update failure	**Possible Causes:** Application settings stored in the registry are damaged. Enabling the firewall will restrict the user to update the software. **Possible Solutions:** Reinstall the application. Disable the firewall settings (Temporarily as required).
Service failure	**Possible Causes:** A file missing in an application. Detection of improper or incompatible drivers on the system. Corrupted file in an application due to malware. **Possible Solutions:** Reinstall the application or the missing file. Ensure that only appropriate or compatible drivers are installed on the system. Reinstall the application.
Hangs on shut down	**Possible Causes:** Misconfigured or corrupted virtual memory. Non-availability of space in the hard disk to read or write the log files during the shutdown process. High CPU utilization. **Possible Solutions:** Reconfigure the virtual memory. Remove unnecessary data from the hard disk. Kill the applications that utilizes maximum CPU capability.

Software Problem	Possible Causes and Solutions
Users cannot print	**Possible Causes:**
	Failure of print spooler.
	Failure of print server driver or services.
	Possible Solutions:
	Debug the print spooler.
	Reinstall the print server driver.

Virtual Memory

Virtual memory is extra virtual RAM that the OS creates by using a part of your hard drive storage space. When there is insufficient space in RAM, or when a program is specifically designed to use virtual memory to improve efficiency, the virtual space created in the hard disk is used as a buffer.

SUDO

The SUDO command, used in UNIX, provides a computer security feature that helps to control system access and system exploits. It prompts the user for the personal password and confirms the user request to execute a command by checking a file, called sudoers, which the system administrator configures.

Fragmentation

Fragmentation is a disk condition in which chunks of a file are scattered around the disk as noncontiguous clusters due to frequent creation, deletion, and modification of files. Fragmentation will lead to inefficient usage of the storage space. This can be corrected using the defragmentation tool.

Print Spooler

Print spooler is a program that enables a user to manage current print tasks.

Software Tools Used for Troubleshooting

There are various software tools used in troubleshooting.

Software Troubleshooting Tool	Description
Defragmentation tool	This is a useful tool on servers where a high number of transactional operations occur. The file systems can quickly become fragmented, dragging down the performance of applications running on your server. To perform a successful defrag, you should really have at least 15% free space left on your disk, so make sure you don't let critical system or data disks fill up too much or they'll be harder to maintain.

Software Troubleshooting Tool	Description
Monitoring tool	A software tool that monitors the state of services or daemons, processes, and resources on a system. The tool tracks one or more *counters,* which are individual statistics about the operation of different objects on the system, such as software processes or hardware components. Some objects can have more than one instance; for example, a system can have multiple CPUs.
	When a counter value reaches a given *threshold,* it indicates that the object of the counter may be functioning outside acceptable limits. Many operating systems include basic performance monitor tools, or you can obtain more complex third-party tools, including network monitors based on the SNMP protocol and remote monitoring systems designed to handle large clusters or server farms.
System logs	It records information, warning, or error messages generated by system components. For example, system log will show you if a driver or service has failed to load.
	It stores the error log in a non-volatile storage device and uses the log data to analyze the causes of recorded errors after the test. The system logs tool saves error logs and enables error analysis even if a remote debugging environment is not available.

ACTIVITY 9-3
Troubleshooting Software Problems

Scenario:
In this activity, you will troubleshoot software problems.

1. What are the possible causes that would not allow a user to log on to the server?

   a) Failure of the encryption service on the system.

   b) Improper User account Control (UAC) configuration.

   c) Improper or insufficient permissions to access the target resources.

   d) Unauthorized device software.

2. What are the possible causes that would hang the system while shutting it down?

   a) Nonavailability of space in the hard disk to read or write log files.

   b) Corrupted file in an application due to malware.

   c) High CPU utilization.

   d) Fragmentation of the hard disk.

3. Match a software tool to its description.

   ___ Defragmentation tool   a. It records information, warning, or error messages generated by system components.

   ___ Monitoring tool   b. It tracks one or more counters.

   ___ System logs   c. It is used on servers where a high number of transactional operations occur.

4. When a counter value reaches a given _____ , it indicates that the object of the counter may be functioning outside acceptable limits.

5. What is the possible solution for an OS boot failure?

   a) Defragment the hard disk.

   b) Repair the corrupted files by using the checkdisk utility.

   c) Take the backup of the log files and clear the event log viewer.

   d) Reinstall the OS.

TOPIC D
Troubleshoot Server Network Problems

You described how to troubleshoot software problems. Even if the hardware components and software applications are properly installed and maintained, there are chances that you may encounter a few problems related to the network. In this topic, you will troubleshoot network problems.

Network problems can arise from a variety of sources outside your control. As a server technician you will need to identify and resolve those problems efficiently. To do that, you will need a strong fundamental understanding of the tools and processes involved in network troubleshooting.

Common Network Problems

There are a few problems you might encounter in a network.

Network Problem	Possible Causes and Solutions
Internet connectivity failure	**Possible Causes:** Bad cables. Failure of the NIC card. Improper IP configuration. Failure of ISP. **Possible Solutions:** Check cables and connections and check for diagnostic LEDs on the network adapter. Replace cables, if necessary. Replace or reinstall the NIC as necessary. On the IP network, check for a missing or incorrect IP address. If the address is manually configured, this could be a data entry error; reconfigure the connection. Contact the ISP and inform them of the problem.
Email failure	**Possible Causes:** Upon enabling the port security, users will not be able to access the email port in the server. Failure of the email protocols such as SMTP or POP3. This may be due to missing files in the protocol. Misconfiguration of host files, which may be due to incorrect entry of the workgroup name in the configuration. **Possible Solutions:** Disable the port security. Reinstall the necessary protocols. Reconfigure the host files in your server by entering the correct work group name.

Network Problem	Possible Causes and Solutions
Resource unavailable	**Possible Causes:** Failure of a component in the resource. Insufficient permissions. Improper subnetting, which may be due to incorrect entry of IP addresses during the IP configuration. **Possible Solutions:** Check to make sure the network components are in working condition. Check to make sure the user has appropriate permissions. Enter the correct IP addresses and reconfigure the IP address in your server.
DHCP server misconfigured	**Possible Cause:** Improper entry of IP address scope in the DHCP configuration. **Possible Solution:** Reconfigure the DHCP protocol by entering the appropriate IP address scope.
Non-functional or unreachable domain	**Possible Causes:** Misconfigured routers or switches due to improper entry in the routing table or the switching table. Misconfiguration of DNS or DHCP protocol due to improper IP addresses and its corresponding host name. **Possible Solutions:** Reconfigure the routing table and switching table entries of the routers and switches. Reconfigure the DNS or DHCP protocol on the system.
Destination host unreachable	**Possible Causes:** Incorrect destination IP address. Bad cables. Failure of the NIC card. Improper subnetting due to invalid entry of the IP addresses that are within the subnets, or either the source or destination device has an incorrect subnet mask. **Possible Solutions:** Enter the correct destination IP address. Visually inspect and replace the cables. Replace the NIC card. Check the TCP/IP configuration and reconfigure the IP addresses and their subnet masks.

Network Problem	Possible Causes and Solutions
Unknown host	**Possible Causes:** Devices are configured to use different VLANs. Invalid value for the host parameter. Host is not available on the network. **Possible Solutions:** Reconfigure the devices under the same VLAN. Check the host name value. Check for the availability of the host on the network. If not found, configure the host to the network.
Default gateway misconfigured	**Possible Causes:** The IP address of the gateway is incorrect for the specified route. Incorrect OS route tables. **Possible Solutions:** Change the IP address of the gateway to the correct address. Reconfigure the OS route table.
Failure of service provider	**Possible Causes:** Damaged cables, power failure, or technical issues at the service providers end. **Possible Solution:** Contact the ISP to find out if there are any problems at their end. Implement alternate Internet connectivity options.
Can reach by IP not by host name	**Possible Causes:** Misconfiguration of DNS due to improper mapping of the IP addresses with their host name. Misconfigured host files due to improper entry of an IP address for the particular host name. **Possible Solutions:** Check the IP configuration settings and verify that the DNS server is running. Check the hosts file to make sure it does not contain incorrect entries.

Network Diagnostic Tools

Network diagnostic tools are applications or utilities that can help you to monitor and test the functionality of a network and its components. There are various diagnostic tools for troubleshooting network problems.

Network Diagnostic Tool	Operating System	Description
ping	Windows 2003/2008 Linux/UNIX	A TCP/IP utility that transmits a datagram to another host. If network connectivity works properly, the receiving host sends the datagram back.
ipconfig	Windows 2003/2008	A TCP/IP utility that verifies network settings and connections.
ifconfig	Linux/UNIX	A TCP/IP utility that displays current network interface configuration information and enables you to assign an IP address to a network interface.
tracert	Windows 2003/2008	A TCP/IP utility determines the route data takes to get to a particular destination. The ICMP protocol sends out Time Exceeded messages to each router to trace the route. Each time a packet is sent, the TTL value is reduced before the packet is forwarded. This allows TTL to count how many hops it is to the destination.
traceroute	Linux/UNIX	Performs the same function as that of tracert.
nslookup	Windows 2003/2008 Linux/UNIX	A DNS utility that displays the IP address of a host name, or the host name of an IP address. It gets this information by querying the appropriate name server (DNS server) on the Internet.
netstat	Windows 2003/2008	A TCP/IP utility that shows the status of each active network connection. Netstat will display statistics for both TCP and UDP, including protocol, local address, foreign address, and the TCP connection state. Because UDP is connectionless, no connection information will be shown for UDP packets.
nbtstat	Windows 2003/2008	Used to view and manage NetBIOS over TCP/IP (NetBT) status information. It can display NetBIOS name tables for both the local computer and remote computers, and also the NetBIOS name cache. With nbtstat, you can refresh the NetBIOS name cache as well as the names registered with the WINS server.
route	Windows 2003/2008	Permits manual updating of the routing table. The route command also distinguishes between routes to hosts and routes to networks by interpreting the network address of the destination variable, which can be specified either by symbolic name or numeric address.

Time To Live

Time to Live (TTL) is a numeric value that specifies how many hops or passes through routers that a packet is allowed to make before it reaches its destination. It also specifies a time limit or span in milliseconds within which a packet has to be delivered at the required destination, failing which the packet is discarded and a message sent to the originator to re-send the particular packet. TTL is specified in the packet header. Every router hop is deducted from the TTL field. When the count reaches zero, the router detecting it, discards the packet and sends a message to the originating host. The default TTL value is 30 hops.

Additional Diagnostic Tools

Although it would be impossible to list every diagnostic tool available for every server, here are some additional tools that you might find useful:

- For servers running on the Windows operating system:
  - The Device Manager utility enables you to check for device conflicts and get driver information.
  - Chkdsk (in Windows 2003/2008) utilities scan the hard drive for errors.
  - Disk Defragmenter enables you to analyze and defragment files.
  - System Monitor (in Windows Server 2003/2008) enables you to view, monitor, and record several categories of server performance.
- For servers running on UNIX and Linux operating systems:
  - The `ps` command enables you to view information about running processes.
  - The `free` command enables you to view information about memory availability and usage.
  - The `vmstat` command enables you to view statistics related to virtual memory.
  - The `df` command enables you to view information about disk free space.
  - The `du` command enables you to view information about disk usage.
  - The `lspci` command enables you to view a list of installed PCI devices.
  - The `sysdiag` utility enables you to view device information and test devices.
  - The `sysfsutils` utility enables you to manage the file system.
  - The `lsvpd` utility enables you to list the vital product data for each device.

ACTIVITY 9-4
Diagnosing Network Problems
Scenario:
In this activity, you will diagnose network problems.

---

1. **What are the possible causes for Internet connectivity failure?**

   a) Failure of the NIC card

   b) Port security being enabled

   c) Bad cables

   d) Misconfigured host files

---

2. **Match a diagnostic tool to its description.**

   ___ ping

   ___ ipconfig

   ___ tracert

   ___ nslookup

   a. Tests and displays the path that a network connection would take to a destination host.

   b. Verifies network settings and connections.

   c. Displays the IP address of a host name or the host name of an IP address.

   d. Transmits a datagram to another host.

---

3. **What are the possible solutions to resolve the destination host unreachable problem?**

   a) Visually inspect and replace the cable.

   b) Check to make sure the user has appropriate permissions.

   c) Replace the NIC card.

   d) Check the TCP/IP configuration and reconfigure the subnets.

---

4. **True or False? DNS failure or DNS misconfiguration is the possible cause for the failure of the service provider.**

   ___ True

   ___ False

TOPIC E

Troubleshoot Server Storage Device Problems

In the previous topic, you described the various networking issues and their solutions. Storage devices are particularly susceptible to wear and tear because they contain moving parts. In this topic, you will describe the various storage device problems and their resolutions.

Traditional storage devices, because they are one of the few system components that contain moving parts, are particularly susceptible to wear and tear. There is a saying that there are two types of storage devices: ones that have failed and ones that are failing. Because these devices support so many system functions, it is not always obvious that the device is the culprit. Yet storage device problems, particularly those involving hard drives, can have a truly devastating effect on a system and on a user's productivity. Therefore, being able to spot, identify, and correct storage device problems early on, before they cause data loss, will be an important skill for you as a server technician.

Common Storage Problems

There are a few common storage problems you may encounter at your workplace.

Storage Problems	Possible Causes and Solutions
Slow file access	**Possible Causes:**
	Detection of bad sectors in the hard disk.
	Insufficient space in the hard disk or in any other the storage media.
	Possible Solutions:
	Reformat the hard disk.
	Delete the unwanted files in the storage device.
OS not found	**Possible Causes:**
	Failure of the backplane.
	Failure of the drive/HBA/media controller. This occurs because the synchronization in the timing between the controller and the hard disk is unsuccessful.
	Detection of corrupted boot files or File Allocation Table (FAT).
	Possible Solutions:
	Replace the backplane
	Replace the drive/HBA/media controller.
	Reformat the hard disk.

Storage Problems	Possible Causes and Solutions
Data not available	**Possible Causes:** Failure of the drive. Improper connections. During the array rebuild process, it is not possible to avail the data because the hard disks are reconfigured and formatted. **Possible Solutions:** Replace the drive. Visually inspect the connectors and ensure that they are connected properly.
Unsuccessful backup	**Possible Causes:** Failure of the storage media. Improper or loose connections, or faulty cables. Insufficient storage space in the storage media. Usage of incompatible storage medium that is not supported by the OS. **Possible Solutions:** Visually inspect the media and repair or replace the media. Visually inspect the connectors and cables and ensure that they are connected properly. Remove the unwanted files in the storage media. Use an appropriate storage medium that is supported by the OS.
Error light	**Causes:** Hard drive has physically crashed, most probably due to RAID controller failure. RAID controller is the circuit that allows the system to communicate with the hard drive. Improper hard disk installation or improper connections to the hard disk. **Possible Solutions:** Replace the drive in the RAID array. Visually inspect and reinstall the hard disk properly.
Unable to mount the drive	**Possible Cause:** Improper disk partition. A mount utility tool mounts volumes on the virtual disk immediately after the tool successfully mounts a VHD file. Sometimes, the volume arrival notification may be delayed for a long time. In this situation, the mount utility tool stops the operation and reports an error. **Possible Solution:** Partition the disk properly using the partitioning tools. A supported hotfix is available from the respective OS vendor to fix this issue.

Storage Problems	*Possible Causes and Solutions*
Drive not available	**Possible Causes:** Improper or loose connections. Failure of backplane or hard drive. **Possible Solutions:** Visually inspect the connectors and cables ensure that they are connected properly. Replace the backplane or the hard drive.
Cannot access logical drive	**Possible Causes:** Improper disk RAID configuration. Mismatched drive, which is due to the improper configuration of the hard disk specification in the BIOS setup program. The drive overlay programs does not get loaded into memory before your server's startup system files. **Possible Solutions:** Reconfigure the RAID. Reconfigure the hard disk specifications in the BIOS setup program. Check the documentation included with your drive overlay software, or contact the hard disk manufacturer for information to access the hard disk.
Data corruption	**Possible Causes:** Improper termination of the system, which may be due to power leakage on the SCSI bus. Detection of bad sectors. The data is affected by a virus or malware. **Possible Solutions:** Ensure proper termination on the SCSI bus. Use an active terminator, instead of passive terminator. Reformat the hard disk or defragment the disk. Use an antivirus software to remove the virus.
Slow I/O performance	**Possible Causes:** Drive is too full or fragmented. The hard drive controller is too slow. An incorrect (and slower) cable was used to connect the drive. **Possible Solutions:** Delete all unneeded files. Defragment the drive. Verify and replace the hard drive cable if necessary.

Storage Problems	Possible Causes and Solutions
Restore failure	**Possible Cause:**
	Failure of the storage media due to a malware or improper handling of the backup media.
	Incomplete data backup due to faulty settings when taking a backup.
	Possible Solution:
	Either repair the affected file or perform a data recovery process to restore the data.
	Ensure that the data has been backed up properly using the right settings and procedure.
Cache failure	**Possible Causes:**
	Failure of the cache battery.
	Cache functionality turned off.
	Possible Solutions:
	Replace the cache battery.
	Manually turn on the cache.
Multiple drive failure	**Possible Cause:**
	Physical damage to more than one drive in an array.
	Improper installation of more hard disks.
	Installation of multiple drivers for a single device.
	Possible Solution:
	Replace the failed drives.
	Reinstall the hard drives.
	Install an appropriate driver for a device.

Driver Overlay Program

A drive overlay program is a program provided by third-party manufacturers to allow access to the entire capacity of your hard disk. The drive overlay program gets loaded into memory before your server's startup system files are loaded. The reasons for installing a drive overlay program includes:

- BIOS of your motherboard does not support hard disks that are larger than 528 MB.
- Your server has incompatible hard disk drives that need to be used together.

Storage Troubleshooting Tools

Apart from system logs and monitoring tools, there are a few more types of storage trouble-shooting tools.

Storage Troubleshooting Tool	Description
Disk Management	It is the primary tool you will use to optimize hard disks on your system by creating, deleting, or formatting partitions to create the most functional disk configuration. For example, you might want to break a large hard disk into one operating system partition and a data partition; when users search for files or documents, they can limit the search to the data partition only and save time.
Monitoring	Monitors storage devices such as storage arrays, tape libraries. The storage monitoring tool provides a complete view of your storage environment thereby reducing the downtime with timely detection of problems. It saves administrative time with effective reporting and escalations.
Partitioning	Divides the storage space of the hard disk into discrete partitions. Upon partitioning the disk, various files and directories are stored in different partitions. The partitioning tool prepares hard disks for installing a new operating system.
Array management	It is used to protect the data in the array disks by controlling the data access, preventing unauthorized alteration, and securely deleting data when it is no longer required. The array management tool controls the drives so that they appear as one or more virtual disk drives to the host operating software.
RAID array management	It is one of the array management tools that is confined to only manage the RAID arrays in your server.
net use	It either connects or disconnects the server from a shared resource, or allows to view the information about current server connections. This command also controls persistent network connections.
mount	All files accessible in a Unix system are arranged in one big tree. These files can be spread out over several devices. The command serves to attach the file system found on some device to the big file tree. Conversely, the umount command will detach it again.

ACTIVITY 9-5

Troubleshooting Storage Problems

Scenario:

In this activity, you will troubleshoot storage problems.

1. **If you are not able to access the logical drive, what actions should you take to resolve the problem?**

   a) Re-configure the RAID

   b) Rearrange the drives

   c) Partition the disk

   d) Replace the drive in the RAID array

2. **What are the possible solutions for slow I/O performance?**

   a) Delete all unneeded files.

   b) Reformat the hard disk.

   c) Rearrange the drives properly.

   d) Defragment the drive.

3. **Match each storage issue to their possible causes.**

   ___ Cannot access logical drive   a. Detection of corrupted boot files or File Allocation Table (FAT).

   ___ Slow file access   b. Improper termination of the system, which may be due to power leakage on the SCSI bus.

   ___ OS not found   c. Improper disk RAID configuration.

   ___ Data corruption   d. Insufficient space in the hard disk or in any other the storage media.

4. **True or False? The disk management tool optimizes hard disks on your system by creating, deleting, or formatting partitions to create the functional disk configuration.**

   ___ True

   ___ False

Lesson 9 Follow-up

In this lesson, you described the various issue that you may encounter while working with servers and the ways to fix them. Knowledge to isolate and troubleshoot the problem will enable you to provide a speedy solution for issues you encounter.

1. **What are common server hardware issues that you have encountered?**

2. **Which troubleshooting tools will you use most often at your workplace?**

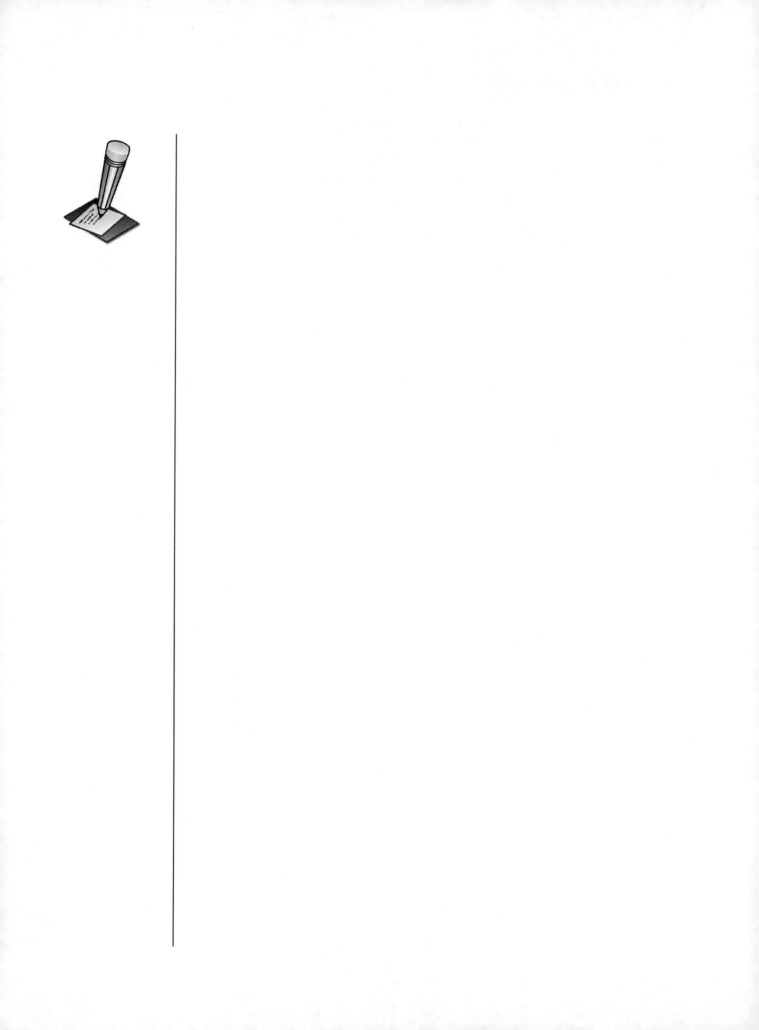

10 | Exploring Disaster Recovery Concepts and Methodologies

Lesson Time: 3 hour(s)

Lesson Objectives:

In this lesson, you will describe disaster recovery concepts and techniques.

You will:

- Examine disaster recovery plans.
- Create and recover a backup.
- Implement replication methods.

Introduction

In the previous lesson, you identified major issues, tools, and techniques for trouble-shooting servers. Unforeseen events damage network resources, including data, and create the need to troubleshoot servers. In the worst case, these events will require you to perform disaster recovery. In this lesson, you will describe the concepts and methodologies related to disaster recovery.

Along with troubleshooting techniques, planning and implementing disaster recovery techniques are critical knowledge areas that you should be familiar with. Server data may be threatened despite all fault tolerance measures you take. You should, therefore, identify both common and uncommon issues that might affect your network and then list the measures to take, resources to use, and guidelines to follow among a host of other essential details before drawing up a robust recovery plan.

This lesson covers all or part of the following CompTIA Server+ (2009) certification objectives:

- Topic A:
  - Objective 5.3: Explain data retention and destruction concepts.
  - Objective 5.4: Given a scenario, carry out the following basic steps of a disaster recovery plan.
- Topic B:

- Objective 5.1: Compare and contrast backup and restoration methodologies, media types and concepts.

- Objective 5.3: Explain data retention and destruction concepts.

- Topic C:

- Objective 5.2: Given a scenario, compare and contrast the different types of replication methods.

TOPIC A
Examine Disaster Recovery Plans

You have addressed the issues and remedies for troubleshooting servers, and now you will address disaster recovery. The most important step in disaster recovery takes place well before any disaster occurs, when you develop and document a solid recovery plan. In this topic, you will examine disaster recovery plans.

Servers are vulnerable to a multitude of threats—not only from hackers, but also from natural disasters and plain old-fashioned decay. Insurance can replace hardware, but lost data is gone for good, and many companies can't survive that. Effectively implementing a disaster recovery plan helps ensure that your organization recovers from any types of disaster.

Disasters and Disaster Recovery

Definition:

A *disaster* is a catastrophic loss of all system functions due to an unavoidable cause. Disasters can affect personnel, buildings, devices, communications, resources, and data. When a disaster strikes, organizations employ a *disaster recovery* strategy for protecting people and resources and try to revive a failed network or system as quickly as possible. Apart from ensuring the safety of all personnel, an organization must assure the continuity of its business functions.

 Disaster recovery is also referred to as fault recovery.

Example:

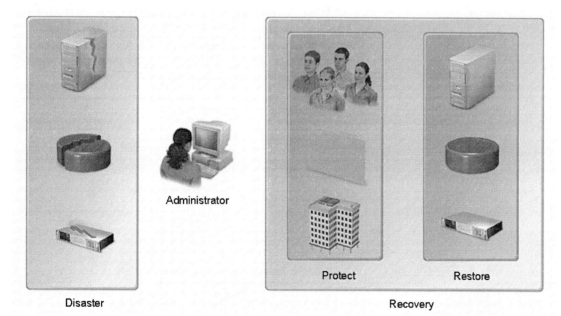

Administrator

Disaster

Protect   Restore

Recovery

Figure 10-1: Disaster recovery protects people and resources and tries to revive a failed network or system.

Disaster Categories

Disasters that can affect a network fall into one of three main categories.

Category	Description
Natural disasters	 **Natural Disaster** Natural disasters include fires, storms, floods, and other destructive forces. Natural disasters involve the involuntary destruction of network servers and associated hardware and software. Data loss is usually related to destruction of the server environment and hardware. The best defense against this type of disaster is excellent documentation and physical security for data backups. In the worst-case scenario, nothing remains of the office after the disaster, and the server has to be completely rebuilt from documentation alone.
Data destruction	 **Data Destruction** Data loss due to causes other than natural disaster is much easier to recover from. This kind of data loss includes accidental deletion, malicious destruction, or a virus attack. Again, the key is a good quality data backup.

Category	Description
Equipment failure	

Equipment Failure

Most day-to-day server disasters relate to failure of server hardware. Not only can hardware failure cause a loss of data, but it can also cause a loss of productivity in the office. Defense against equipment failure can be as simple as having a relationship with a vendor who can get replacement parts quickly or contracting a service provider that stocks parts. Many companies keep high-risk spares on hand in order to quickly replace failures. One major mistake that many server administrators make is to standardize an exotic piece of hardware or rely too heavily on older hardware that might be hard to replace. If a server goes down because older equipment fails, it could be down for an unacceptable length of time while a replacement is found or the server is reconfigured.

Disaster Recovery Plans

Definition:

A *disaster recovery plan* is a policy or a set of procedures that documents how people and resources will be protected in case of a disaster, and how the organization will recover from the disaster and restore normal functioning. The plan should be developed and implemented cooperatively by different functional groups.

The disaster recovery plan incorporates many components, including:

* A complete list of responsible individuals.

* A critical hardware and software inventory.

* Detailed instructions on how to reconstruct the network.

 A complete disaster recovery plan will be highly detailed and completely customized to suit the needs and circumstances of a particular organization.

Example:

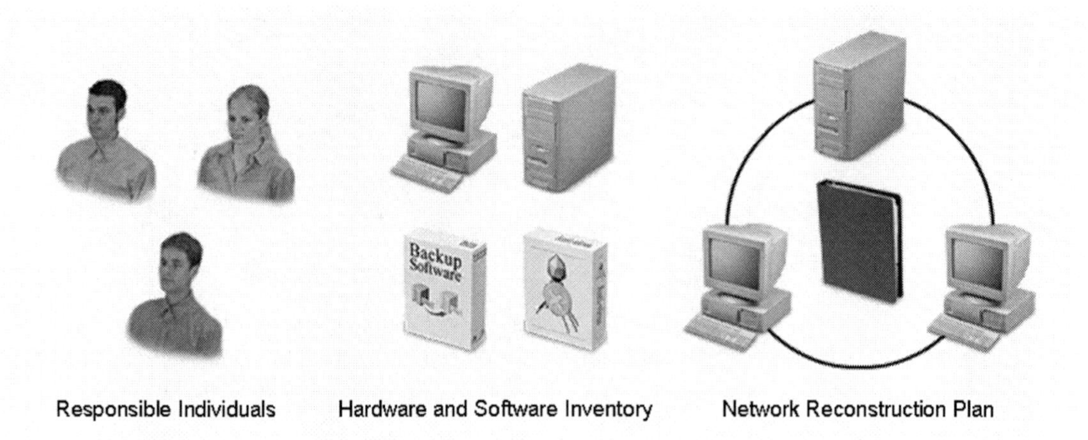

Responsible Individuals   Hardware and Software Inventory   Network Reconstruction Plan

Figure 10-2: Components incorporated in the disaster recovery plan.

Roles and Responsibilities

To efficiently implement all aspects of a complex disaster recovery plan, you'll need to create specific teams with specific plans. You'll need to define your project's scope based on your company's needs and resources, and then create appropriate teams, each with its own team leader. As with your project teams, each team needs to clearly and specifically document the roles and responsibilities of its members, so that in the event of an emergency there is no question as to who is doing what. Have each team identify which resources are necessary to get the operations up and running following a disaster.

Backups and External Team Members

It's a good idea to assign a backup to each member and train him or her. If you find that you need to use external people on your teams, create contracts specifying the circumstances under which you'll require their time, such as training or recovery.

Team Meetings

To keep abreast of what is going on with each team, hold meetings periodically and talk about any problems or concerns. These meetings should be designed to resolve problems, taking whatever actions deemed necessary.

Responsible Individuals

A documented contact list of individuals responsible for various elements of the network speeds the disaster recovery process.

Responsible Individuals	Information to Include
Network administrators	Office, home, pager, and cell phone numbers and home addresses. Document each person's role on the network.
Office managers	Office and human resources managers, department supervisors, and anyone who might have a say in network reconstruction.

Responsible Individuals	Information to Include
Security officials	Anyone with access to safes or storage locations containing offsite data and contacts for data and record storage companies. Also include how to recover offsite data. Include public fire and safety authorities if your disaster situation could affect public safety.
Vendors	Vendors your company deals with regularly and the type of equipment they provide. List sales contacts, cell phone numbers, and home numbers, if possible.
Service providers and contractors	Contractors used regularly and all providers of customized software or custom services.
Manufacturer technical contacts	Contact numbers and websites for manufacturers of all network software and hardware. Include account numbers applicable to the company.
Past IT personnel	Anyone who had a hand in building the network. It is a last resort, but they could contract in to help rebuild or at least provide guidance or information not otherwise available.

Testing and Training

Once you have everything down on paper, test the disaster recovery plan by creating simulation exercises—both announced and unannounced, simple and complex, informal and formal—so that you can find holes in the plan. You can then fix the problems and develop helpful training materials.

Types of Disaster Readiness Tests

Testing of plans can be done at various levels and intensities.

Testing Type	Description
Simulated testing on paper or checklist test	When all of the personnel involved in the recovery effort have been given sufficient time to study their roles in the recovery process, they should walk through the steps in a sort of dry run of the procedures involved. This is also known as a checklist test or a simulated paper test. Different disaster scenarios are recorded on a whiteboard, and the various personnel start filling in the blanks to the recovery plan based on the role(s) allocated to them. This is akin to reading through a script before staging a rehearsal for a play.

Testing Type	Description
Limited environment simulation or structured walk-through test	Once a backup system is in place, then the recovery system should be put through its paces to make sure it works. When various departments in an organization that normally interact with each other in a certain way now find that there are other interaction channels, situations may arise. Typical problems that occur have to do with the hierarchical nature of most large organizations. A person at a senior level in one department may feel that he or she does not have to answer to a person in a peer position in another department. These issues should be cataloged, then the backup and recovery plan should be reviewed to take them into account.
	An example of limited environment simulation that many of you might be familiar with is when the electronic surveillance monitoring and security systems are first installed at your premises. After the alarm system has been installed, a select few people with certain levels of responsibility in the company are informed of the code to enter upon opening the premises. The contact phone numbers for these people are given to the company that installed the security system. Upon installation of the system and initial testing, the system alarm is tripped, and the alarm is automatically sent to the security company. The security company personnel look up their list of phone numbers for your company and proceed to call each one, in turn, down the list. If none of the people on that list answer the phone, then the local police are called in to investigate a potential break-in.
	Performing a limited simulation is different than having an unannounced drill, where the occupants are caught by surprise, and the sanctity of the drill is maintained by carrying it out at irregular intervals.

Testing Type	Description
Full-scale environment simulation or full interruption test	In a full-scale simulation test, a disaster scenario is chosen and the recovery plan for that scenario is actually executed, step by step, to see if it works. Restrictions to the availability of resources are mimicked as with an actual disaster. The simulation may be designed so that any backup or recovery mechanisms that are available at a hot, warm, or cold site that needs to be accessed to expedite recovery can be accessed.
	Unexpected or unpredictable events can occur during a simulation test. As with the structured walk-through tests, such events should be recorded, then the backup and recovery plan should be reviewed to take them into account. Once the reason for the unexpected event is understood, then the backup and recovery plan should be modified to take this into account. In an actual simulation test, the organization's day-to-day workings are not disturbed, because only those personnel involved in the recovery operations are affected.
	A full-scale simulation can also be undertaken so that all aspects of a recovery process are tested. This kind of a test is performed infrequently and retests spaced far apart, as it is disruptive to the organization. The majority of the people in the company are not told in advance that it is a test. Such a test, also called a full interruption test, will actually test the reaction of all the personnel within the organization. Not everybody reacts well under stress, and this test will help in identifying those people who can be trusted to undertake critical jobs in an emergency.

Disaster Recovery Plan Maintenance Types

As with anything else, your disaster recovery plan requires maintenance for it to be updated. You can perform scheduled maintenance at regular intervals to review the plan and modify it, if necessary. You can also perform unscheduled maintenance when a security-related event occurs.

Plan Maintenance

Changes in things like personnel, responsibilities, and organizational structure are a matter of course for the professional world, and you need to make sure your plan reflects them. No one person or group alone should be responsible for plan maintenance; it's just too big a job. So consider assigning team leaders the responsibility of making sure their parts of the plan are updated as necessary.

Disaster Declaration

Because of the great monetary loss that is involved in a salvaging operation, it is often a member of the executive management team that is responsible for declaring a crisis as a disaster. In any case, the designated executive must discuss the event with the appropriate people and come up with a suitable plan. Sometimes a situation doesn't start out as disastrous as anticipated but it can quickly escalate into one. You need to have guidelines in place for declaring a disaster and sequencing the communication flow.

Disaster Recovery Plan Implementation

When creating a disaster recovery plan, you should consider how much mission-critical data is stored on the network, the cost (in dollars/hour) of downtime in the case of a failed server, and the data backup and restore needs of your company. You can implement the plan using any of the following methods:

- Mirroring or duplexing hard drives.
- Implementing a hot-swappable server.
- Implementing server clustering or other high-availability solutions.
- Keeping an inventory of spare server parts, such as hard drives and boards.
- Replicating data to an offsite server.
- Storing server backups at a remote site.

Built-In Recovery Services

Your operating system might include some recovery services that you need to become familiar with. For example, Microsoft's Last Known Good Configuration feature, which makes available a copy of the system's hardware configuration and driver settings from the last time the operating system successfully booted. In addition to services provided by the operating system (or if your operating system doesn't include recovery services), your disaster recovery plan could include restoring data from valid backup media, by using third-party tools, or by using a professional service.

Professional Data Recovery Services

If you're considering using a professional data recovery service, think about the following:

- Professional services are typically expensive. Weigh the cost of the service against the cost of re-creating the data. If the data is critical, it's easier to justify the cost of the service.
- You usually have to send the damaged disk to the vendor. However, onsite service might be available at extra cost.
- Utilities that write to the disk or re-create the volume can render the data unrecoverable by a service. If you think that a problem might lead to using a data-recovery service, make sure you use these utilities only for reading or copying data.
- Re-installing the operating system can render original data unrecoverable by a service.

Emergency Procedures

An emergency procedure is a series of steps that are followed during an unforeseen event such as a natural disaster, network failure, fire accident, or malicious attack, most of which call for immediate action or assistance. Emergency procedures are the foundation for any disaster recovery plan. Organizations should ensure that all employees are aware of the steps to be followed during an emergency situation. It also helps if mock drills are conducted to gauge the effectiveness of the procedure and identify gaps.

While there are no standardized emergency procedures, the following guidelines must be part of any emergency plan:

● The first and foremost objective of any emergency procedure should be to ensure the safety of every person. Never let the employees place themselves in dangerous situations or take unnecessary risks.

● Coordinate the entire disaster recovery operation with the emergency response team.

● Follow the procedures laid out in the disaster recovery plan to facilitate the recovery of data, hardware, and software, and to focus on resuming critical operations.

● Based on the critical nature of a particular service or operation, prioritize the recovery operations. For instance, the most critical resources and operations are restored first.

● Inform all concerned stakeholders about the extent of damage; the methodologies implemented to recover data, hardware, and software; the possible recovery time; and the operational, legal, and financial implications.

Fire Suppressants Used in Server Rooms

In case of fire in a server room, use the right type of fire suppressants to extinguish the fire and minimize damage to the organization's assets and equipment. Typically, aerosol based fire suppressors are used in server rooms. Aerosol is a colorless, liquefied compressed gas. It is dispensed as a colorless electrically nonconductive vapor that does not obscure vision and has acceptable level of toxicity for use. Its benefits include:

● Fast and effective

● Leaves no residue

● Zero ozone depleting potential

● Low global warming potential

● Electronically nonconductive

● Minimal storage requirement

● Extensively tested, recognized, and approved worldwide

● Effective on site installation

Escalation Procedures for Emergencies

An escalation procedure, as part of disaster recovery planning, has two functions: resource escalation and notification escalation. The resource escalation procedure specifies select procurable resources to those individuals striving to recover from a disaster. The notification escalation procedure specifies the people to be notified in case of serious problems. In other words, the escalation procedure ascertains that all necessary resources are made available as required and that everyone has been informed and is aware of the situation.

The following are some of the escalation procedures to be followed in case of an emergency situation:

- Escalate the level of damage and the estimated recovery time to all stakeholders, including the clients, supervisors, and senior management.

- Inform the local police or fire department of the incident.

- Notify the stakeholders about the legal, contractual, and financial implications.

- Escalate the availability of resources to those individuals who can provide technical support for the recovery.

- Escalate the level of damage to vendors so that they can provide immediate support to recover servers and other hardware and software.

Classification and Prioritization of System Recovery

The disaster recovery plan should include a complete inventory of all components in each network, server, and workstation, as well as all associated software that must be restored. Prioritize inventory by identifying the most critical resources that must be restored first.

Resource Type	Description
Critical resource	Loss of any resource or services that has been classified as critical will result in a major disruption of services and operations and impedes the performance of mission-critical functions. It can also lead to a significant financial, production, or information loss. Such resources are assigned the highest priority during the recovery process.
	An example of a critical resource is an organization's database server that contains the complete operational information and data of the organization. The employees perform their daily operations by accessing this database and failure of this database server will lead to significant amount of system downtime, productivity loss, and defaulting on client commitments.

Resource Type	Description
Necessary resource	Failure of a resource that has been classified as a necessary resource will most probably result in the failure of a particular service or function. Moreover, failure of these resources will not impede the critical operations of an organization. Therefore, once the critical resources are restored, the necessary resources can be taken care of.
	An example of a necessary resource is the mail server that is used to transfer email. Failure of this server will only lead to the disruption of email services; however, it will not interrupt the organization's critical operations since other channels of communication can be set up to compensate the loss of this service.
Deferrable resource	Failure of a deferrable resource will result in the failure of a particular privilege in a service. Failure of this operation will not impede the operation of the service. Therefore, when the resources are prioritized for the recovery, the issues with deferrable resources are the ones that is resolved finally.
	An example of a deferrable resource is the resource that provides the facility to perform group chat. Failure of this service in the mail server will only lead to the lack of group chat privilege; however, it will not interrupt the service as a whole.

ACTIVITY 10-1
Discussing the Disaster Recovery Plan Implementation

Scenario:
In this activity, you will discuss issues related to the implementation of a disaster recovery plan.

1. **Which events always require a disaster recovery plan to be updated?**

   a) Loss of a team leader.

   b) Scheduled review and testing of the plan.

   c) Successful recovery from a declared disaster.

   d) Failed data recovery after a hurricane.

2. **Which type of disaster readiness test is synonymous to reading through a script before staging a rehearsal for a play?**

3. **What do you think are the primary responsibility of every member of a disaster recovery team?**

4. **True or False? An escalation procedure has two functions: resource escalation and notification escalation.**

   ___ True

   ___ False

5. **Which of these guidelines must be part of any emergency procedure?**

   a) Ensure the safety of every person.

   b) Coordinate the entire disaster recovery operation with the emergency response team.

   c) Inform all concerned stakeholders about the extent of damage.

   d) Escalate the availability of resources to those individuals who can provide technical support for the recovery.

TOPIC B
Implement Disaster Recovery Methodologies

Previously, you examined how to implement disaster recovery plans. The disaster recovery plan also includes fault tolerance measures such as data backup. In this topic, you will examine how to perform data backup.

As part of a fault-tolerant system, you need to consider backup options and make sure you have an efficient backup plan in place, so that you are able to restore crashed servers to functional capacity in the event of a critical failure or disaster.

Backups

The term *backup* refers to the process of making copies of files or databases and storing them in a different location so that they can be used for restoring data in case of a system failure or other such events. Making a backup of data is a mandatory requirement for huge operations. In personal computers, however, making a backup is a necessary but neglected task. The process of retrieving files from a backup is referred to as restoring.

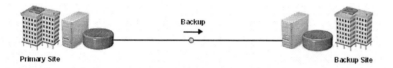

Figure 10-3: Backup makes copies of files or databases and stores them in a different location.

Backup Utilities
A backup utility is a software program that archives data that is typically located on a hard disk to any removable medium. Some utilities compress data before storing it, which can be more efficient than simply copying data to the backup medium. Network operating systems usually contain built-in backup utilities.

Difference Between an Archive and a Backup
A backup is a secondary copy of data used for data protection. In case the source files are damaged, the data can be restored from the backup. In contrast, an archive is the primary data, which is moved to a less expensive type of media, such as a tape, for long-term, low-cost storage. Also, the purpose of an archive is only to access the information and not to restore it.

Last Known Good Configuration
The Last Known Good Configuration (LKGC) option was first introduced in Microsoft Windows 2000/2003 and is available in all later versions of Windows operating systems. This feature enables a user to load the last working version of Microsoft Windows in the safe mode. Running the last known good configuration will restore your last good system settings and will not delete anything. The only thing you may have to reinstall are the programs you have recently installed because the configuration for those programs may have been lost.

Backup Plans

While it is impossible to be completely prepared for every natural disaster or other occurrence that can crash your network, you should have a good backup plan to help maximize fault recovery efforts. Good backup plans include answers to questions such as:

● What should be backed up?

● How large will the backups be?

● Which backup medium (or media) should be used?

● When should backups occur?

● Who is responsible for initiating and maintaining backups?

● Where should the backup media be stored?

● How often should backups be tested?

● What should be done when data is lost?

● How fast can the system be restored?

Identifying the Data to Back Up

The actual data that needs to be backed up regularly will vary according to the company's needs, but your backup plan should at least include measures for backing up any data that is considered to be mission-critical. You also need to consider whether backing up the server is enough, or if data on individual workstations also needs to be backed up. If users consistently save their important data files to the network, then a workstation backup is probably not as necessary as when users save the majority of their data files on their local hard disks.

Workstation Configurations

Another thing to consider is whether you need to back up workstation configuration information. If bringing down the server for backups is prohibited, try using online backup software instead.

Backup Types

All utilities support several types of backups.

Backup Type	Description
Full	Backs up all information, regardless of whether it was previously backed up. Also known as a normal backup.
Incremental	Backs up files new or modified since the last full or incremental backup.
Differential	Backs up files new or modified since the last full backup.
Copy	Backs up any selected files, regardless of whether or not the archive bit is turned on, and leaves the archive bit the same as before the backup. Commonly used between full and incremental backups.
Daily	Only backs up files that were changed during the current day and leaves the archive bit unchanged.
Appended	An option that backs up files until media runs out of space, then overwrites from oldest to newest. This relates more to the backup media than to the specific backup types.

Operating System and Their Backup Types

The following table describes backup types for different operating systems.

NOS	Backup Type	What Gets Backed Up	Reset Archive Bit?	Time Issues
Windows Server 2003/2008	Normal (Full)	All selected data	Yes	Longest to back up; shortest to restore
	Copy	All selected data	No	Long to back up; short restore
	Differential	All files created or changed since the last normal or incremental backup	No	Longer to back up each day; short restore
	Incremental	All files created or changed since the last normal or incremental backup	Yes	Shortest to back up; longest to restore
	Daily	All files created or changed on that day	No	Depends on the number of files changed that day
UNIX/Linux	Full	All files	Not applicable	Longest to back up; shortest to restore
	Differential	All files created or changed since the last full backup	Not applicable	Longer to back up each day; short restore
	Incremental	All files created or changed since the last full or incremental backup	Not applicable	Shortest to back up; longest to restore

Backup Combinations

Typically, the fastest type of backup is an incremental backup combined with a regular full backup, but it requires that you restore the last full backup and every incremental backup since the last full backup (in chronological order), which can be extremely time-consuming. What you can do instead is use differential backups combined with a regularly scheduled full backup, because all new or modified files since the previous full backup are included and you would only need two media sets for a full restore. Each differential backup following the last full backup will take an increasing amount of time.

Because differential backups are based on the last backup that cleared the archive bit, you shouldn't mix incremental and differential backups. Differential backups count on the archive bit not being cleared. Any differential backups following an incremental backup wouldn't back up all modified files since the last full backup because the incremental backup cleared the archive bit. Keep in mind that the backup methods you implement will also directly impact your restore time.

If you opt to do full backups each time you back up your data, be aware that doing so takes the most time. However, it also includes the fastest full restores because you only need to restore data from one media set. The following table summarizes backup and restore times for each backup type.

Backup Type	Relative Time Necessary for a Full Backup	Relative Time Necessary for a Full Restore
Full backup only	Longest	Shortest
Combination incremental and full	Shortest	Longest
Combination differential and full backup	Time increases daily; shorter than full backup overall but longer than incremental	Shorter than incremental but longer than full

Specialized Data Backups

Certain data types may require specialized procedures or additional software components to perform a successful backup.

Specialized Backup Type	Description
Open files	Files that are opened by an application are locked to ensure that only one client makes changes at a time. It is a nice feature, but also one that causes a few problems for network backup software. Specifically, the backup software has to deal with a client making changes during the backup, which can create errors in the backup (remember that backups are relatively slow). It also has to deal with the locked files. To help, you can deploy an open files agent with the backup software. When the backup software encounters a locked file, it uses the open files agent to take a snapshot of the file. The snapshot temporarily disables the file's ability to be edited and copies the file to a temporary location on the drive. The backup software then backs up the snapshot. This happens very quickly and does not disrupt the client using the file.

Specialized Backup Type	Description
Databases	They are essentially big, open files. Some backup software handles simple databases with nothing more than an open files agent. However, larger databases have special considerations. In a database, the actual data on the drive might not be current because of write-behind caching; a technique that temporarily stores database changes in server memory while the server is busy. Sometimes, database logs need to be reset when a database is backed up. Log files are often stored on a different drive than the database itself. These databases may require either a manual backup procedure to close open files and clear logs, or the use of a database agent, which can back up the database and reset the logs while the database is online.
Email	Email servers are essentially modified database servers that store users' mailboxes. Data is still in a database data store, which means that the email server can be backed up just like a database server. In fact, a standard backup and restore of a mail server contains all the same elements that backing up a database does. When a mail server is backed up, like a database, one restore option is to restore all the data and then extract the damaged mailbox. There is another type of mail server backup called the brick-level backup, which uses a special agent that is aware of the database's data structure. Brick-level backups enable a database to be backed up mailbox by mailbox, which takes longer, and then restored one mailbox at a time. Some agents even enable the mail to be restored message by message.
Power user workstation	Some power users on your network might have sensitive data on their personal workstations that you would choose to include in a backup plan. Workstations are easy to back up when they have an agent installed that enables backup software to access them. However, they have to be powered on to be backed up. This used to be a problem, but today most network cards and PCs support a technology called Wake on LAN (WOL), in which backup software sends a signal to the workstation (awakens it), waits for it to boot up, backs it up, and then turns it off again.

Specialized Backup Type	Description
Mobile user workstation	When remote users are on the network, they are backed up the same way that workstations are. However, when they are primarily offline, backups require a different solution. Many backup software manufacturers use a remote agent to back up remote users when the users connect to the network. The agent copies changed data from the laptop to a network drive. This is always a partial backup, so it is faster than copying all the data off the laptop. But how do you back up remote users if they are not connected to the network? Some backup software uses over-the-web backups. The process is the same as already described except that the user attaches to a secure website and uploads data.
Enterprise	Many companies have moved to an enterprise-wide solution for data backups. A high-performance backup solution is deployed from a central location and all backup data is stored in the central location. Many of these solutions cross manufacturers' boundaries, enabling one setup to get backups from PC servers, UNIX mainframes, mid-range servers, and workstations, regardless of manufacturer and operating system.
Snapshots	They can be used to take complete backups of drives and databases. There are a number of different snapshot technologies implemented in software, in hardware, or in combinations of the two. Depending on the technology in use, snapshots might clone an entire copy of a volume to another physical drive, or they might record only file changes or only pointers to file locations. See your storage or backup vendors for specifics on the snapshot backup implementation they offer.
Bare metal	Based on disk imaging technology, bare metal allows you to not only back up your documents and media, but also backup operating system with all drive boot records and system information. The main challenge with bare metal backups is that information cannot be backed up to the drive that includes an operating system running on it. Active operating systems exclusively lock their data, thereby, protecting third parties to access it, either on files or on sector levels. Therefore, a different drive is required to back up your main system drive.

Off-Site Storage

Moving at least one full backup per week to an off-site location is a good idea. There are a lot of companies that offer this kind of service. The drawback is that when you want to restore the data you need to go through a third party to get it.

Rotation Method

Backups should be performed systematically and on a regular basis to protect against data loss. Most large organizations implement a structured backup scheme that includes a backup schedule and details about which files are backed up, where the backup is stored, and how it can be retrieved. The backup scheme will specify the backup *rotation method,* which determines how many backup tapes or other media sets are needed, and the sequence in which they are used and reused. Designated administrators will have the responsibility for designing and managing the backup scheme and for restoring data when needed.

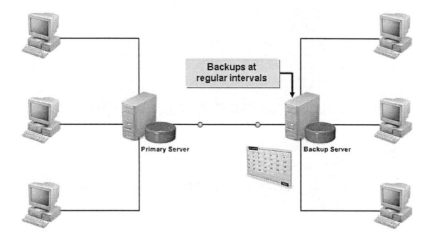

Figure 10-4: Every backup scheme will specify the backup rotation method.

The Grandfather-Father-Son Backup Rotation Method

In the Grandfather-Father-Son method, daily tape sets are used Monday through Thursday, weekly tape sets every Friday, and monthly tape sets on the last day of each month. It is a usual practice to rotate daily tape sets weekly, weekly tape sets monthly, and monthly tape sets annually.

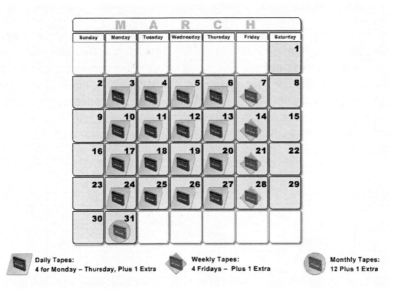

Daily Tapes:
4 for Monday – Thursday, Plus 1 Extra

Weekly Tapes:
4 Fridays – Plus 1 Extra

Monthly Tapes:
12 Plus 1 Extra

Figure 10-5: Grandfather-Father-Son process for securely backing up new and modified data.

The Grandfather-Father-Son method is secure and involves assigning one backup set for Mondays, another for Tuesdays, another for Wednesdays, and another for Thursdays. On each of those days, you can reuse the assigned set. On Fridays of that month, however, you may use a new set, which you can reuse in the next month too in the same order. It will be helpful if you can label each daily backup set with the name of the day, weekly tapes with number 1 through 4 for each Friday, and monthly tapes with the name of the month. At the end of each month, you can replace the backup sets used from Monday to Thursday. You may then choose to either reuse the old ones the following year or keep them as permanent records.

Leaning Tower Method

In the leaning tower method, also known as the Tower of Hanoi method, tape sets are staggered with one tape set for every two days, and different sets every four, eight, sixteen, and thirty-two days, respectively.

Day	1	2	3	4	5	6	7	8	9	10	11	12	13	14	15	16
Media Set	A		A		A		A		A		A		A		A	
		B				B				B				B		
				C								C				
								D								
																E

Media Set	Used Every
A	2 Days
B	4 Days
C	8 Days
D and E	16 Days alternating between set D and E

Figure 10-6: Leaning tower process for securely backing up new and modified data.

The leaning tower method involves using five media sets. Media set A is used every two days; media set B every fourth day; media set C every eighth day; media set D every sixteenth day; and, media set E is alternated with media set D, doubling the backup history with each media set used—2, 4, 8, or 16 days until the media is overwritten. This way you can have media sets with most recent versions of the files. It will help if you can label each of the media sets with a letter or number (media set A or 1). You can apply this rotation method to either a daily or weekly rotation schedule. If you're doing a daily rotation, you'll need at least five media sets; a weekly rotation requires eight.

Backup Media

The *backup medium* is the place where you store backed up data. The backup medium may include tape drives, disk, WORM, optical drives, and flash drives.

Medium	Description
Small-capacity removable disks	Magnetic disks that hold less than 500 MB and can be removed from disk drives and replaced as they get full. Although they don't hold a lot of data, they're popular for partial workstation backup because of their low cost and ease of use, and because many newer computers come equipped with one or more of them.
Large-capacity removable disks	The same as small-capacity removable disks except that they store more than 500 MB of data. They cost more than the small-capacity disks, but hold more data and can easily be used for more complete workstation backups. However, they have limited server use because one disk isn't usually sufficient backup for most servers.
Removable optical disks	Use a laser or other light source to read and write information stored on disk. They tend to have larger capacities (650 MB to 17 GB) than magnetic removable disks, but also tend to be slower. Optical jukeboxes, which can contain hundreds of disks, can expand capacities into the hundreds of terabytes. There is also a hybrid category called magneto-optical (MO) disks that combine the benefits of both magnetic and optical storage methods.
Tape backups	Probably the most common, because tape drives are reliable, inexpensive, and widely supported. Common tape backup formats include QIC, Travan, DAT, DLT, and 8 mm.
Flash drives	Stores data using flash memory. These flash drives can be USB drives or memory sticks. A third party tool, which is generally compatible with the OS, is used to perform backup or recovery of data whenever a flash drive is connected to the computer system.

Backup Best Practices

You need to keep the following in mind if you wish to create and maintain a durable backup file or database:

- Use the appropriate operating system services to identify any open files and then close them. Most backup software gives you the option to back up open files either with or without locks.
- Follow the manufacturer's instructions for maintaining the backup device. For example, if you're using a tape backup, periodically clean the tape heads (with a cleaning tape) to minimize intermittent errors caused by dirty recording heads.
- Store a copy of the backup media off-site.
- Store the on-site copy of the backup in a fireproof safe.

Backup Security

The are various best practices for ensuring security of backup data. They include:

- Authentication of users and backup clients to the backup server.
- Role based access control lists for all backup and recovery operations.
- Data encryption options for both backup transmission and storage.
- Backup of remote clients to a centralized location behind firewalls.
- Use segregation of duties enforced by policy for all personnel handling backup data. Document all access, testing, backup, and restore cycles.

Backup Verification Steps

Before using a backup device to restore data, test it to make sure it's reliable. To test the backup device:

- Try restoring from more than one external hard drive if possible, to ensure that the hard drive is properly aligned.
- Try restoring some of the backed-up data into a test directory, making sure you don't overwrite any data when doing so.
- Configure the backup software to verify after it writes.
- Verify that the backup contains all the required files.

OS Restore vs. Data Restore

OS restore is a feature first introduced in Windows XP. It allows users to restore their computers to a previous state without losing personal data files. The OS restore feature automatically reverts your system to the original configuration.

Data restoration restores the lost or logically damaged data from FAT and NTFS supported file system. It is easy to use and does not require any technical skills to operate computer data recovery software.

Features of data restoration:

- Recovers data from former existing partitions.
- Support for FAT and NTFS file systems.
- Recovers deleted files and folders even after use of the Shift+Del key and clearing the Recycle Bin.
- Provides best graphical user interface (GUI) for easy and quick data recovery.

- Recovers data lost due to deleted, formatted, damaged or corrupted partitions in all logical crashes.
- Restore data from bad sectors.

Legal Requirements for Data Retention and Destruction

Every organization should have a well defined legal policy concerning the retention and destruction of data. Corporate policy and legal and regulatory requirements dictate how to retain and destroy data records. Because it is difficult to attain legal and regulatory compliance, corporate legal departments must assume advisory roles and act as internal consultants to ensure adherence to these standards. Failing to properly retain information may result in legal issues and fines.

The legal policy should include:

- Standards and guidelines on how long different types of documents should be retained to meet legal or policy requirements.

- Plans for consistent and secure storage, and retrieval of all document types. Storage recommendations take into account the nature of information, the physical media on which it is stored, and the security measures for documents.

- Plans for disposal or destruction of outdated documents. Some documents can simply be recycled or thrown away. However, confidential information must have an approved destruction method to ensure that the data cannot be retrieved. The destruction method depends upon the sensitivity of the data and the media it is stored on, and can range from shredding and burning paper documents, to reformatting computer disks multiple times.

Material Safeguarding

Safeguarding classified materials entails developing and implementing policies, guidelines, standards, and procedures that specify how to maintain the confidentiality of classified information. Access controls, either physical or logical, are at the heart of this process. The first step is deterring unauthorized individuals from accessing classified materials.

Declassification

As risks associated with the disclosure of classified information are reduced, the information can be declassified. The data owner determines the point in time of declassification. Security administrators are required to follow the local standards for declassification.

Policy Requirements for Data Retention and Destruction

To ensure proper management of data, it is essential that organizations have an internal policy governing the retention and destruction of information.

Policy	Guidelines
Data retention	<ul><li>Identify and classify the data that needs to be stored or backed up.</li><li>Determine the appropriate storage media.</li><li>Specify the data retention time based on contractual obligations, legal requirements, and any other statutory or mandatory requirements.</li><li>Check the need for a backup plan to ensure protection against inadvertent loss of data.</li><li>Ensure data back up is performed regularly, consistently, and safely.</li><li>Restrict access to any data that is retained for legitimate business purposes and make sure that it is physically secure.</li><li>Ensure that your data retention policies are compliant with local laws and regulations.</li></ul>
Data destruction	<ul><li>Prior to the permanent destruction of data, confirm that the information is no longer required.</li><li>Get proper authorization from the senior management and the concerned stakeholders before destroying the data.</li><li>Obtain recorded statements authorizing the destruction of data. This will help prevent legal issues that may arise at a later point of time.</li><li>Maintain a permanent list or database of the destroyed files.</li><li>Use a wipe or over-write program to destroy information on hard drives before disposing it.</li><li>Alternately, destroy tapes, optical disks, or any electronic storage device containing sensitive information before their disposal.</li><li>Ensure that the disposal of any electronic waste material is done in compliance with the local pollution control laws.</li><li>Ensure that your data destruction policies are compliant with local laws and regulations.</li></ul>

Material Destruction

Destroying classified materials is a required (Operations security) OPSEC activity. With governmental activities, there is a set of standards that determines methods for destroying various types of classified information. Destruction specialists must have a clearance level that matches the level of destroyed material. They must also follow specific processes that include:

- Degaussing—Reducing or eradicating unwanted magnetic fields.
- Drive wiping by writing binary zeros on an entire drive using approved processes.
- Complete physical destruction of media through incineration, shredding, or pulping.

Material Reuse

Often, the media erasure process leaves readable data, which includes swap files or hidden files, in places and slack space or unused or vacant cluster space reserved on a disk for data storage. This is because file deletion does not actually delete a file but removes pointers to it. Programs can undelete a file and retrieve the deleted information. If it is necessary to reuse media, systems can force a true deletion and data wipe if the proper options are used.

Policy Awareness

If your organization has a policy concerning the retention and destruction of data—ensure that all employees are made aware of the policy guidelines, perform regular audits and inspections to ensure its compliance, and ensure that the policy guidelines are current and updated.

How to Create and Recover a Backup

Procedure Reference: Create a Data Backup

The specific steps for backing up data will vary depending upon the backup utility and platform you are using. In general, to back up data:

1. Connect to the storage device.
2. Run the backup utility.
3. Select the data you want to back up.
4. Specify the backup destination and any other parameters for the backup.
5. Run the backup.

Procedure Reference: Recover Backup Data

The specific steps for recovering of data will vary depending upon the recover utility and platform you are using. In general, to recover the backed up data:

1. Connect to the storage device.
2. Run the backup recover utility.
3. Select the data you want to recover.
4. Specify the destination and any other parameters for restoration.
5. Perform data recovery.
6. Verify the recovered files and folders.

Backing Up Data Stored on Linux Servers

Most Linux distributions include several utilities that can be used as part of an overall backup solution. For example, you can use the tar or cpio utilities that are built into the operating system, or you can use a third-party solution such as Amanda, Afbackup, or Arkeia.

ACTIVITY 10-2
Backing Up Data in an External Device

> There is a simulated version of this activity available on the CD-ROM shipped with this course. You can run this simulation on any Windows computer to review the activity after class, or as an alternative to performing the activity as a group in class. The activity simulation can be launched either directly from the CD-ROM by clicking the Interactives link and navigating to the appropriate one, or from the installed data file location by opening the C:\ServerPlus\Data\Simulations\Lesson 10\10-2 folder and double-clicking the executable Backing Up Data in an External Device_guided.exe file.

Setup:

1. Verify that the data files for this activity have been installed on your server. These files reside in the C:\ServerPlus\Data\Exploring Disaster Recovery Concepts and Methodologies\Sales Data folder at the root of the C drive.

2. Obtain and install a removable media device, preferably an external hard disk, or follow your instructor's directions to access a location for storing the backup.

Scenario:

You are a network administrator for Ristell & Sons Publishing, a small publishing house with a growing client base. All client information is stored on a central file server, and the largely remote sales force has full permission to read, write, and execute these files. The file server currently is scheduled to automatically back itself up at regular intervals. Because of a federal holiday, no one will be in the office during the next scheduled backup, and so you want to force a single backup session ahead of time. You want to back up the file server that contains some sales information that multiple users have access to. You only want to back up the file server once.

What You Do	How You Do It
Sever Computer	
1. Install the Windows Server Backup utility.	a. Choose **Start→Administrative Tools→ Server Manager.**
	b. In the **Server Manager** window, in the left pane, right-click **Features** and choose **Add Features.**
	c. In the **Add Features Wizard**, on the **Select Features** page, in the **Features** list box, scroll down and expand the **Windows Server Backup Features.**
	d. Check the **Windows Server Backup.**
	e. Check the **Command-line Tools** check box. Observe that the **Add Features Wizard** dialog box pops up.
	f. In the **Add Features Wizard** dialog box, click **Add Required Features**.
	g. Observe that the **Command-line Tools** check box is now checked and then, click **Next**.
	h. In the **Confirm Installation Selections** page, click **Install.**

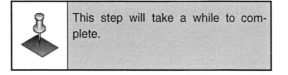

This step will take a while to complete.

i. In the **Installation Results** page, observe that the **Installation succeeded** message is displayed and click **Close** to close the **Add Features Wizard.**

j. Close the **Server Manager** window.

| 2. | Back up the disk partition volume of the server. | a. | Choose **Start→Administrative Tools→ Windows Server Backup.** |

b. In the **Windows Server Backup** window, in the **Actions** pane, click **Backup Once.**

c. In the **Backup Once Wizard**, in the **Backup options** page, accept the default settings and click **Next.**

d. In the **Select backup configuration** page, select **Custom** and click **Next.**

e. In the **Select backup items** page, uncheck **Enable system recovery** check box, check the **Local Disk (C:)** check box, and click **Next.**

f. In the **Specify destination type** page, verify that the **Local drives** option is selected and click **Next.**

g. In the **Select backup destination** page, from the **Backup destination** drop-down list, verify that the external hard drive is selected, and then click **Next.**

h. In the **Specify advanced option** page, verify that the **VSS copy backup (recommended)** option is selected and click **Next.**

i. In the **Confirmation** page, click **Backup.**

This step will take a while to complete depending on the size of the data to be backed up.

j. In the **Backup progress** page, when the backup is complete, click **Close.**

k. Close the **Windows Server Backup** window.

3. Verify the creation of a backup file.

a. Choose **Start**→**Computer.**

b. In the **Computer** window, double-click your external drive partition.

c. In the your external drive partition window, double-click the **WindowsImageBackup** folder.

d. In the **WindowsImageBackup** window, double-click **deptserver.**

e. Double-click the **Backup** folder that contains the current date.

f. Verify that a **VHD** file is located on your external hard drive window and close the window.

ACTIVITY 10-3

Restoring Data from an External Storage Device

> There is a simulated version of this activity available on the CD-ROM shipped with this course. You can run this simulation on any Windows computer to review the activity after class, or as an alternative to performing the activity as a group in class. The activity simulation can be launched either directly from the CD-ROM by clicking the Interactives link and navigating to the appropriate one, or from the installed data file location by opening the C:\ ServerPlus\Data\Simulations\Lesson 10\10-3 folder and double-clicking the executable Restoring Data from an External Storage Device_guided.exe file.

Setup:

Ensure that the removable media device, in which the backup was taken, is attached to the server.

Scenario:

A user has accidentally deleted some critical client files from his server. Fortunately, you have a backup copy of the files stored in an external storage device.

What You Do	How You Do It

Sever Computer

1. Create a simulation of a user accidently deleting a folder.

   a. Choose **Start→Computer.**

   b. In the **Computer** window, double-click **Local Disk (C:)** .

   c. In the **Local Disk (C:)** window, double-click the **Data** folder.

   d. In the **Data** window, double-click the **Exploring Disaster Recovery Concepts and Methodologies** folder.

   e. Right-click **Sales Data** and select **Delete.**

   f. In the **Delete Folder** message box, click **Yes** to delete the folder.

   g. Close the **Data** window.

   h. Right-click **Recycle Bin** and select **Empty Recycle Bin.**

   i. In the **Delete Folder** message box, click **Yes.**

2. Recover the deleted files from the backup.

a. Choose **Start→Administrative Tools→ Windows Server Backup.**

b. In the **Windows Server Backup** window, in the **Actions** pane, click **Recover.**

c. In the **Recovery Wizard**, on the **Getting started** page, verify that **This server (DEPTSERVER)** is selected, and click **Next.**

d. In the **Select backup date** page, verify that the date corresponds to the most recent backup, and click **Next.**

e. On the **Select recovery type** page, verify that the **Files and folders** option is selected and click **Next.**

f. On the **Select items to recover** page, expand **deptserver→Local Disk (C:)→ Data** and select **Sales Data.**

g. Verify that **Proposal.rtf** and **Specifications.rtf** appear in the right pane and click **Next.**

h. On the **Specify recovery options** page, in the **Recovery destination** section, verify that the **Original location** option is selected and click **Next.**

i. On the **Confirmation** page, click **Recover.**

j. When the wizard has finished recovering the two files, click **Close.**

k. Close the **Windows Server Backup** window.

3. Verify that the backup files have been restored.

a. Choose **Start→Computer** and double-click **Local Disk (C:).**

b. Double-click the **Data** folder.

c. Double-click the **Sales Data** folder.

d. Verify that the **Proposal.rtf** and **Specifications.rtf** files are present.

e. Close the **Sales Data** window.

PRACTICE ACTIVITY 10-4
Designing a Backup-and-Restore Plan

Scenario:

You've been asked to develop a tape rotation plan for an insurance office with data and files stored on a single server. They require a monthly archive on the first Monday of every month, to be retained for one year. They want reports run on the data every Monday and stored for two months. Lastly, they would like the security of at least one week's worth of tapes stored offsite. This office has production hours from 8:00 A.M. to 7:00 P.M., Monday through Friday. They generate many changes daily and you want to minimize the amount of time required for each backup operation.

1. What backup schedule will you implement?

2. How many tapes would be required for a year's worth of backups, assuming that you do not need extra tapes for the transit to offsite?

3. What would be a good time during the week to transfer the tapes to offsite storage?

4. It is Monday afternoon, and your office manager is looking at a file that she swears she edited on Friday, but the file appears to be the old one from the previous Thursday. With your plan, how do you restore the file?

5. The company experiences a complete disk failure at 10 A.M. on Thursday. How do you restore the data?

6. **What are the essential guidelines in a data retention policy?**

_____

TOPIC C
Implement Replication Methods

You examined how to backup data using various methods. Apart from the data backup methods, there are few replication methodologies implemented on a server to ensure data redundancy. In this topic, you will examine the various methods of replicating data.

Disaster recovery planning provides contingency procedures in the event of catastrophic events that you cannot reasonably foresee or prevent. In contrast, fault-tolerance and availability planning is intended to prevent the negative impact of mishaps that you can reasonably foresee, such as a temporary power outage or the inevitable failure of a hard disk. Therefore, by implementing a few replication methods, you can enhance the availability of data in distributed systems and keep these minor occurrences from turning into disasters for your organization.

Replication

Replication is the process of sharing and synchronizing data across multiple devices or servers. The replication process can be performed by one of three methods: disk-to-disk replication, server-to-server replication, and site-to-site replication.

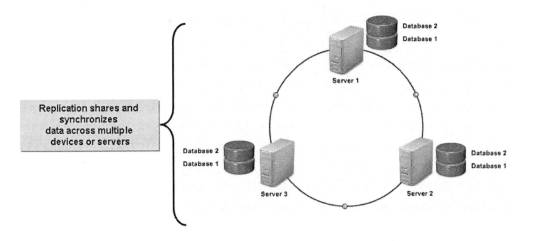

Figure 10-7: Replication shares data across multiple devices.

Disk-to-Disk Replication

Disk-to-disk replication is the process of replicating data across multiple storage disks to ensure consistency among redundant resources. The disk-to-disk replication method functions as a random-access storage. It allows the device to send and receive multiple concurrent streams of data, or to recover individual files without the need to scan the entire backup volume. Therefore, this replication method can enhance the availability of data in a distributed system. The disk-to-disk replication is usually performed using the disk mirroring technique. The advantage of this type of replication is its high-speed access to the replicated data.

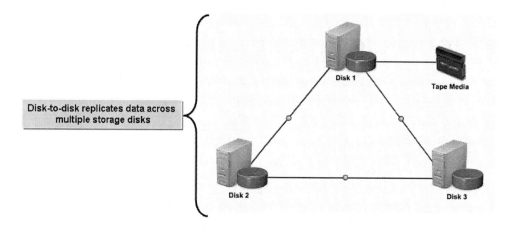

Figure 10-8: *Disk-to-disk replication functions as a random-access storage.*

Server-to-Server Replication

The server-to-server method is the process of replicating data across multiple servers. The changes made on one server are replicated simultaneously on different servers. Continuously maintaining updated copies of the data allows the read activity to be scaled across multiple servers. Sever-to-server replication is implemented in scenarios that demand high throughput. It includes improving data scalability and availability, data warehousing and reporting, integrating data from multiple sites, integrating heterogeneous data, and batch processing.

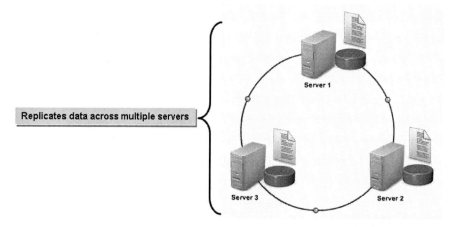

Figure 10-9: *The changes made on one server is replicated simultaneously on different servers.*

Clustering

Server-to-server replication is achieved by implementing an appropriate clustering technique. *Clustering* is the process of grouping two or more servers with a high-speed channel to share the workload between them. If one fails, others take over the workload. Clustering is also used in special-purpose computers, such as array processors, which provide concurrent processing on data sets. It is primarily used for very large computational problems in the engineering and scientific fields.

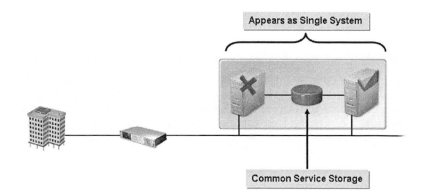

Figure 10-10: Clustering groups two or more servers with a high-speed channel to share workload between them.

Cluster Configurations

There are three general cluster configurations that support service failover. Nodes in all of these clusters need to have access to at least one common storage device.

Cluster Configuration	Description
Active/Active	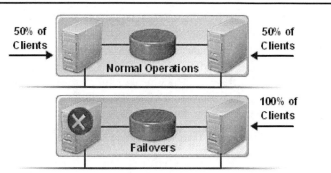 A cluster that has all nodes online, constantly providing services. This cluster type has the greatest resource efficiency because all nodes serve clients. If a node fails, the cluster resources fail over to one of the remaining nodes. That node will lose some performance as it takes on the resources and workload of the failed node. Latency in failover can range from seconds to minutes, depending on cluster configuration and the services on each cluster.

Cluster Configuration   Description

Active/Passive

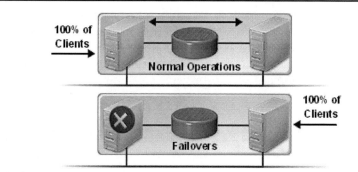

A cluster that includes at least two nodes, at least one of which is in active mode and handles the full workload, while one node is in passive or standby mode to act as a backup server. The standby node does not own any resources in the cluster. If an active server fails, the passive node will not receive a heartbeat from the failed node and will take over the resources from the failed active node. Performance during failover is relatively unaffected as long as the passive server is equal to the failed active server in performance. Latency in failover can range from seconds to minutes, depending on cluster configuration and the services on each cluster.

Fault-Tolerant or High-availability

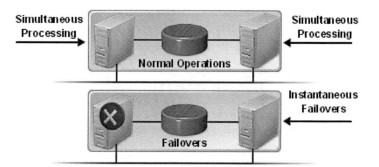

A general term for implementations that use clustering, RAID, redundant hardware, and other technologies to achieve 99.999% of uptime. In "shared everything" clusters, nodes share common hardware resources such as processors, memory, and disks, and can execute commands simultaneously so that a node can take over immediately if one fails. Failover times are in milliseconds, and there is often no performance degradation at all. High-availability clustering solutions are complicated to set up, configure, and maintain, and can cost hundreds of thousands of dollars to implement. However, they offer the highest level of failover performance and are the best choice for organizations, such as banks, brokerage firms, and airlines, that require "five nines" of uptime for financial or other reasons. Even just a few minutes of downtime in these organizations can be expensive.

Site-to-Site Replication

Site-to-site replication is the process of replicating data across multiple sites. The disaster recovery plan should include provisions for offsite locations that can be used as temporary offices. In the event of a disaster, these sites will keep the business up and running.

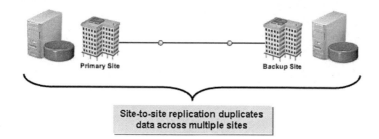

Figure 10-11: *Site-to-site replication provide offsite locations that can be used as temporary offices.*

Site Types

Backup site locations and replacement equipment can be classified as hot, warm, or cold, depending on how much configuration would be necessary to bring the location or spare equipment online.

Site Type	Description
Hot site	An alternate facility already equipped with resources and equipment ready for immediate disaster recovery. The hot site's size and physical location should be adequate to handle the equipment and resources your company needs. Hot sites are also referred to as alternate processing sites, backup sites, recovery sites, or recovery centers. Hot site would minimize the latency to restart an operation during any disaster.
Warm site	A cross between a cold site and a hot site; it's only partially equipped.
Cold site	An alternate facility that doesn't have any resources or equipment except for elevated floors and air conditioning. In order to reproduce your company's critical business functions, all of the equipment and resources would have to be installed. Basically, a cold site is simply a structure with potential. They can also be referred to as alternative sites, backup sites, recovery sites, or shell-sites.

Distance Requirements for the Site Types

Replication/alternative backup arrangements should be far away from the primary site as necessary to avoid being subject to the same set of risks as the primary location and should not rely on the same infrastructure components used by the primary site. The replication standards does not specify any specific distance requirements for implementing replication methods. Generally, hot sites are placed very close to the primary site to provide immediate access data incase of disaster, warm site are placed few kilometers away from the primary site, and cold sites are placed thousands of miles away from the primary site.

ACTIVITY 10-5

Discussing Replication Methods

Scenario:

In this activity, you will examine various replication methods.

---

1. **What is the best description of a cluster?**

    a) A specialized file server that is designed and dedicated to support data storage needs.

    b) A group of separate disks configured to work as a unit.

    c) A private network dedicated to data storage.

    d) A group of servers working together to provide fault tolerance and load balancing.

---

2. **What is the advantage of the disk-to-disk replication method?**

---

3. **Match the cluster type to its description.**

    ___ Active/active   a. A cluster with nodes that handle the full workload during normal operations, and other nodes in standby mode.

    ___ Active/passive   b. A cluster in which servers can provide almost instantaneous failover.

    ___ Fault-tolerant or high-availability   c. A cluster that has all nodes online, constantly providing services.

---

4. **True or False? The active/passive cluster type has the best failover response time.**

    ___ True

    ___ False

---

5. **What is the advantage of hot site replication?**

---

6. **In an active/passive configuration, how does the passive server know that the active server has failed?**

    a) The active server sends a message.

    b) The administrator brings the standby server online.

    c) The server heartbeat stops.

    d) The passive server reboots.

7. **What are the operations that require server-to-server replication?**

Lesson 10 Follow-up

In this lesson, you identified issues and technologies related to disaster recovery. As a server professional, one of your most important responsibilities will be to protect the server and its data, and ensure that the server can resume functioning as quickly as possible if it is damaged.

1. **What are the replication methods implemented in your organization to safeguard data?**

2. **Explain why good data backups and effective fault tolerance measures reduce the need for disaster recovery.**

Follow-up

In this course, you discussed the objectives related to installing, configuring, upgrading, maintaining, and troubleshooting server hardware and software. You also examined the issues relating to server IT environment and the disaster recovery concepts. The information and skills covered in this course will be helpful to professionals working with servers on the job, and also to prepare for the CompTIA Server+ certification examination, 2009 objectives. (exam number SK0-003).

1. **What are the various issues that you will consider before planning to install a server in your organization?**

2. **What are the various applications for which you need a server in your organization?**

3. **What are the various fault tolerant methods that you may want to implement for your server?**

What's Next?

The material in *CompTIA® Server+® Certification (2009 Objectives)* provides foundational information and skills required in any server-related career. It also assists you in preparing for the CompTIA® Server+® certification exam. Once you have completed *CompTIA® Server+® Certification (2009 Objectives)*, you might wish to take any number of vendor-specific technology or administration courses from Element K, including courses leading to professional-level certifications from Microsoft and Novell.

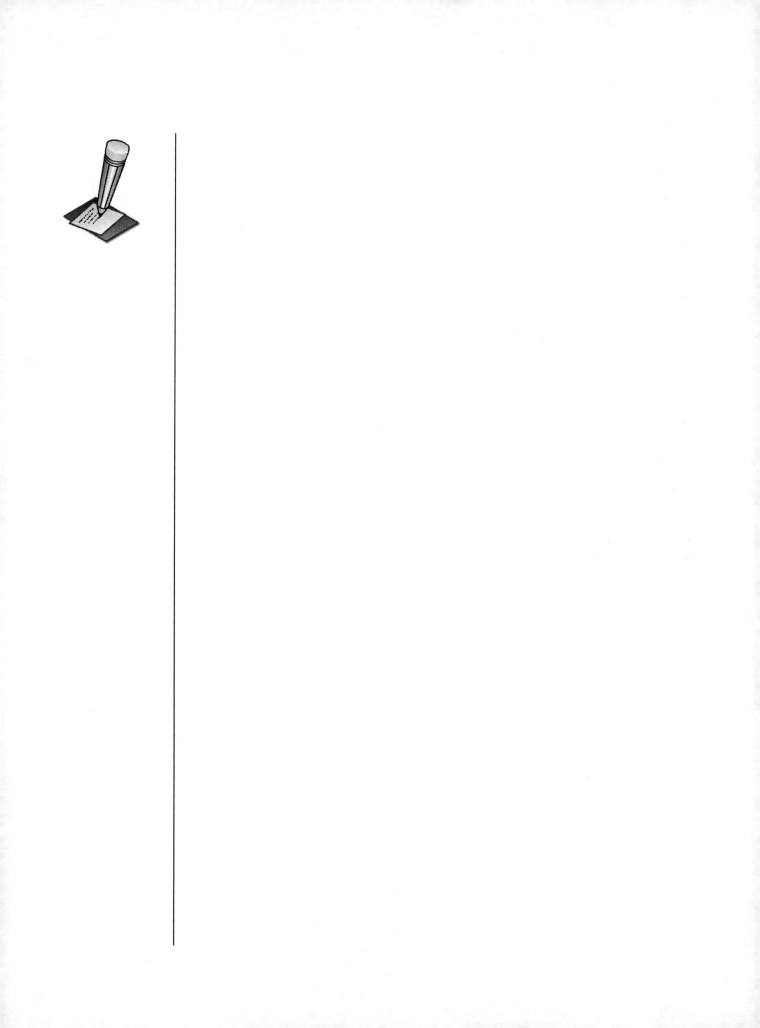

A | Mapping Server+ Course Content to the CompTIA® Server+® Exam Objectives

The following tables will assist you in mapping the Server+ course content to the CompTIA Server+ certification exam objectives.

1.0 System Hardware

Exam Objective	Server+ Certification Lesson and Topic Reference	Server+ Certification Activity Reference
1.1 Differentiate between system board types, features, components and their purposes.		
● Dip switches / jumpers	Lesson 2, Topic A	
● Processor (single and multi)	Lesson 2, Topic B	
● Bus types and bus speeds	Lesson 2, Topic A	
● On board components	Lesson 2, Topic A	
● NICs	Lesson 2, Topic A	
● Video	Lesson 2, Topic A	
● Audio	Lesson 2, Topic A	
● USB	Lesson 2, Topic A	
● HID	Lesson 2, Topic A	
● Serial	Lesson 2, Topic A	
● Parallel	Lesson 2, Topic A	
● Expansion slots	Lesson 2, Topic A	
● PCI	Lesson 2, Topic A	
● PCIe	Lesson 2, Topic A	
● PCIx	Lesson 2, Topic A	
● AGP	Lesson 2, Topic A	

Exam Objective	Server+ Certification Lesson and Topic Reference	Server+ Certification Activity Reference
1.1 Differentiate between system board types, features, components and their purposes.		
● ISA	Lesson 2, Topic A	
● BIOS	Lesson 2, Topic A	
● Riser Card / backplane	Lesson 2, Topic A	
● Storage connectors	Lesson 4, Topic B	
● SCSI	Lesson 4, Topic B	
● SATA	Lesson 4, Topic B	
● IDE	Lesson 4, Topic B	
● Floppy	Lesson 4, Topic A	

Exam Objective	Server+ Certification Lesson and Topic Reference	Server+ Certification Activity Reference
1.2 Deploy different chassis types and the appropriate components		
● Cooling	Lesson 2, Topic D	
● Fans	Lesson 2, Topic D	
● Water cooled	Lesson 2, Topic D	
● Passive	Lesson 2, Topic D	
● Active	Lesson 2, Topic D	
● Shroud	Lesson 2, Topic D	
● Ducts	Lesson 2, Topic D	Activity 7–3
● Redundant cooling	Lesson 2, Topic D	
● Hot swappable	Lesson 2, Topic D	Activity 7–6
● Ventilation	Lesson 2, Topic D	Activity 7–14
● Form Factor (tower, rack, blade)	Lesson 1, Topic B	
● Space utilization (U size, height, width, depth)	Lesson 1, Topic B	
● Power	Lesson 2, Topic D	
● Connectors	Lesson 2, Topic D	
● Voltages	Lesson 2, Topic D	
● Phase	Lesson 2, Topic D	

Exam Objective	Server+ Certification Lesson and Topic Reference	Server+ Certification Activity Reference
1.2 Deploy different chassis types and the appropriate components		
• Redundant power	Lesson 2, Topic D	
• Shut off switches – chassis intrusion	Lesson 2, Topic D	
• Power buttons	Lesson 2, Topic D	
• Reset buttons	Lesson 2, Topic D	
• Diagnostic LEDs	Lesson 2, Topic D	
• Expansion bays	Lesson 2, Topic A	

Exam Objective	Server+ Certification Lesson and Topic Reference	Server+ Certification Activity Reference
1.3 Differentiate between memory features / types and given a scenario select appropriate memory		
• Memory pairing	Lesson 2, Topic C	
• ECC vs. non ECC	Lesson 2, Topic C	
• Registered vs. non-registered	Lesson 2, Topic C	
• RAID and hot spares	Lesson 4, Topic C	
• Types	Lesson 2, Topic C	
• DDR	Lesson 2, Topic C	
• Fully buffered DIMM	Lesson 2, Topic C	
• DDR2	Lesson 2, Topic C	
• SDRAM	Lesson 2, Topic C	
• DDR3	Lesson 2, Topic C	
• Memory compatibility	Lesson 2, Topic C	
• Speed	Lesson 2, Topic C	
• Size	Lesson 2, Topic C	
• Pins	Lesson 2, Topic C	
• CAS latency	Lesson 2, Topic C	
• Timing	Lesson 2, Topic C	
• Vendor specific memory	Lesson 2, Topic C	
• On board vs. riser card	Lesson 2, Topic A	

Exam Objective	Server+ Certification Lesson and Topic Reference	Server+ Certification Activity Reference
1.4 Explain the importance of a Hardware Compatibility List (HCL)		
• Vendor standards for hardware	Lesson 2, Topic B	
• Memory and processor compatibility	Lesson 2, Topic C	
• Expansion cards compatibility	Lesson 2, Topic A	
• Virtualization requirements	Lesson 3, Topic B	

Exam Objective	Server+ Certification Lesson and Topic Reference	Server+ Certification Activity Reference
1.5 Differentiate between processor features / types and given a scenario select the appropriate processor		
• Multicore	Lesson 2, Topic B	
• Multiprocessor	Lesson 2, Topic B	
• Cache levels	Lesson 2, Topic B	
• Stepping	Lesson 2, Topic B	
• Speed	Lesson 2, Topic B	
• VRMs	Lesson 2, Topic B	
• Execute disable (XD) or not execute (NX)	Lesson 2, Topic B	
• Hyperthreading	Lesson 2, Topic B	
• VT or AMD-V	Lesson 2, Topic B	
• AMD vs.Intel (non-compatible CPUs)	Lesson 2, Topic B	
• Processor architecture (RISC, CISC)	Lesson 2, Topic B	
• Vendor slot types	Lesson 2, Topic B	
• 64 bit vs. 32 bit	Lesson 2, Topic B	
• Heat dissipation (heat sinks, fans, liquid cooling)	Lesson 2, Topic D	

Exam Objective	Server+ Certification Lesson and Topic Reference	Server+ Certification Activity Reference
1.6 Given a scenario, install appropriate expansion cards into a server while taking fault tolerance into consideration.		
● Manufacturer specific	Lesson 2, Topic A	
● Fax cards	Lesson 2, Topic A	
● PBX cards	Lesson 2, Topic A	
● Camera cards	Lesson 2, Topic A	
● VoIP	Lesson 2, Topic A	
● HBAs	Lesson 2, Topic A	
● NICs	Lesson 2, Topic A	Activity 5–3
● Video	Lesson 2, Topic A	
● Audio	Lesson 2, Topic A	
● Storage controller (SCSI, SATA, RAID)	Lesson 4, Topic B Lesson 4, Topic C	
● SCSI low voltage / high voltage (LVD/HVD)	Lesson 4, Topic B	
● SCSI IDs	Lesson 4, Topic B	
● Cables and connectors	Lesson 4, Topic B	
● Active vs. passive termination	Lesson 4, Topic B	
● Port expansion cards	Lesson 2, Topic A	
● USB	Lesson 2, Topic A	
● IEEE 1394	Lesson 2, Topic A	
● Serial	Lesson 2, Topic A	
● Parallel	Lesson 2, Topic A	

Exam Objective	Server+ Certification Lesson and Topic Reference	Server+ Certification Activity Reference
1.7 Install, update and configure appropriate firmware.		
● Driver / hardware compatibility	Lesson 3, Topic A	
● Implications of a failed firmware upgrade (redundant BIOS)	Lesson 7, Topic C	

Exam Objective	Server+ Certification Lesson and Topic Reference	Server+ Certification Activity Reference
1.7 Install, update and configure appropriate firmware.		
• Follow manufacturer instructions and documentation	Lesson 8, Topic A	

2.0 Software

Exam Objective	Server+ Certification Lesson and Topic Reference	Server+ Certification Activity Reference
2.1 Install, deploy, configure and update NOS (Windows / *nix).		
• Installation methods (Optical media, USB, network share, PXE)	Lesson 3, Topic A	
• Imaging — System cloning and deployment (Ghost, RIS/WDS, Altris, Virtualization templates)	Lesson 3, Topic A Lesson 6, Topic A	
• Bootloader	Lesson 3, Topic A	
• File systems:	Lesson 3, Topic A	
• FAT	Lesson 3, Topic A	
• FAT 32	Lesson 3, Topic A	
• NTFS	Lesson 3, Topic A	
• VMFS	Lesson 3, Topic A	
• ZFS	Lesson 3, Topic A	
• EXT3	Lesson 3, Topic A	
• Driver installation	Lesson 6, Topic A	
• Driver acquisition	Lesson 6, Topic A	
• Installation methods	Lesson 6, Topic A	
• Require media	Lesson 6, Topic A	
• Configure NOS:	Lesson 6, Topic A	
• Initial network	Lesson 6, Topic A	Activity 6–1, activity 6–2, activity, 6–3. activity 6–5, activity 6–6
• User	Lesson 6, Topic A	Activity 6–1, activity 6–2, activity, 6–3. activity 6–5, activity 6–6
• Device	Lesson 6, Topic A	Activity 6–1, activity 6–2, activity, 6–3. activity 6–5, activity 6–6

Exam Objective	Server+ Certification Lesson and Topic Reference	Server+ Certification Activity Reference
2.1 Install, deploy, configure and update NOS (Windows / *nix).		
● Roles	Lesson 6, Topic A	Activity 6–1, activity 6–2, activity, 6–3. activity 6–5, activity 6–6
● OS environmental settings	Lesson 6, Topic A	Activity 6–1, activity 6–2, activity, 6–3. activity 6–5, activity 6–6
● Applications and tools	Lesson 6, Topic A	Activity 6–1, activity 6–2, activity, 6–3. activity 6–5, activity 6–6
● Patch management	Lesson 3, Topic A	

Exam Objective	Server+ Certification Lesson and Topic Reference	Server+ Certification Activity Reference
2.2 Explain NOS security software and its features.		
● Software firewall	Lesson 3, Topic C	
● Port blocking	Lesson 3, Topic C	
● Application exception	Lesson 3, Topic C	
● ACL	Lesson 3, Topic C	
● Malware protection software	Lesson 3, Topic C	
● Antivirus	Lesson 3, Topic C	
● Antispyware	Lesson 3, Topic C	
● Basics of file level permissions vs share permissions	Lesson 3, Topic C	

Exam Objective	Server+ Certification Lesson and Topic Reference	Server+ Certification Activity Reference
2.3 Given a scenario, implement and administer NOS management features based on procedures and guidelines		
● User management	Lesson 3, Topic B	
● Add and remove users	Lesson 3, Topic B	
	Lesson 6, Topic A	
● Setting permissions	Lesson 3, Topic B	
● Group memberships	Lesson 3, Topic B	
● Policies	Lesson 3, Topic B	
	Lesson 6, Topic A	
● Logon scripts	Lesson 3, Topic B	

Exam Objective	Server+ Certification Lesson and Topic Reference	Server+ Certification Activity Reference
2.3 Given a scenario, implement and administer NOS management features based on procedures and guidelines		
• Resource management	Lesson 3, Topic B	
• ACLs	Lesson 3, Topic B	
• Quotas	Lesson 3, Topic B	
• Shadow Volumes	Lesson 3, Topic B	
• Disk management	Lesson 3, Topic B	
• Performance monitoring	Lesson 3, Topic B	
• Baselining	Lesson 3, Topic B	
• Monitoring (tools and agents)	Lesson 3, Topic B Lesson 6, Topic B	
• SNMP (MIBs)	Lesson 3, Topic B Lesson 6, Topic B	Activity 6–4
• WBEM (WMI)	Lesson 3, Topic B Lesson 6, Topic B	

Exam Objective	Server+ Certification Lesson and Topic Reference	Server+ Certification Activity Reference
2.4 Explain different server roles, their purpose and how they interact		
• File and print server	Lesson 1, Topic B	
• Database server	Lesson 1, Topic B	
• Web server	Lesson 1, Topic B	
• Messaging server	Lesson 1, Topic B	
• DHCP server	Lesson 1, Topic B	
• Directory services server	Lesson 1, Topic B	
• DNS server	Lesson 1, Topic B	
• Application server	Lesson 1, Topic B	
• Update server and proxy server	Lesson 1, Topic B	
• Filtering server	Lesson 1, Topic B	
• Monitoring server	Lesson 1, Topic B	
• Dedicated server	Lesson 1, Topic B	
• Distributed server	Lesson 1, Topic B	
• Peer to peer	Lesson 1, Topic B	

Exam Objective	Server+ Certification Lesson and Topic Reference	Server+ Certification Activity Reference
2.4 Explain different server roles, their purpose and how they interact		
• Remote access server	Lesson 1, Topic B	
• Virtualized services	Lesson 3, Topic B	
• NTP server	Lesson 1, Topic B	
• Explain the difference between a workstation, desktop, and a server	Lesson 1, Topic A	
Server shut down and start up sequence (One server vs multiple servers vs attached components.	Lesson 6, Topic A	

Exam Objective	Server+ Certification Lesson and Topic Reference	Server+ Certification Activity Reference
2.5 Summarize server virtualization concepts, features and considerations		
• Resource utilization	Lesson 3, Topic B	
• Configuration	Lesson 3, Topic B	
• Interconnectivity	Lesson 3, Topic B	
• Management server	Lesson 3, Topic B	
• Reasons for virtualization	Lesson 3, Topic B	
• Cost benefits	Lesson 3, Topic B	
• Redundancy	Lesson 3, Topic B	
• Green initiative	Lesson 3, Topic B	
• Disaster recovery	Lesson 3, Topic B	
• Testing environment	Lesson 3, Topic B	
• Ease of deployment	Lesson 3, Topic B	

Exam Objective	Server+ Certification Lesson and Topic Reference	Server+ Certification Activity Reference
2.6 Describe common elements of networking essentials		
• TCP/IP	Lesson 3, Topic D	
• Subnetting	Lesson 3, Topic D	
• DNS	Lesson 3, Topic D	

Exam Objective	Server+ Certification Lesson and Topic Reference	Server+ Certification Activity Reference
2.6 Describe common elements of networking essentials		
● DHCP	Lesson 3, Topic D	
● Classes	Lesson 3, Topic D	
● Gateways	Lesson 3, Topic D	
● Static vs dynamic	Lesson 3, Topic D	
● IP stack	Lesson 3, Topic D	
● Ports	Lesson 3, Topic D	
● Ethernet	Lesson 3, Topic D	
● Types	Lesson 3, Topic D	
● Speeds	Lesson 3, Topic D	
● Cables	Lesson 3, Topic D	
● VPN	Lesson 3, Topic D	
● VLAN	Lesson 3, Topic D	
● DMZ	Lesson 3, Topic D	

3.0 Storage

Exam Objective	Server+ Certification Lesson and Topic Reference	Server+ Certification Activity Reference
3.1 Describe, RAID technologies and its features and benefits		
● Hot spare	Lesson 4, Topic C	
● Software vs hardware	Lesson 4, Topic C	
● Cache read / write levels (data loss potential)	Lesson 4, Topic C Lesson 2, Topic C	
● Performance benefits and tradeoffs	Lesson 4, Topic C	

Exam Objective	Server+ Certification Lesson and Topic Reference	Server+ Certification Activity Reference
3.2 Given a scenario, select the appropriate RAID level		
● 0, 1, 3, 5, 6, 10, 50	Lesson 4, Topic C	Activity 5–8

Exam Objective	Server+ Certification Lesson and Topic Reference	Server+ Certification Activity Reference
3.2 Given a scenario, select the appropriate RAID level		
• Performance benefits and tradeoffs	Lesson 4, Topic C	

Exam Objective	Server+ Certification Lesson and Topic Reference	Server+ Certification Activity Reference
3.3 Install and configure different internal storage technologies		
• Hot swappable vs non-hot swappable	Lesson 4, Topic C	
• SCSI, Ultra SCSI, Ultra320 (termination), LUNs	Lesson 4, Topic B	
• SAS, SATA	Lesson 4, Topic B	
• Tape	Lesson 4, Topic A	
• Optical	Lesson 4, Topic A	Activity 5–7
• DVD	Lesson 4, Topic A	
• DVD-R	Lesson 4, Topic A	
• CD-ROM	Lesson 4, Topic A	
• CD-R	Lesson 4, Topic A	
• CD-RW	Lesson 4, Topic A	
• Blu-Ray	Lesson 4, Topic A	
• Flash	Lesson 4, Topic A	
Floppy (USB)	Lesson 4, Topic A	
Controller (firmware levels)	Lesson 4, Topic C	
Hard drive (firmware, JBOD)	Lesson 4, Topic A	

Exam Objective	Server+ Certification Lesson and Topic Reference	Server+ Certification Activity Reference
3.4 Summarize the purpose of external storage technologies		
• Network attached storage	Lesson 4, Topic D	
• Storage area network	Lesson 4, Topic E	
• Tape library	Lesson 4, Topic A	

Exam Objective	Server+ Certification Lesson and Topic Reference	Server+ Certification Activity Reference
3.4 Summarize the purpose of external storage technologies		
• WORM	Lesson 4, Topic A	
• Optical jukebox	Lesson 4, Topic A	
• Transport media	Lesson 4, Topic E	
• iSCSI	Lesson 4, Topic E	
• SATA	Lesson 4, Topic B	
• SAS	Lesson 4, Topic B	
• SCSI	Lesson 4, Topic B	
• Fiber Channel	Lesson 4, Topic E	

4.0 IT Environment

Exam Objective	Server+ Certification Lesson and Topic Reference	Server+ Certification Activity Reference
4.1 Write, utilize, and maintain documentation, diagrams and procedures		
• Follow pre-installation plan when building or upgrading servers	Lesson 8, Topic A	
• Labelling	Lesson 8, Topic A	
• Diagram server packs and environment topologies	Lesson 8, Topic A	
• Hardware and software, installation, configuration, server role, and repair logs	Lesson 7, Topic B	
• Document server baseline (before and after service)	Lesson 7, Topic B	Activity 7–2
• Original hardware configuration, service tags, asset management and warranty	Lesson 7, Topic B	
• Vendor specific documentation	Lesson 8, Topic A	
• Reference proper manuals	Lesson 8, Topic A	
• Websites	Lesson 8, Topic A	
• Support channels (list of vendors)	Lesson 8, Topic A	

Exam Objective	Server+ Certification Lesson and Topic Reference	Server+ Certification Activity Reference
4.2 Given a scenario, explain the purpose of the following industry best practices		
● Follow vendor specific server best practices	Lesson 8, Topic A	
● Documentation	Lesson 8, Topic A	
● Tools	Lesson 8, Topic A	
● Websites	Lesson 8, Topic A	
● Explore ramifications before implementing change — determine organizational impact.	Lesson 8, Topic A	
● Communication with stakeholders before talking action and upon completion of action	Lesson 8, Topic A	
● Comply with all local laws / regulations, industry and corporate regulations	Lesson 8, Topic A	
● Purpose of Service Level Agreement (SLAs)	Lesson 8, Topic A	
● Follow change control procedures	Lesson 8, Topic A	
● Equipment disposal	Lesson 8, Topic A	

Exam Objective	Server+ Certification Lesson and Topic Reference	Server+ Certification Activity Reference
4.3 Determine an appropriate physical environment for the server location		
● Check for adequate and dedicated power, proper amperage and voltage	Lesson 8, Topic A	
● UPS systems (check load, document service, periodic testing)	Lesson 8, Topic A	
● UPS specifications (run time, max load, bypass procedures, server communication and shut down, proper monitoring)	Lesson 8, Topic A	
● Server cooling considerations — HVAC	Lesson 8, Topic A	
● Adequate cooling in room	Lesson 8, Topic A	

Exam Objective	Server+ Certification Lesson and Topic Reference	Server+ Certification Activity Reference
4.3 Determine an appropriate physical environment for the server location		
● Adequate cooling in server rack	Lesson 8, Topic A	
● Temperature and humidity monitor	Lesson 8, Topic A	

Exam Objective	Server+ Certification Lesson and Topic Reference	Server+ Certification Activity Reference
4.4 Implement and configure different methods of server access		
● KVM (local and IP based)	Lesson 8, Topic B	
● Direct connect	Lesson 8, Topic B	
● Remote management	Lesson 8, Topic B	
● Remote control	Lesson 8, Topic B	Activity 8–2
● Administration	Lesson 8, Topic B	
● Software deployment	Lesson 8, Topic B	
● Dedicated management port	Lesson 8, Topic B	

Exam Objective	Server+ Certification Lesson and Topic Reference	Server+ Certification Activity Reference
4.5 Given a scenario, classify physical security measures for a server location		
● Physical server security	Lesson 8, Topic B	
● Locked doors	Lesson 8, Topic B	
● Rack doors	Lesson 8, Topic B	
● CCTV	Lesson 8, Topic B	
● Mantraps	Lesson 8, Topic B	
● Security personnel	Lesson 8, Topic B	
● Access control devices (RFID, keypads, pinpads)	Lesson 8, Topic B	
● Biometric devices (fingerprint scanner retina)	Lesson 8, Topic B	
● Security procedures	Lesson 8, Topic B	

Exam Objective	Server+ Certification Lesson and Topic Reference	Server+ Certification Activity Reference
4.5 Given a scenario, classify physical security measures for a server location		
● Limited access	Lesson 8, Topic B	
● Access logs	Lesson 8, Topic B	
● Limited hours	Lesson 8, Topic B	
● Defense in-depth — multiple layers of defense	Lesson 8, Topic B	
● Reason for physical security	Lesson 8, Topic B	
● Theft	Lesson 8, Topic B	
● Data loss	Lesson 8, Topic B	
● Hacking	Lesson 8, Topic B	
● Server documentation related to servers	Lesson 8, Topic B	
● Passwords	Lesson 8, Topic B	
● System configurations	Lesson 8, Topic B	
● Logs	Lesson 8, Topic B	

5.0 Disaster Recovery

Exam Objective	Server+ Certification Lesson and Topic Reference	Server+ Certification Activity Reference
5.1 Compare and contrast backup and restoration methodologies, media types and concepts		
● Methodologies (full, incremental, differential)	Lesson 10, Topic B	
● Snapshot	Lesson 10, Topic B	
● Copy	Lesson 10, Topic B	
● Bare metal	Lesson 10, Topic B	
● Open file	Lesson 10, Topic B	
● Databases	Lesson 10, Topic B	
● Data vs. OS restore	Lesson 10, Topic B	
● Rotation and retention (grandfather, father and son, leaning tower)	Lesson 10, Topic B	
● Media types	Lesson 10, Topic B	

Exam Objective	Server+ Certification Lesson and Topic Reference	Server+ Certification Activity Reference
5.1 Compare and contrast backup and restoration methodologies, media types and concepts		
● Tape	Lesson 10, Topic B	
● Disk	Lesson 10, Topic B	
● WORM	Lesson 10, Topic B	
● Optical	Lesson 10, Topic B	
● Flash	Lesson 10, Topic B	
● Backup security and off-site storage	Lesson 10, Topic B	
● Importance of testing the backup and restoration process	Lesson 10, Topic B	Activity 10–2 Activity 10–3

Exam Objective	Server+ Certification Lesson and Topic Reference	Server+ Certification Activity Reference
5.2 Given a scenario, compare and contrast the different types of replication methods		
● Disk to disk	Lesson 10, Topic C	
● Server to server	Lesson 10, Topic C	
● Clustering	Lesson 10, Topic C	
● Active/active	Lesson 10, Topic C	
● Active/passive	Lesson 10, Topic C	
● Site to site	Lesson 10, Topic C	
● Site types	Lesson 10, Topic C	
● Cold site	Lesson 10, Topic C	
● Hot site	Lesson 10, Topic C	
● Warm site	Lesson 10, Topic C	
● Distance requirements	Lesson 10, Topic C	

Exam Objective	Server+ Certification Lesson and Topic Reference	Server+ Certification Activity Reference
5.3 Explain data retention and destruction concepts		
● Awareness of potential legal requirements	Lesson 10, Topic B	
● Awareness of potential company policy requirements	Lesson 10, Topic B	
● Differentiate between archiving and backup	Lesson 10, Topic B	

Exam Objective	Server+ Certification Lesson and Topic Reference	Server+ Certification Activity Reference
5.4 Given a scenario, carry out the following basic steps of a disaster recovery plan		
● Disaster recovery testing process	Lesson 10, Topic A	
● Follow emergency procedures (people first)	Lesson 10, Topic A	
● Use appropriate fire suppressants	Lesson 10, Topic A	
● Follow escalation procedures for emergencies	Lesson 10, Topic A	
● Classification of systems (prioritization during recovery)	Lesson 10, Topic A	

6.0 Troubleshooting

Exam Objective	Server+ Certification Lesson and Topic Reference	Server+ Certification Activity Reference
6.1 Explain troubleshooting theory and methodologies		
● Identify the problem and determine the scope	Lesson 9, Topic A	

Exam Objective	Server+ Certification Lesson and Topic Reference	Server+ Certification Activity Reference
6.1 Explain troubleshooting theory and methodologies		
• Question users/ stakeholders and identify changes to the server / environment	Lesson 9, Topic A	
• Collect additional documentation / logs	Lesson 9, Topic A	
• If possible, replicate the problem as appropriate	Lesson 9, Topic A	
• If possible, perform back-ups before making changes	Lesson 9, Topic A	
• Establish a theory of probable cause (question the obvious)	Lesson 9, Topic A	
• Determine whether there is a common element of symptom causing multiple problems	Lesson 9, Topic A	
• Test the theory to determine cause	Lesson 9, Topic A	
• Once theory is confirmed determine next steps to resolve problem	Lesson 9, Topic A	
• If theory is not confirmed re-establish new theory or escalate	Lesson 9, Topic A	
• Establish a plan of action to resolve the problem and notify impacted users	Lesson 9, Topic A	
• Implement the solution or escalate as appropriate	Lesson 9, Topic A	
• Make one change at a time and test/confirm the change has resolved the problem	Lesson 9, Topic A	
• If the problem is not resolved, reverse the change if appropriate and implement new change	Lesson 9, Topic A	

Exam Objective	Server+ Certification Lesson and Topic Reference	Server+ Certification Activity Reference
6.1 Explain troubleshooting theory and methodologies		
• Verify full system functionality and if applicable implement preventative measures	Lesson 9, Topic A	
• Perform a root cause analysis	Lesson 9, Topic A	
• Document findings, actions and outcomes throughout the process	Lesson 9, Topic A	

Exam Objective	Server+ Certification Lesson and Topic Reference	Server+ Certification Activity Reference
6.2 Given a scenario, effectively troubleshoot hardware problems, selecting the appropriate tools and methods		
• Common problems	Lesson 9, Topic B	
• Failed POST	Lesson 9, Topic B	
• Overheating	Lesson 9, Topic B	
• Memory failure	Lesson 9, Topic B	
• Onboard component failure	Lesson 9, Topic B	
• Processor failure	Lesson 9, Topic B	
• Incorrect boot sequence	Lesson 9, Topic B	
• Expansion card failure	Lesson 9, Topic B	
• Operating system not found	Lesson 9, Topic B	
• Drive failure	Lesson 9, Topic B	
• Power supply failure	Lesson 9, Topic B	
• I/O failure	Lesson 9, Topic B	
• Causes of common problems	Lesson 9, Topic B	
• Third party components or incompatible components	Lesson 9, Topic B	
• Incompatible or incorrect BIOS	Lesson 9, Topic B	
• Cooling failure	Lesson 9, Topic B	

Exam Objective	Server+ Certification Lesson and Topic Reference	Server+ Certification Activity Reference
6.2 Given a scenario, effectively troubleshoot hardware problems, selecting the appropriate tools and methods		
• Mismatched components	Lesson 9, Topic B	
• Backplane failure	Lesson 9, Topic B	
• Environmental issues	Lesson 8, Topic A	
• Dust	Lesson 8, Topic A	
• Humidity	Lesson 8, Topic A	
• Temperature	Lesson 8, Topic A	
• Power surge / failure	Lesson 8, Topic A	
• Hardware tools	Lesson 9, Topic B	
• Power supply tester (multimeter)	Lesson 9, Topic B	
• System board tester	Lesson 9, Topic B	
• Compressed air	Lesson 9, Topic B	
• ESD equipment	Lesson 9, Topic B	

Exam Objective	Server+ Certification Lesson and Topic Reference	Server+ Certification Activity Reference
6.3 Given a scenario, effectively troubleshoot software problems, selecting the appropriate tools and methods		
• Common problems	Lesson 9, Topic C	
• User unable to logon	Lesson 9, Topic C	
• User cannot access resources	Lesson 9, Topic C	
• Memory leak	Lesson 9, Topic C	
• BSOD / stop	Lesson 9, Topic C	
• OS boot failure	Lesson 9, Topic C	
• Driver issues	Lesson 9, Topic C	
• Runaway process	Lesson 9, Topic C	
• Cannot mount drive	Lesson 9, Topic C	
• Cannot write to system log	Lesson 9, Topic C	
• Slow OS performance	Lesson 9, Topic C	
• Patch update failure	Lesson 9, Topic C	

Exam Objective	Server+ Certification Lesson and Topic Reference	Server+ Certification Activity Reference
6.3 Given a scenario, effectively troubleshoot software problems, selecting the appropriate tools and methods		
● Service failure	Lesson 9, Topic C	
● Hangs no shut down	Lesson 9, Topic C	
● Users cannot print	Lesson 9, Topic C	
● Cause of common problems	Lesson 9, Topic C	
● Malware	Lesson 9, Topic C	
● Unauthorized software	Lesson 9, Topic C	
● Software firewall	Lesson 9, Topic C	
● User Account Control (UAC/SUDO)	Lesson 9, Topic C	
● Improper permissions	Lesson 9, Topic C	
● Corrupted files	Lesson 9, Topic C	
● Lack of hard drive spaces	Lesson 9, Topic C	
● Lack of system resources	Lesson 9, Topic C	
● Virtual memory (misconfigured, corrupt)	Lesson 9, Topic C	
● Fragmentation	Lesson 9, Topic C	
● Encryption	Lesson 9, Topic C	
● Print server drivers/ services	Lesson 9, Topic C	
● Print spooler	Lesson 9, Topic C	
● Software tools	Lesson 9, Topic C	
● System logs	Lesson 9, Topic C	
● Monitoring tools (resource monitor, performance monitor)	Lesson 9, Topic C	
● Defragmentation tools	Lesson 9, Topic C	

Exam Objective	Server+ Certification Lesson and Topic Reference	Server+ Certification Activity Reference
6.4 Given a scenario, effectively diagnose network problems, selecting the appropriate tools and methods		
● Common problems	Lesson 9, Topic D	

Exam Objective	Server+ Certification Lesson and Topic Reference	Server+ Certification Activity Reference
6.4 Given a scenario, effectively diagnose network problems, selecting the appropriate tools and methods		
● Internet connectivity failure	Lesson 9, Topic D	
● Email failure	Lesson 9, Topic D	
● Resource unavailable	Lesson 9, Topic D	
● DHCP server misconfigured	Lesson 9, Topic D	
● Non-functional or unreachable	Lesson 9, Topic D	
● Destination host unreachable	Lesson 9, Topic D	
● Unknown host	Lesson 9, Topic D	
● Default gateway misconfigured	Lesson 9, Topic D	
● Failure of service provider	Lesson 9, Topic D	
● Can reach by IP not by host name	Lesson 9, Topic D	
● Causes of common problems	Lesson 9, Topic D	
● Improper IP configuration	Lesson 9, Topic D	
● VLAN configuration	Lesson 9, Topic D	
● Port security	Lesson 9, Topic D	
● Improper subnetting	Lesson 9, Topic D	
● Component failure	Lesson 9, Topic D	
● Incorrect OS route tables	Lesson 9, Topic D	
● Bad cables	Lesson 9, Topic D	
● Firewall (misconfiguration, hardware failure, software failure)	Lesson 9, Topic D	
● Mis-configured NIC, routing / switch issues	Lesson 9, Topic D	
● DNS and/or DHCP failure	Lesson 9, Topic D	
● Mis-configured hosts file	Lesson 9, Topic D	
● Networking tools	Lesson 9, Topic D	

Exam Objective	Server+ Certification Lesson and Topic Reference	Server+ Certification Activity Reference
6.4 Given a scenario, effectively diagnose network problems, selecting the appropriate tools and methods		
● ping	Lesson 9, Topic D	
● tracert / traceroute	Lesson 9, Topic D	
● ipconfig / ifconfig	Lesson 9, Topic D	
● nslookup	Lesson 9, Topic D	
● net use / mount	Lesson 9, Topic E	
● route	Lesson 9, Topic D	
● nbstat	Lesson 9, Topic D	
● netstat	Lesson 9, Topic D	

Exam Objective	Server+ Certification Lesson and Topic Reference	Server+ Certification Activity Reference
6.5 Given a scenario, effectively troubleshoot storage problems, selecting the appropriate tools and methods		
● Common problems	Lesson 9, Topic E	
● Slow file access	Lesson 9, Topic E	
● OS not found	Lesson 9, Topic E	
● Data not available	Lesson 9, Topic E	
● Unsuccessful backup	Lesson 9, Topic E	
● Error lights	Lesson 9, Topic E	
● Unable to mount the device	Lesson 9, Topic E	
● Drive not available	Lesson 9, Topic E	
● Cannot access logical drive	Lesson 9, Topic E	
● Data corruption	Lesson 9, Topic E	
● Slow I/O performance	Lesson 9, Topic E	
● Restore failure	Lesson 9, Topic E	
● Cache failure	Lesson 9, Topic E	
● Multiple drive failure	Lesson 9, Topic E	
● Causes of common problems	Lesson 9, Topic E	
● Media failure	Lesson 9, Topic E	

Exam Objective	Server+ Certification Lesson and Topic Reference	Server+ Certification Activity Reference
6.5 Given a scenario, effectively troubleshoot storage problems, selecting the appropriate tools and methods		
• Drive failure	Lesson 9, Topic E	
• Controller failure	Lesson 9, Topic E	
• HBA failure	Lesson 9, Topic E	
• Loose connectors	Lesson 9, Topic E	
• Cable problems	Lesson 9, Topic E	
• Mis-configuration	Lesson 9, Topic E	
• Improper termination	Lesson 9, Topic E	
• Corrupt boot sector	Lesson 9, Topic E	
• Corrupt file system table	Lesson 9, Topic E	
• Array rebuild	Lesson 9, Topic E	
• Improper disk partition	Lesson 9, Topic E	
• Bad sectors	Lesson 9, Topic E	
• Cache battery failure	Lesson 9, Topic E	
• Cache turned off	Lesson 9, Topic E	
• Insufficient space	Lesson 9, Topic E	
• Improper RAID configuration	Lesson 9, Topic E	
• Mis-matched drives	Lesson 9, Topic E	
• Backplane failure	Lesson 9, Topic E	
• Storage tools	Lesson 9, Topic E	
• Partitioning tools	Lesson 9, Topic E	
• Disk management	Lesson 9, Topic E	
• RAID array management	Lesson 9, Topic E	
• Array management	Lesson 9, Topic E	
• System logs	Lesson 9, Topic C	
• Net use / mount command	Lesson 9, Topic E	
• Monitoring tools	Lesson 9, Topic C	

B | CompTIA® Server+® Acronyms

The following is a list of acronyms that appear on the CompTIA Server+ exam covering 2009 objectives. Candidates are encouraged to review the complete list and attain a working knowledge of all listed acronyms as a part of a comprehensive exam preparation program.

Acronym	Associated Term
*nix	Unix/Linux/Solaris/OS X/BSD
AD	Active Directory
AGP	Advanced Graphics Port
AMD-V	AMD Virtualization
BIOS	Basic Input/Output System
BSOD	Blue Screen of Death
CPU	Central Processing Unit
CRU	Customer Replaceable Unit
DC	Domain Controller
DHCP	Dynamic Host Control Protocol
DMZ	Demilitarized Zone
DNS	Domain Name Service
DSRM	Directory Services Restore Mode
EISA	Extended Industry Standard Architecture
FAT	File Allocation Table
FRU	Field Replaceable Unit
FTP	File Transfer Protocol
HBA	Host Bus Adapter
HCL	Hardware Compatibility List
HID	Human Interface Device
HTTP	Hyper Text Transport Protocol
HTTPS	Secure Hyper Text Transport Protocol
IMAP4	Internet Mail Access Protocol
ISA	Industry Standard Architecture

Acronym	Associated Term
iSCSI	Internetworking Small Computer Serial Interface
JBOD	Just a bunch of disks
LAN	Local Area Network
LDAP	Lightweight Directory Access Protocol
LKGC	Last Known Good Configuration
LUN	Logical Unit Number
NOS	Network Operating System
NTFS	New Technology File System
NTP	Network Time Protocol
NX	No Execute
OS	Operating System
OSPF	Open Shortest Path First
PCI	Peripheral Component Interconnect
POP3	Post Office Protocol
RAID	Redundant Array of Independent Disks
RAM	Random Access Memory
SAS	Serial Attached SCSI
SATA	Serial ATA
SCSI	Small Computer Serial Interface
SLA	Service Level Agreement
SMTP	Simple Mail Transport Protocol
SNMP	Simple Network Management Protocol
TCP/IP	Transmission Control Protocol / Internet Protocol
USB	Universal Serial Bus
VLAN	Virtual Local Area Network
VM	Virtual Machine
VMFS	VMWare File System
VoIP	Voice over IP
VPN	Virtual Private Network
VT	Virtualization Technology
WBEM	Web-based Enterprise Management
WMI	Windows Management Instrumentation
WORM	Write Once Read Many
XD	Execute Disable

Lesson Labs

Due to classroom setup constraints, some labs cannot be keyed in sequence immediately following their associated lesson. Your instructor will tell you whether your labs can be practiced immediately following the lesson or whether they require separate setup from the main lesson content.

Lesson 1 Lab 1

Discussing Server Fundamentals

Activity Time: 15 minutes

Scenario:
In this activity, you will discuss common network architecture and server types.

1. What is the difference between the client/server architecture and the centralized network architecture?

2. What are the various functions performed by a server on a network?

3. What are the various services provided by a web server?

4. List some common applications of a peer-to-peer network configuration.

Lesson 2 Lab 1

Discussing Server Hardware Components

Activity Time: 15 minutes

Scenario:
In this activity, you will discuss server hardware components.

---

1. You encounter various problems when you switch on a server. The POST test reveals errors at different stages. What components are checked at each stage in the POST test?

---

2. What is the advantage of implementing the memory pairing feature on your server?

---

3. Why is RAM that works properly in a workstation often incompatible with RAM used in the server?

---

4. You have been asked by your manager to install a redundant cooling system on a server and PC. Although the redundant cooling feature has its benefits when installed on a server, installing it on PC has disadvantages. List some of the disadvantages.

---

5. Discuss the advantages of the PCI bus technology.

---

6. **In a server running on Microsoft Windows Server 2008, how do you verify the size of RAM currently installed on the server without opening the chassis and examining the memory modules?**

Lesson 2 Lab 2

Identifying Server Hardware Components

Activity Time: 25 minutes

Objective:

Identify Server Hardware Components

Data Files:

Exploring the Server Hardware_Crossword.htm

Before You Begin:

From the C:\ServerPlus\Data\Exploring the Server Hardware folder, open the Exploring the Server Hardware_Crossword.htm file.

Scenario:

In this activity, you will identify the various server hardware components.

---

1. Complete the crossword provided in the Exploring the Server Hardware_Crossword.htm document.

---

2. Check your answers with the Crossword_Solution_lesson2.htm file provided in the solution folder.

Lesson 3 Lab 1

Discussing Server Software

Activity Time: 15 minutes

Scenario:
In this activity, you will discuss the applications and features of server software.

1. What are the various factors that will influence your choice of a NOS?

2. What are the various factors that you will consider while choosing a file system?

3. Compare the advantage and disadvantage of booting by network share and boot devices.

4. What are the various resource management features supported by a NOS?

5. What are the advantages of server virtualization?

Lesson 4 Lab 1

Discussing the Server Storage Systems

Activity Time: 15 minutes

Scenario:

In this activity, you will discuss the server storage systems.

---

1. List the benefits of a WORM storage system.

---

2. What are the main differences between the IDE and SCSI technologies?

---

3. What are the risks of a SCSI bus that does not have terminations?

---

4. You company is currently planning to install an enterprise-wide server that will be used for heavy transactional data. Management has requested a fast, fault-tolerant system. Which RAID system will you suggest to implement?

Lesson 5 Lab 1

Discussing Server Hardware Installation

Activity Time: 15 minutes

Scenario:
In this activity, you will discuss server hardware installation.

---

1. When installing server hardware, what safety precautions should you always take?

---

2. In a rackmount server setup, how is the rack space measured?

---

3. What is the purpose of protecting devices from ESD and how will you achieve it?

---

4. Once the system board is replaced, do components have to be installed in a particular order?

---

5. After installing a new CPU, what critical precaution must you take prior to powering up the system?

Lesson 6 Lab 1

Discussing Server Configuration Practices

Activity Time: 15 minutes

Scenario:
In this activity, you will discuss server configuration practices.

1. **True or False? When installing Windows Server 2008 on a new server, you must provide third-party device drivers near the end of the installation process.**

   ___ True

   ___ False

2. **Your company has bought an external CD tower to hold several proprietary software packages used in the course of business. This CD tower needs to be connected to the main server. Place the installation steps in the proper order.**

   Power on the server.

   Install device drivers.

   Set permissions for employees to access the tower.

   Check for updated device drivers.

   Connect the tower to the main server.

   Power on the tower.

3. **Match each management protocol to its description.**

___	SNMP	a.	Includes network traffic monitoring probes.
___	DMI	b.	Agents store management information in MIFs.
___	RMON	c.	Agents store management information in MIBs.

4. **True or False? The main reason for keeping server documentation current is to assist in troubleshooting efforts.**

   ___ True

   ___ False

5. **What are the various user policies that you will implement on your organization's domain?**

Lesson 7 Lab 1

Discussing Issues Related to Upgrading a Server

Activity Time: 15 minutes

Scenario:

In this activity, you will discuss some server upgrade issues.

1. **Place these upgrade checklist steps in the proper order.**

    Research documentation pertaining to the upgrade.

    Schedule downtime.

    Test and pilot the upgrade.

    Locate and obtain the necessary software.

    Implement the upgrade.

2. **Match each installation or upgrade issue to its corresponding hardware component.**

    ___ Termination and cabling   a. Processors
    ___ IRQs   b. Memory
    ___ Stepping   c. Hard drives
    ___ ECC or non-ECC   d. UPS
    ___ Battery disposal   e. Adapters and peripherals

3. **Match each server software type to the possible reason for upgrading it.**

    ___ BIOS and firmware   a. Implement a new MIB for a replacement UPS.

    ___ NOS   b. Enhance performance of peripheral devices.

    ___ Drivers   c. Fix known security holes.

    ___ Monitoring agents and service tools   d. Enable the system board to support new hardware.

4. What are the various best practices that a network administrator must follow before performing an upgrade of the server?

Lesson 8 Lab 1

Discussing the Best Practices of Deploying a Server the IT Environment

Activity Time: 15 minutes

Scenario:

In this activity, you will discuss the best practices of installing a server in the IT environment.

1. What devices can be used for securing the server room?

2. What are the various factors you will consider before installing CCTVs inside the server room?

3. What kind of information can be included in a security related documentation?

4. What are the various agreements included in an SLA?

Lesson 9 Lab 1

Discussing Server Issues

Activity Time: 15 minutes

Scenario:
In this activity, you will discuss how to troubleshoot servers.

1. What is an important role of the troubleshooting process?

2. What are the steps involved in a troubleshooting process?

3. A user calls the help desk and says he cannot open a file. The server where the file is stored is located in a different building. What are the first steps you need to take to be able to diagnose the problem?

4. Through your diagnostic questions, you establish that the file is a word-processing document stored on a network file server. The user last accessed the file three months ago. By reviewing the activity logs on the file server, you find that there is a bi-monthly cleanup routine that automatically backs up and removes user data files that have not been accessed since the last cleanup date. The backups are stored in an offsite facility for one year. Given this information, what is your action plan, how will you implement it, and what potential side effects of the plan do you need to consider?

5. A 30-GB hard drive was installed, but the system reports that the drive is about 500 MB. What can be done to resolve this problem?

Lesson 10 Lab 1
Discussing Disaster Recovery

Activity Time: 15 minutes

Scenario:
In this activity, you will discuss various aspects of the disaster recovery process.

1. What distinguishes disaster recovery planning from fault tolerance planning?

2. List some of the different personnel roles involved in designing and implementing a disaster recovery plan.

3. **What do you feel is the most important aspect of a disaster recovery plan? Why?**

_____

4. **Why is it important to update a disaster recovery plan regularly?**

_____

5. **How many tape sets are required when using the grandfather-father-son rotation method?**

_____

6. **List and describe the three major backup types.**

_____

7. **What are some special issues involved in backing up databases?**

_____

Lesson 10 Lab 2

Identifying Disaster Recovery Concepts

Activity Time: 25 minutes

Data Files:

Exploring Disaster Recovery Concepts and Methodologies_Crossword.htm

Before You Begin:

From the C:\ServerPlus\Data\Exploring Disaster Recovery Concepts and Methodologies folder, open the Exploring Disaster Recovery Concepts and Methodologies_Crossword.htm file.

Scenario:

In this activity, you will identify the various disaster recovery concepts and methodologies.

---

1. Complete the crossword provided in the Exploring Disaster Recovery Concepts and Methodologies_Crossword.htm document.

---

2. Check your answers with the Crossword_Solution_lesson10.htm file provided in the solution folder.

Solutions

Lesson 1

Activity 1-1

1. **Match the type of computer to its description.**

   c   Server

   a   Workstation

   b   Desktop Computer

   a. High-end computers designed for technical or scientific applications.

   b. A system deployed as a general purpose computer to be operated directly by a single user.

   c. Computers that are designed to facilitate the sharing of resources between other computers on the network.

2. **Which statements are valid for a peer-to-peer network?**

   a) Access to shared files is controlled by centralized servers.

   ✓ b) No centralized server is required.

   c) Clients in a peer-to-peer network do not have any processing power of their own.

   ✓ d) No centralized data storage is used.

3. **True or False? A server computer can support a multiuser operating system.**

   ✓ True

   ___ False

4. **Which networks are based on a type of interaction between the server and client computer?**

   ✓ a) Client-server networks

   b) TCP/IP networks

   ✓ c) Centralized computer networks

   ✓ d) Peer-to-Peer computer networks

Activity 1-2

1. **Which server type can be used as part of a firewall solution?**

   a) File

   ✓ b) Proxy

   c) Print

   d) DHCP

2. **Which of these are server form factors?**

   ✓ a) Rackmount

   ✓ b) Blade

   c) Database

   ✓ d) Tower

3. **Match each application server model to its description.**

c	Peer-to-peer	a.	They are designed to run primarily on a single computer.
b	Distributed	b.	They are designed to run on more than one computer.
a	Dedicated	c.	They do not need a server to act as a go-between among participating clients.

4. **Which Internet functionality allows a server to assign IP addresses to clients that log on to the network?**

   a) FTP

   b) Proxy

   ✓ c) DHCP

   d) DNS

5. **Match each internetworking device with its description.**

c	Gateway	a.	Prevents unwanted data from entering into the network.
b	Router	b.	Manages the exchange of information from network to network, or between network segments.
a	Firewall	c.	Translates the protocols between dissimilar networks.

Lesson 1 Follow-up

Lesson 1 Lab 1

1. **What is the difference between the client/server architecture and the centralized network architecture?**

   In client/server architecture, client nodes have some processing capabilities of their own and may not depend on the server for all functions. In centralized network architecture, client nodes do not perform any processing on their own and are totally dependent on the centralized server for all data processing. Client nodes act as dumb terminals that simply receive input from users and provide them with the output generated by the server.

2. **What are the various functions performed by a server on a network?**

   Answers will vary, but may include: functions such as facilitating the sharing of files, printers, and storage resources, securing the network from untrusted users, transferring email messages, and processing requests from clients.

3. **What are the various services provided by a web server?**

   Answers will vary, but may include: services such as resolving the IP addresses from the domain names, assigning IP address to client nodes, blocking data from untrusted sources, and acting as a proxy for an organizations network.

4. **List some common applications of a peer-to-peer network configuration.**

   Answers will vary, but may include: applications such as VoIP, instant messaging, online chat, streaming media, and online gaming. The configuration can also be used for file sharing, though the bandwidth requirement would be very high.

Lesson 2

Activity 2-1

1. **A 32-bit PCI bus is operating at a clock speed of 66 MHz. What is the total bandwidth of the bus?**

   ✓ a) 264 Mb/s

   b) 512 Mb/s

   c) 528 Mb/s

   d) 544 Mb/s

2. **Which PCI technology uses a point-to-point bus topology to ensure that devices have constant access to the system bus?**

   a) Bus mastering

   ✓ b) PCIe

   c) PCIx

   d) AGP

3. **True or False? Server system boards are most often identified by their form factors.**

___ True

_✓_ False

4. **Match a bus type to its description.**

_b_ Processor bus

a. Handles traffic between the CPU, chipset, and RAM.

_a_ Memory bus

b. Handles traffic between the CPU and the chipset.

_c_ I/O buses

c. Handles traffic between hardware components and the processor.

5. **What is the advantage of using a riser card?**

The riser card enables you to connect additional adapters to the system in an orientation that is parallel to the system board, thereby saving on space within the system case.

Activity 2-2

1. **Which feature provides protection against buffer overflow attacks?**

✓ a) XD

b) AMD-V

c) Hyperthreading

d) Mutliprocessing

2. **True or False? The processor first checks the L1 cache residing on the processor.**

_✓_ True

___ False

3. **Match an instruction set to its description.**

_c_ CISC

a. A design strategy for computer architecture that is meant to simplify and streamline CPU operation by taking advantage of advancements in compiler technology and by combining the best of two design strategies.

_b_ RISC

b. A design strategy for computer architecture that depends on a combination of hardware and software to perform complicated instructions.

_a_ EPIC

c. A design strategy for computer architecture that depends on hardware to perform complicated instructions.

4. **Which feature enhances the processor design by implementing virtualization on it?**

a) XD

b) Mutliprocessing

✓ c) AMD-V/VT

d) Hyperthreading

5. **What is the key factor that you must consider when selecting a CPU for a server?**

   a) Power supply

   b) Expansion slots

   c) RAM

   ✓ d) System board

6. **What are the factors that you should keep in mind when installing a CPU?**

   ✓ a) Power

   ✓ b) Removal

   ✓ c) Cooling

   d) RAM

Activity 2-3

1. **Which of these is a characteristic of buffered memory?**

   a) It contains a register that delays incoming data.

   b) It holds data until it can be written to the disk drive.

   ✓ c) It helps to minimize the load of information transfer.

   d) It holds data in a secondary cache to speed up processes.

2. **What are the speed and cost differences between SRAM and DRAM?**

   a) SRAM memory is slower and less expensive than DRAM.

   b) DRAM memory is slower and more expensive than SRAM.

   ✓ c) SRAM memory is faster and more expensive than DRAM.

   d) DRAM memory is faster and less expensive than SRAM.

3. **True or False? RAMBUS is the fastest type of RAM available.**

   ✓ True

   ___ False

4. **Match a RAM memory type to its description.**

b	DRAM	a.	Runs at high clock speeds and is synchronized with the CPU bus.
c	EDO	b.	A type of RAM that needs to be refreshed.
a	SDRAM	c.	Memory access cycles overlap, saving about 10 nanoseconds per bit of data accessed.

5. **True or False? Memory interleaving provides for concurrent memory requests, so read and write operations can occur almost simultaneously.**

   ✓ True

   ___ False

Activity 2-4

1. **Which provides sufficient cooling even if an air moving device fails?**

    a) Vent cooling system

    b) Hot swappable cooling system

    c) Liquid cooling system

    ✓ d) Redundant cooling system

2. **True or False? A diagnostic LED is an electronic device that lights up when electricity is passed through it to provide a quick visual notification of the status of the server and FRUs.**

    ✓ True

    ___ False

3. **Match a power connector to the peripheral devices that uses it.**

_c_	Berg	a.	Serial ATA drives
_b_	Molex	b.	SCSI drives
_a_	SATA	c.	Floppy disk drives

4. **What is the power required by the PCI bus?**

    a) 12.1 watts

    ✓ b) 56.1 watts

    c) 5 watts

    d) 20 to 25 watts

Lesson 2 Follow-up

Lesson 2 Lab 1

1. **You encounter various problems when you switch on a server. The POST test reveals errors at different stages. What components are checked at each stage in the POST test?**

    POST is a built-in diagnostic program that is run every time a server starts up. Initially, the power supply is tested and, when optimum power is fed to the system, the CPU, BIOS, and RAM are checked. Finally, the I/O drives and controllers are tested.

2. **What is the advantage of implementing the memory pairing feature on your server?**

    Memory pairing increases RAM capacity, thereby enabling you to open more files and programs simultaneously. Newer servers use DIMMs (dual in-line memory modules) that you can install singly, although some Dual DDR (also called dual-channel DDR) motherboards perform better when RAM is installed in paired sets.

3. **Why is RAM that works properly in a workstation often incompatible with RAM used in the server?**

    Servers usually use ECC RAM; they will not operate properly if non-ECC RAM is installed on them.

4. **You have been asked by your manager to install a redundant cooling system on a server and PC. Although the redundant cooling feature has its benefits when installed on a server, installing it on PC has disadvantages. List some of the disadvantages.**

    Answers will vary, but may include: providing redundant cooling by exploiting more air moving devices than is needed for a nonredundant case has several disadvantages. Disadvantages include the cost of extra air moving devices, cost of supplying extra power capacity to drive the extra air moving devices, and need for extra space to accommodate the extra air moving devices. This is a serious concern because the room occupied by fans cannot be used for electronics. Due to these drawbacks, redundant cooling is implemented only on a server.

5. **Discuss the advantages of the PCI bus technology.**

    Answers will vary, but may include: This technology expands the serial and parallel I/O devices' accessibility, increases data transfer speed, increases system performance, increases bandwidth, and eliminates bus bottlenecks.

6. **In a server running on Microsoft Windows Server 2008, how do you verify the size of RAM currently installed on the server without opening the chassis and examining the memory modules?**

    In a server running on Microsoft Windows Server 2008, the System Properties window of the server displays how much memory is currently installed on the system. You can also access the BIOS and view how much memory is installed.

Lesson 3

Activity 3-1

1. **Which operating system is a NOS?**

    a) Microsoft Windows XP

    ✓ b) Microsoft Windows Server 2008

    c) Microsoft Windows 2000

    d) Microsoft Windows Vista

2. **Which file system is an example of the journaling file system?**

    a) FAT32

    b) FAT

    c) NTFS

    ✓ d) EXT3

3. **Which program acts as an interface between a hardware device and its operating system?**

    a) BIOS

    b) File system

    ✓ c) Device driver

    d) Patch

4. **Which file systems can be used with Windows-based computers?**

   ✓ a) FAT

   b) VMFS

   ✓ c) NTFS

   d) ZFS

5. **Which of these require the implementation of PXE?**

   a) Personal computer

   ✓ b) Centralized network of a library

   ✓ c) Office networks

   d) Peer-to-peer network

Activity 3-2

1. **Which of these is a user management feature?**

   a) ACL

   ✓ b) Group level permission

   c) Disk quotas

   d) Shadow copy

2. **Which are the resource management features of a NOS?**

   a) Setting up permissions

   ✓ b) Virtualization support

   ✓ c) Shadow copy

   d) Maintaining logon scripts

3. **Which statements are valid for server virtualization?**

   ✓ a) Server virtualization leads to reduction in space, power, and cooling requirements.

   ✓ b) It is possible to use a single physical server as a sandbag for testing multiple applications at the same time.

   c) All virtual servers need to run the same operating system.

   ✓ d) Server virtualization reduces the cost.

4. **True or False? Virtual server migration is possible between physical hardware made by different manufacturers.**

   ___ True

   ✓ False

5. **Which disk quota indicates the effective limit of the data that can be stored by a user on the shared disk?**

   a) Soft quota

   ✓ b) Hard quota

   c) Grace quota

   d) File quota

6. **In which operating system, the shadow volume copy is known as Volume Snapshot Service (VSS)?**

   In all windows operating systems, the shadow volume feature is known as Volume Snapshot Service (VSS).

Activity 3-3

1. **Which statements are valid for antivirus software?**

   a) They cannot detect any spyware.

   ✓ b) An antivirus can remove any code that resembles a virus.

   c) Antivirus software is always deployed on gateway servers at the network perimeter.

   ✓ d) Antivirus software is capable of monitoring a system for activities common to virus programs.

2. **Which statements are valid for share-level permissions?**

   a) They prompt the user for user name and password each time the shared resource is accessed.

   ✓ b) Any user who logs into the user's computer can access the protected resources.

   c) They are more secure than file-level permissions.

   ✓ d) All shared files are stored on user's computer.

3. **The firewall implementation in which the communication channel used by the malware is blocked is known as** *port blocking* .

4. **What is the name of the folder that can be remotely accessed from other computers through a local area network as if it were a resource in the local machine?**

   The folder that can be remotely accessed from other computers through a local area network as if it were a resource in the local machine is known as network share.

Activity 3-4

1. **Which class of IP address is set aside for research and experimentation purpose?**

   a) Class A

   b) Class B

   c) Class D

   ✓ d) Class E

2. **Match the classes of IP addresses to their range.**

a	Class A	a.	1.0.0.0 to 127.255.255.255
c	Class B	b.	240.0.0.0 to 255.255.255.255
e	Class C	c.	128.0.0.0 to 191.255.255.255
d	Class D	d.	224.0.0.0 to 239.255.255.255
b	Class E	e.	192.0.0.0 to 223.255.255.255

3. **Match the TCP port types to their range.**

c	Well known ports	a.	1024 through 49151
a	Registered ports	b.	49152 through 65535
b	Dynamic ports	c.	1 through 1023

4. **True or False? A VPN network infrastructure is owned by a single organization.**

___ True

✓ False

5. **Which utility of TCP/IP provides dynamic configuration of IP addresses?**

    a) Subnetting

    b) DNS

✓ c) DHCP

    d) FQDN

6. **Which Ethernet types use the star topology?**

    a) 10 BASE 5

    b) 10 BASE 2

✓ c) 10 BASE T

✓ d) Switched Ethernet

Lesson 3 Follow-up

Lesson 3 Lab 1

1. **What are the various factors that will influence your choice of a NOS?**

   Answers will vary, but may include: factors such as compatibility with hardware, the management features provided, the security features available, the various file systems that can be supported, and support for virtualization.

2. **What are the various factors that you will consider while choosing a file system?**

   Answers will vary, but may include: factors such as ease of deployment and access to data, support provided by the operating system in use, support provided by the storage hardware in use, and the amount of data that can be stored.

3. **Compare the advantage and disadvantage of booting by network share and boot devices.**

   The main advantage of network share booting is that it provides consistency across the network on centralized networks. However, it is slower than booting from boot devices and should always be carried out from a trusted network.

4. **What are the various resource management features supported by a NOS?**

   Answers will vary, but may include: resource management features such as ACLs, disk quotas, shadow copies, baselining, and SNMP.

5. **What are the advantages of server virtualization?**

   Answers will vary, but may include: benefits such as reduced space requirements, reduced cooling and power requirements, reduced cost of installation and maintenance, and testing multiple applications in a single server.

Lesson 4

Activity 4-1

1. **Which storage system does not involve any moving parts to read and write data?**

   ✓ a) Flash storage

   b) Optical jukebox

   c) Optical storage

   d) Tape libraries

2. **Match the storage device to its appropriate description.**

_c_	Floppy disk drive	a.	Records data magnetically; most often used for backups.
_d_	Hard disk drive	b.	Records and reads data by using a laser.
_b_	Optical disk drive	c.	Records data magnetically on removable disks.
_a_	Tape drive	d.	Records data magnetically on nonremovable disks.
_e_	Flash drive	e.	Records data in nonvolatile memory.

3. **Which optical drive media types enable you to write to an optical disk only once?**

   a) CD-RW

   b) DVD-RW

   ✓ c) CD-R

   d) DVD-RAM

4. **Which tape drive provides the maximum storage capacity of 800 GB on a single tape with a transfer rate of 160 MB/s?**

   a) QIC

   b) DLT

   c) 4 mm digital audio tape

   ✓ d) Ultrium-3

5. **A user wants to transfer several megabytes of data between two computers that are not connected by a network. What storage device would you recommend?**

   ✓ a) A USB thumb drive

   b) A floppy disk

   c) An external tape drive

   d) A CD-ROM or DVD-ROM drive

Activity 4-2

1. **What is the bus speed of the first SCSI standard?**

   a) 8 bits wide at 7 MB/s

   b) 16 bits wide at 5 MB/s

   ✓ c) 8 bits wide at 5 MB/s

   d) 8 bits wide at 8 MB/s

2. **Which is the common name for an ATA-4 device that uses Ultra DMA mode 2?**

   a) ATA/ATAPI

   ✓ b) Ultra ATA 33

   c) Ultra ATA 66

   d) EIDE

3. **Why was performance an issue in the PIO transfer mode?**

   In the PIO transfer mode, performance suffered because the CPU had to execute all of the instructions for every data transfer, consuming processing time that could be used for other processes.

4. **True or False? IDs identify physical devices and LUNs identify logical devices.**

   ✓ True

   ___ False

5. **For each SCSI ID, what is the maximum number of LUNs that you can have on a 16-bit bus?**

   a) 7

   b) 8

   ✓ c) 16

   d) 32

6. **True or False? You cannot connect two ATA devices with an 80-conductor cable and still implement the Cable Select feature.**

   ___ True

   ✓ False

7. **Which SCSI type supports a data transfer rate of 80 MB/s?**

   a) Wide SCSI

   b) Ultra-320

   ✓ c) Wide Ultra-2

   d) Ultra-160

8. **Match each type of SCSI termination to its appropriate characteristic.**

d	Active	a.	Special terminators needed.
b	Forced Perfect	b.	Uses diode clamps.
a	HVD	c.	Simplest form of termination.
c	Passive	d.	Uses voltage regulators.

Activity 4-3

1. **A user wants some fault tolerance on her workstation. She has two physical disk drives available. Which level of RAID could she employ?**

   a) RAID 0

   ✓ b) RAID 1

   c) RAID 2

   d) RAID 5

2. **What is the minimum hardware requirement for a hardware-based RAID 5 implementation?**

   a) Two disks and a RAID controller

   ✓ b) Three disks and a RAID controller

   c) Four disks and a RAID controller

   d) Six disks and a RAID controller

3. **True or False? Software RAID provides the same reliability and performance as hardware RAID.**

   ___ True

   ✓ False

4. **What is the role of a hot spare drive in a RAID configuration after a primary drive has failed?**

   a) To continually be idle in the array.

   b) To return the system to its normal operational mode.

   c) To reconstruct lost data.

   ✓ d) To assume the role of the failed drive.

5. **What is the total available disk space for seven 10 GB drives running in a RAID 5 array?**

   a) 20 GB

   b) 40 GB

   ✓ c) 60 GB

   d) 80 GB

Activity 4-4

1. **What protocols are commonly used with NAS systems?**

   ✓ a) TCP/IP

   b) HTTP

   ✓ c) NFS

   ✓ d) SMB

2. **True or False? Implementing a NAS system is a cost-effective alternative to traditional file servers.**

___ True

✓ False

3. **What are the options for connecting a NAS?**

Clients can access a NAS either directly or through a server. When users connect directly, it is like connecting to any other server or share. When a server provides connectivity, it either acts as a gateway to the NAS, or hosts a distributed file system that provides the client with access to the data on the NAS. In either case, the client is unaware of the NAS as a separate device. The client does not need to be reconfigured if the data structure on the NAS changes.

4. **What are the benefits of using a NAS?**

Answers will vary, but may include: the NAS system is often more reliable and less prone to downtime than a traditional file server, which improves data availability.

The NAS system can scale efficiently because it is relatively inexpensive to add additional storage devices once the NAS is implemented.

Because the NAS system is dedicated to storage management, data storage and retrieval performance is very high.

NAS systems are easier to secure than traditional file systems because there are fewer points of access to the device. For example, without a keyboard and monitor, no one can log on directly to the system console.

The NAS facilitates data backups because the data can be backed up over a local bus system inside the NAS while it continues to serve client requests. Or, a separate high-performance network link can be created between the NAS and a backup server.

Activity 4-5

1. **How does a SAN differ from a NAS implementation?**

    a) SANs are dedicated to data storage.

    b) SAN devices use high-speed network connections.

✓ c) SAN devices have redundant connections for high reliability.

✓ d) SAN data traffic is separated from the production network traffic.

2. **True or False? Unlike SCSI NAS devices, SAN arrays can be distributed throughout the network.**

✓ True

___ False

3. **With which SCSI specification was Fiber Channel introduced?**

    a) SCSI-2

✓ b) SCSI-3

    c) Ultra 2

    d) Ultra 160

4. **Where can iSCSI be implemented?**

iSCSI can be used over already ubiquitous Ethernet connections, theoretically reducing the Total Cost of Ownership (TCO). iSCSI can run on 1-Gigabit Ethernet and 10-Gigabit Ethernet networks.

5. **What are the drawbacks of a SAN?**

Answers will vary, but may include: SANs can be complex to implement and the required redundancies mean they are quite expensive.

Lesson 4 Follow-up

Lesson 4 Lab 1

1. **List the benefits of a WORM storage system.**

Answers will vary, but may include: greater shelf life (up to 30 years), highest levels of data integrity, lower cost, and higher data storage capacity.

2. **What are the main differences between the IDE and SCSI technologies?**

Answers will vary, but may include: IDE is less expensive, simpler to implement, provides good performance, and is best implemented in an desktop environment. SCSI is more expensive, offers excellent performance, can be implemented in RAID systems, easier to expand, and is best suited for higher end server environment.

3. **What are the risks of a SCSI bus that does not have terminations?**

Electrical signals traversing along an unterminated SCSI bus yields unintended results by reflecting back and forth and interfering with more recent signals. To eradicate these reflections, terminating resistors are installed at each end of the line. Poor or improper terminations can be a major source of SCSI-related problems, including failed system startups, hard drive crashes, and random system failures.

4. **You company is currently planning to install an enterprise-wide server that will be used for heavy transactional data. Management has requested a fast, fault-tolerant system. Which RAID system will you suggest to implement?**

Because this is a high-end transaction database system, high read/write performance is required. Moreover, larger storage capacity with fault-tolerance ability is warranted. To meet these requirements, RAID 30 or RAID 50 is a better choice.

Lesson 5

Activity 5-1

1. **Match the hardware component with the appropriate installation recommendation.**

   <u>d</u> System board
   <u>f</u> Hard drive
   <u>c</u> Processor
   <u>e</u> Memory
   <u>a</u> Internal cable
   <u>b</u> Internal fan
   <u>g</u> External device

   a. Ensure length provides for slack to allow for clearance.
   b. When possible, attach it before installing the system board.
   c. Make sure that cache sizes match.
   d. Attach heat sink before installation.
   e. Fill the slots in order from lowest to highest number.
   f. If needed, set jumpers.
   g. If needed, verify that the power supply can handle the additional load.

2. **What are the most important overall best practices when installing any internal system hardware components?**

   Verify that the system is powered down and all power sources have been disconnected from the server. Follow all ESD prevention techniques.

3. **When you are installing a system board, which part can cause the board to short circuit if not properly installed?**

   ✓ a) Standoff screws

   b) Management software

   c) RAID controller card

   d) DVD drive

4. **What specific safety precautions are recommended for installing a power supply?**

   ✓ a) Ensure that both of the power supply connectors are switched off when you plug them in.

   b) Place the power supply in the top rack of a rackmount system.

   ✓ c) Unplug the power cord from the power supply before you do any other work on it.

   ✓ d) Remove any unused power supply connectors.

5. **True or False? When installing memory, you must use the same size memory sticks in all slots in the server.**

   ___ True

   ✓ False

6. **In which CPU slot should a single processor be installed in a dual processor system board?**

   When installing a single processor into a dual processor system board, the processor should be installed in the CPU 0 slot.

Activity 5-9

1. **True or False? When examining a system board, you will often find that very few components on the board are repairable.**

   ✓ True

   ___ False

2. **When installing or upgrading a system board, what should you do while disconnecting cables from the board?**

   a) Remove them completely from the case, so they are out of the way.

   ✓ b) Mark each cable as you go, so you can easily reconnect them later.

   c) Unscrew the system board from the case.

   d) Disconnect all external devices.

3. **True or False? When installing a CPU, you need to verify that you have an appropriate and compatible cooling system to cool the new processor.**

   ✓ True

   ___ False

4. **When installing and configuring a power supply, what step should you complete first?**

   a) Unplug the power supply from the system board.

   b) Unplug the electrical power cord from the electric outlet and from the power supply.

   c) Toggle the power switch on the computer on and off to discharge any remaining electricity stored in the computer's capacitors.

   ✓ d) Shut down and turn off the system.

Activity 5-11

1. **What is the audio error code and video output for a system board failure?**

   a) Continuous tone without any display.

   ✓ b) One long, one short beep without any display.

   c) Two short beeps without any display.

   d) One or more short beeps with DOS prompt on the display.

2. **Match a POST error code with its problem.**

_b_	0106	a.	Memory error
_c_	0602	b.	System board
_a_	0201	c.	Disk failure

3. **True or False? 1714 indicates drive not ready.**

   ✓ True

   ___ False

Activity 5-12

1. **What is the main benefit of implementing tower servers?**

   ✓ a) Cost savings

   b) Space savings

   c) Energy savings

   d) Best performance

2. **What issues should you consider when implementing a tower server setup?**

   ✓ a) Airflow

   ✓ b) Cable management

   c) Number of slots on the backplane

   ✓ d) Power

3. **What is the main benefit of implementing blade servers?**

   a) Cost savings

   ✓ b) Space savings

   c) Energy savings

   d) Easy implementation

4. **Your company has purchased a new server rack with locking doors. The plan is to install the rack in the main server room, which has a security system and environmental controls already in place. A colleague asks you if you would lock the rack. What would be your response and reasoning?**

   a) Lock the rack, because there is no such thing as too much security.

   b) Lock the rack, but fans might need to be installed inside the rack to ensure proper airflow and cooling.

   ✓ c) No, the server room environment provides adequate security, and airflow should not be an issue.

   d) No, because it will be easier to work on the system if it is unlocked.

5. **You've been asked to install a new tower server into an existing small business environment. The three existing servers are situated in a locked utility closet. To have enough room for the UPS, monitors, keyboards, and mice, the servers are stacked on the floor. Each server is also connected to an Ethernet switch via a short cable that needs to be unplugged when the server needs to be moved. What recommendations would you make to improve this installation environment?**

   ✓ a) Place the servers and the UPS on metal racks or shelves.

   ✓ b) Implement a KVM switch.

   ✓ c) Use longer network cables, and organize all cables with ties or fasteners.

   ✓ d) Remove all input and output devices, and implement remote console management for the servers.

   e) Provide sliding rails and hinged cases for easy access.

Lesson 5 Follow-up

Lesson 5 Lab 1

1. **When installing server hardware, what safety precautions should you always take?**

   Power down the server and unplug all power cords before opening the case to prevent electrical shock.

   Use an ESD kit to prevent damage to computer components.

2. **In a rackmount server setup, how is the rack space measured?**

   Rack space is measured in Units (U). 1U is equal to 1.75 inches. Each server being installed on a rack will have its own unit measurement. For instance, a medium size server will have a rack height of 7U, whereas a small size server will have only 1U. A standard rack height is approximately 42U; therefore, you must calculate and allocate sufficient space for all servers in the rack.

3. **What is the purpose of protecting devices from ESD and how will you achieve it?**

   Electrostatic discharge can cause damage to the server components. An antistatic wrist strap effectively grounds the technician to discharge any electrostatic buildup.

4. **Once the system board is replaced, do components have to be installed in a particular order?**

   Although there is no need to install all components in a particular order, it is recommended to install the CPU and memory modules, then the adapter cards, and then the cables. This will vary depending on the system board and chassis layout, because it is possible that certain components will interfere with others if installed first. For example, a CD-ROM or hard disk drive can partially limit access to memory modules or IDE cable connections.

5. **After installing a new CPU, what critical precaution must you take prior to powering up the system?**

   Once the CPU is secured in the slot, it is critical that the heatsink and fan are properly installed. Improper installation of the heatsink and fan can result in overheating and damage in a matter of seconds.

Lesson 6

Activity 6-4

1. **Match each shutdown procedure to its appropriate NOS.**

_c_	Choose Start→Shut Down, type a comment in the Comment text box, and click OK.	a.	OS/2 Warp Server
_b_	Switch to the console prompt, type down, press Enter, and power down the computer.	b.	Linux
_a_	Switch to the Workplace Shell GUI and click Shut-down.	c.	Windows Server 2008

2. **True or False? One way to verify a NOS installation is to ping the newly set up server from another computer.**

   ✓ True

   ___ False

3. **True or False? Using the proper shutdown procedure for a NOS can help prevent data corruption.**

   ✓ True

   ___ False

4. **True or False? Any peripheral connected to the main server is automatically accessible to all users.**

   ___ True

   ✓ False

5. **You've been asked to help set up a dedicated remote access server for the company. What external peripheral devices would you install on this server?**

   a) Printer

   b) Drive array

   ✓ c) Modem subsystem

   ✓ d) UPS

Activity 6-6

2. **Which event type is of the highest significance to the user?**

   a) Information

   b) Warning

   ✓ c) Error

   d) Success audit

3. **Which log files are present in Windows operating systems?**

   ✓ a) system.log

   b) console.log

   ✓ c) security.log

   ✓ d) application.log

Activity 6-7

1. **Which information could be considered for high-priority server documentation?**

    ✓ a) IP address

        b) Warranty information

        c) Phone list

    ✓ d) NOS version

    ✓ e) Hardware configuration

2. **Your company's server documentation practices require a copy of the server management plan to be included with each server's documentation. What management-related documentation should also be included?**

        a) Hardware manuals

    ✓ b) Server baseline information

        c) BIOS information

        d) Support phone numbers

3. **True or False? It is a good practice to maintain more than one copy of server documentation.**

    ✓ True

    ___ False

4. **True or False? It is essential to have a description of the various problems encountered and their solutions in the logs.**

    ✓ True

    ___ False

Lesson 6 Follow-up

Lesson 6 Lab 1

1. **True or False? When installing Windows Server 2008 on a new server, you must provide third-party device drivers near the end of the installation process.**

    ___ True

    ✓ False

2. Your company has bought an external CD tower to hold several proprietary software packages used in the course of business. This CD tower needs to be connected to the main server. Place the installation steps in the proper order.

   4 Power on the server.

   5 Install device drivers.

   6 Set permissions for employees to access the tower.

   1 Check for updated device drivers.

   2 Connect the tower to the main server.

   3 Power on the tower.

3. Match each management protocol to its description.

   c SNMP   a. Includes network traffic monitoring probes.

   b DMI   b. Agents store management information in MIFs.

   a RMON   c. Agents store management information in MIBs.

4. True or False? The main reason for keeping server documentation current is to assist in troubleshooting efforts.

   ✓ True

   ___ False

5. What are the various user policies that you will implement on your organization's domain?

Answers will vary, but may include: policies such as restricting access to certain websites on the Internet, restricting the ability to modify the system settings, and prompting users to change passwords after the first login.

Lesson 7

Activity 7-1

1. What are the benefits of using upgrade checklists?

   ✓ a) They act as a visual reminder.

   ✓ b) They ensure consistent methodology across the organization.

      c) They improve server performance.

   ✓ d) They act as a training tool.

2. **You have been assigned to perform a hardware upgrade. What types of software might you need to accomplish this assignment?**

   a) None. It's a hardware upgrade.

   ✓ b) Device drivers

   ✓ c) NOS updates

   d) User applications

3. **What types of information should always be documented with each upgrade that you perform?**

   ✓ a) A completed upgrade checklist.

   ✓ b) A description of problems encountered and their solutions.

   c) Data relating to return on investment (ROI) resulting from the upgrade.

   ✓ d) An updated server baseline.

4. **You need to upgrade a mission-critical database application that is installed on several servers across the network. You decide to test the implementation on some servers in a non production environment. What should you do before you implement the upgrade?**

   ✓ a) Baseline the performance of each server in the test bed.

   ✓ b) Research issues and guidelines that can have an impact on the upgrade's success.

   c) Nothing. Testing the upgrade in a non-production environment is sufficient preparation.

   ✓ d) Schedule downtime.

Activity 7-3

1. **One of the processors in a multiprocessor server appears to be failing, so you want to replace it immediately. What compatibility issues do you face?**

   ✓ a) Stepping

   ✓ b) CPU speed

   ✓ c) Cache size

   d) External ventilation

2. **True or False? Before upgrading RAM with additional capacity, it is recommended to test its compatibility with the older version.**

   ✓ True

   ___ False

3. **Your office has recently experienced several lengthy power outages during business hours. During a couple of these outages, the UPS battery was completely drained. What UPS component could you upgrade to minimize downtime and data loss?**

   a) User application management software

   ✓ b) Battery

   ✓ c) Cabling

   d) NOS

4. A departmental server contains a RAID 5 array with eight 73 GB SCSI drives and one 73 GB hot spare. The controller supports up to 15 hard drives. The department has grown dramatically and now needs this array to hold twice as much data. You decide to replace the existing drives with identical 146 GB drives. What issues should you consider?

✓ a) Termination and cabling

b) Brand compatibility

✓ c) Master/slave reconfiguration

d) Array reconfiguration

Activity 7-4

2. True or False? Each time you receive a notice that there is a BIOS upgrade for a server's system board, you should immediately implement the upgrade.

___ True

_✓_ False

3. What are the reasons to upgrade device drivers?

✓ a) To solve known hardware problems or problems with corrupted driver files.

✓ b) To increase the performance and functionality of peripherals.

c) To avoid flashing the BIOS.

✓ d) To increase NIC throughput.

4. True or False? While upgrading a device driver, it is advisable to retain a copy of the old device driver.

_✓_ True

___ False

5. True or False? A server computer can have only a single BIOS.

___ True

_✓_ False

Lesson 7 Follow-up

Lesson 7 Lab 1

1. Place these upgrade checklist steps in the proper order.

_2_ Research documentation pertaining to the upgrade.

_4_ Schedule downtime.

_3_ Test and pilot the upgrade.

_1_ Locate and obtain the necessary software.

_5_ Implement the upgrade.

2. **Match each installation or upgrade issue to its corresponding hardware component.**

_c_	Termination and cabling	a.	Processors
_e_	IRQs	b.	Memory
_a_	Stepping	c.	Hard drives
_b_	ECC or non-ECC	d.	UPS
_d_	Battery disposal	e.	Adapters and peripherals

3. **Match each server software type to the possible reason for upgrading it.**

_d_	BIOS and firmware	a.	Implement a new MIB for a replacement UPS.
_c_	NOS	b.	Enhance performance of peripheral devices.
_b_	Drivers	c.	Fix known security holes.
_a_	Monitoring agents and service tools	d.	Enable the system board to support new hardware.

4. **What are the various best practices that a network administrator must follow before performing an upgrade of the server?**

   Answers will vary, but may include: best practices such as evaluating the impact of the upgrade in a test setup before implementing in the entire network, informing the clients about the required downtime for the upgrade, informing the clients about the impact of the upgrade on the organizations network, and getting the backups of all the necessary data and software on external hard disks so as to roll back the upgrade if necessary.

Lesson 8

Activity 8-1

1. **Which statements are valid for server rack diagrams?**

   ✓ a) Server rack diagrams are pictorial representation of the rack locations.

   b) All server rack diagrams are prepared using software tools.

   ✓ c) Server rack diagrams help in planning the network topology.

   d) Server rack diagrams do not indicate the location of electrical power outlets.

2. **Which statements are valid for service level agreements?**

   ✓ a) SLAs can vary from one organization to another.

   ✓ b) SLAs may require the service provider to allot a system administrator for the organization's network.

   c) Service providers can be expected to provide services for products that are out of the scope of SLA.

   ✓ d) SLAs involve discussion on the maintenance schedule routine.

3. **Which statement is not a best practice for server installation?**

    a) Ensuring adequate power supply and backup for server components.

    ✓ b) Installing individual servers racks very close to each other to reduce the utilization of space.

    c) Installing cooling mechanisms for each individual rack of the server.

    d) Following all vendor specified installation procedures.

4. **True or False? Administrators must inform end users about any down time required for the upgrading process.**

    ✓ True

    ___ False

Activity 8-3

1. **Which devices can be classified as biometric sensors?**

    a) RFID tags

    ✓ b) Fingerprint scanners

    ✓ c) Retina scanners

    d) Keypad locks

2. **Which statement is not valid for the defense-in-depth mechanism?**

    a) It involves more than one layer of security around the server location.

    b) It is expensive to implement.

    ✓ c) It is impossible to break through the security layers.

    d) There is no limit on the maximum number of layers that an organization can have.

3. **Which access control device emits radio waves for its detection and identification?**

    ✓ a) RFID tag

    b) Keypad locks

    c) Biometric Sensors

    d) PIN pads

4. **Which statements are valid for remote management of a server?**

    a) Remote management is performed using KVM switches.

    ✓ b) Remote management should be enabled on both the client and server computers.

    ✓ c) It is possible to remotely manage a server running on Windows Server 2008 from a workstation running on Windows XP.

    ✓ d) It is possible to deploy some software on the workstation through remote management.

Lesson 8 Follow-up

Lesson 8 Lab 1

1. **What devices can be used for securing the server room?**

   Answers will vary, but may include: devices such as mechanical locks, RFID tags and readers, biometric sensors, PIN pads, and keypad locks.

2. **What are the various factors you will consider before installing CCTVs inside the server room?**

   Answers will vary, but may include: factors such as the cost of installation of CCTV cameras, number of cameras required, location of cameras, resolution of cameras, and cost of the equipment being monitored.

3. **What kind of information can be included in a security related documentation?**

   Answers will vary, but may include: information such as the user name and password of each individual user, security setting and configuration of each workstation, and access keys and passwords for accessing the server room.

4. **What are the various agreements included in an SLA?**

   Answers will vary, but may include: agreements such as point of contact, maintenance schedule and routine, provision for consultation on hardware and software related issues, hours of service, and termination and renewal of contracts.

Lesson 9

Activity 9-1

1. **Users on the third floor cannot connect to the Internet, but they can log on to the local network. What should you check first?**

   a) Router configuration tables

   b) If viruses exist

   c) If the power cable to the hub is connected

   ✓ d) If users on other floors are having similar problems

2. **Which techniques will help you to identify an affected area for a logon problem?**

   a) Ask the user open-ended questions about the problem.

   ✓ b) Try to replicate the problem on another workstation nearby.

   c) Make a list of problems that can all cause the same symptoms.

   ✓ d) Find out if users in other parts of the building are having the same problem.

3. **A user calls to say that his server will not boot. He mentions that everything was fine until a brief power outage occurred on his floor. What stage of the troubleshooting process can this information help you with most directly?**

    a) Selecting the most probable cause.

    b) Implementing an action plan and solution, including recognizing potential effects.

    c) Documenting the solution and process.

    ✓ d) Establishing what has changed.

4. **What are the steps you will follow to identify the results and effects of a solution?**

    Answers will vary, but may include: verify that the user agrees that the problem is solved before you proceed with final documentation and closing the request. Think about those potential effects and test for them before you close out the issue. If a major change was made, it may be advisable to continue monitoring and testing the system and network for several days or even weeks after the problem is addressed.

5. **What are some of the steps you will follow in the process of implementing an action plan and solution?**

    Answers will vary, but may include: once you have determined the probable cause, you should create an action plan before you start making changes, detailing each step that you will take while attempting to resolve the issue. You should also make sure that you are able to restore the system to the condition it was in before you began troubleshooting, in case things do not go as planned. You also need to think about how the action plan will affect the user or other aspects of the network. If you think ahead, you can help ensure that productivity does not suffer and that downtime is minimized.

6. **A user calls the help desk and says that he cannot open a file. What are some of the questions you should ask?**

    Ask the user to describe his system and his physical location. What application is he using to open the file? Can he open other files with that application? If so, the problem is with the file and not the software. Ask him to describe the specific problem he is having. Can he find the file but receives an error when he opens it? Or does the file open but looks corrupted? To localize the problem, ask where the file is saved; is it on a local disk or on a network drive? Can he open other files from that location? If not, it may be a problem with the storage media itself. Or is it in an email attachment? Find out when he could last open the file, if ever. If he could open the file previously, find out anything that might have occurred since that time to change the situation. If the file is in a network location, review network activity logs to see if there have been any issues or changes to that server.

Activity 9-2

1. **What are the possible causes for the 'OS not found' problem?**

    a) Data cable is not connected or incorrectly connected to the drive.

    ✓ b) The hard disk is damaged.

    c) Overheating of the processor.

    ✓ d) Sector 0 of the physical hard disk drive has an incorrect Master Boot Record (MBR).

2. **What are the main causes for onboard component failure?**

   ✓ a) Improper power supply to the server onboard components.

   b) Incorrect BIOS startup settings.

   ✓ c) Overheating of the components due to the lack of adequate cooling system.

   ✓ d) Backplane failure.

3. **Match a hardware problem to its causes.**

c	Failed POST	a.	Incompatible memory installation.
d	Overheating	b.	UPS failure.
a	Memory failure	c.	Improperly seated or faulty internal component.
b	Power failure	d.	Dust on the internal components.

4. **What is the possible cause for incorrect boot sequence?**

   a) Improper power supply to the server onboard components.

   b) Improper installation of the expansion card.

   c) Overheating of the processor.

   ✓ d) Drive disconnected, damaged, or not recognized by the BIOS.

5. **What is the application of compressed air canister?**

   A compressed air canister has a nozzle that can be aimed at components to blow dust out. This is often used when removing dust from the interior of a server. Be sure to blow the dust away from the power supply and drives. It can also be used to blow dust out of the power supply fan area, from keyboards, and from the ventilation holes on other peripherals.

Activity 9-3

1. **What are the possible causes that would not allow a user to log on to the server?**

   ✓ a) Failure of the encryption service on the system.

   ✓ b) Improper User account Control (UAC) configuration.

   c) Improper or insufficient permissions to access the target resources.

   d) Unauthorized device software.

2. **What are the possible causes that would hang the system while shutting it down?**

   ✓ a) Nonavailability of space in the hard disk to read or write log files.

   b) Corrupted file in an application due to malware.

   ✓ c) High CPU utilization.

   d) Fragmentation of the hard disk.

3. **Match a software tool to its description.**

_c_	Defragmentation tool	a.	It records information, warning, or error messages generated by system components.
_b_	Monitoring tool	b.	It tracks one or more counters.
_a_	System logs	c.	It is used on servers where a high number of transactional operations occur.

4. When a counter value reaches a given _threshold_ , it indicates that the object of the counter may be functioning outside acceptable limits.

5. What is the possible solution for an OS boot failure?

    a) Defragment the hard disk.

    b) Repair the corrupted files by using the checkdisk utility.

    c) Take the backup of the log files and clear the event log viewer.

    ✓ d) Reinstall the OS.

Activity 9-4

1. What are the possible causes for Internet connectivity failure?

    ✓ a) Failure of the NIC card

    b) Port security being enabled

    ✓ c) Bad cables

    d) Misconfigured host files

2. Match a diagnostic tool to its description.

_d_	ping	a.	Tests and displays the path that a network connection would take to a destination host.
_b_	ipconfig	b.	Verifies network settings and connections.
_a_	tracert	c.	Displays the IP address of a host name or the host name of an IP address.
_c_	nslookup	d.	Transmits a datagram to another host.

3. What are the possible solutions to resolve the destination host unreachable problem?

    ✓ a) Visually inspect and replace the cable.

    b) Check to make sure the user has appropriate permissions.

    ✓ c) Replace the NIC card.

    ✓ d) Check the TCP/IP configuration and reconfigure the subnets.

4. True or False? DNS failure or DNS misconfiguration is the possible cause for the failure of the service provider.

    ___ True

    ✓ False

Activity 9-5

1. **If you are not able to access the logical drive, what actions should you take to resolve the problem?**

   ✓ a) Re-configure the RAID

   ✓ b) Rearrange the drives

      c) Partition the disk

      d) Replace the drive in the RAID array

2. **What are the possible solutions for slow I/O performance?**

   ✓ a) Delete all unneeded files.

      b) Reformat the hard disk.

      c) Rearrange the drives properly.

   ✓ d) Defragment the drive.

3. **Match each storage issue to their possible causes.**

_c_	Cannot access logical drive	a.	Detection of corrupted boot files or File Allocation Table (FAT).
_d_	Slow file access	b.	Improper termination of the system, which may be due to power leakage on the SCSI bus.
_a_	OS not found	c.	Improper disk RAID configuration.
_b_	Data corruption	d.	Insufficient space in the hard disk or in any other the storage media.

4. **True or False? The disk management tool optimizes hard disks on your system by creating, deleting, or formatting partitions to create the functional disk configuration.**

   ✓ True

   ___ False

Lesson 9 Follow-up

Lesson 9 Lab 1

1. **What is an important role of the troubleshooting process?**

   Answers will vary, but may include: the troubleshooting process serves as a framework for correcting a problem efficiently without introducing further problems or making unnecessary modifications to the system.

2. **What are the steps involved in a troubleshooting process?**

    The troubleshooting process involves several steps. They include:

    Step 1: Gather information.

    Step 2: Identify the affected area.

    Step 3: Determine what has changed.

    Step 4: Establish the theory of the most probable cause.

    Step 5: Test the theory to determine the cause.

    Step 6: Create an action plan and solution.

    Step 7: Implement and test the solution.

    Step 8: Identify the results and effects of the solution.

    Step 9: Document the process and solution.

3. **A user calls the help desk and says he cannot open a file. The server where the file is stored is located in a different building. What are the first steps you need to take to be able to diagnose the problem?**

    Answers will vary, but may include: you need to define the specific symptoms of the problem so that you can begin to consider potential causes; you need to find out if other users are affected and, if so, who; and you need to find out if anything has changed on the user's system or the network since he could last access the file.

4. **Through your diagnostic questions, you establish that the file is a word-processing document stored on a network file server. The user last accessed the file three months ago. By reviewing the activity logs on the file server, you find that there is a bi-monthly cleanup routine that automatically backs up and removes user data files that have not been accessed since the last cleanup date. The backups are stored in an offsite facility for one year. Given this information, what is your action plan, how will you implement it, and what potential side effects of the plan do you need to consider?**

    You need to locate the tape containing the archived copy of the document and restore it to the network location. You might need to work with your company's backup administrator to identify the tape and retrieve it from the offsite storage location. You need to ensure that you identify the correct file and restore only that file so that you do not overwrite later data.

5. **A 30-GB hard drive was installed, but the system reports that the drive is about 500 MB. What can be done to resolve this problem?**

    The system may contain an old BIOS version that doesn't recognize large drives. Update the BIOS so that the entire drive can be recognized. Some drive manufacturers also supply a driver or install program that can be installed to enable the old BIOS and the new large drive to work together.

Lesson 10

Activity 10-1

1. **Which events always require a disaster recovery plan to be updated?**

    ✓ a) Loss of a team leader.

    ✓ b) Scheduled review and testing of the plan.

       c) Successful recovery from a declared disaster.

    ✓ d) Failed data recovery after a hurricane.

2. **Which type of disaster readiness test is synonymous to reading through a script before staging a rehearsal for a play?**

    The simulated testing on paper or checklist test. In this test, when all of the personnel involved in the recovery effort have been given sufficient time to study their roles in the recovery process, they should walk through the steps in a sort of dry run of the procedures involved. This is also known as a checklist test or a simulated paper test. Different disaster scenarios are recorded on a whiteboard, and the various personnel start filling in the blanks to the recovery plan based on the role(s) allocated to them.

3. **What do you think are the primary responsibility of every member of a disaster recovery team?**

    The primary responsibility of every member of a disaster recovery team is to read, understand, and follow the recovery plan.

4. **True or False? An escalation procedure has two functions: resource escalation and notification escalation.**

    ✓ True

    __ False

5. **Which of these guidelines must be part of any emergency procedure?**

    ✓ a) Ensure the safety of every person.

    ✓ b) Coordinate the entire disaster recovery operation with the emergency response team.

    ✓ c) Inform all concerned stakeholders about the extent of damage.

       d) Escalate the availability of resources to those individuals who can provide technical support for the recovery.

Activity 10-4

1. **What backup schedule will you implement?**

    One possible schedule would be a full backup every Monday at 8:00 P.M., plus incremental backups Tuesday through Friday at the same time.

2. **How many tapes would be required for a year's worth of backups, assuming that you do not need extra tapes for the transit to offsite?**

    A total of 29 tapes: 12 tapes for the monthly Monday archives; 9 tapes for the weekly Monday reports (in case one of the two months in the reporting period contains five Mondays); and 8 tapes for the Tuesday–Friday backups (4 stored onsite, 4 offsite).

3. **What would be a good time during the week to transfer the tapes to offsite storage?**

Tuesday afternoon or Wednesday morning, to allow time to test the Monday backups before archiving them but to avoid retaining them onsite any longer than necessary.

4. **It is Monday afternoon, and your office manager is looking at a file that she swears she edited on Friday, but the file appears to be the old one from the previous Thursday. With your plan, how do you restore the file?**

The tape from last Friday should be offsite, so it will have to be retrieved. The tape needs to be cataloged, and the file found and marked for restore. The restore job should be run, and the file stored in an alternate location and checked to verify that it is the correct file. If it is the correct file, it can be moved into the correct directory.

5. **The company experiences a complete disk failure at 10 A.M. on Thursday. How do you restore the data?**

Replace the hard disk and then restore the full backup tape from Monday, the incremental backup from Tuesday, and the incremental backup from Wednesday. To the extent possible, users will have to manually repost any changes and transactions that occurred between the Wednesday incremental backup and the Thursday morning disk failure.

6. **What are the essential guidelines in a data retention policy?**

The essential guidelines of data retention policy include identifying and classifying the data that needs to be stored or backed up, determining the appropriate storage media, specifying the data retention time based on contractual obligations, legal requirements, and any other statutory or mandatory requirements, checking the need for a backup plan to ensure protection against inadvertent, ensuring data backup is performed regularly, consistently, and safely, restricting access to any data that is retained for legitimate business purposes and ensuring that it is physically secure.

Activity 10-5

1. **What is the best description of a cluster?**

   a) A specialized file server that is designed and dedicated to support data storage needs.

   b) A group of separate disks configured to work as a unit.

   c) A private network dedicated to data storage.

   ✓ d) A group of servers working together to provide fault tolerance and load balancing.

2. **What is the advantage of the disk-to-disk replication method?**

   The advantage of disk-to-disk replication is its high speed of access to the replicated data.

3. **Match the cluster type to its description.**

_c_	Active/active	a. A cluster with nodes that handle the full workload during normal operations, and other nodes in standby mode.
_a_	Active/passive	b. A cluster in which servers can provide almost instantaneous failover.
_b_	Fault-tolerant or high-availability	c. A cluster that has all nodes online, constantly providing services.

4. **True or False? The active/passive cluster type has the best failover response time.**

 ___ True

 _✓_ False

5. **What is the advantage of hot site replication?**

 Answers may vary, but can include: Hot site replication would minimize the latency to restart an operation during any disaster.

6. **In an active/passive configuration, how does the passive server know that the active server has failed?**

 a) The active server sends a message.

 b) The administrator brings the standby server online.

 ✓ c) The server heartbeat stops.

 d) The passive server reboots.

7. **What are the operations that require server-to-server replication?**

 Answer may vary, but can include: sever-to-server replication is implemented in scenarios which demand high throughput. It includes improving data scalability and availability, data warehousing and reporting, integrating data from multiple sites, integrating heterogeneous data, and batch processing.

Lesson 10 Follow-up

Lesson 10 Lab 1

1. **What distinguishes disaster recovery planning from fault tolerance planning?**

 Answers will vary, but may include: disaster recovery planning enables you to restore network services in the event of a catastrophic damage that is either not foreseeable or preventable. Fault tolerance measures enable systems to keep functioning in the event of a mishap that can reasonably be predicted. Without fault tolerance measures in place, those events could actually trigger a disastrous system loss.

2. **List some of the different personnel roles involved in designing and implementing a disaster recovery plan.**

 Answers will vary, but may include: network administration personnel are primarily responsible for designing, testing, and documenting the plan. Corporate managers and administrators must provide input to the plan and understand their responsibilities if the plan is implemented. Key vendors and contractors should be aware of the role they will be expected to play in the plan, and the level of service they will be expected to provide.

3. **What do you feel is the most important aspect of a disaster recovery plan? Why?**

 Answers will vary, but may include: documenting the plan adequately is probably the most important aspect. The people who composed the plan might not be those who implement it, so detailed documentation is critical to implementing it successfully. Another important aspect of a disaster recovery plan is testing the plan by doing a walkthrough or some other form of test.

4. **Why is it important to update a disaster recovery plan regularly?**

   Answers will vary, but may include: primarily to make sure that records of passwords, responsible parties, and recovery agents are current, and that all procedures are still valid. The plan can fail if the security information is incorrect.

5. **How many tape sets are required when using the grandfather-father-son rotation method?**

   One set each for Monday through Thursday (four), one set for each Friday of the month (four; if there are five Fridays, the fifth Friday will be the month-end tape), and 12 month-end sets (one for the last business day of each month), for a total of 20. If you use an extra daily, weekly, and monthly tape, the total is 23.

6. **List and describe the three major backup types.**

   In a full backup, all information is backed up.

   In an incremental backup, new files and those created or modified since the last full or incremental backup are backed up and the archive bit is cleared. While each backup is quick, a full recovery can be slow because of the necessity to restore from multiple tapes.

   In a differential backup, all files created or modified since the last full backup are backed up and the archive bit is not cleared. While each backup takes longer, recovery only requires the most recent full and differential backups.

7. **What are some special issues involved in backing up databases?**

   Answers will vary, but may include: the database must be closed, or there must be agent software to back it up while open. The transaction logs may need to be cleared when the backup is complete. These logs may need to be replayed if there is a restore, so that the database can be brought to the most current state possible.

Glossary

802.1X server
It uses one of the several certificate-based mechanisms to authenticate wireless users on a network.

ACL
(Access Control List) A list of permissions set up by a user or an administrator and attached to a shared resource.

active termination
Adds voltage regulators to the resistors used in passive termination to allow for more reliable and consistent termination of the bus.

antispyware
Software that is designed for removing or blocking a spyware.

antivirus software
An application that scans files for executable code that matches patterns known to be common to viruses, and monitors systems for activity associated with viruses.

application server
A computer in a client/server environment that performs the business logic (the data processing).

backup medium
The place where you store backed up data.

backup utility
A software program that archives data on a hard disk to a removable medium.

backup
The process of copying files or databases to another location so that they will be used to restore data in case of equipment failure or other catastrophic events.

BIOS chip
(Basic Input Output System chip) A ROM or Electrically Erasable Programmable ROM (EEPROM) chip that stores the BIOS program code, which allows system devices to communicate with each other.

BIOS
(Basic Input Output Sequence) A program that is run first when a computer is switched on.

blade server
It consists of a chassis (or backplane) that contains one or more server blades.

boot device
A device from which the operating system is loaded into the hard disk during the booting or installation process.

bootloader
A piece of code that is run before running any operating system.

buffered memory
It is memory that contains buffer logic chips that re-drive signals through memory chips and enable modules to include more memory chips.

bus

An electrical pathway to which various server components are connected in parallel so that signals are transferred among them.

cache memory

A random access memory that is located closer to the processor and allows the processor to execute instructions and to read and write data at a higher speed than the regular RAM.

centralized network

A network in which a single computer or server controls all network communication and performs data processing and storage on behalf of its clients.

chip creep

A problem that can occur if equipment is repeatedly exposed to temperature fluctuations. The expansion and contraction due to temperature variance causes the chips to loosen in their sockets.

CISC

(Complex Instruction Set Computer) A design strategy for computer architecture that depends on hardware to perform complicated instructions.

client/server network

A network in which some nodes act as servers to provide services to other nodes. The nodes that receive services from the servers are known as clients.

clustering

A process of grouping two or more servers with a high-speed channel to share workloads between them.

cold site

An alternate facility that doesn't have any resources or equipment except for elevated floors and air-conditioning.

cold swap

Powering off a system before doing repairs or maintenance.

computer network

A group of computers connected to communicate with each other and share resources.

cooling system

A system unit component that prevents damage to computer parts by dissipating the heat generated inside a computer chassis.

counter

An individual statistic about the operation of system objects such as software processes or hardware components, monitored by a performance monitor.

data collector set

The set of objects or components selected for the purpose of baselining.

database server

A computer in a LAN dedicated to database storage and retrieval.

daughter board

An expansion board connected directly to the motherboard to facilitate the computer with an added feature such as modem capability.

DDR memory

(Double Data Rate memory) SDRAM's replacement, it transfers data twice per clock cycle.

DDR2 memory

(Double Data Rate 2 memory) The next-generation DDR memory technology that features faster speeds, higher data bandwidths, lower power consumption, and enhanced thermal performance.

DDR3 memory

(Double Data Rate 3 memory) The memory technology that transfers data at twice the rate of DDR2 and uses 30% less power in the process.

defense-in-depth

A security strategy in which multiple layers of physical security are provided to help reduce the risk of one component or layer of the defense mechanism being compromised or circumvented.

desktop computer

A general term used to designate any system deployed as a general purpose computer to be operated directly by a single user.

device driver

A computer program that acts as an interface between the operating system and a hardware device.

DHCP

(Dynamic Host Configuration Protocol) A network service that provides automatic assignment of IP addresses and other TCP/IP configuration information.

disaster recovery plan

A policy and set of procedures that documents how people and resources will be protected in case of a disaster, and how the organization will recover from the disaster and restore normal functioning.

disaster recovery

The administrative function of protecting people and resources while bringing a failed network or system back online as quickly as possible.

disaster

A catastrophic loss of system functioning due to a cause that cannot reasonably be foreseen or avoided.

disk mirroring

A complete duplication of data on two separate physical drives.

disk striping

It provides enhanced performance by interleaving bytes or groups of bytes across multiple drives, so that several disks can read and write at the same time.

DMA modes

Single word (two bytes of data) and multiple-word (bursts of data) modes are defined for the IDE/ATA interface.

DMA

(Direct Memory Access) Any transfer protocol where a peripheral device transfers information directly to or from memory, without the CPU being required to perform the transaction.

DMI

(Desktop Management Interface) A standard for managing and tracking components in a desktop or notebook PC or in a server.

DMZ

(Demilitarized zone) A small section of a private network that is located between two firewalls and made available for public access.

DNS

(Domain Name System) A TCP/IP name resolution service that translates FQDNs into IP addresses.

domain name space

It consists of information about the hierarchy of domains and the hosts under each domain, which is referred by the name servers for mapping domains.

DRAM

(Dynamic RAM) A type of RAM that needs to be refreshed.

DSA

(Directory System Agent) Server software feature that enables an LDAP server to process queries from the clients and access data from a database.

ECC

(Error Checking and Correction memory) A type of RAM that includes a fault detection/correction circuit to test the accuracy of data as it passes in and out of memory.

EDO

(Extended Data-Out) Provides improved performance over equivalent Fast Page Mode devices, but the performance increase isn't available unless the computer's chipset supports EDO.

EPIC

(Explicitly Parallel Instruction Computing) A design strategy for computer architecture that is meant to simplify and streamline CPU operation by taking advantage of advancements in compiler technology and by combining the best of the CISC and RISC design strategies.

Ethernet

A family of LAN technologies developed to enable communication between different computers over a shared broadcasting medium. It is also known as IEEE 802.3.

expansion card

A circuit board that is inserted into an expansion slot located on the main motherboard to allow a new feature to be added to the server.

expansion slot

A socket on the computer system board that is designed to hold expansion cards.

fax server

It provides a bank of fax modems, allowing users to fax out and remote users to fax in over the next available modem.

FC-AL

(Fiber Channel-Arbitrated Loop) A Fiber Channel implementation that can connect up to 127 nodes without using a switch. All devices share the bandwidth, and only two can communicate with each other at the same time, with each node repeating the data to its adjacent node.

FCIP

(Fiber Channel over IP) Provides connectivity between Fiber Channel storage networks over an IP-based network.

FDD

(Floppy Disk Drive) A computer storage device that reads data from and writes data to removable disks made of flexible Mylar plastic covered with a magnetic coating in a stiff, protective, plastic case.

Fiber Channel

A high-speed transmission technology, originally developed for connecting mainframe computers to various peripheral and storage devices.

file quota

A disk quota that limits the number of files and directories that can be created by a user.

file server

It is usually a high-speed computer on a network that stores the programs and data files shared by users.

file system

A database maintained by an operating system on the storage media for the storage, organization, manipulation, and retrieval of data.

file-level permission

A security feature that allows users to set access control to the individual files instead of the folders.

firewall

Hardware or software that regulates data flow to a secured network by filtering data originating from unsecured or untrusted sources.

flash storage

A storage device that stores data using flash memory.

FPT

(Forced Perfect Termination) Diode clamps are added to the circuitry to force the termination to the correct voltage.

FQDN

(Fully Qualified Domain Name) A domain name that denotes the specific location in the DNS hierarchy from the top domain to the last.

FTP

(File Transfer Protocol server) A special type of file server that stores files for download from, or upload to, the Internet or an intranet running the TCP/IP protocol stack.

gateway
A computer that performs conversion between different types of networks or applications.

grace quota
A disk quota that allows users to temporarily violate their allotted limits by certain amounts if necessary.

hard quota
The effective limit of allotted disk quota.

HDD
(Hard Disk Drive) A computer storage device that uses fixed media and magnetic data storage.

hot site
An alternate facility already equipped with resources and equipment ready for immediate disaster recovery.

hot spare
An extra drive configured in your system that is kept inactive unless another drive fails.

hot-swapping
The ability to exchange computer hardware "on the fly" without interrupting the computer's service or, at least, minimizing the interruption.

HVD SCSI
(High Voltage Differential SCSI) A scheme with a total cable length of 25 meters that is less susceptible to noise than SE SCSI.

HVD
(high-voltage differential) A SCSI signaling scheme that uses two wires, one for data and one for the inverse of data. HVD devices use high voltage and cannot be used on a single-ended SCSI chain.

hyperthreading
A technique that enables a single CPU to act like multiple CPUs.

imaging
The process of copying the contents of one computer hard disk to another hard disk of identical configuration so as to create an identical clone of the source disk.

instruction
A fundamental operation that the processor can execute.

iSCSI
(Internet SCSI) A protocol that serializes SCSI commands so that they can be transferred over a TCP/IP network.

JBOD
(Just a Bunch of Disks) Also referred to as spanning, it is a storage method that uses a number of external physical hard drives organized into a single logical drive to store data.

KVM switch
A hardware device that allows a user to control multiple computers from a single keyboard, video unit and mouse.

LDAP server
(Lightweight Directory Access Protocol server) It uses Specialized Directory System Agents (DSAs) that process queries and updates to an LDAP directory.

LUNs
(Logical Unit Numbers) An identifier used on a SCSI bus to distinguish between up to eight devices (logical units) with the same SCSI ID.

LVD or LVDS
(Low Voltage Differential signaling) Supports cable lengths up to 12 meters, and uses 3.3 Volt logic that reduces power usage, dissipates less heat, and is faster than HVD SCSI.

LVD
(low-voltage differential) A SCSI signaling technique that uses two wires, one for data and one for the inverse of data. LVD devices use a low voltage and can be used on a single-ended SCSI chain.

mail server
A computer in a network that provides "post office" facilities by storing incoming mail for distribution to users and forwards outgoing mail through appropriate channels. It is also known as message server.

memory interleaving

The process of splitting main memory into several physically separate components called banks or modules.

memory pairing

A technique to couple two physical memory banks and enhance server performance.

memory

A repository that allows temporary storage of information that your processor needs to make calculations, run programs, open documents.

motherboard

Another term for the system board.

multiprocessing

The concurrent execution of instructions by more than one processor.

NAS

(Network-Attached Storage) A specialized file server that is designed and dedicated to support only data storage needs.

NOS

(Network Operating System) An operating system that controls the functioning of a network by implementing necessary protocol stacks and device drivers appropriate for the network hardware.

NTP

(Network Time Protocol) A protocol for synchronizing the clocks of computer systems over packet-switched, variable-latency data networks.

optical disk

An internal storage device that stores data optically, rather than magnetically.

optical jukebox

An automated external storage system that houses many optical disks with multiple read/write drives to archive and store data.

passive termination

Uses simple resistors to terminate short, low-speed SE SCSI-1 buses.

patch management

The process of planning what patches should be applied to which systems at a specified time and developing an appropriate strategy.

patch

A piece of software designed to fix problems or update a computer program or its supporting data.

peer-to-peer network

A network in which resource sharing, processing, and communications control are completely decentralized.

performance counters

The performance parameters associated with an object or a server component.

physical port

A hardware interface that helps external devices to communicate with servers.

PIO mode

An I/O mode where the CPU executes the instructions for every data transfer, taking processing time that could be used for other processes.

port number

A 16-bit nonnegative integer, ranging from 0 to 65535 that is used to identify a specific port.

POST

(Power-On Self Test) A built-in diagnostic program that is run every time a server starts up.

power connector

An electrical connector that carry electrical power from the power supply to every server component.

power supply

An internal server component that converts line voltage AC power from an electrical outlet to the low-voltage DC power needed by system components.

print server

It enables many network users to share printers.

processor cache

A type of high-speed memory that is directly linked to the CPU.

processor speed

The number of processing cycles that a microprocessor can perform in a given second.

processor

The main chip on the system board that executes program instructions that drive the computer. It is also called the Central Processing Unit (CPU).

proxy

An application that enables a sender and a receiver to communicate without actually setting up a direct connection between the computers. It acts as a go-between to provide security.

PXE

(Preboot Execution Environment) A booting or installation technique in which a computer loads the operating system from a connected network rather than from a boot device. Also known as network share booting.

rackmount server

It provides sliding rails and hinged cases for easy access, and many components such as hard drives, power supplies, expansion cards, and fans are usually hot-swappable, enabling you to replace faulty parts without downing the server.

RADIUS server

(Remote Authentication Dial-In User Service server) It stores permissions and configuration information for RADIUS-compatible hardware to authenticate remote network users.

RAID cache

A form of disk or peripheral cache.

RAID cache

A form of disk or peripheral cache.

RAM

(Random Access Memory) It is the computer's main memory. RAM is volatile and requires a constant source of electricity to keep track of the data it is storing.

RAS server

(Remote Access Service server) A server running Windows NT Server or Windows 2000 Server that provides a subset of wide area networking services, including packet forwarding and remote connections for Windows-based clients, and enables you to implement VPNs over the Internet or other public network.

RDRAM

(RAMBUS DRAM) It has a data rate higher than SDRAM and DDR and is similar to DDR. An 800 MHz RDRAM chip can handle two operations per clock cycle.

redundancy power

The ability of the power supply to provide fault tolerance for the system's power and to prevent server shutdown due to a power supply failure.

registered memory

A special type of buffered memory, the Synchronous DRAM (SDRAM) version of buffered memory.

remote alert

A message that apprises you of a problem that happens when your operating system is in a sleep mode, hasn't booted yet, or freezes up.

remote management

A feature of NOS that allows the server hardware and applications on it to be managed from any remote location in the network.

replication

The process of sharing and synchronizing data across multiple devices or servers.

RISC

(Reduced Instruction Set Computer) A design strategy for computer architecture that depends on a combination of hardware and software to perform complicated instructions.

riser card
A board that is plugged into the system board and provides additional slots for adapter cards.

RMON
(Remote Monitoring) An SNMP extension that provides additional functionality over and above that provided by standard SNMP.

rotation method
The schedule that determines how many backup tapes or other media sets are needed, and the sequence in which they are used and reused.

router
A device that manages the exchange of information from network to network, or between network cabling segments.

RRAS server
(Routing And Remote Access Service server) RAS implementation found in Windows Server 2003.

SAN
(storage area network) A special-purpose high-speed network that is dedicated to data storage.

SAS
(Serial Attached SCSI) A serial version of the SCSI interfaces. SAS is a point-to-point architecture that uses a disk controller with four or more channels operating simultaneously. SAS also supports serial ATA (SATA) drives, which can be mixed with SAS drives in a variety of configurations.

SDRAM
(Synchronous DRAM) Runs at high clock speeds and is synchronized with the CPU bus.

SE SCSI
(Single-Ended SCSI) Drives that use one signal line against ground. Susceptibility to noise limits the maximum allowable cable lengths.

server baselining
The method of analyzing the performance of a sever by comparing its current performance with the performance before an upgrade or modification.

server blade
It consists of a single circuit board holding components such as processors, memory, and network connections that are usually found on multiple boards.

server rack diagram
A graphical representation of the location of individual server racks, electrical power connections, and network connections to be used for a server.

server virtualization
A resource management feature that allows the operating system to isolate the physical characteristics of the server hardware from users.

server
A computer that provides services to client computers as well as to other servers on a network.

shadow copy
A feature that allows users to make manual or automatic backup copies or snapshots of a file or folder on a specific volume at a specific point in time.

share-level permissions
Permissions set for network shares.

SLAs
(Service Level Agreements). The various agreements made with the vendors of server components to ensure a reliable post installation servicing and maintenance of the components.

SNMP
(Simple Network Management Protocol) The Internet standard protocol developed to manage nodes on an IP network. It can be used to monitor network devices and their functions.

soft quota

A warning level of the disk quota, at which users are informed that they are nearing their allotted limit.

SSA

(Serial Storage Architecture) A fault-tolerant peripheral interface that transfers data at 80 and 160 MB/s. SSA uses SCSI commands, allowing existing software to drive SSA peripherals such as disk drives.

standalone operating systems

An operating system that is designed for supporting a single computer.

storage device

A hardware device that is used to store data.

subnetting

The technique of dividing a large network into smaller interconnected domains to prevent excessive rates of packet collision.

system board

A printed circuit board that houses processor or memory chips, controller circuits, buses, slots, and sockets. It is also referred as motherboard.

tape drive

An internal storage device that stores data magnetically on a removable tape.

tape libraries

An external storage device that stores, retrieves, reads, and writes data on multiple magnetic tape cartridges.

TCP port

An end-point to a logical connection and it is generally application specific.

terminal server

A specialized server that aggregates multiple communication channels together.

TFTP

(Trivial File Transfer Protocol) A protocol used for loading the operating system on a PXE client from a PXE server on TCP/IP based networks.

threshold

It is the value that signals that an object or a component functioning outside the acceptable performance limits.

tower server

It looks like a traditional desktop PC but includes more opportunities for expansion. Tower servers take up more physical space than newer form factors, but they often provide the best value for smaller companies and departmental networks.

troubleshooting model

Any standardized step-by-step approach to the troubleshooting process.

troubleshooting

The recognition, diagnosis, and resolution of problems affecting a server.

TTL

(Time to Live) A numeric value that specifies how many hops or passes through routers that a packet is allowed to make before it reaches its destination.

unbuffered/unregistered memory

It is Memory where no buffers or registers are included in the memory module.

usage quota

A disk quota that limits the amount of disk space that can be used by a user. Also known as block quota.

VLAN

(Virtual LAN) A logical subgroup within a local area network established via software rather than manually shifting cables in the wiring closet.

VPN

(Virtual Private Network) A network that uses a public telecommunication infrastructure, such as the Internet, to provide remote offices or individual users with secure access to their organization's network.

VRM

(Voltage Regulator Module) A replaceable module installed on the system board to stabilize the voltage fed into the processor.

VSS

(Volume Snapshot Service) An implementation of the shadow copy feature in the releases of Microsoft Windows server operating systems.

VT

(Virtualization Technology) A feature to enhance the processor design by implementing virtualization on it. It is also known as AMD Virtualization (AMD-V).

wait state

A period during which a CPU or bus remains idle, often due to differences in clock speeds among various components.

Wake-on-LAN

A concept that enables users to remotely power-on client systems simply by sending a specially formatted network packet known as a magic packet.

warm site

A cross between a cold site and a hot site that is only partially equipped.

WBEM

(Web-Based Enterprise Management) Management of a network performed using web browsers that retrieve information from web servers and display it using web pages.

web server

A computer that provides World Wide Web services on IP networks, including the Internet.

WINS

(Windows Internet Naming Service server) It provides name resolution for Windows-based networks.

workstation

A class of high-end computers designed for technical, scientific, and commercial applications.

WORM

(Write Once Read Many) An external storage system that allows information to be written once on storage media, however the data can be read several times.

write-back cache

A caching method where changes to data stored in L1 cache aren't copied to the main memory until absolutely necessary.

write-through cache

It performs all write operations in parallel; data is simultaneously written to the main memory and the L1 cache.

XD

(Execute Disable) A security feature to provide protection against buffer overflow attacks by preventing the execution of code in the segregated memory space. This is called No Execute (NX).

ZIF socket

(Zero Insertion Force socket) A type of processor socket that uses a lever to tighten or loosen pin connections between the processor chip and the socket.

Index

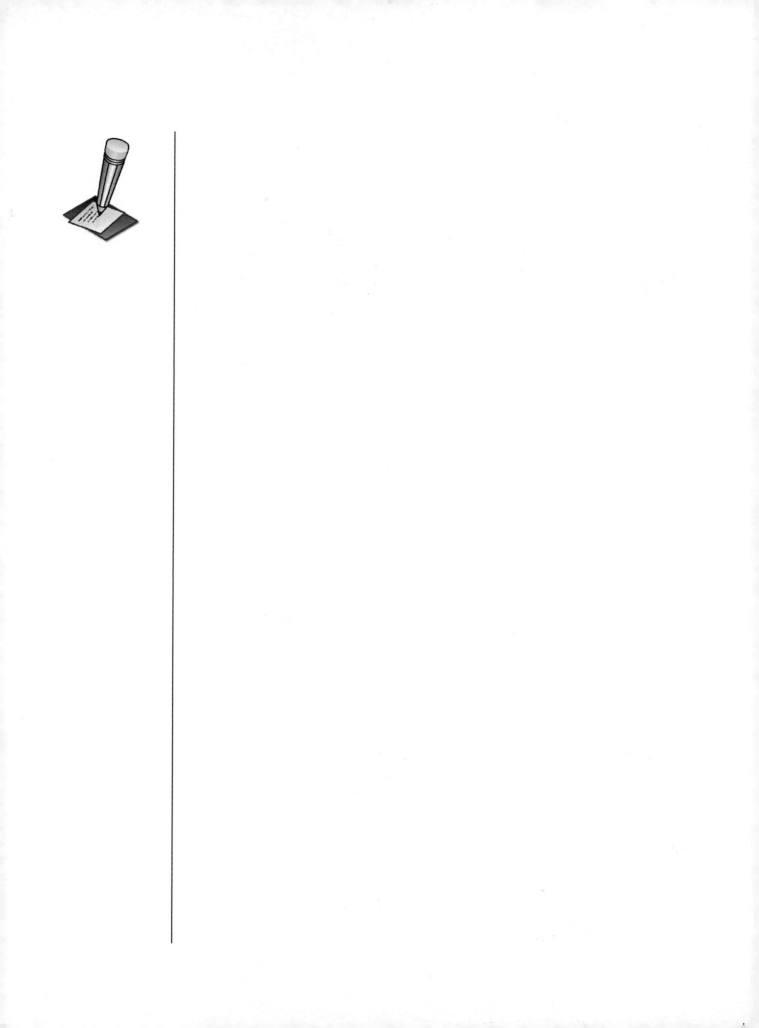

085055 S3PB rev 1.0
ISBN-13 978-1-4246-1388-0
ISBN-10 1-4246-1388-8

9 781424 613380